SOVIET SCHOLARS AND
SOVIET FOREIGN POLICY

SOVIET SCHOLARS AND SOVIET FOREIGN POLICY

A case study in Soviet policy towards India

Augsburg College
George Sverdrup Library
Minneapolis, Minnesota 55454

RICHARD B. REMNEK

Foreword by
W. W. KULSKI

CAROLINA ACADEMIC PRESS
Durham, North Carolina
1975

Copyright © Richard B. Remnek
All rights reserved

Carolina Academic Press
2206 Chapel Hill Road
Box 8791 Forest Hills Station
Durham, N.C. 27707

Library of Congress catalog card number: 74-21938
ISBN: 0-89089-011-0

This edition may not be sold outside the U.S.A. and Canada

Printed in India

*To the memory of
my beloved father Alfred Remnek*

FOREWORD

This book by Professor Richard B. Remnek is a major contribution to the knowledge and understanding of an important aspect of Soviet foreign policy, namely the policy toward India and, by repercussion, toward the whole Indian subcontinent. But it is more than that. The author seeks in his analysis of Soviet policy toward India the answer to the question which puzzles the Western specialists and to which they offer disagreeing replies: do the Soviet scholars bear any influence on the formulation of Soviet foreign policy? He compares the views of Soviet specialists, especially the economists, with the development of Soviet policy during the years of 1947 to 1971 (the Epilogue completes the story for the later seventies). His conclusion is that the Soviet specialists have begun to influence the actual policy in the post-Khrushchev period, while before they were forced to serve mostly as apologists for what the Soviet government did or decided to do. This is the result of a pragmatic nature of policies followed by the post-Khrushchev leadership. The evidence presented in this book provides empirical support for this view.

An additional benefit of this study is the recognition of the importance of Soviet academic literature as a valuable data source for a better understanding of Soviet foreign policy. In the first place, important policy-relevant debates appear in the scholarly literature which do not surface in the popular press. Secondly, without consulting the Soviet scholarly literature misleading inferences regarding Soviet foreign policy motives and attitudes are likely to be drawn. The author's presentation of the Soviet scholarly literature on India not only elaborates the contours of Soviet policy toward India but also provides insights into the attitudinal dimension of Soviet foreign policy behavior. Thus, for example, it is all the more apparent that the Soviet-Indian friendship is based from the Soviet perspective not upon transient factors, such as the personalities of the leadership or the attitudes toward Indian domestic policies (indeed Khrushchev in 1959 made some major commitments to India at a time of general academic disenchantment with Nehru's policies), but on calculations attuned to the geopolitical realities of the region.

The Soviet official friendliness toward India does not prevent Soviet specialists either from expressing views critical of economic and social weaknesses of India or from offering advice as to how Soviet economic aid could be handled more rationally and effectively.

The author's views are vouched by the ample use not only of Soviet but also of Indian and Western materials.

With respect to Soviet policy toward India, the author does not challenge the general view that the USSR, if forced to choose, has always chosen India over Pakistan for among other reasons that both countries have unfriendly relations with China which in turn entertains friendly relations with Pakistan.

I feel sure that this important book will be of great interest not only to Western readers but also and above all to Indian and Pakistani readers.

Durham, North Carolina

WLADYSLAW W. KULSKI
*Emeritus James B. Duke Professor
Duke University*

PREFACE

Social science, as with all intellectual endeavors in the Soviet Union, must serve the public interest as determined by the Communist Party of the Soviet Union. While there is very little reason to doubt that Soviet social scientists, no less than their Western counterparts, harbor a sense of social responsibility to work in the public service, controversy today centers upon how best to perform this function within the delicate framework of balancing expertise against *'partiinost'* (party-mindedness). To be sure, so long as that "coryphaeus" of human wisdom, Joseph Stalin, was alive, such uncertainty did not exist, for the role of Soviet scholars was precisely defined. Given his prescience, it is not surprising that the value of social science in the formation of public policy went largely unrecognized. Suspicious of all things personally incomprehensible to him as potentially subversive, Stalin checked the development of all scientific life. As one observer of the debilitating effects of Stalinism in economics noted, Stalin placed "... docile and obedient sycophants in powerful positions in the Institute of Economics and elsewhere. These faithful executioners of Stalin's will were content to guard doctrinal purity and to produce a generation of economists who could not even recognize, much less analyze, important economic problems."[1] What is true of economics was true of other disciplines as well. Denied a role in the policy-making process, Soviet scholars were called upon mainly to provide elaborate support for officially prescribed interpretations. Conclusions already established were thus to be confirmed by research. Dogmatic deduction which "fitted" the facts to conform to Stalin's ideas was a surrogate for inductive research. In short, Soviet social scientists served mainly as official ideologues.

In the two decades since Stalin's death, this state of affairs has significantly changed as the party leadership has gradually come to recognize the instrumental value of social science research in the

[1] Richard W. Judy, "The Economists," in *Interest Groups in Soviet Politics*, edited by M. Gordon Skilling and Franklyn Griffiths (Princeton, N. J.: Princeton University Press, 1971), p. 224.

search for solutions to the complex problems of an increasingly industrialized society. The steady removal of ideological constraints has been correlated with the attainment of methodological sophistication in several fields, which has equipped social scientists to proffer policy-oriented prescriptions to Soviet decision-makers. The significant impact of scholars in various arenas of domestic policy-making has already been documented by Western analysts of interest group interaction in Soviet politics.[2]

However, whether Soviet scholars play a similar role in foreign policy-making is less well understood. A disparity in roles between those social scientists oriented to domestic problems and those concerned with foreign affairs has been intimated by the authors of a review of the emergence of political science as a recognized discipline in the Soviet Union and Eastern Europe, in which they note that Soviet scholars in the fields of local government and public administration have been encouraged to generate policy-oriented studies whereas the fields of comparative government and international relations are still dominated by ideologues.[3] Yet, the evidence that Soviet specialists in foreign affairs have not participated in the general metamorphosis of Soviet social science in the post-Stalin era is by no means conclusive. While some observers have continued to regard these experts as ideologues whose opinions do not carry much weight in official deliberations,[4] others have observed an increasing orientation of these specialists towards policy prescriptive roles.[5]

The major objective of the present study, then, is to clarify the role of Soviet scholars in the foreign policy-making process, using

[2] See, especially the excellent case studies in the field of education reform by Joel Schwartz and William R. Keech, "Group Influence on the Policy Process in the Soviet Union," *The American Political Science Review*, LXII (September 1968), 840-51, and Philip D. Stewart, "Soviet Interest Groups and the Policy Process," *World Politics*, XXII (October 1969), 29-50.

[3] David E. Powell and Paul Shoup, "The Emergence of Political Science in Communist Countries," *The American Political Science Review*, LXIV (June 1970), 577.

[4] See, particularly, John Keep, "The Soviet Union and the Third World," *Survey*, 72 (Summer 1969), 29.

[5] This has been persuasively argued by William Zimmerman in his excellent study, *Soviet Perspectives on International Relations, 1956-1967* (Princeton, N. J.: Princeton University Press, 1969).

Soviet policy towards independent India as an empirical referrent. More specifically, we propose to examine the Soviet experts' role over time to determine whether it has become more policy-oriented, and if so, whether a perceptible impact on Soviet policy towards India can be detected. Given the lacunae of information regarding the foreign policy-making process in the Soviet Union as well as the absence of the type of debate over foreign policy which marked, for example, Soviet education and economic policy in the post-Stalin period, we intend simply to extract policy-relevant analyses and prescriptions from Soviet scholarly literature on contemporary India and the problems of developing countries and to determine whether they later found reflection in Soviet policy towards India. We are concerned here only with positive influence which eventuates in concrete policy change, since negative influence which restrains alteration of policy cannot be discerned by this approach. It is also recognized that this approach, due to the influence of several intervening factors, cannot provide conclusive evidence of either the presence or absence of a scholarly input in the decision-making process. For example, even if a scholar's recommendation for a new form of economic assistance was later incorporated in an aid agreement, it may nevertheless be the case that the impetus for the new idea came from a higher official source and/or that the temporal lag, which at first glance suggested the presence of a scholarly input, was to be explained by various delays in the negotiating process, some of which might have been beyond the control of the Soviet government. Or, it may also be that a scholar's recommendation has been adopted by Soviet officials, but has not yet been actualized in concrete form. Furthermore, it is quite probable that Soviet experts give advice to Soviet leaders on an informal and confidential basis, without the substance of this advice ever reaching print. Thus, at the outset, it is acknowledged that this method of correlating scholarly analyses with Soviet policy offers, at best, an imprecise approximation of the degree of scholarly influence in the foreign policy-making process.

In view of these formidable difficulties, it was reasoned that the selection of the Indian case study might improve prospects for the detection of a scholarly input. Following the hypothesis of Schwartz and Keech that expert influence is likely to be greater the more problematic and technical the issue,[6] we assumed that the impact of scholarly expertise would be more apparent in economic relations which usually involve some degree of professional evaluation of prospects than in political relations which are more clearly subject to the vicissitudes of the international environment. With the long history of the Soviet aid program in India within the context of fairly steady, good relations, it was anticipated that any alteration in this aid program might likely be the consequence of an expert reevaluation of the effectiveness of this aid. It is recognized, however, that in a country as large and relatively independent of Soviet political influence as India, Soviet aid planners might not have the same leverage as in smaller countries more dependent upon Soviet political and material support. Yet, this consideration is outweighed by the fact that there is more abundant and reliable information from non-Soviet sources on Soviet-Indian relations than on Soviet relations with virtually any other developing country. Indeed, much valuable information on this subject is engendered from the Indian side by the very fact that Soviet-Indian relations have themselves become something of a political issue widely discussed and frankly reported in the pages of the independent Indian press. The prospects for achieving a more accurate appraisal of any Soviet scholarly influence in India are therefore presumably greater than in non-democratic countries with government-controlled news media.

In order to delineate the relationship between scholarly analysis and policy, we shall examine both separately. Soviet policy towards India is considered in chapter one, before the academic analysis, since this provides an empirical referrent which sensitizes the reader to the policy relevance of the scholarly analysis. In the remaining chapters, the academic literature is examined chronologically, with each chapter corresponding to an important temporal phase of Soviet policy towards India.[7] We have employed a chronological rather than topical organization of the chapters which deal with the scholarly literature primarily because it facilitates comparison with Soviet policy. The chronological framework provides the additional benefit of examining changes in Soviet

---

[6] Schwartz and Keech, *op. cit.*, 848.

[7] For an explanation of the periodization selected in this study, see below, pp. 5-6.

perceptions of India, which reflect not only responses to external events but also the changing character of the Soviet leadership itself.

While the changing role of the Soviet scholar is our primary concern, a major by-product of this study is the more profound comprehension of Soviet policy towards India to be gained by contrasting scholarly analysis with official policy. Although some Western analysts have denigrated the value of published Soviet sources and urged that inferences about Soviet foreign policy be drawn almost exclusively from the observation of actual Soviet conduct,[8] such approach might generate misleading interpretations based on values and modes of analysis alien to Soviet thinking. It is the conviction of this author, however, that the examination of Soviet scholarly perceptions may furnish insights into the attitudes and motivations which guide the conduct of Soviet foreign policy. Even where academic analyses seem at variance with official policy, more accurate calculations of Soviet intentions might result. Thus, for example, the fact that Soviet commentators were already making a critical appraisal of the Nehru government in the late 1950's suggests that the Soviet decision to support India in her confrontation with China was based more upon a realistic calculation of national self-interest than on illusory images of Nehru's progressiveness. Thus, an examination of the Soviet scholarly literature should illuminate to a certain extent the well-springs of the conduct of Soviet policy towards India.

Data for the first part of this study on Soviet policy towards India was gathered from the Soviet, Indian and Western press, supplemented by the published research of Western and Indian scholars on the subject. Primary data sources for the Soviet scholarly literature reviewed in the second part consist of scholarly books and articles from major academic journals. While books have been relied upon to supplement the relative paucity of published research in the late 1940's and 1950's, for subsequent years we have depended more heavily upon journal articles and summaries of academic conferences and discussions, which furnish a wealth of policy opinions, often divergent, in capsulized form.

[8] See, Keep, *op. cit.*, 29.

PREFACE

I would like to acknowledge with true gratitude Duke University, the Ottis Green Foundation and the Research Triangle Foundation which provided financial support for the conduct of much of the research. In addition, it is my great pleasure to express my indebtedness to the following people: first, to my wife, Katia, without whose endurance and management this work could not have been accomplished; second, to Professor Emeritus W. W. Kulski of Duke University whose friendly encouragement, sound guidance and sage advice have helped shape this work, and moreover, whose personal example as a humanitarian and a dedicated scholar has set a very high standard by which to measure one's own life; and third, to Professor Vladimir G. Treml of Duke University for his perceptive comments and advice on the economic section of this work.

Memphis, Tennessee   RICHARD B. REMNEK

CONTENTS

1. SOVIET POLICY TOWARDS INDIA, 1947-1971 .. 1

   Introduction .. 1
   The Stalinist Background .. 6
   The Post-Stalinist Rapprochement, 1953-1959 .. 11
   The Chinese Divergence and its Impact on Soviet
       Policy, 1959-1964 .. 26
   The Post-Khrushchev Period, 1964-1971 .. 50
   Soviet Economic Policy Towards India .. 82

2. THE STALINIST BACKGROUND, 1947-1953 .. 101

   The Emergence of Modern Soviet Indology .. 101
   Soviet Scholarship under Stalin .. 110

3. THE EARLY KHRUSHCHEV YEARS, 1953-1959 .. 127

   The Post-Stalin Interim, 1953-1955 .. 127
   Reappraisal and Resistance .. 130
   Defining the National Bourgeoisie .. 139
   The Reassessment of Indian State Capitalism .. 143
   The Role of Foreign Private Capital .. 150
   The Impact of Agrarian Reforms .. 152
   The Refinement of Economic Development
       Strategies .. 156
   The Perspective on Foreign Aid .. 159
   The Reassessment of Nationality Problems in India .. 162
   The Reevaluation of Indian Foreign Policy .. 165

4. THE LATE KHRUSHCHEV YEARS, 1960-1964 .. 171

   The Effect of the Sino-Indian Border Dispute .. 171
   The Growing Influence of Indian Monopolies .. 173
   The Changing Perspective of Foreign Capital
       Investment .. 181
   The Assessment of India's Current Revolutionary
       Potential .. 185

India and the Third World	.. 190
Towards a Realistic Perspective of Economic Development	.. 198
Soviet Aid to India	.. 205
Evaluating the Performance of the Indian State Sector	.. 207
Perceptions of the Agrarian Question in India	.. 212

5. THE POST-KHRUSHCHEV PERIOD, 1965-1971 .. 223

The Shifting View of the Indian Political Scene	.. 223
Towards a Realistic Assessment of the "Non-Capitalist Path of Development"	.. 232
New Directions in the Soviet View of Economic Development	.. 241
The Reevaluation of Socialist Economic Relations with Developing Countries	.. 250
Recognition of the Problems of Agrarian Over-population and Employment	.. 257
The Food Problem and Agrarian Reforms	.. 263
Reassessing the Possibilities of Economic Development Planning	.. 272
Changing Perspectives of Socio-Political Processes in the Third World	.. 279
The View of Caste	.. 283

CONCLUSION .. 290

EPILOGUE: SOVIET POLICY TOWARDS INDIA SINCE BANGLADESH .. 297

Indo-Soviet Economic Collaboration	.. 298
Indo-Soviet Political Relations	.. 304
The Role of Great Power Rivalries	.. 309
Future Contingencies and Prospects	.. 318

Selected Bibliography	.. 321
Index	.. 333

1.
SOVIET POLICY TOWARDS INDIA, 1947–1971

INTRODUCTION

The determination of Soviet policy towards independent India poses certain conceptual and methodological problems. In the context of international relations, the term policy usually connotes a purposive set of attitudes and actions on the part of one country towards another. Policy may be designed and consistent or incremental and incoherent. Although policy is intrinsic to a relationship between two countries, it is not coextensive with the composite sum of those relations and must be distinguished from them. For, at the very least, relations are a product of policies of each partner in the relationship. Moreover, external factors may intervene to complicate the transactions between states, although, it should be noted, responses to these external forces may, in fact, be influenced by policy, pre-dispositions themselves. In the context of Indo-Soviet relations then, one must not equate Soviet policy towards India with the entire scope of these relations. Yet, the secretive nature of much important international transactions not only obstructs our ability to examine these relations in depth but also precludes the possibility of ascertaining Soviet policy with precision. So too, there are specific events which are surrounded by such complex and furtive circumstances that the attempt to understand the interplay of Soviet as distinct from Indian policy seems futile. Thus, the determination of Soviet policy is at best an approximation. Nevertheless, it is only when we have isolated Soviet policy towards India over the time period covering Stalin's last years from 1947-53 to the consolidation of power by Madame Gandhi that we may begin to evaluate the impact and interrelationship between observations and prescriptions proffered in Soviet academic writings on modern-day India and the formulation and implementation of Soviet policy.

A second conceptual dilemma relates to problems of what constitutes policy in the Soviet context. To be sure, an important component in any state's policy towards another consists of the sum total of transactions with another country which that state initiates. These transactions may be of a tangible nature such as trade relations, economic and military assistance; they may also be politically supportive, but no less important, such as expressions of official support on foreign policy issues of interest to the other state. Soviet support for India on the issues of Goa and Kashmir are but two examples.

While such statements are integral to the foreign policies of all states, the problem peculiar to the Soviet context is that of distinguishing official from unofficial policy. In Western states where there is a clear distinction between public and private realms, this poses no great difficulty. Statements made by government ministers are deemed official, commentaries by analysts in private news media are unofficial. In the Soviet political system, which aspires towards complete politicization of society and the merger of private with public realms of social activity, any published statement has official authorization. Thus, one might challenge the assumption that there are official as distinct from unofficial policy statements in the Soviet context. Yet, it seems appropriate at least to posit the existence of a hierarchical ordering of published statements. The most authoritative pronouncements would be those made by high party and government officials at important party-state functions such as Party Congresses, Supreme Soviet sessions, etc. Speeches by Soviet officials and statements in joint communiques would also rank as highly authoritative statements. Below these in order of significance would be news reports and commentaries in the mass circulation Soviet press. It should be noted that in times of crisis especially, the way in which an event is reported may itself reveal official policy at the highest level. Indeed, one of the contrasts between the Western and Soviet press is that the controlled Soviet press serves as an accurate barometer of official thinking. Commentaries by important political observers or correspondents of the mass circulation press often have quasi-official status insofar as such commentaries occasionally preview major policy decisions as we shall see below.

It may also be reasonably argued that the writings of Soviet scholars in academic journals and books should also be considered official in that censorship ensures that all published material will reflect the Party line. However, since our purpose is to analyze the relationship of scholarly expertise to Soviet foreign policy, we shall be considering academic literature separately. Moreover, Soviet academic literature occasionally reveals debates and divergences of viewpoint which are not to be found in the popular press. A problem, however, arises when a Soviet scholar has an article published in the popular press. This was a fairly common occurrence in the Stalinist period, but has occurred less frequently in recent years as the number of qualified journalists has increased. In certain cases, the publication of an analytic essay by a prestigious academician in the popular press may resolve certain issues which had been under discussion in the scholarly literature. In some cases, such articles may also convey important policy decisions.[1] Thus, dependent upon the specific context, analytic

---

[1] An interesting case is that of Professor R. A. Ul'ianovskii, who besides being widely published in the academic press, also has the official position of Assistant Chief of the International Department of the Central Committee of the CPSU, and serves presumably as a liaison between the academic community and higher party echelons. His articles in the popular press must of course be considered as authoritative.

articles in the popular press penned by scholars may be considered either in this chapter or in subsequent chapters.

A methodological problem pertinent to the task of delineating Soviet policy towards India concerns the utility of the Soviet press itself as an information source. While we have noted that the Soviet press presents an accurate reflection of official thinking, it is nonetheless evident that not all important policy decisions will be disclosed to the Soviet public. This is especially true of the more sensitive aspects of Indo-Soviet relations such as arms deliveries. Indeed, the author could only find an indirect admission, in a 1969 speech by Kosygin,[2] that the Soviets had ever engaged in a military assistance program for India, which in fact had commenced in the early 1960's. Thus, the author has had to consult additional sources, especially the Indian press, to fill in the omissions in the Soviet press.

In analyzing Soviet policy towards India, it must be kept in mind that Indo-Soviet relations do not occur in a geo-political vacuum. Soviet policy is influenced by broader considerations such as the security of its Central Asian borderlands and the Sino-Soviet split. External factors may also alter, at least temporarily, the conduct of this policy; such was the case, for example, in October 1962 when the exigencies of the Cuban missile crisis subdued the Soviet reaction to the Chinese military invasion of the Indian territories of Ladakh and NEFA. Moreover, in view of the basic enmity and distrust surrounding Indo-Pakistani relations, Soviet-Pakistani relations themselves must be considered in any analysis of the relationship between India and the Soviet Union. In fact, Soviet policy towards India must be evaluated in the broader context of Soviet policy towards the South Asian subcontinent. Cognizant of the major role of external factors, we shall nevertheless consider these influences only in the context of our major concern, Indo-Soviet relations.

In this chapter we shall then examine the evolution of Soviet policy towards India since independence. Since our aim is to trace changes over time, we shall not cover in detail Soviet actions during

---

[2] See, his address at the funeral of Indian President Zakir Husain as reported in *Pravda*, May 7, 1969, p. 4, in *Current Digest of the Soviet Press* (hereinafter *CDSP*), XXI, No. 19, 17.

crises in the subcontinent, such as the 1962 Chinese invasion and the 1965 Indo-Pakistani war. Not only have these crises been treated in depth elsewhere,[3] but, due to the temporal dimension, it is probable that the impact of academic expertise upon Soviet crisis behavior is minimal. Certainly if there is any influence, it would be through private consultations of the party leadership with individual scholars. Since we are not privy to such information, the effort to relate scholarly expertise to crises decision-making seems quite futile. It is our underlying assumption that if Soviet academic expertise does influence the process of foreign policy formation, it should be manifest in the gradual evolution of Soviet policy over time.

The year 1947 seems to be a logical point of departure for this study since it was not only the year of Indian independence but also marked the important shift in Soviet post-war foreign policy initiated by Zhdanov's enunciation of the "two-camp" thesis at the founding meeting of the Cominform. Having considered the late Stalinist period of foreign policy retrenchment as a background, we shall seek to delineate the evolution of Soviet policy towards India in the following chronological subsections: the post-Stalinist rapprochement, from 1953-1959; the impact of the Chinese divergence, 1959-1964; and the post-Khrushchev period, 1964-1971. A final subsection concerning Soviet economic policy in India has also been included. It is recognized that the very process of establishing a periodization of Indo-Soviet relations poses certain difficulties dependent upon the perspective adopted. Since our concern is with Soviet policy, we are employing a periodization which best approximates major foreign policy shifts in the evolution of that policy. Fortuitously, such a periodization also accommodates important changes in the Indian context; for example, the fall of Khrushchev follows by six months the death of Nehru and the commencement of the post-Nehru succession struggle. This chronological periodization, nonetheless, does impose a certain artificial segmentation upon the evolution of Indo-Soviet relations. Thus, for example, although Indo-Soviet relations dramatically improved following

---

[3] See, for example, Bhabani Sen Gupta, *The Fulcrum of Asia* (New York: Pegasus, 1970), Chapters 3 and 4. His coverage of Soviet diplomatic maneuvering during the 1965 India-Pakistan conflict is especially comprehensive.

Stalin's death, there are indications that Stalin had already begun to reevaluate his India policy several months before his death. Therefore, it should be noted that there is a continuity in the evolution of Soviet policy that transcends such organizational devices.

THE STALINIST BACKGROUND

Although it is common to find mention of traditional Indo-Soviet friendship in the Soviet press in recent years, it should nevertheless be remembered that these relations had inauspicious beginnings. Despite immediate formal recognition and exchange of ambassadors, the Soviets, it would seem, were ideologically ill-prepared to accept the fact of India's peaceful attainment of political independence in 1947. At a time of Communist successes elsewhere in Asia, the peaceful transfer of power in India seemed to be some sinister British ruse to blunt and divert the growing revolutionary struggle elsewhere. Despite the formal transfer of power, the Soviets were not convinced that the British had lessened their grip on the subcontinent. From the Soviet viewpoint, the Mountbatten plan for the partition of India into two separate states would only serve to perpetuate political turmoil in the subcontinent and, thereby, enable the British to play an arbiter role according to the formula "divide and rule." So too, the Soviets felt that the princely states would continue to serve as a bulwark for conservative reaction through which the British could continue to intervene. The fact that the Indian National Congress accepted the plan indicated to the Soviets that the Indian bourgeoisie, whose political agent was the Congress, had gone over to the side of reaction and joined the camp of Imperialism. At best, then, India had changed its status from a colony to a semi-colony, not a significant step in the Marxist typology.

The Soviet perspective of Indian independence was colored by the Soviet response to the post-war shift in the structure of world power relations. The Zhdanov speech marked the beginning of a period of hostile retrenchment in foreign affairs. India was but a pawn in this global class struggle and lacked an independent identity. The very concept of Nehru's foreign policy of nonalignment contradicted the "two camp" formula which posited: "If you are not with us, you are against us." Moreover, despite Nehru's verbal denunciation of colonialism and expression of a desire for good relations with the Soviet Union, the Soviets' suspicion of his insincerity was reinforced by India's diplomatic docility in the first few years after independence. Specifically, the Soviets were irked by India's assumption of a pro-Western posture on the issues of Korean unification and the Greek Civil War and also by her agreement in 1948 to participate in a joint Commonwealth military aid program to crush Communist insurgency in Burma.

However, it was Nehru's trip to the United States during the following year which brought the sharpest fire. The offer of American aid was interpreted as an initial step in drawing India into a Western military alliance aimed at the Soviet Union. Playing on anti-Western nationalism, the Soviet press depicted Nehru's trip as showing his willingness to make concessions to the United States.[4] It was at this time, moreover that Stalin extended a surprise invitation to the Prime Minister of Pakistan, Liaquat Ali Khan, to visit the USSR. Although never accepted, the offer itself constituted a Soviet counter to Nehru's Washington trip.

While the Soviets suspected the Nehru government of being a camp follower of the West, it must also be recognized that their actions were making this assumption a self-fulfilling prophecy. By encouraging a Communist insurrection in India,[5] the Soviets were, in fact, pushing the Nehru government closer to the West. Encouraged by the successes of Communist armed insurrection elsewhere in Asia, Moscow gave the green light to the adoption of the left strategy by the Indian Communists. With the post-war 'spheres of influence' still unsettled, Stalin may have been gambling for a Communist take-over in India.

Underlying the inimical initial Soviet reception of Indian inde-

---

[4] See, for example, A. D'iakov, "Anglo-American Plans in India," *Pravda*, Nov. 25, 1949, p. 3, in *CDSP*, I, No. 48, 33-34.

[5] The CPSU directive calling for an armed uprising, which erupted in Telengana district of Hyderabad state in 1948, was apparently conveyed to the Communist Party of India at a Southeast Asian Youth Conference held in Calcutta in February, 1948. For a detailed account of the Moscow-CPI interaction during this period, consult, John Kautsky, *Moscow and the Communist Party of India* (New York: John Wiley and Sons, Inc., 1956).

pendence were certain fundamental state interests. In the aftermath of the cruel experience of German invasion in World War II, the Soviets were preoccupied with the future security of their borderlands. It would seem that India was not a great concern since she was separated from Soviet territory by high mountains which formed a natural defensive barrier. Historically, ties between Russia and India were sparse indeed.[6] The first official Soviet representative in India was a Tass correspondent who arrived in 1942.[7] However, in the nuclear age, foreign military bases in India would expose the USSR's southern flank to attack. Moreover, a hostile neighbor might broadcast racial and religious propaganda to set Central Asians against Russians. Thus, the Soviets were hypersensitive to Western and especially American penetration in the area. The Soviet attitude towards Kashmir was specifically shaped by such anxieties. While abstaining during UN Security Council debates on the subject, the Soviets interpreted the dispute as an artificial issue that had been externally instigated. The American proposal to convert the area into a UN trust territory was seen as an effort to convert Kashmir into a military base directed at Soviet territory.

Thus, it was Soviet security needs which, to a large degree, determined their interests in South Asia. Soviet policy was predicated on the goal of eliminating Western influence in the subcontinent. Indeed, this prime objective continued to form the basis of Soviet India policy in the post-war Stalin period, with the difference being in the strategies chosen to secure these objectives. In the Stalinist frame of mind, which left no room for buffer states, the only guarantee of the security of Soviet borderlands was their encirclement by a *cordon sanitaire* in reverse; i.e., a ring of subservient Communist states. Yet, this strategy, while successful elsewhere, failed in India. The Communist-led insurrection in Telengana district proved to be only a minor irritant to the government as compared with the post-partition problems of refugees and the war in Kashmir. The Communists had become even more isolated on the Indian political scene as party strength

---

[6] Contacts seemed to have been limited to infrequent personal sojourns such as that of the 16th Century Russian merchant Afanasy Nikitin.

[7] Arthur Stein, *India and the Soviet Union* (Chicago: University of Chicago Press, 1969), p. 10.

plummeted from an estimated 90,000 to 20,000.

While much emphasis has been given to the post-Stalin diplomatic offensive in India and elsewhere, it is nevertheless clear that Stalin had begun to reevaluate his India policy soon after the turn of the new decade. Ironically, it was the Communist Chinese victory in 1949 that set in motion this process, since Nehru's reaction towards this and subsequent events afforded the first demonstration that non-alignment was more substantive than illusory. India's early recognition of the CPR and support for the Chinese Communists' seating at the UN, which were followed by her efforts to mediate the Korean War, forced the Soviet government to revise its attitude. An article responding to the Indian position on the Korean conflict positively evaluated the decision taken but attributed it to submission before mass public pressure.[8] While this appraisal may at first glance seem consistent with previous Soviet analyses, it nevertheless suggests that the Nehru government was responsive to public sentiment. Also, the article noted without comment the existence of quarrels among the Indian leaders on communal problems and Indo-Pakistani relations, thus suggestive of a more discriminating approach to the Nehru government.

Indian refusal to sign a Japanese peace treaty in San Francisco during the following year brought a more positive indirect response. During the summer of 1951 a limited cultural exchange program commenced. More significantly, the Soviets with much publicity began to ship wheat and other foodstuffs to help India tide over food crises in 1951 and especially the following year.[9] Although it was probably motivated by factors independent of state relations, Moscow's redirection of CPI activities onto the parliamentary path undoubtedly redounded to the Congress government's advantage. Also, on the diplomatic front, the Soviet UN delegate, Jacob Malik, rejected the idea of a UN plebiscite during a 1952 Security Council debate on Kashmir, thereby moving closer to the Indian position, while at the same time, not burning his bridges with Pakistan.[10] Officially, the Soviets remained neutral on this

---

[8] *Izvestia*, Sept. 23, 1950, p. 4, in *CDSP*, II, No. 38, 26.

[9] See, for example, *Pravda*, June 10, 1951, p. 3, in *CDSP*, III, No. 23, 14.

[10] J. A. Naik, "Soviet Policy on Kashmir," *India Quarterly*, XXIV, No. 1 (Jan.-Mar., 1968), 52-53.

critical issue.[11]

A visible shift in Soviet policy towards the Third World in general came at an ECAFE session in Singapore in October 1951. This initial debut by a Soviet representative at an ECAFE meeting was marked by a Soviet offer to enter trade negotiations with developing countries on the basis of Soviet deliveries of machinery and industrial equipment in exchange for the traditional exports of these countries.[12] This historic offer was soon followed up by Soviet participation in an industrial exhibition held in Bombay in January 1952,[13] which was reciprocated by Indian attendance at the Moscow Economic Conference a few months later, at which a Soviet trade offer of machinery was accepted. However, negotiations were not consummated in the form of a trade agreement until after Stalin's death. Nevertheless, underlying the Soviet economic offensive was the concept that trade could be used to drive a wedge between the Third World and the West. This view in itself was based upon the assumption that the newly liberated countries were not merely Western pawns and that such leaders as Nehru had demonstrated an ability to cope with the international environment in a flexible manner. Thus, the Soviet adoption of an activist economic policy in the Third World was part of a positive reevaluation of newly independent regimes.

This change, to be sure, was only dimly perceptible at the surface. An important sign of this shift came at the Nineteenth Party Congress in 1952. Delivering the major report, Malenkov spoke of the growth of "national resistance" in India, Iran and Egypt,[14]

[11] However, they did support Indian claims to French and Portuguese colonial enclaves in India. A September 23, 1950 *Izvestia* article, for example, mentions without comment the section of a Congress Party resolution calling for annexation of French and Portuguese enclaves, a position which is suggestive of passive support for the Indian position. See, *Izvestia*, Sept. 23, 1950, p. 4 in, *CDSP*, II, No. 38, 26.

[12] Prior to this offer, Soviet trade with the Third World was extremely limited, inasmuch as the Soviets viewed their trade only as a means to overcome temporary domestic shortages of raw materials. The first barter trade deal was signed with India in 1949. Yet, the volume of Indo-Soviet trade, insignificant to begin with, declined during these years, the pattern to be reversed only after the signing of a five-year trade agreement in December, 1953. For a listing of Indo-Soviet trade volume since 1938, see, Stein, *op. cit.*, Appendix 3, p. 297.

[13] *Pravda*, Jan. 7, 1952, p. 3, in *CDSP*, IV, No. 1, 11.

[14] *Pravda*, Oct. 6, 1952, pp. 2-9, in *CDSP*, IV, No. 38, 31.

which gave official approbation to India's independent foreign policy.

Thus, the seeds of rapprochement with the Indian government were sown in the closing months of Stalin's rule. The abandonment of the left strategy was an acknowledgement of its bankruptcy in India and elsewhere.[15] It must have certainly become obvious that the Soviets had a good deal to gain by establishing good relations with India. Under Nehru, India was at the height of its influence among the newly emergent countries. Thus, once the Soviets had decided to develop relations with these countries, India represented the natural bridge to the Third World. Indeed, it was this consideration that explains a good deal of the attention focused upon India in the 1950's.

THE POST-STALINIST RAPPROCHEMENT, 1953-1959

Although the signs of change in Soviet foreign policy were discernible on the eve of Stalin's death, the departure from the scene of this dictator, whose name evoked much distrust and suspicion among informed circles in India, did much to facilitate the dramatic improvement in Indo-Soviet relations during the next two years.

The appointment as ambassador in October 1953 of M.A. Menshikov, a foreign trade specialist who spoke fluent English, was a harbinger of this change. Menshikov's informality and outgoingness coupled with his laying a wreath at Gandhi's tomb suggested an important positive overture. Menshikov's presence hastened the conclusion of a five-year trade agreement which was signed in December 1953.[16] The slackened demand for Indian tea and jute following the Korean War boom also propelled the Indians to seek new markets for her exports. Consonant with earlier trade offers at ECAFE sessions, the trade agreement provided for Soviet deliveries of machinery and industrial equipment in return for India's

---

[15] Marshall Shulman in his *Stalin's Foreign Policy Reappraised* (Cambridge, Mass.: Harvard University Press, 1963) observed a similar shift in tactics in Western Europe at about the same period of time.

[16] Although the negotiations had been concluded several weeks earlier, the pact was signed while Vice-President Nixon was in New Delhi on a goodwill tour. This deliberate slight was India's counter to American encouragement of Pakistan to enter a military alliance. *New York Times*, Dec. 5, 1953, p. 1.

traditional exports—a trade pattern which would continue into the next decade.

A further sign of Soviet willingness to aid India's industrial development came with Soviet decision to develop its own foreign aid program. Although the Soviets under Stalin consistently warned newly emergent countries of the evils of Western foreign aid, they had themselves remained inactive in this area. To be sure, in the period of intensive post-war reconstruction, the Soviets were in no position to engage in an extensive assistance program. As some observers have noted, it was only in the 1950's that the Soviets developed the surplus industrial capacity to enable them to initiate a foreign assistance program.[17]

The first indication of this policy change came at a session of the UN Economic and Social Council at Geneva on July 15, 1953. There, the Soviet delegate, A. Arutiunian, announced the Soviet decision to contribute to the UN Technical Assistance Program for the first time. A *Pravda* article covering the Geneva session noted that Soviet aid, in contrast to American assistance, would serve to strengthen the "economic independence" of recipient countries without attaching any binding preconditions.[18] This pronouncement had specific relevance to India, for that country became the first major recipient of Soviet aid. The Soviet offer to build a steel mill at Bhilai came a year later, with a formal agreement signed in February 1955. As the first major Soviet aid project, Bhilai was a model of Soviet aid programs, and indeed, the Soviets took great pains to ensure its success. The Bhilai offer was itself a barometer of the extent to which Indo-Soviet relations had improved. It was preceded by a growing appreciation on the part of the Soviet leadership of the value of the Nehru government.

Not only was India praised for its constructive role during the Korean War, but also Nehru's firm rejection of the Dullesian strategy of states forming anti-Communist military alliances was lauded. In the South Asian context, as Soviet relations with India improved, Pakistan grew closer to the United States. This, in turn, pushed the Soviets even closer to India although Nehru still

---

[17] See, Milton Kovner, "Soviet Aid Strategy in Developing Countries," *Orbis* (Fall, 1964), 631. See also P. L. Tandon, "Vital Role of Trade with USSR," *Commerce* (Bombay, April 11, 1970), 38.

[18] *Pravda*, July 17, 1953, p. 4, in *CDSP*, V, No. 29, 15.

maintained India's equidistance between both blocs. Within three years of Stalin's departure, in fact, the Soviet leadership was to make important commitments to India from which they could not easily extricate themselves in the future. A closer examination of the unfolding of events in this process is in order.

In an important address before the Supreme Soviet in August 1953,[19] Malenkov announced the new Soviet line when he praised India's contributions in Korea and gave official blessing to Nehru's foreign policy. However, while noting with approval the improvement in Indo-Soviet relations, he, at the same time, expressed a hope for a similar improvement in relations with Pakistan. This Soviet overture did not have the desired effect. As Indo-Soviet relations noticeably improved, Pakistan, desirous of gaining Western support on Kashmir, grew more receptive to American efforts to draw her into a military alliance. Indeed, over the same period of time when India and the Soviet Union were putting the final touches on the Bhilai agreement, Pakistan formally joined SEATO (September 1954) and the Baghdad Pact (February 1955).

The Soviet response to these negotiations was predictable. A series of articles warning against Pakistani entry into a military alliance was published in the Soviet press.[20] The Soviets also delivered a diplomatic note of protest to Pakistan objecting to her adhesion to a military compact with the United States. In an effort to dissuade Pakistan, the Soviets at this stage suggested that Kashmir be resolved through bilateral negotiations between the parties concerned without outside interference.[21] Whether they held out the carrot or the stick,[22] the Soviets were unable to alter Pakistan's course, and as a result, the Cold War arrived on the subcontinent.

[19] *Pravda*, Aug. 9, 1953, pp. 1-4, in *CDSP*, V, No. 30, 10.

[20] *Pravda*, Jan. 25, 1954, p. 4, in *CDSP*, VI, No. 4, 15. *Pravda*, Aug. 25, 1954, p. 4, in *CDSP*, VI, No. 34, 17.

[21] Naik, *op. cit.*, 54.

[22] A Soviet threat to sell arms to India in response to Pakistan's entry into a Western military pact cannot be excluded. The *New York Times* reported on Dec. 15, 1953, that Ambassador Menshikov had made an informal bid to discuss the sale of military equipment to India should the United States decide to arm Pakistan. Although the Indian Foreign Office later denied this report, a few days later it was reported that the Indian government was circulating a memorandum in Western capitals hinting that India would turn to the Soviet Union for arms if Pakistan received U.S. military assistance. See, *New York Times*, Dec. 17, 1953, p. 24; Dec. 25, 1953, p. 8.

A potential stumbling block to further improvement in Indo-Soviet relations was removed in 1954 when a Sino-Indian agreement on Tibet was reached; this settlement, by which India withdrew her troops stationed in Tibetan trading centers and recognized Chinese sovereignty in the region and received in return special trade privileges, was noted approvingly in the Soviet press.[23] The Nehru visit to Peking which followed set the stage for the historic exchange of visits with Soviet leaders during the following year. During the course of that year Nehru's foreign policy received favorable comment in the Soviet press. Specifically, the Soviet press lauded Nehru's proposals on ending the Indochina war.[24] In appreciation, the Soviets gave manifest support to Indian claims to the Portuguese enclave of Goa.[25] By the end of the year, some fourteen Indian delegations, ranging from a soccer team to industrialists, visited the Soviet Union. Returning Soviet artists noted the charms of India[26] —a practice which sharply contrasted with Stalinist accounts of the abject poverty of India.

The momentous year of 1955 which marked the culmination of the Soviet efforts to court India commenced with a significant *Pravda* editorial commemorating India's Republic Day.[27] Not only was the foreign policy of "the outstanding statesman Jawaharlal Nehru" praised, but the domestic accomplishments of the Indian government in the fields of agriculture, education and public health were listed as well. Indicative of the current Soviet policy of amplifying India's voice in world affairs, the editorial noted: "Peace-loving peoples had great confidence in India and authorized her to head international commissions for implementing truce terms in Korea and Indochina." Establishing the ideological rationale for the Soviet aid to India, the editorial accused British and American capital of hampering India's independent development through their competitive struggle to dominate the Indian market.

[23] *Pravda*, April 30, 1954, p. 4, in *CDSP*, VI, No. 17, 18.
[24] *Pravda*, May 31, 1954, p. 4, in *CDSP*, VI, No. 22, 22. According to Arthur Stein, Nehru attached considerable importance to the moderate Soviet position displayed at the Geneva Conference ending the Indochina War. Remaining doubts having evaporated, Nehru moved towards closer cooperation with the Soviets after this point. See, Stein, *op. cit.*, p. 51.
[25] *Pravda*, Aug. 4, 1954, p. 2, in *CDSP*, VI, No. 31, 15.
[26] *Literaturnaia Gazeta*, September 2, 1954, p. 1, in *CDSP*, No. VI, 35, 12.
[27] *Pravda*, January 26, 1955, p. 3, in *CDSP*, VII, No. 4, 33.

Soviet aid, therefore, would help India resist Western economic penetration and contribute to her struggle for economic independence. Thus, whereas under Stalin economic dependence was taken as proof of Indian political submissiveness, now Indian political independence was acknowledged as fact with the battle for economic independence still in the forefront. The editorial then prepared the Soviet public for the signing only a few days later of the Bhilai agreement on terms more generous than those offered by other Western countries for similar projects in India.[28]

In April the Bandung Conference of Asian and African nations was held with much fanfare. The conference, which was co-sponsored by the Indian and Chinese, not only marked a high water mark in Sino-Indian relations, but also promulgated the much heralded Pancha Shila, or five principles of international affairs, which have served as a diplomatic bridge upon which close relations between Communist and non-Communist states could be constructed. In preparation for Nehru's forthcoming visit, the Soviets took pains to remove any remaining obstacles to the Indo-Soviet rapprochement. Thus, an editorial in the May issue of *Kommunist* reversed the previously hostile appraisal of Gandhi by positively evaluating his role in the independence movement.[29] In the same month, writing in *Pravda*, O. Orestov supported the Congress government's linguistic policy which called for the continued utilization of English as the official language with its gradual displacement by Hindi.[30] This marked a reversal of the previous Soviet posture which strongly opposed the retention of English and encouraged the development of state and regional languages.[31] Inasmuch as linguistic policy is closely associated with the problem of national integration in India, the new Soviet

---

[28] Soviet aid for the Bhilai steel mill was given through the extension of a credit at 2.5% interest to be paid back over a 12-year time period following delivery of all equipment.

[29] "For the Further Advance in Soviet Oriental Studies," *Kommunist*, No. 8 (May 1955), 74-83, in *CDSP*, VII, No. 28, 22.

[30] *Pravda*, May 10, 1955, p. 3, in *CDSP*, VII, No. 19, 14-15.

[31] For a standard exposition of this position, see N. Sosina, "On the Question of the State Language in the Union of India," in I. M. Reisner and N. M. Goldberg, eds., *Studies in the Modern History of the Countries of the Middle East, India, Afghanistan and Iran* (Moscow, 1951), as reviewed by A. M. Osipov in *Sovetskaia Kniga*, No. 8 (1951), 64-68, in *CDSP*, IV, No. 2, 13-14.

posture suggested Soviet support for a strong, unified Indian nation state, whereas the previous position had tended to encourage regional movements, which would weaken central authority in India.

The Orestov article also touched upon the peculiar position of the CPI. The Indian Communists were now called upon "to strengthen even more the friendly ties now binding Soviet and Indian peoples." While noting the CPI's endorsement of several Nehru foreign policy initiatives, Orestov, perhaps reproachfully, indicated that CPI support for Nehru's domestic program was not forthcoming. The reticence of the CPI to follow the Soviet lead *vis-a-vis* the Nehru government was natural. During the delicate diplomatic incubation period since Stalin's death, Nehru had not altered his contemptuous attitude toward Indian Communists to facilitate the Indo-Soviet rapprochement. On the contrary, in December 1954, the Preventive Detention Act, which enabled the government to detain troublesome Communists as well as communal extremists without trial, was extended for a three-year period. This was neither the first nor the last instance of Moscow's sacrificing the interests of local Communists on the altar of improving state relations. Yet it was indicative of the extent to which the Soviets were desirous of establishing close relations with India.

The sincerity of Moscow's intent to cultivate good relations with India was graphically evident during the historic sixteen-day visit of Prime Minister Nehru in June. According to foreign correspondents, Nehru was accorded the most tremendous reception ever given to a visiting foreign statesman.[32] Nehru was accorded the privilege of being the first non-Communist leader to address a public gathering in the Soviet Union. It is clear then that the Soviets were using the visit not only to announce to the world its determination to abide by the policy of peaceful coexistence, but also to impress as many neutral and nonaligned states as possible.

The Soviet performance during this visit gained exceedingly high marks. Sensitive to a possible American overreaction to the visit, Nehru, prior to his departure for Moscow, went out of his way to moderate his previously critical attitude towards U.S. policy and paid a compliment to President Eisenhower; during the visit itself, he continually emphasized the theme of peace. The Soviet leaders,

---

[32] *New York Times*, June 23, 1955, p. 1.

for their part, deferred to Indian sensitivities on this subject and refrained from any criticism of the United States or Great Britain during the duration of the visit.[33] In what must have been a welcome contrast to some of their Western counterparts, the Soviet leaders were careful not to slight Indian pride and self-respect.[34] As an Indian journalist, K. Rangaswami, who accompanied the Nehru entourage to both Peking and Moscow, later put it:

> "It may be said that the Russians scored where others have failed. Their study and understanding of India's national sentiments and susceptibilities as well as individual preferences and aversions is almost something uncanny.... Never once was there a public mention or private reference made by Soviet leaders to their agreement to set up a steel plant in India. It would have been justifiable if they sought to make some political capital out of the deal. But they have gained from the experience of others and have refrained from touching on the subject."[35]

Rangaswami also noted that Nehru was profoundly impressed by the personal conduct and approach to problems displayed by Soviet leaders.[36]

The communique which closed the visit was an adoption of the Indian draft and emphasized the themes of peace and non-interference in each others internal affairs. Moreover, any mention

---

[33] *Pravda,* June 7, 1955, p. 1, in *CDSP,* VII, No. 23, 11.

[34] The Soviets also paid strict attention to Indian customs. During an official reception for Nehru at which all alcoholic beverages were replaced by tomato juice in deference to Hindu custom, Anastas Mikoyan was reported to have said: "We will do anything for peace...even give up Vodka." *New York Times,* June 23, 1955, p. 1.

[35] *Hindu,* July 2, 1955, quoted in Stein, *op. cit.,* p. 68.

[36] A good illustration of Soviet tact may be seen in the response given to Nehru's public speech before a crowd of 50,000-70,000 at Moscow's Dynamo Stadium, in which he claimed that India was establishing a "socialist society by peaceful means." Bulganin, who shared the podium with the Indian statesman, responded: "The Soviet people are watching with great interest and sympathy the efforts which are being made by the great *Indian people* to create in their country a society on a socialist pattern." [Emphasis added.] *New York Times,* June 22, 1955, p. 4. Thus, without becoming involved in ideological recriminations, Bulganin adroitly sidestepped Nehru's claim.

of either the West or Pakistan was omitted although it is probable that these important matters were discussed.

In retrospect, the visit seems less substantive than emotional and symbolic.[37] The visit meant more than forging firm Indo-Soviet friendship. It also helped to remove the remaining vestiges of diplomatic isolation to which Stalinist post-war policy had led. India, being the first major developing nation to establish warm relations with the Soviet Union, now served as a bridge upon which the Soviets could now expand their ties with other developing countries of Asia and Africa. Nehru himself became a spokesman for the new Soviet image. In a visit to London in July, for example, Nehru claimed that the Soviets were earnestly interested in reducing international tension.[38]

The return visit which Bulganin and Khrushchev paid at the end of the year was more than symbolic, for it led to certain significant policy commitments. Thus, it is worth examining in some detail.

It will be remembered that the lengthy eighteen-day tour was in itself a spectacular event—one of the first "Bulganin and Khrushchev road shows." The reception afforded the Soviet leaders was no less impressive than Nehru's. At Calcutta alone it was estimated that over two million turned out to greet the leaders.[39] Warming to the welcome, Bulganin and especially Khrushchev, who seems to have taken center stage during the tour,[40] displayed an aptitude for political showmanship unmatched by most Western leaders. Whether it was kissing babies, sampling buffalo's milk or donning turbans, the tandem did much to enhance their popularity if not demonstrate their statesmanship.

Indeed, in contrast to the treatment accorded Nehru, the Soviet leaders embarrassed the Indian government by engaging in political diatribes against the West, which provoked a protest from the

[37] Indicatively, Nehru is reported to have said on his departure from Moscow: "I am leaving part of my heart behind." *New York Times*, June 24, 1955, p. 3. Characteristic of American anxieties at that time, the *New York Times* editorial on the same day rejoined that Nehru had also left a part of his common sense behind.

[38] *New York Times*, July 11, 1955, p. 1.

[39] *New York Times*, November 30, 1955, p. 14.

[40] In the course of their visit, it was reported that Bulganin was beginning to look tired while Khrushchev remained ebullient. *New York Times*, November 25, 1955, p. 4.

British Foreign Office.⁴¹ Nehru was, in fact, forced to indirectly reprimand his guests when he stated at a Calcutta rally that India had refrained from criticizing other countries unless "compelled to do so by circumstances," the intent clearly being that Bulganin and Khrushchev had not behaved accordingly.⁴²

Although rankled by the tactless conduct of the Soviet leaders, the Indian government had good reasons to be pleased by the visit. Materially, the Indians profited a good deal from it, as the Soviet leaders gave promises of additional aid. Bulganin, noting that a team of Soviet oil technicians had already been dispatched to India, said that the Soviet Union was prepared to share its experience in industry and the development of atomic energy for peaceful purposes.⁴³ Khrushchev emphasized India's need for heavy industry and offered to initiate educational exchange programs in order to train Indian engineers and technicians.⁴⁴ Just prior to their departure, the Soviet leaders presented a gift of ten million dollars' worth of farm machinery for a state agricultural farm at Suratgarh.

Yet, it was not Soviet material generosity which counted most. Besides strong statements of support on Goa, the Soviets for the first time enunciated a distinctly pro-Indian position on Kashmir. In a speech at Srinagar on December 10, Khrushchev dropped a political bombshell when he remarked that the "people of Kashmir had already decided to join the Indian Union"—an allusion to the decision taken two years before by the Kashmiri Constituent Assembly to join the Indian Union.⁴⁵ Although Nehru was later

---

⁴¹ *New York Times*, November 27, 1955, p. 9.

⁴² *New York Times*, December 1, 1955, p. 4. The accompanying Soviet delegation was apparently more sensitive to the Indian position. Members of that delegation reportedly asked Indians and foreigners for a reaction to the tour and nodded acknowledgingly when told that the tough anti-Western language was embarrassing to India. See, *New York Times*, December 9, 1955, p. 1. In what may have been a belated apology to the Indian leaders, Khrushchev, in a speech before the Supreme Soviet on his return, underlined Soviet respect for Indian nonalignment in the following words: "India really is a neutral state and deserves confidence and respect from us and from other states." *Pravda*, December 30, 1955, pp. 3-5, in *CDSP*, VII, No. 52, 17.

⁴³ *Pravda*, November 20, 1955, pp. 1-2, in *CDSP*, VII, No. 47, 1.

⁴⁴ *New York Times*, November 21, 1955, p. 1.

⁴⁵ *New York Times*, December 11, 1955, p. 1.

reported to have said that the Soviet leaders "expressed their opinion (on Kashmir) after due consideration and great deliberation,"[46] there is strong indication that this momentous decision was taken rather suddenly, perhaps on Khrushchev's personal behest, for there had been no prior indication of this major policy shift. In a speech the day before, Bulganin, for example, spoke only of the renewal of ancient contacts between the peoples of the Soviet Union and this northern Himalayan state, thus avoiding any hint of what was to follow.[47] In fact, the very decision to go to Kashmir had been announced only mid-way through the tour. The Kashmir itinerary was added onto the return leg of the trip after the Soviet leaders had paid a brief visit to Burma. The mere announcement of the visit was enough to draw an official protest from the Pakistani government, which termed it an "unfriendly act."

Indeed, it would appear that Pakistan figured prominently in this decision. As previously mentioned, the Soviets had become quite indignant at Pakistani entry into a Western military alliance and had tried various measures to dissuade Pakistan from this course.[48] Having failed to prevent a Pakistani signature on the Baghdad Pact, the Soviet leaders displayed a sharp pique during their Indian tour. Thus, Bulganin issued a strong threat when he warned that territories housing foreign-controlled military bases would "be turned into fields of war and annihilation."[49] Indeed, Khrushchev's Srinagar statement was itself ensconced in an anti-Pakistani diatribe. Referring to the aforementioned Pakistani protest as "an unprecedented interference on Pakistan's part in another country's internal affairs...," Khrushchev angrily commented, "No other power in the past had dared to tell us what we should do and whom to choose as our friends."[50] The rambunctious First Secretary went so far as to question the very legitimacy of Pakistan, by reiterating the Stalinist formulary that the 1947 partition was not brought about by religion, but by "some third state" (i.e., Great

---

[46] Stein, *op. cit.*, p. 76.

[47] *New York Times*, December, 10, 1955, p. 4.

[48] As one lever of pressure, the Soviets had been supporting Afghan demands for the creation of an independent Pushtunistan to be formed from Pushtu regions of West Pakistan. See, *Pravda*, April 5, 1955, p. 4, in *CDSP*, VII, No. 14, 41.

[49] *New York Times*, November 29, 1955, p. 1.

[50] *New York Times*, December 11, 1955, p. 1.

Britain) in pursuance of its policy of divide and rule.

Thus, the dialectics of Cold War politics had led the Soviets to make a firm commitment to the Indian position on Kashmir. This support was to be demonstrated in 1957 and again in 1962 when the Soviets cast their veto on UN Security Council resolutions in defense of India's position on Kashmir. To the extent that Soviet support hardened India's resolve on this issue, the Soviets indirectly helped to make the problem even more intractable to solution, thereby, perpetuating Indo-Pakistani discord.[51] Moreover, in making this commitment, the Soviet leaders had pushed the Pakistani government even more into the Western camp. Judging from their remarks at the time, the commitment to support India on Kashmir was in large part a punitive measure against Pakistan.[52] As one Indian scholar observed, Khrushchev's statement at Srinagar was the equivalent of three Bhilais,[53] and moreover, it was gratis, for the Soviets did not win any commensurate concessions from the Indian side. The joint communique did not disclose any Indian concessions to Soviet positions in world affairs beyond those which had been taken previously. Moreover, throughout the visit, Nehru was careful to reaffirm Indian non-alignment.

Thus, the Kashmir commitment had the effect of solidifying Indo-Soviet ties. The Soviet partisan role in the politics of the subcontinent became the hallmark of Soviet policy in the Khrushchev era. It should be noted, herein, that the Chinese, who were also enjoying good relations with the Indians at this time, did not feel compelled to commit themselves on this issue. When the Cold War alignments began to dissolve in the subcontinent in the early 1960's, their discretion was to afford the Chinese much greater leverage with which to maneuver.

In the wake of this historic visit, there ensued a period of official

---

[51] The Pakistani High Commissioner to India observed that Khrushchev's speech could result in setting back efforts to reach a settlement and accused the Soviet leaders of trying to convince the peoples of both countries that further negotiations were pointless. *New York Times*, December 13, 1955, p. 6.

[52] An additional consideration may have been the conviction that a Kashmir secure in Indian hands would not be turned into a foreign military base. See, Bulganin's post-visit report before the Supreme Soviet. *Pravda*, December 30, 1955, pp. 1-2, in *CDSP*, VII, No. 51, 15.

[53] Harish Kapur, "The Soviet Union and Indo-Pakistani Relations," *International Studies (New Delhi)*, VIII, Nos. 1-2, (July-October, 1966), 156.

euphoria over India. In their post-trip reports before the Supreme Soviet, Bulganin and Khrushchev not only praised Indian foreign policy, but also commended various aspects of the government's domestic program, such as community development, state agricultural farms and the public sector.[54] At the Twentieth Party Congress, which officially discarded the Stalinist two-camps in favor of the broader "peace zone" consisting of both socialist and non-socialist states of Europe and Asia, India was accorded pride of place among developing nations, being mentioned immediately after China in Khrushchev's report.[55] In the Soviet perspective, India had joined the ranks of the great powers.

It was at this time that the Soviets, sensing a broad consensus with Nehru on many areas of foreign affairs, promoted Indian representation on many major international bodies, such as disarmament commissions, truce commissions, etc. Indeed, when a Middle East crisis broke out in 1958, Khrushchev went as far as to call for a Geneva summit meeting to include the United States, Great Britain, France, the Soviet Union and India, an offer which surely rankled the Chinese, who were beginning to fear that the Soviets valued "bourgeois" India over Communist China.

The Chinese, who were also having their troubles with India over border demarcation, must have been irritated with the whitewash that India received in the Soviet press. The Soviets refrained from making critical comment on Indian domestic politics.[56] Thus, the Soviet press interpreted the CPI victory in Kerala during the 1957 general elections in a rather low key, noting only that the elections had shown majority support for India's foreign policy.[57] Furthermore, the separatist movement among the Naga Hill tribes was viewed as being fabricated by "Imperialist intrigues."[58] On the diplomatic front, the Soviets continued to demonstrate their support for Indian

---

[54] *Pravda*, December 30, 1955, pp. 1-2, in *CDSP*, VII, No. 51, 13.

[55] *Pravda*, February 15, 1956, pp. 1-11, in *CDSP*, VIII, No. 4, 6-7.

[56] It should be noted that Nehru exhibited remarkable restraint as well, when, for example, he remained silent on Soviet intervention in Hungary in 1956. For further detail on the Indian response to this event, see, Stein, *op. cit.*, pp. 88ff.

[57] Perevoshchikov, "Elections in India," *Izvestia*, April 9, 1957, p. 4, in *CDSP*, IX, No. 14, 27.

[58] *Pravda*, September 18, 1957, p. 6, in *CDSP*, IX, No. 37, 16-17.

claims to Kashmir and Goa.[59]

A major beneficiary of this "honeymoon" period was the Indian economy. To complement the Bhilai steel mill, the Soviets extended a $125 million credit in November 1957 for several projects in the state sector including a heavy machinery plant, a coal-mining machinery plant, a thermal power station and coal-mining projects. In addition, the Soviets set up facilities at Bhilai to train Indian metallurgists and technicians for the plant. More advanced training for Indian engineers was arranged in the Soviet Union. Also, as part of its UNESCO contribution, the Soviets financed and helped set up the Indian Institute of Technology at Bombay. Moreover, to reduce Indian dependence on Western oil refineries, the Soviets, as early as 1955, dispatched a team of oil experts to conduct geological surveys which led to the discoveries first of natural gas and then of oil in the Cambay Gulf and Ankleshwar. In 1960, the Soviets delivered petroleum products on such favorable terms that it forced the three Western-owned oil refineries in India to lower prices.

Soviet economic assistance might have taken even larger proportions had it not been for apparent resistance from the Indian side. Thus, for example, in a March 1956 visit, Mikoyan offered India Soviet expertise in Indian economic planning, an offer which was turned down.[60] Later in the year it was reported that when a Soviet team recommended the construction of a heavy machine building plant at Bokaro, the more conservative members of the Nehru cabinet, including Morarji Desai, T. T. Krishnamachari and G. V. Pant, forced the adoption of a plant one-half the recommended size.[61]

Although Soviet aid to India was small in comparison with American assistance, its impact was proportionately much greater,

---

[59] The use of the Security Council veto on the Kashmir issue has been already noted. The Soviets, who had consistently supported India's claim to the Portuguese enclave of Goa, were forced to use their UN veto in 1961 to block a Security Council resolution condemning India as an aggressor for having taken over Goa. In the period under review, the Soviets regarded American support for Portuguese interests as a ploy to involve Portuguese Goa in SEATO and thus apply additional pressure on India. See *Pravda*, September 18, 1957, p. 6, in *CDSP*, IX, No. 37, 16-17.

[60] Cited in Bhabani Sen Gupta, *op. cit.*, p. 85.

[61] *Economic Weekly*, December 22, 1956, 1492.

since it was concentrated on a few large projects in the state sector, which from both the Soviet and Indian perspective was the key to industrialization.

Indo-Soviet trade also increased dramatically following the Bulganin and Khrushchev visit. In fact, by 1958 the volume of trade had increased so rapidly that India ranked as the Soviet Union's fourth largest trading partner, in terms of total trade turnover, in the non-Communist world.[62] Moreover, to accommodate India's need to save on hard currency expenditures, the Soviets agreed to incorporate in the bilateral trade agreement signed in 1958 a provision which allowed for payment in rupees without conversion into a convertible currency.[63] The Soviets also agreed to parity tonnage for Soviet and Indian ships to conduct this trade, a measure which helped resuscitate a lagging Indian shipping industry.[64]

This trade and aid offensive suggests that the Soviets were desirous of forging solid and long-term economic ties with India which would strengthen Indo-Soviet political ties as well. In view of these extensive aid and trade commitments, it is worthwhile to inquire what Soviet expectations were with regard to India.

It will be remembered that one of the basic objectives of Soviet policy towards India was to reduce or eliminate Western influence there. Soviet economic commitments were rationalized as contributions to India's quest for economic independence, which was a more or less subtle euphemism for the abovementioned goal. By providing India with a non-Western alternative source of aid and trade, the Soviets believed that they thereby enabled India to resist Western political pressures. At a time when the United States was applying the Zhdanov "two-camp" thesis in reverse by seeking to forge an anti-Communist military alliance system, Indian nonalignment and prestige among other Third World countries were highly valued.

---

[62] *Vneshniaia Torgovlia*, No. 7 (July, 1959), 13-20, in *CDSP*, XI, No. 34, 6. Between 1953 and 1958, Indian imports from the USSR increased from $900,000 to $45,600,000 and exports to the USSR from $700,000 to $49,000,000. See, Stein, *op. cit.*, App. B, p. 297.

[63] *Pravda*, November 17, 1958, p. 5, in *CDSP*, X, No. 46, 27-28. The 1953 trade agreement employed a system of clearing accounts in pounds sterling.

[64] *Pravda*, April 7, 1956, p. 3, in *CDSP*, VIII, No. 14, 33.

As far as influencing the course of Indian domestic politics is concerned, there is little evidence that the Soviets harbored grandiose ambitions. To be sure, the Soviets were flattered by such institutions as planning and the state sector, which were inspired by Soviet economic development. Although a 1956 *New Times* article by M. Rubinshtein spoke of "objective conditions in India for obviating the continued growth of monopoly capital," and for "taking the socialist path" by "peaceful methods,"[65] an article appearing in *Kommunist* at the end of the year dismissed as impossible the notion, suggested by Rubinshtein, that socialism could somehow be built by reforms in India.[66] Until Castro's Cuba raised Soviet expectations regarding new revolutionary possibilities among developing countries, the achievement of political and economic independence was as much as the Soviets could hope for short of a Communist take-over by "peaceful means." Thus, India ranked in the top echelon of non-Communist developing countries in the typology which the Soviets employed at this time.

Given the generous aid and trade terms extended to India, it would appear that Soviet objectives there were rather modest. It must be remembered that this formative phase in the development of close Indo-Soviet ties was a delicate period. In order to counteract the Stalinist image and cultivate a climate of trust, the Soviet leadership may have overcommitted itself both politically and economically. Certainly, it is known that the Chinese greatly resented the significant amount of Soviet assistance to India. Indeed, this point of view may have won over a part of the Soviet leadership as well. The foreign aid program, it now appears, was one of the targets of the so-called 'anti-Party group's' general opposition to Khrushchev's policies.[67] Just how important India had become to the Khrushchevite leadership would be seen more clearly in 1959 when the Chinese threw down a challenge to the Soviets over India.

[65] M. Rubinshtein, "A Non-Capitalist Path for Under-developed Countries," *New Times*, Nos. 28, 32, 1956, as quoted in Gupta, *op. cit.*, p. 80.
[66] V. Semenov, "The Disintegration of the Colonial System of Imperialism and Questions of International Relations," *Kommunist* (December 1956), 97, in *CDSP*, IX, No. 10, 6.
[67] See, Saburov's speech at the Twenty-First (1959) Party Congress, reported in Kovner, *op. cit.*, 633.

THE CHINESE DIVERGENCE AND ITS IMPACT ON SOVIET POLICY, 1959-1964

The events of 1959 were to effect a major shift in Soviet policy towards India. In that year tensions along the Sino-Indian border received worldwide attention. An unsuccessful rebellion in Tibet, which ended with the Dalai Lama's seeking refuge in India, was followed by major border incidents along the mountain passes in the summer. As a result, the Chinese and Indians, who had co-authored the Pancha Shila four years earlier, were set at loggerheads. While these events have been adequately described elsewhere,[68] what concerns us here is the Soviet reaction to them.

The border conflict placed the Soviets in the precarious position of choosing between a "fraternal" state with whom relations were deteriorating rapidly or a "bourgeois" state with whom relations were being carefully cultivated. The stakes in this decision were quite high. Confronted by a direct military threat from a Communist power, the Indian government might have overreacted by swinging sharply to the West for military and political support, and perhaps even abandoning the policy of non-alignment. Certainly, a clear demonstration of Soviet support for the Chinese position would not only have undone years of painstaking effort to establish an Indo-Soviet rapprochement, but also have made the continuation of Nehru's foreign policy infeasible. This possibility would then have confirmed Chinese accusations that the Indian "bourgeois" government had become firmly aligned with the American "Imperialists." Moreover, it would have dealt a telling blow to the Khrushchevian global strategy of peaceful coexistence, in which India played an important part. Finally, it had to be considered that Indian military dependence upon the West might have led to the construction of American military bases in the border areas, contiguous not only to China but also to the Soviet Union. Thus, the cardinal objective of Soviet policy towards India since Stalin's day was involved.

It was these considerations which influenced the Soviet leaders not to allow the Chinese to disrupt their foreign policy objective.

---

[68] See, Stein, *op. cit.*, pp. 111-22; Gupta, *op. cit.*, pp. 117-40, Neville Maxwell, *India's China War* (New York: Random House, 1971).

Challenging Peking on an issue in which the Chinese felt they had a strong case, Moscow issued the following Tass statement in response to a major border clash in the Longju sector of the North East Frontier Agency:

> "The incident on the Chinese-Indian border is certainly deplorable.... The Chinese and Soviet peoples are linked by the unbreakable bonds of fraternal friendship.... Friendly cooperation between the USSR and India is successfully developing in keeping with the idea of peaceful coexistence.... Its (the dispute's) inspirers are trying to discredit the idea of peaceful coexistence between states with different social systems and to prevent the strengthening of the Asian people's solidarity in the struggle for consolidation of national independence."[69]

This historic document, which brought the Sino-Soviet dispute into the open, marked the first instance in which a Communist state professed "neutrality" in a dispute between a fellow Communist state and a bourgeois government. As Bhabani Sen Gupta remarks: "If Moscow had remained neutral, leaving the dispute to be settled exclusively between Peking and New Delhi, and trying to bring both to a compromise, it might have been regarded by the Chinese as a tolerable position. But Khrushchev decided not to remain neutral by declaring Soviet neutrality."[70]

The decision to release the statement was not lightly taken. That the Soviets were aware that the stake involved was nothing less than a defense of basic Soviet foreign policy goals is suggested by the pointed reference to supposedly Western (but which could just as easily be Chinese) efforts to sabotage the principle of peaceful coexistence between states with different social systems. Moreover, it is known that the statement was made public despite strong Chinese attempts to block such a move.[71]

---

[69] *Pravda*, September 10, 1959, as quoted by Stein, *op. cit.*, p. 116.

[70] Gupta, *op. cit.*, p. 87.

[71] *Ibid.*, p. 88. Gupta records that Peking sent Moscow a copy of a letter which Chou En-lai was about to send to Nehru laying claim for the first time to some 35,000 square miles of territory which India regarded as her own. By not releasing the Tass statement, the Soviets might thus have bargained for a withdrawal of this dramatic escalation of the Chinese territorial claim.

Furthermore, not only did the Soviets render indirect political support for the Indian position,[72] but they also chose this moment to announce their largest credit to India up to this time—a $378 million loan for various projects in India's Third Five Year Plan. With India's defense budget now being sharply increased in response to the Chinese military threat, the Soviets had thus emphasized that they would continue to help underwrite Indian economic development under even more burdensome conditions.

While the Soviets maintained their "neutrality" on the border dispute, urging a peaceful, negotiated settlement of it, they were more pointed in their criticism of the Chinese behind the scenes. The Chinese later disclosed that the CPSU Central Committee had informed the CPC in a verbal notification that "one cannot possibly seriously think that a state such as India which is militarily and economically immeasurably weaker than China would really launch a military attack on China and commit aggression against it."[73] In addition, in a closed session at a Communist gathering at Bucharest in June, 1960, Khrushchev vilified the CPC for having acted as "pure nationalists" on the border dispute.[74]

Furthermore, it is questionable just how intent the Soviets were to arrive at an amicable resolution of the dispute. Although there was speculation among Indian journalists at the time that the Soviet Union was trying to mediate the dispute,[75] if this was so, then very little came of it. Although Khrushchev might have prevailed upon Nehru to receive Chou En-lai in April, 1960, there is no evidence that he succeeded in modifying India's bargaining position. Indeed, the talks between the two governments were fruitless, since the positions of both sides had become too rigid. It may be argued, moreover, that the Soviet response itself contributed

---

[72] The Tass statement had the desired effect of dissociating the Soviet from Chinese positions on the border conflict in the minds of Indian officials. Commenting on the statement, Nehru said: "Considering everything, the statement was a fair one and an unusual one for the Soviet government to sponsor." *Hindu*, September 12, 1959, quoted in Stein, *op. cit.*, p. 117.

[73] "The Truth About How the Leaders of the CPSU Have Allied Themselves with India Against China," *People's Daily*, November 2, 1963, quoted in Harish Kapur, "India and the Soviet Union," *Survey*, XVI, No. 1 (Winter, 1970), 204.

[74] Cited in Richard Siegel, "Chinese Efforts to Influence Soviet Policy," *India Quarterly*, XXIV, No. 3 (July-September, 1968), 224.

[75] *New York Times*, September 14, 1959, p. 11.

to the intractability of the dispute. Thus, as a leading Indian scholar observes, "Soviet support persuaded Nehru that no flexibility in his basic stand on the border was called for."[76] This support for India also seems to have hardened the Chinese negotiating position since in his September 8th letter to Nehru, Chou En-lai virtually withdrew the earlier offer to recognize the MacMahon line.[77]

In retrospect then, the Soviet response indicated that the maintenance of good relations with India was valued over "proletarian solidarity" with China. India itself became a focal point in the Sino-Soviet dispute. From this point in time Indo-Soviet relations took on a new dimension. As the Sino-Soviet dispute grew in intensity, India was to have an increasingly important role in the emergent Soviet strategy to contain China.

It should be noted, however, that although the Soviets did not accept the Chinese case against Nehru, neither did they cling to their previous rose-colored image of India. In fact, it would appear that Chinese criticism of the Nehru government had made some impression upon the Soviet leaders.

The imposition of Presidential rule in Kerala toppling the Communist-led government, the emergence of the right wing Swatantra Party, and President Eisenhower's successful tour of India in 1959 definitely suggested to the Soviets that a shift towards a conservative course was under way in India. Moreover, the Nehru government showed that it was no longer reticent to express criticism of the Soviet Union. Thus, for example, shortly after the resumption of Soviet atmospheric nuclear tests in 1961, Nehru, who had been attending the Belgrade Conference of non-aligned states, paid a short visit on Khrushchev and reprimanded him for the test resumption. In fact, the joint communique ended on the discordant note that there had been a "wide, frank exchange of views on current problems of the international situation...."[78] Thus, India had ceased to be a proponent of Soviet foreign policy goals in the

---

[76] Gupta, *op. cit.*, p. 129.

[77] *Ibid.*, p. 129.

[78] *Pravda*, September 8, 1961, p. 1, in *CDSP*, XIII, No. 36, 6. This was not the sole occasion on which Nehru voiced sharp criticism. On his visit to the United States in October, 1961, he sided with the Americans on the Berlin issue and castigated the Soviets for the first time for their repression of the Hungarian uprising.

world arena. So too, with the achievement of independence by a large number of African states and with the growing stature of other Afro-Asian leaders such as Nasser and Nkrumah, India's prestige among the developing countries had ebbed and with it, her importance in Soviet eyes.

Although criticism of various aspects of Nehru's domestic and foreign policies were voiced in the Soviet press as early as late 1958,[79] a more thoroughgoing reappraisal of Indian development emerged as part of a general reevaluation of Soviet policy towards developing countries. With the wave of colonial emancipation in Africa, the problems of post-independent development now absorbed Soviet attention. Operating within the ideological framework of Marxism-Leninism, the Soviets could not but dwell on the phenomena of class divisions in the post-liberation phase. This meant that the earlier simplistic image of the positive role of the national bourgeoisie in the Third World was jettisoned, and a more critical assessment of the ruling national bourgeoisie and their institutions began to emerge. Thus, for example, in one of the more critical articles in this period, B. N. Ponomarev, the Central Committee Secretary in charge of relations with foreign Communist parties,[80] took note of the "contradictory policy" of the national bourgeoisie,

---

[79] Thus, for example, in response to an earlier article by Nehru, critical of Soviet society, (J. Nehru, "The Basic Approach," *A. I. C. C. Economic Review*, May 15, 1958), P. Iudin, then Soviet Ambassador to China, in an article in the December 1958 *World Marxist Review*, accused the Indian bourgeoisie and landlords of using the state machinery as an instrument of violent repression against the masses and debunked Nehru's socialism as bearing "very little real likeness to real socialism." It is questionable, however, whether Iudin's article reflected the majority position of the Soviet leadership. Its publication in *World Marxist Review* rather than *Pravda*, and the fact that Iudin was recalled as Ambassador in November 1959 because of his open support for the Chinese position on the border dispute, suggests that his views reflected those of a leftist section of the Kremlin leadership. For a more detailed examination of this article (P. Iudin, "Can We Accept Pandit Nehru's Approach," *World Marxist Review*, December, 1958), see, Stein, *op. cit.*, pp. 106-10. That Iudin's point of view was not dominant is further suggested by a review of the proceedings of the 21st Party Congress, at which an Uzbek party official declared that India was progressing in a "democratic" manner (this, in the face of mounting attacks on the CPI-led Kerala government). *Pravda*, January 31, 1959, pp. 7-8, in *CDSP*, XI, No. 8, 28.

[80] B. Ponomarev, "Concerning the National-Democratic State" *Kommunist*, No. 8 (May, 1961), 33-40, in *CDSP*, XIII, No. 22, 3-7.

which, while opposed to colonialism and domination by foreign monopolies, was nevertheless dependent on a continuous flow of foreign capital from the "Imperialist" powers. Moreover, in a major revision of the earlier rose-colored view of the state sector in developing countries, Ponomarev emphasized that its progressiveness was dependent on the socio-economic context and warned that the bourgeoisie supported the state sector only insofar as it promoted their interests. Although India was not mentioned by name, this analysis was definitely applicable. In order to justify their large aid commitment to India, the Soviets argued that Indian state capitalism, while not as progressive as those in other Afro-Asian states, was nevertheless not to be equated with state monopoly capitalism of the West, since the former arose as a means of creating an independent national economy and should thus be considered generally progressive, whereas the latter was a product of overripe capitalism.[81]

Whereas, in view of his liaison position with foreign Communist parties, Ponomarev could be expected to support the more left wing orientation towards the third world, his was by no means an isolated position. Although different assessments as to which elements of the bourgeoisie could still play a progressive role in the developing countries were aired in the Soviet press,[82] the general tenor of Soviet analyses was much more critical. Even Khrushchev, who was personally identified with the pristine image of the bourgeoisie, conceded at the 21st Party Congress that the upper bourgeoisie and landlords were seeking to tie the developing countries to the world capitalist system.[83]

A second major aspect of this reappraisal was the elaboration of a new development model—the national democratic state. As

---

[81] See, for example, R. Avakov and R. Andreasian, "The Progressive Role of the State Sector," in the symposium on "The National Liberation Movement at the Present Stage," *Kommunist*, No. 13 (September, 1962), 89-109, in *CDSP*, XIV, No. 41, 9-10.

[82] The most conclusive evidence of divergent attitudes surfaced during the deliberations over the 1961 Party Program in which a statement noting that the bourgeoisie would have to make concessions as developing countries travel further along the non-capitalist path of development was deleted from the draft program in favor of a milder formulary. See, *Pravda*, No. 2, 1961, pp. 1-9, in *CDSP*, XIII, No. 45, 13.

[83] *Pravda*, Oct. 19, 1961, pp. 1-10, in *CDSP*, XIII, No. 45, 24.

defined in the communique of the meeting of eighty-one communist parties in Moscow in November 1960, the national democratic state was:

> "a state which consistently upholds its political and economic independence; fights against Imperialism and its military blocs, against military bases on its territory; a state which fights against the new forms of colonialism and the penetration of Imperialist capital; a state which rejects dictatorial and despotic methods of government; a state in which the people are ensured broad democratic rights and freedoms (freedom of speech, press, assembly, demonstrations, establishment of political parties and social organization), the opportunity to work for the enactment of an agrarian reform and other domestic and social changes and for participation in shaping government policy."[84]

Designed initially as a blueprint for newly liberated states, the state of national democracy was soon viewed as a kind of halfway house towards socialism or, in Marxist terms, a transitional form leading towards a non-capitalist path of development. Indeed, the term non-capitalist development, which had previously been employed in reference to socialist construction in underdeveloped Asian states under Communist rule,[85] gradually was reinterpreted as being applicable to progressive non-Communist Afro-Asian states. Giving maximum publicity to the non-capitalist path of development, the Soviets at this juncture warned that developing states remaining within the world capitalist system would take centuries to catch up with the advanced industrial states.

It should be noted that the two concepts of the national democratic state and the non-capitalist path of development were as yet rather vague. Whether any non-Communist state was actually traveling this path and exactly how such a state would

---

[84] This may be found in John Gittings, ed., *Survey of the Sino-Soviet Dispute* (London: Oxford Univ. Press, 1968), Appendix Q, pp. 355-69.

[85] The term was originally employed by Lenin to explain the hypothetical situation of successful proletarian revolutions in advanced countries coming to the aid of underdeveloped areas, thus obviating the necessity of passing through a capitalist stage of development.

evolve were still unanswered problems. At this stage in the evolution of Soviet thought on the process of development, the more traditional view that the transition to socialism was possible only under the leadership of Communist parties prevailed.[86] The answers to economic problems of development were still posited in ideological terms. Thus, for example, in the article by Ponomarev previously cited, the solution to the food problem in these countries was tied exclusively to agrarian social reforms and the abolition of the feudal landholding system.[87] Nevertheless, Castro's Cuba must certainly have affected Soviet strategy and whetted Soviet expectations regarding revolutionary possibilities in the Third World.[88]

Thus, the Indian development model, exemplified by the 'political and economic independence' formulary, was gradually eclipsed as other developing countries appeared more attractive. Although as late as 1960 India was still placed in the forefront of Afro-Asian progressive states,[89] in subsequent years she was relegated to an inferior category, below a group of progressive states such as Egypt, Ghana, Indonesia and others, but above a category of dependent countries, such as most Latin American states, the Philippines, Pakistan, etc. In fact, while India was considered to be a bourgeois state rooted in the world capitalist economic system, her government was nevertheless seen to be committed (though not wholeheartedly) to achieving economic independence, and, on these grounds, Soviet aid and support for that country

[86] An emphatic statement of this position may be found in G. Starushenko, "Through General Democratic Transformations to Socialist Transformation," in "The National Liberation Movement at the Present Stage," *Kommunist*, No. 13 (Sept. 1962), 89-109, in *CDSP*, XIV, No. 41, 13-14.

[87] Ponomarev, *op. cit.*, p. 6.

[88] It should be recalled that the Soviets were very reticent to acknowledge the socialist direction of Castro's revolution. Academician E. Zhukov, writing in 1960, for example, stated that Cuba was "pursuing by no means a socialist but a general democratic national policy." Zhukov, moreover, did not even single out Cuba for special commendation, but merely linked it with other progressive states. See, E. Zhukov, "Significant Factors of Our Times—On Some Questions of the Present Day National Liberation Movement," *Pravda*, August 26, 1960, pp. 3-4, in *CDSP*, XII, No. 34, 18-19.

[89] See, Zhukov, *Ibid.*, 19. Zhukov states that general democratic measures were being carried out in varying degrees in India, Indonesia, Egypt and Iraq.

continued. It is evident, therefore, that Soviet defense of the Indian position during the Sino-Indian border conflict did not extend to continued ideological support for India's political evolution. In fact, although not as condemnatory as the Chinese posture, the Soviet attitude towards India became increasingly more critical. The brief 'honeymoon' period was definitely at an end.

Whether the diminished view of India affected the Soviet aid program to any degree is difficult to determine. The $ 347 million credit agreement, signed in the fall of 1959, for the expansion of Bhilai to 2.5 million tons output per year, the construction of 2.5 million ton oil refinery at Barauni and other state sector projects have already been mentioned. Another $ 125 million in credits for additional projects was extended in February 1961.[90] Moreover, it was reported in the Indian press that the Soviets were in contact with a leading unspecified Indian firm for the purpose of setting up a large engineering plant, but nothing ever came of this.[91] Thus, Soviet economic assistance to India continued without interruption.[92]

A more significant development was the commencement of Soviet military assistance to India with the shipment of military transports and helicopters in 1961. Leaving little doubt that this military aid was designed to meet the growing Chinese threat, the Soviets proceeded to train Indian crews in the Soviet Union to fly these planes in the mountainous border areas.[93] In addition, in August 1962 an agreement was finalized according to which the Soviets would sell India twelve MIG-21's (a plane which the

---

[90] Consult Marshall I. Goldman, *Soviet Foreign Aid* (New York: Praeger, 1967), Table IV-1, pp. 102-03, for a more detailed listing of Soviet credits until 1963.

[91] *Economic Weekly*, November 19, 1960, 1671.

[92] There is an Indian report, however, that Morarji Desai, then Finance Minister, was informed by Mikoyan during a 1962 trip to the Soviet Union that all funds for Indian assistance provided under the current plan had been exhausted and that additional aid would not be forthcoming. *Economic Weekly*, April 28, 1962, 692. It cannot be concluded on the basis of this evidence that the Soviets had decided to curtail their aid program at this time.

[93] *Asian Recorder*, VII, No. 2 (May 14-20, 1961), 3950. It was reported that the Soviets at this time also began to dispatch road building equipment to make some border areas accessible to Indian troops. See, Sisir Gupta, "India and the Soviet Union," *Current History*, March, 1963, 142.

Chinese did not possess), with the delivery of the first six set for December, and build in India a plant for the assembly and production of these jets.[94] This represented a definite Soviet commitment to the defense of India against the Chinese threat and, as such, drew Chinese ire. Yet, we cannot be sure that the Soviets were motivated solely by fear of the growing Chinese military threat. It is known, for example, that Soviet interest in supplying military aircraft to India dates back to 1956,[95] long before a major Chinese military threat to India could be taken seriously. Given the general justification that Soviet aid contributed to India's economic independence, the offer of military equipment, predating the Sino-Indian military conflict, most likely was extended in that spirit, i.e., that Soviet military aid would reduce India's dependence on Western suppliers and hence strengthen her political independence. Certainly, with the recognition that India's defense requirements had augmented considerably after the 1959 border conflict, the Soviets may have been prompted to step in to assume a part of this military burden. Indeed, following the October 1962 Chinese invasion, Khrushchev, in a secret letter to the Communist parties, defended Soviet military aid to India precisely on the grounds that it kept India from being forced to turn to the United States and Great Britain.[96] Thus, the Soviet decision to supply military arms to India may have been motivated by a confluence of earlier desires to offset Western influence with growing anxiety over Chinese territorial ambitions. Certainly, it was this latter factor which acquired much greater importance following the major Sino-Indian border conflict of October 1962.

The eruption of hostilities along the Sino-Indian border in October 1962 may be considered a second major crisis in Indo-

---

[94] Richard Siegel, "Evaluating the Results of Foreign Policy: Soviet and American Efforts in India," *Monograph Series in World Affairs*, Graduate School of International Studies, Univ. of Denver, Monograph No. 4-1968-69 (Denver: Univ. of Denver, 1969), 10-11.

[95] Lorne J. Kavic, *India's Quest for Security* (Berkeley, Calif: Univ. of California Press, 1967), p. 104. It was only after she failed to receive satisfactory terms from Western suppliers to offset a recent Pakistani purchase of U.S. Lockheed F-104's that India turned to the Soviets for MIG-21's.

[96] Cited in David Floyd, *Mao Against Khrushchev* (New York: Praeger, 1963) p. 366. In fact, the CPSU letter went so far as to claim that these arms supplies "represented a tremendous victory over the United States and England."

Soviet relations. Much has been written about this crisis, and a detailed examination seems redundant.[97] However, in analyzing the Soviet response to the border conflict, it should be kept in mind that the question of responsibility cannot be easily ascertained. Indeed, the consensus of Western scholars writing on this subject is that Indian obstinacy and shortsightedness stood in the way of a peaceful settlement of the border dispute.[98] Yet, the Soviets decided to sidestep this issue entirely.

Certainly the timing of the Chinese military action placed a much greater strain on Indo-Soviet relations than the 1959 hostilities.[99] Preoccupied with the Cuban Missile crisis, the Soviets tended to placate China to line up Communist support for the Soviet position on Cuba. Thus, the Soviets issued the well-known *Pravda* editorial of October 25,[100] in which the validity of the MacMahon line, which India claimed as its legal border, was questioned and India was urged to accept China's three-point peace offer—proposals which were clearly unacceptable to the Indians. The editorial went even further towards adopting the Chinese line by stating that the conflict served the interests of "certain reactionary circles in India that have cast their lot with foreign capital" and warned that "even progressive people may succumb and take a chauvinist stand"—a clear reference to the patriotic positions taken by the right wing of the CPI.[101] However, the document stopped short of endorsing the Chinese claim that India had been the aggressor.

The Soviets also worked behind the scenes to bring about a quick negotiated resolution to this embarrassing conflict. Both at

---

[97] See, in particular, Neville Maxwell, *India's China War* (New York: Random House, 1971).

[98] This is the conclusion of Harold Hinton, *Communist China in World Politics* (Boston: Houghton Mifflin, 1966), p. 299. Hinton's position is supported by both Gupta, *op. cit.*, p. 163, and Stein, *op. cit.*, p. 145. This is also the main thesis of Neville Maxwell's *India's China War*.

[99] Although Moscow was apparently consulted by the Chinese prior to the showdown, Stein believes that they did not anticipate the proportions which the Chinese military operations would take. Stein, *op. cit.*, p. 154.

[100] *Pravda* (Editorial), October 25, 1962, p. 1, in *CDSP*, XIV, No. 43, 16-17.

[101] Many of the more radical CPI members were jailed at this time under the Defence of India Act. In fact, the border conflict precipitated a formal split within the CPI between pro-Moscow and pro-Peking wings.

the UN and through private diplomatic channels the Soviets at the height of the Cuban crisis urged India to accept the Chinese cease-fire proposal by withdrawing her troops twenty kilometers from the battle line.[102] Moreover, although the Soviets did suspend military aid,[103] they did not employ any other sanctions. Within one week of the outbreak of hostilities, Moscow reaffirmed its aid commitment to India when the visiting Indian Minister for Fuel was informed that the Soviet government would speed up aid for India's coal, oil and power industries.[104]

The initial Soviet response was a calculated risk as far as Soviet-Indian relations were concerned. The Indian public was by and large shocked at the Soviet stand. According to one Indian scholar, informed Indian circles had apparently come to believe on the eve of the conflict that the Soviets would remain neutral.[105] Fortunately, Nehru, although seriously shaken by this crisis, did not succumb to public discontent and showed a keen understanding of the Soviet difficulties at this time. Furthermore, to allay Soviet suspicions, Nehru's first diplomatic action during this crisis was to inform the Soviet Ambassador that the Indian government would not request more Western arms than was absolutely necessary to repulse the Chinese. Fear of India's military dependence on the West was, as we have seen, a prime Soviet concern. Nehru's sensitivity and patience was duly rewarded.

Once the Cuban crisis subsided, the Soviets returned to a position of neutrality on the border conflict. Announcing this shift, a *Pravda* editorial on November 5th neither mentioned the Mac-Mahon line nor supported the Chinese peace proposals.[106] Rather the Soviets urged a negotiated settlement and claimed that the prolongation of the conflict only drained uselessly the material resources of both sides. However, the Soviets, in reply to Chinese

---

[102] Consult R. Vaidyanath, "The Reaction of the Soviet Union and Other Communist States," *International Studies*, V, Nos. 1-2 (July-October, 1963), 71.

[103] The first deliveries of MIG's did not arrive until February 1963, two months overdue. Also, it was announced in New Delhi on November 27th that an Indian request for emergency supplies of Soviet arms was refused. See, Gupta, *op. cit.*, p. 175. However, it should be noted, the Soviets were not critical of Nehru's appeals for American and British arms at this time.

[104] Stein, *op. cit.*, p. 155.

[105] Vaidyanath, *op. cit.*, 70.

[106] *Pravda* (Editorial), November 5, 1962, p. 1, in *CDSP*, XIV, No. 43, 18-19.

denunciations of the Soviet stand on Cuba, soon issued a scathing criticism of Peking's role in the border conflict. In a major policy speech before the Supreme Soviet on December 12,[107] Khrushchev belabored the fact that a negotiated settlement had not been reached and took the Chinese to task for getting involved in a conflict over territory of no value. With his usual rhetorical innuendo, he interpreted the Chinese troop withdrawal in the following manner:

> "It may be asked—How can you claim that this was a reasonable step, when it was taken after so many lives had been laid down and so much blood shed? Would it not have been better if the sides had not resorted to hostilities at all? Yes, of course this would have been better. But if the course of events could not be changed, it was better to display courage now and stop the conflict. Is this not wisdom worthy of a statesman? Of course people could be found who say: Here is the CPR, now withdrawing its troops actually to the line on which the conflict began; wouldn't it have been better not to have moved from positions where they formerly stood?..."

Returning the Chinese charge of Soviet capitulation before American arms over Cuba, he went on to say:

> "But, comrades, there are people who try to put another interpretation on the decision taken by the government of the CPR. They say: Is this not a retreat? And this question too is asked: Is this not a concession on the part of the Chinese comrades?...Some are already saying that China ceased hostilities apparently because India began to receive support from the American and British Imperialists who are providing that country with arms. Consequently, say such people, the CPR felt that if the conflict were to develop further it might grow into a major war that would require even greater sacrifice. Yet, evidently the Chinese friends took account of the situation...."

[107] *Pravda*, December 13, 1962, pp. 1-5, in *CDSP*, XIV, No. 52, 7-8.

Arguing that the conflict was a setback for the democratic movement in India and had only strengthened the forces of reaction there, Khrushchev stated:

> "Tomorrow, if the war continues, anyone who utters a word against the war will be considered a Communist. Consequently, pacifists will also be placed in this category. Here you have a debauch by reactionary forces, by the most brazen militarists and reactionaries. Evidently the Chinese comrades also took this into account when they decided the question of a cease-fire and withdrawal of troops."

Khrushchev's pointed condemnation of the Chinese role in the border conflict was followed up by a more reasoned defense of the Soviet position, which is contained in a CPSU secret letter dispatched in January 1963 to other Communist parties.[108] While acknowledging the MacMahon line as "artificial," the letter nevertheless maintained that this was no reason for provoking military operations "which were bound to throw India into the arms of the capitalists...." The letter went on to defend Soviet arms supplies and Indo-Soviet relations, stating that:

> "The policies of India and the USSR have much in common. India tried genuinely to find a path to neutral absolute independence, and there were many socialist elements which it was worth encouraging."

Underlining Soviet solicitude for India in the past, the letter noted that "the establishment of this state of mutual trust (in Indo-Soviet relations) required many years of difficult negotiations and patience before the fruits of mutual confidence and friendship were apparent."

The CPSU was, in fact, arguing that the Chinese had tried to undo years of patient Soviet effort. Suggestive of the strong Soviet concern to bring about a quick negotiated

---

[108] Cited in Floyd, *op. cit.*, p. 366.

settlement,[109] the letter stated in emotional terms:

> "We begged—yes, we begged—the Chinese to stop their military operations immediately and we offered immediate mediation, for which India was ready. We wanted to prevent India from being forced to turn for military aid to the United States and Great Britain, who had been waiting for such an opportunity from the Chinese, who call themselves Communists. Thus, years of hard striving for Indian friendship and Indian neutrality went for nothing. Not only that—and let us be straight—today the capitalists are supplying arms to India because Chinese aggression forced them to do so. The Chinese aggression also had the consequence that we lost one of our most faithful friends[110] among the Indian leaders and that because he relied on our help."

Thus the border conflict had become a prime issue in the Sino-Soviet dispute. In fact, the bitter recriminations surrounding both the Cuban missile crisis and the Sino-Indian border conflict precipitated a major escalation of the Sino-Soviet dispute with a vitriolic wave of polemics the following year. The Soviets accused the Chinese of deliberately seeking to sabotage Indo-Soviet relations and driving India into Western hands. Certainly, at the very least, the display of Chinese military superiority had pricked the balloon of Indian pride as a world power and a co-equal of the Chinese—an image which the Soviets had been promoting. The border conflict was also a major blow to Nehru's foreign policy, and definitely eroded his domestic base of support. Not only did Nehru's personal prestige wane, but, for the remainder of the decade, India turned inwards, beset by problems of political instability and economic stagnation aggravated in part by a major increase in defense commitments. It was these latter

---

[109] It should be noted, however, that once the Cuban crisis subsided, the Soviets withdrew their pressure on India to accept Chinese terms and instead, sought an international agreement against the use of force to resolve territorial disputes.

[110] A reference to Krishna Menon who was forced to step down from his cabinet position of Defense Minister.

considerations which underlay Soviet anxieties over India for the next several years.

While we have noted how Nehru acted immediately to reassure Moscow, the Soviets were nevertheless quite alarmed over the future conduct of Indian foreign policy. Even though they tacitly accepted India's reception of some $100 million in Western military aid in the months following the crisis, they warned against any involvement in a military alliance with the West. In fact, in a *Pravda* article, dated December 25, 1962,[111] the Soviets went so far as to give a strong hint that should India forsake its policy of non-alignment (at least between the West and the Soviet bloc, since genuine non-alignment was already a dead letter), the Soviets might forfeit their support for the Indian position on Kashmir. The Soviet press viewed the detention of Indian Communists, the joint Anglo-American air maneuvers in India,[112] and the general debates over the policy of non-alignment as indicative that the forces of reaction were on the rise in India and specifically urged all "progressive forces" to rebuff the right wing advances.[113] Indeed, for the remainder of the decade, such anxieties over the course of Indian domestic and foreign policy continually surfaced in the Soviet media.

Soviet concern was particularly heightened following Nehru's death in the spring of 1964. Not only did the Soviet press praise Nehru as an "outstanding statesman" and a friend of the Soviet Union, but it paid close attention to his successor, noting that Shastri would continue Nehru's policy "at least for the immediate

---

[111] *Pravda*, December 25, 1962, p. 3, in *CDSP*, XIV, No. 52, 32-33.

[112] In the summer of 1963, a joint Anglo-American air exercise was held in India, with long-range fighter aircraft flying in to operate from Indian Air Force bases. Despite the fact that Nehru had requested this form of military assistance in November 1962, this was not known at the time. In fact, the Indian government tried to play down their significance by denying that the maneuvers entailed any commitment by the British and American governments to assist India in the event of a Chinese attack. See, on this point, Maxwell, *op. cit.*, p. 467.

[113] A. Kuznetsov, "Strengthen the Unity of Progressive Forces." *Pravda*, August 24, 1963, p. 3, in *CDSP*, XV, No. 34, 36. Interestingly, the post-Cuba crisis Soviet position was a strong prop for Indian maintenance of non-alignment, for Nehru consistently argued that it was Soviet neutrality on the border conflict itself which justified the continuation of his foreign policy. See, Stein, *op. cit.*, p. 162.

future."[114] In another unusual commentary,[115] I. Serebriakov assessed the composition of the Shastri cabinet, lauding the inclusion as Minister of Information and Broadcasting of Indira Gandhi and other close supporters of Nehru but taking issue with the participation in the government of S. K. Patil, the Bombay Congress leader, T. T. Krishnamachari, and M. Desai, all linked with big business interests. Moreover, Serebriakov acknowledged that reactionary forces had support within Congress ruling circles and warned that they "may become a serious threat to the future of the country."

The public expression of Soviet preferences regarding the Nehru succession is rather curious. Certainly, this would have been unthinkable during the formative phase of constructing friendly relations, when the Soviets paid scrupulous attention to Indian sensitivities. The fact that the Soviets were now playing a partisan role with respect to domestic Indian politics suggests, at the very least, that the Soviets felt confident enough in their relations with India, following the crucial test of October 1962, to risk disfavor with three potential successors to Nehru's mantle. It might also be added that by broadcasting their preferences they were giving the Indian right wing the opportunity to argue Soviet interference in India's domestic affairs—something which they obviously did not desire. Whatever the rationale regarding the partisan role which the Soviets assumed, the possibility that they would have withdrawn their political and economic support had Morarji Desai assumed leadership and/or India acceded to a military alliance with the West cannot be ruled out. Certainly, it would seem that the Soviets were walking a tightrope—seeking to thwart the growing influence of the political right in India and at the same time wary of any threats to Indian political stability from the far left. For the remainder of the decade the Soviets would then concentrate their efforts on forging a stable left-center coalition in India, under the Marxist rubric of a national democratic front.

It should also be noted that, despite their concerns, the Soviets had apparently decided not to wait cautiously upon events but to

---

[114] *Pravda*, May 28, 1964, p. 3, in *CDSP*, XVI, No. 22, 20.

[115] I. Serebriakov, "Good Hopes," *Pravda*, June 11, 1964, p. 5, in *CDSP*, XVI, No. 24, 22-23.

assume a more active commitment to India. Thus, although there was some tendency to withhold military arms in the wake of the border conflict,[116] the military aid pipeline was soon flowing again and by May 1964 the total value of arms obtained since the Chinese invasion amounted to $130 million.[117] Moreover, in September 1964 India received a new loan of $140 million to be repaid at 2% interest over a ten-year period for the purchase of two additional squadrons of MIG-21's, 50 surface-to-air missiles, 70 light tanks, 6 submarines, helicopters and other assorted weapons.[118] It was precisely during this period that the USSR overtook the US as the chief supplier of military arms to India.

While the growing Chinese threat appears to be a cardinal factor in the Soviet decision to dramatically escalate its military assistance to India, the desire to offset Western influence also figured in their deliberations. It was reported, for example, that an American offer to afford India the protection of an air umbrella sparked Soviet interest in extending an offer to establish missile manufacturing facilities in India.[119] Both this offer and the previous agreement to establish a MIG plant in India were consistent with the stated purpose of Soviet aid, i.e., to promote India's political and economic independence. In any event, the September 1964 military aid agreement, signed on the occasion of President Radhakrishnan's warm reception in Moscow, probably was staged as a demonstration that Indo-Soviet relations were as warm as ever—this coming during the period of uncertainty following Nehru's death.

Soviet economic assistance during this period seems to have followed a more or less similar pattern. Thus, after a lull in new aid commitments, the Soviets stepped in, after years of fruitless and acrimonious Indo-American negotiations, to sign an agreement to

---

[116] R. K. Nehru, a high ranking Indian foreign ministry official, was unable to procure additional Soviet arms in January 1963. Three months later, Soviet Defense Minister Malinovskii declined to include a stopover in India on a visit to Indonesia. This was regarded as a sign that the Soviets were deliberately dissociating themselves from any further military assistance to India. See, Stein, *op. cit.*, p. 162.

[117] *New York Times*, May 13, 1964, p. 1.

[118] See, H. Kapur, *op. cit.*, 206.

[119] Romesh Thapar, "Umbrellas, Missiles and Talk," *Economic Weekly*, February 15, 1963, 311-12.

build the Bokaro steel plant in April 1964. Their propaganda coup was somewhat tarnished, however, by the fact that the preliminary design work done by the Indian firm of Dastur and Company was shelved as the Soviets assumed the bulk of the work themselves. This brought a sharply critical response in the Indian press. The *Economic Weekly*, for example, charged the Soviets with perpetrating a form of technological colonialism.[120]

However, at the same time when the Soviets were renewing their military and economic commitments to India, their policy towards the subcontinent as a whole began to change perceptibly. It should be recalled that during the previous decade 'Cold War' politics had become enmeshed in Indo-Pakistani relations, as Pakistan sought American support on Kashmir. Yet, insofar as the Sino-Indian border conflict resulted in India's becoming the pivot of Soviet and American efforts to stem the Chinese tide, the patterns of power relations in the subcontinent were upset. Pakistan, frustrated in its hopes for firm American support, began to reduce her military pact commitments and look elsewhere for an ally, with China being the logical choice. In December 1962 a border agreement was signed with China which afforded *de facto* recognition to Pakistan's claim to Kashmir. The implications of the new friendship became manifest when, after a visit to Peking in March 1963, Z. A. Bhutto told the Pakistani parliament that an attack on Pakistan by India would involve "the largest state in Asia."[121] The Soviets, who as late as 1960 belligerently threatened Pakistan over the consequences of allowing American bases on their soil, took a rather jaundiced view of these proceedings and

---

[120] See, R. Thapar, "Our Soviet Link," *Economic Weekly*, August 22, 1964, 1378-79. R. Thapar, "Bokaro, Made in USSR," *Economic Weekly*, October 17, 1964, 1674. *Economic Weekly* (Editorial), December 5, 1964, 1905-06. In fairness to the USSR, it should be added that the Soviets were not solely responsible for this decision. It was later revealed that the Indian Steel Minister, S. Reddy, had pushed the Soviet Union towards accepting the project on a turn key basis, since he was anxious that the next steel plant in the state sector be built in his native state of Andhra Pradesh on a similar basis with an Anglo-American consortium. See, R. Thapar, "The Passing Scene," *Economic Weekly*, January 23, 1965, 117-18.

[121] Robert H. Donaldson, "The Soviet Approach to India: Doctrinal Assessment and Operational Strategy," (unpublished Ph.D. dissertation, Harvard University, 1968), p. 412.

tried to offset Chinese influence.[122]

Thus, by 1964, the Soviets began to backtrack on the Kashmir issue. In contrast to previous practice, no mention was made of Kashmir in the joint communiques issued on the occasions of Shastri's visit in June 1964 and of Radhakrishnan's in September 1964. Indeed, Mikoyan is reported to have informed Shastri during his visit that it was time for India and Pakistan to seek a settlement of their differences.[123] In subsequent years, the Soviets would remain silent on this subject. The option for a "low profile" on Kashmir was the minimum price the Soviets had to pay to improve relations with Pakistan.

As we shall see below, this and other Soviet overtures to Pakistan sent shock waves throughout India and seriously undermined the confidence in Indo-Soviet relations that had been so carefully cultivated during the previous decade. Although Moscow's shift towards a balanced policy in the subcontinent led to the Soviet Union's assuming the role of the major external political power in the subcontinent, it also meant that the 'special relationship', which many informed Indian circles thought had characterized Indo-Soviet relations, was at an end. It should also be added that in opening the door towards Pakistan, the Soviets must have been aware that they were giving additional opportunities for right wing assaults on Indian foreign policy. In this and in the aforementioned case of broadcasting their political preferences in the Nehru succession struggle, Moscow must have been reasonably confident that Indo-Soviet relations would survive intact.

It appears then that Soviet policy towards India, shorn of the ideological halo of an earlier period, rested on the more solid bedrock of mutual self-interest. This contrasted sharply with the

---

[122] While the Soviets commented favorably upon the anti-Western trend in Pakistani foreign policy, in their polemics with the Chinese, they chastized the latter for befriending a member of an "aggressive Imperialist" military bloc. At a February 1964 Central Committee Plenum, Suslov went so far as to denounce the Chinese for associating with the "reactionary regime of Pakistan." See, *Pravda*, April 3, 1964, pp. 1-8, in *CDSP*, XVI, No. 13, 12. At a time when the Soviets themselves were courting Pakistan, this pronouncement is, at the very least, quite inconsistent. It seems that Moscow was trying to have it both ways—i.e., to woo Pakistan and yet denounce Peking for doing the same.

[123] Selig Harrison, "Troubled India and Her Neighbors." *Foreign Affairs* XLIII, No. 2 (January 1965), 323.

vagaries of the Soviet line toward other developing nations following the Sino-Indian border conflict. Indeed, it would seem that the major escalation of the Sino-Soviet dispute in 1963 removed all remaining constraints on the Soviet perspective toward the Third World.

This 'revisionist' direction was marked by the official adoption of such concepts as 'revolutionary democrats,' identified as the radical intelligentsia and leadership in the more progressive developing states who could serve as a proxy for a Communist party where the proletariat had not yet formed.[124] Indeed, the role of Communist parties was deliberately down-played with attention being riveted on the 'revolutionary democrats.' Moreover, the more progressive states from the Soviet perspective, such as Egypt, Algeria, Ghana, Mali, Burma and others, were frequently identified as traveling on the non-capitalist path of development leading towards socialism, with India relegated to a secondary category of bourgeois-ruled independent states.[125] Another departure was the development of closer inter-party relations with many ruling parties in these states, such as the National Liberation Front of Algeria, the Arab Socialist Union of Egypt, the Democratic Party of Guinea, etc. Unlike the other innovations of the last years of the Khrushchev era, this practice would be maintained and further developed with many officials of these parties receiving additional training in Moscow.[126]

Towards the close of his rule, Khrushchev made a rather bold departure when, on a trip to Egypt in June 1964, he referred to that country as one that had "embarked on the path of socialist construction" and at the same time awarded the title of Hero of the Soviet Union to President Nasser and Vice-President Abdal

---

[124] Khrushchev gave official sanction to the term 'revolutionary democrat' when he used it in a December 1963 interview with journalists from the developing states. See, *Pravda*, December 22, 1963, pp. 1-2, in *CDSP*, XV, No. 51, 13.

[125] Consult the typology presented by Suslov in his February 1964 Central Committee plenum address. *Pravda*, April 3, 1964, pp. 1-8, in *CDSP*, XVI, No. 13, 14.

[126] An agreement of such nature was recently concluded with the ruling Democratic Party of Guinea. See, "Joint Soviet-Guinean Communique," *Pravda*, May 25, 1971, p. 5, in *CDSP*, XVIII, No. 21, 19-20.

Hakim Amer.[127] Although these titles and attributes were received warmly in Cairo, this action must have certainly alarmed the other Presidium leaders. At a time when Soviet foreign policy in general was on the defensive following the Cuban crisis, Khrushchev was now extending rather gratuitously Soviet commitments in the Third World.

Khrushchev's magnanimity did not go unchallenged and indeed, as Uri Ra'anan suggests, may have contributed to his ouster.[128] Speaking at this time, for example, Suslov was very careful not to extend such ideological endorsements to specific regimes.[129] Khrushchev himself was forced to backtrack when, speaking before an International Youth Forum in September, he deleted any mention of either Egypt or Algeria building socialism.[130] Moreover, the communique issued on the occasion of Egyptian Prime Minister Ali Sabry's visit omitted any reference to "socialist development" in Egypt.[131]

Although there were some mild reverberations of Khrushchev's adventurist line following his ouster,[132] the new CPSU leadership pursued a much more conservative approach. References to Afro-Asian countries building socialism ceased. Rather, the theme that some progressive countries were undergoing deep social and economic transformations on the non-capitalist path of development was stressed.

[127] *Pravda*, May 15, 1964, p. 1, in *CDSP*, XVI, No. 20, 10. *Pravda*, May 18, 1964, p. 3, in *CDSP*, XVI, No. 20, 8. This statement was not inadvertent. Khrushchev's characterization of Egypt as a country "along the road of socialist development" was repeated in his television speech in Moscow on his return. See, *Pravda*, May 28, 1964, pp. 1-2, in *CDSP*, XVI, No. 21, 17-18. Incidentally, Amer was later dismissed and denounced for pro-Western sympathies after the June 1967 six-day war.

[128] Uri Ra'anan, "Moscow and the 'Third World'," *Problems of Communism*, XIV, No. 1 (January-February 1965), 22-31.

[129] *Pravda*, April 3, 1964, pp. 1-8, in *CDSP*, XVI, No. 13, 5-16.

[130] *Pravda*, September 22, 1964, pp. 1-2, in *CDSP*, XVI, No. 38, 8-10.

[131] *Pravda*, September 24, 1964, p. 2, in *CDSP*, XVI, No. 39, 32.

[132] For example, at a gathering of Arab Communist parties in December 1964, it was suggested that the Algerian National Liberation Front and Egyptian Arab Socialist Union would lead the march towards socialism. Cognizant that this might be interpreted as a 'revisionist' approach, the Soviet observer noted: "This does not contradict Marxism-Leninism, but on the contrary supports and enriches it." See, *Pravda*, December 11, 1964, p. 5, in *CDSP*, XVI, No. 50, 17-18.

By the close of the Khrushchev era then, Soviet thinking on the development process in the Third World had come a long way since the mid-1950's. Inspired by the example of Castro's Cuba and the radical nationalism of many Afro-Asian states, the Soviets enriched their conceptual framework to accommodate these developments. As Soviet expectations grew, their perspective of 'bourgeois' India diminished. Yet, although India had been dropped from the pantheon of Third World 'favorites,' she nevertheless remained the major recipient of Soviet aid among non-Communist developing states. How then could the Soviets justify this economic assistance to India, especially in the face of Chinese accusations that this aid was being used to prop up bourgeois monopolist circles there?

Certainly the large Soviet economic investment in India was in itself sufficient reason for its continuation. Once engaged in the construction of large industrial projects, the Soviets assumed the responsibility for their proper functioning and utilization. In the Indian political context, moreover, any precipitous Soviet action in this area would only have served as a pretext for right wing political groups to pressurize India towards adopting a more pro-Western policy. Soviet prestige was on the line not only in India but also in other Afro-Asian states, since India, as the oldest major recipient of Soviet aid, served as a model of Soviet economic aid. So too, as the Sino-Soviet schism passed beyond the polemical stage, the economic as well as military aid programs could be justified on the basis that an economically sound and militarily strengthened India would relieve some of the pressure from the Sino-Soviet border.

However, these sound arguments did not find expression in the Soviet press. Instead, the familiar theme that Soviet aid contributed to India's economic independence persisted. Yet, there was a distinctly defensive posture towards Soviet aid at this time. In sharp contrast to Khrushchev's admissions in the late 1950's that Soviet aid constituted something of a sacrifice for the Soviet Union, the Soviet public was now reminded of the positive benefits of their aid, such as the consumer goods which the USSR received in return for industrial credits.[133] Soviet aid was also justified on the grounds

---

[133] V. Tiagunenko, "Internationalism in Action—USSR Economic Cooperation with Young Independent States," *Pravda*, June 11, 1963, p. 3, in *CDSP*, XV, No. 23, 19.

that it contributed to the growth of an indigenous proletariat.[134] Specific to the Indian case, B. N. Ponomarev explained to the Seventh CPI Congress in December 1964 that Soviet aid not only furthered India's industrialization but also strengthened the state sector to make it capable of withstanding the pressures of "Imperialist monopolists and the selfish interests of local monopolistic groups." Moreover, he defended Soviet aid as a contribution to the "growth of the working class and the formation of a domestic scientific-technical intelligentsia."[135] In trying to counter the Chinese contention that their aid above all benefited the ruling bourgeoisie, it would seem that the Soviets were rather hard pressed to come up with convincing rejoinders.

In retrospect then, the decade of the 1960's marked a growing divergence between the theory and practice of Soviet policy towards India. It would seem that the Soviet practical commitments to India were no longer buttressed by a highly positive ideological perspective of developments in that country. Rather, as we have suggested earlier, Indo-Soviet relations were based on the firmer foundation of national self-interest and mutual advantage. This may be the key to understanding the durability of Indo-Soviet friendship.

Furthermore, if during the mid-1950's the cardinal Soviet concern was to lessen Western influence in an area contiguous to their southern borders, then by the early 1960's Soviet preoccupation with China had definitely affected that policy. It should be stressed, however, that the Chinese factor did not suddenly supplant this earlier Soviet concern. As we have seen in the case of Soviet military assistance, these two objectives overlapped. To be sure, as the Chinese threat grew in intensity, India emerged as the focal point of parallel Soviet and American efforts to contain China. Yet, it should be recognized that Soviet and American policies towards India did not converge. As their press clearly reveals during this period, the Soviets were very much concerned about a possible rightward shift in India's domestic and foreign policies resulting in India's adhesion, either formally or informally, to a Western military pact that would have undone years of careful Soviet effort.

[134] *Pravda*, August 7, 1963, p. 4, in *CDSP*, XV, No. 32, 5-6.
[135] *Pravda*, December 15, 1964, p. 3, in *CDSP*, XVI, No. 50, 19.

Another major consequence of the Chinese divergence was the Soviet move towards a more balanced policy towards India and Pakistan in order to establish a stable zone on the Soviet's southern flank. Although the first steps in this direction were already taken in Khrushchev's last year in power, they did not bear fruit until after his departure.[136]

THE POST-KHRUSHCHEV PERIOD, 1964-1971

While the signs of change were already evident in Khrushchev's last months of power, the post-Khrushchev leadership moved even more rapidly to extricate the Soviet Union from its overinvolvement with India by retracting its visible support for the Indian position on Kashmir.[137] To be sure, this entailed some calculated risk as far as relations with India were concerned. Yet, underlying the Soviet willingness to improve relations with Pakistan was both the recognition of Indian dependence on Soviet support against the Chinese and the long-expressed view that the Kashmir issue was artificially instigated by the West in order to sow dissension in the subcontinent and optimally to gain a forward base along Soviet Central Asian borders. Indeed, the possibility that the Soviets underestimated the intensity and complexity of the dispute cannot be ruled out.

Nevertheless, the need for a stable and peaceful subcontinent must have outweighed all other considerations. The Soviets undoubtedly did not want to see China outflank them in South

---

[136] There is a certain parallel here between the effect of Khrushchev's fall and Stalin's death on Soviet policy in the subcontinent. Just as Stalin's death removed some of the suspicion regarding Soviet intentions in India, so, too, the ouster of Khrushchev, who was so closely identified with Indo-Soviet friendship ever since his famous Srinagar pronouncement on Kashmir, must have certainly facilitated the thaw in Soviet-Pakistani relations which was to follow.

[137] A good example of the Soviet "low profile" on Kashmir was *Pravda* coverage of Aruna Asaf Ali's acceptance speech for the Lenin Peace Prize which deleted her reference to Indian gratitude for Soviet support on Kashmir. See, *Pravda*, August 13, 1965, cited in R. Vaidyanath, "Some Recent Trends in Soviet Policies Towards India and Pakistan," *International Studies*, VII, No. 3 (January, 1966), 436. It should be added, however, that when pressed, the Soviets reaffirmed their support to India. Thus, during Security Council discussions during the 1965 Indo-Pakistani conflict, the Soviets publicly stated that Kashmir was an integral part of India. See, Kapur, *op. cit.*, 211.

Asia. The Soviets, thus, committed themselves to ensuring the stability and security of the subcontinent as a whole.

The first important sign of a positive response to these Soviet signals was the April 1965 visit of President Ayub Khan, the first ever by a Pakistani chief of state. Although important differences remained between the two sides,[138] Ayub was nevertheless hailed as a "great statesman" and Pakistani foreign policy was given favorable treatment in the Soviet press.[139] His visit also marked the occasion of the signing of scientific-cultural, technical assistance and trade agreements. On the decisive political issue, the communique included a vague formula of support for national liberation movements which the Pakistani press broadly interpreted as being applicable to Kashmir.[140] However, the communique also reaffirmed the doctrine of the peaceful settlement of all disputes, which should have quashed speculation regarding any significant concessions over Kashmir.

Soon after Ayub's visit, Indian Prime Minister Shastri arrived in Moscow to discuss the recent flare-up of Indo-Pakistani fighting in the Rann of Kutch and other important matters.[141] In an effort

[138] Thus, the discussions with Soviet leaders were characterized as a "frank exchange of opinions." See, *Pravda*, April 6, 1965, p. 1, in *CDSP*, XVII, No. 14, 18.

[139] Thus, for example, *Pravda* took note of Pakistan's protest of U.S. Seventh Fleet maneuvers in the Indian Ocean, a position which India had refused to take. See, A. Kutsenkov, "Time for Reflection and Hope," *Pravda*, March 23, 1965, p. 3, in *CDSP*, XVII, No. 12, 30-31.

[140] See, Gupta, *op. cit.*, p. 265.

[141] While Indo-Pakistani relations were the main subject of attention, Chinese possession of the atomic bomb, Vietnam and other issues were brought up. India's decision not to produce nuclear weapons was lauded in the official communique. Indeed, Soviet pressure on India to refrain from producing her own bomb was matched by an awareness on the part of Indian government circles that their acquisition of the bomb would force Pakistan to seek a Chinese nuclear umbrella which would only deepen tensions on the subcontinent. Although China was most probably discussed, no overt statement of Soviet support on the Sino-Indian border problem was forthcoming, since the Soviets wished not to needlessly provoke the Chinese at this time. For the joint communique, consult, *Pravda*, May 20, 1965, p. 1, in *CDSP*, XVII, No. 20, 11-12.

With respect to Vietnam, there is a clear indication that the Soviets were irritated at India's rather mild posture. During the talks, Kosygin stated that "those who only recently experienced the burden of colonial enslavement themselves should support other peoples struggling for national liberation." See, *Pravda*, May 16, 1965, pp. 1-2, in *CDSP*, XVII, No. 20, 8.

to quell Indian anxieties consequent to Ayub's recent visit, Kosygin remarked: "There is nothing in the development of Soviet-Indian ties that could be directed against other peace-loving countries and peoples and when the Soviet Union strives to improve relations with other countries, it does not do so at the expense of Soviet-Indian friendship."[142] The purpose of that friendship, Kosygin explained, was to "stabilize the situation in South Asia." Thus, the Soviet leadership urged India to seek a negotiated solution to the hostilities in the Rann of Kutch.[143] Kosygin, moreover, warned against any outside interference and specifically admonished those "people who like to warm their hands on hostility between states"— a thinly veiled reference to the Chinese.[144] Although Kosygin did not explicitly disclose any mechanism by which Indo-Pakistani relations could be improved, his reference to the fact that Indo-Soviet friendship had developed through the growth of diversified economic relations might have been intended as a blueprint for Pakistanis and Indians to emulate. This gradualist approach, designed to first normalize Indo-Pakistani relations and then cultivate over time a climate of trust before coping with the Kashmir issue, was the one later advanced by the Soviet leadership during the Tashkent negotiations.

In order to appreciate the Soviet success in bringing both sides to the negotiating table at Tashkent, following the major outbreak of hostilities in Kashmir in September 1965, it should be noted that Moscow had, within a few short months of Khrushchev's ouster, been able to disengage itself from a partisan role in the Indo-Pakistani dispute. With the Chinese firmly committed to Pakistan and the Americans bogged down in Vietnam, the Soviets had maneuvered themselves into the role of a mediator, whose interest in preserving peace in the subcontinent had been clearly demonstrated.

The reaction of the major foreign powers to the Indo-Pakistani war was a good illustration of the changed power balance in the

---

[142] *Pravda*, May 16, 1965, pp. 1-2, in *CDSP*, XVII, No. 20, 7. It might also be noted, herein, that this formulary could also be used by India to maintain close relations with the United States; it also leaves the door open for India to improve relations with China.

[143] *Pravda*, May 9, 1965, p. 3, in *CDSP*, XVII, No. 19, 25.

[144] *Pravda*, May 16, 1965, pp. 1-2, in *CDSP*, XVII, No. 20, 9.

subcontinent.¹⁴⁵ The Chinese, who had earlier supported Pakistan on the Rann of Kutch, openly supported Pakistan on Kashmir and took steps apparently designed to keep Pakistan from accepting a cease-fire.¹⁴⁶ The United States suspended arms deliveries to both countries, which especially hurt Pakistan's capability of waging mechanized warfare for more than a few weeks and probably made their acceptance of a Security Council cease-fire resolution, strongly supported by the US and USSR, inevitable. The Soviets were deeply interested in seeking a negotiated end to this conflict, which, from their viewpoint, not only served to buttress domestic reaction in both countries but also severely jeopardized their objective of achieving stability in South Asia. Besides sponsoring the cease-fire resolution, Moscow also put pressure on both sides to avoid further escalation of the conflict. Yet, it was the Chinese ultimatum, which threatened to turn the conflict into a wider war,¹⁴⁷ that elicited the unprecedented Soviet offer to mediate the dispute. Alarmed by Chinese belligerent tones, the Soviets may also have given the Indians some assurances of support in the event of a Chinese attack. Some indication of this can be seen in Kosygin's letter to Shastri offering Soviet good offices for a negotiated settlement. In it, Kosygin called attention to a September 13, 1965 Tass statement which was Moscow's most pointed admonition to Peking, stating: "Those whose inciting statements,

---

[145] According to an Indian interpretation, the war itself was the result of Pakistani fears of the complete integration of Kashmir within India. Pakistan sent infiltrators into the disputed territory who caused disturbances. India regarded them as irregulars of the Pakistani army, and full scale hostilities commenced. For further detail on the causes of the war, consult, Gupta, *op. cit.*, pp. 196-200.

[146] On September 16, Peking handed the Indian Charge d'affaires a note demanding the dismantling within five days of Indian forward military posts along the Chinese-Sikkim border. However, the ultimatum was allowed to lapse. Gupta (p. 224) argues that the ultimatum actually hastened the adoption by Pakistan of a UN cease-fire resolution, while at the same time convincing Pakistan of Chinese readiness to come to their aid. He suggests that the Chinese desired the fighting to end before the numerically stronger Indian army could inflict a major defeat on Pakistani forces.

[147] Consult, V. Maevskii's statement in *Pravda*, January 6, 1966, that "certain bellicose circles" tried to engage the parties in a larger war and tried to prevent the Tashkent meeting from taking place. V. Maevskii, "First Step," *Pravda*, January 6, 1966, in *CDSP*, XVIII, No. 1, 5.

whose policy helps fan the conflict must be warned by the entire world, by all states that they assume a heavy responsibility for such a policy, for such actions."[148] In any event, when, it became evident to the belligerents that the conflict might take on dangerous proportions, a cease-fire was arranged and the Soviet offer for both sides to meet at Tashkent was accepted.

The Tashkent meeting in January 1966 was in itself a diplomatic victory for the Soviet Union, for it marked the first time that two non-Communist states had sought the good offices of a Communist power. Yet, though a cessation of hostilities had been achieved, the task of reaching a negotiated settlement of Indo-Pakistani differences proved to be a far more difficult matter.[149] The talks at Tashkent soon got bogged down over Indian insistence that a non-aggression pact be penned before discussing Kashmir, and Pakistani determination to settle Kashmir first. Indeed, the conference almost broke up over Pakistan's insistence that Kashmir be included in the final communique. It was only as a result of Kosygin's last minute efforts that a declaration was signed at all.[150]

The Tashkent declaration which was signed on January 10 was a compromise formula.[151] On the crucial issue of Kashmir both sides stated their respective positions and pledged themselves not to resort to force. Other than this, the declaration remained silent

---

[148] Cited in Sheldon W. Simon, "The Kashmir Dispute in Sino-Soviet Perspective," *Asian Survey*, VII, No. 3 (March 1967), 180.

[149] For fuller treatment of these negotiations, see, Gupta, *op. cit.*, pp. 220-32. See also J. A. Naik, "Soviet Policy on Kashmir," *India Quarterly*, XXIV, No. 1 (January-March, 1968), 50-61.

[150] Indeed, the Soviet diplomatic performance at Tashkent deserves high marks. The Soviet high level delegation, led by Kosygin and including Foreign Minister Gromyko, Defense Minister Malinovskii and Marshal Sokolovskii, that attended the talks could not but impress the disputees of the seriousness of the Soviet purpose. So too, Kosygin took pains not to appear to be intervening in any way and made it clear that his long private meetings with the two South Asian leaders were at their requests. Moreover, Soviet publicists and diplomats carefully tried to build up an atmosphere of optimism and a climate of goodwill. The only hint of negativism appeared in a *Pravda* article written just prior to the close of the talks, which drew attention to the complexity of the problems under discussion, apparently to prepare Soviet readers for the anticipated failure of the negotiations. See, Iu. Zhukov and V. Maevskii, "In Spite of Difficulties," *Pravda*, January 10, 1966, p. 4, in *CDSP*, XVIII, No. 2, 3.

[151] *Pravda*, January 11, 1966, p. 1, in *CDSP*, XVIII, No. 2, 4-5.

on this critical issue. Rather, it seems that Soviets, apparently convinced that the solution to Kashmir could be found only in a climate of trust, were trying first to clear the atmosphere of the hostility which surrounded Indo-Pakistani relations. Thus, the declaration called not only for mutual troop withdrawals behind the lines held on August 5 as well as the resumption of normal diplomatic relations, but also urged both sides to discourage hostile propaganda against the other and to restore economic and trade relations, communications linkages and cultural exchanges.

The accord was hailed in the Soviet press. Kosygin noted that the declaration "marks a new stage in the development of relations between India and Pakistan, puts an end to military conflict and points out ways of overcoming the difficulties that stand in the way of the normalization of relations between the two major Asian powers and...lays a real foundation for creation of conditions of peace in this highly important area of Asia."[152] It is unfortunate, however, that Indian Prime Minister Shastri died suddenly on the night of January 10, for his death removed whatever mutual understanding that might have been reached during the meetings.[153] In retrospect, even though the Tashkent meeting was an important Soviet diplomatic success, it had but a marginal effect on bringing the disputees closer together. The reaction in Pakistan to the Tashkent agreement was one of shock and disappointment, insofar as it brought them no gain on Kashmir. Riots broke out in several major West Pakistani cities, and Ayub's position was badly shaken. Although India made the unilateral gestures of reopening border trade and releasing impounded non-military cargo, these were interpreted in Pakistan as mere ruses. By January 1967, Indian officials had become increasingly pessimistic on the prospects for a genuine rapprochement.[154]

The Soviets, nevertheless, continued over the next few years to apply pressure on both sides to seek a *modus vivendi*. Thus, Kosygin in a letter to President Ayub and Prime Minister Gandhi offered Soviet assistance in mediating a dispute on the use of the Ganges River. So persistent had Moscow become on modifying India's

---

[152] *Pravda*, January 11, 1966, p. 2, in *CDSP*, XVIII, No. 2, 5.
[153] This possibility has been strongly suggested by Gupta, *op. cit.*, p. 231.
[154] Simon, *op. cit.*, 184.

position on Kashmir that the Indian Defense Minister in April 1969 warned that there was a limit to which India could be pushed on Kashmir.[155] The Soviets also tried to interest India and Pakistan along with Iran and Afghanistan in developing a regional economic trade area, but Pakistan declined to attend a 1969 conference at Kabul organized for this purpose.[156]

With the passage of time the Soviets became more reconciled to the intractable nature of the problems involved in Indo-Pakistani relations. Though on the first anniversary of the Tashkent Declaration the Soviets expressed optimism that the declaration was paving the way for normalization of relations, a year later a *Pravda* article reviewing the progress of Indo-Pakistani relations pessimistically concluded that the signing of the declaration could not in itself remove all the contradictions between India and Pakistan which had accumulated over a long period of time.[157]

Moscow's inability to diminish the hostility between India and Pakistan soon began to have an adverse affect on their relations with both countries. As Harish Kapur aptly observes: "Having once decided to maintain and develop relations with the two contending nations, Moscow found itself increasingly obliged to adopt policies that vitiated the development of relations with both of them."[158]

Soviet military aid to South Asia is a good case in point. Moscow, as we have noted, became New Delhi's main supplier of military hardware even before Washington suspended arms deliveries during the Indo-Pakistan war. In contrast to American behavior, the Soviets during the conflict concluded an agreement to sell submarines to India.[159] After the fighting, the Soviets began to replenish Indian losses in a big way. During the next two years,

---

[155] *Statesman Weekly*, April 12, 1969, p. 2.

[156] J. A. Naik, "Sino-Soviet Confrontation: Repercussions on Soviet Foreign Policy," *Economic and Political Weekly*, January 3, 1970, 26.

[157] Contrast the two *Pravda* articles commemorating the Tashkent agreement: V. Maevskii, "A Year Later," *Pravda*, January 10, 1967, p. 3, in *CDSP*, XIX, No. 2, 24-25, and Erik Alekseev, "A Good Basis," *Pravda*, January 10, 1968, p. 5, in *CDSP*, XX, No. 2, 18.

[158] Kapur, *op. cit.*, 209.

[159] This marked the first instance in which India, previously dependent on Great Britain for her naval ordinance, was forced to turn to the Soviet Union for naval equipment. *Economic Weekly*, August 14, 1965, 1254.

the Soviets furnished naval surface craft, submarines, ground-to-air missiles, tanks and Sukhoi-7 fighter-bombers. This military build-up had a pronounced negative impact on Pakistan. Although the Soviets had come forth with increasing amounts of economic assistance,[160] their reluctance to either curtail military supplies to India or furnish Pakistan with them placed a severe strain on the development of Soviet-Pakistani ties.

It was Chinese military aid to Pakistan which forced both the Americans and Russians to reconsider their positions.[161] The United States responded by authorizing Italy to supply tanks and Iran to transport aircraft to Pakistan. Unable to avail themselves of such indirect means, the Soviets had to deal with Pakistan directly. Limited military assistance in 1967 was followed by a substantial commitment in the summer of 1968 by which the Soviets agreed to supply tanks and other weapons. The report of the arms deal was met by widespread public indignation in India, especially on the part of those who had an axe to grind against the Soviet Union.[162] Although the official response was more subdued,[163] an article in the *A. I. C. C. Economic Review*, generally close to government opinion, contended that India should now develop maximum self-reliance and restore her political maneuverability by mending fences with the Chinese.[164] As we shall discuss below, this was the course

---

[160] After Tashkent, the Soviets stepped up their trade and economic aid markedly. By September 1966 it was estimated that they were involved in the construction of twenty-one projects in Pakistan. In 1968 the Soviets announced that they would help build a steel mill in West Pakistan and a nuclear power station in East Pakistan. During the following year Moscow also committed itself to the construction of a large steel mill in Karachi. See, S. P. Seth, "Russia's Role in Indo-Pak Politics," *Asian Survey*, IX, No. 8 (August, 1969), 619.

[161] A military aid agreement worth $120 million was signed in 1966 by which China would furnish Pakistan with 100 tanks, 80 MIG-19's and other aircraft.

[162] According to Harish Kapur, the information was leaked by some government officials in the hope that the anticipated public reaction might persuade Moscow to backtrack from its original decision. See, Kapur, *op. cit.*, 211.

[163] In a speech on this subject, Indira Gandhi, while taking care to stress that Indian foreign policy would not undergo any change, said that the Soviets had in fact aggravated tensions on the subcontinent and argued that the arms deal would only make Pakistan more intransigent in its negotiations with India. See, *Statesman Weekly*, July 13, 1968, p. 1.

[164] Sadiq Ali, "Soviet Arms Supply to Pak," *A. I. C. C. Economic Review*, August 1, 1968, 3-4.

which the government soon adopted.

This consequence was certainly not intended. The Soviet leaders, who had been keeping the Indian government informed about these developments, insisted that this deal was symbolic and would not upset the military balance in South Asia.[165] It could further be argued that limited Soviet military assistance to Pakistan was beneficial in that it would increase the Soviets' leverage there—an influence which would be exercised against any military venture.[166]

From the Soviet viewpoint the 1968 arms agreement was only a symbolic act (this was also the way the Pakistani press interpreted it), designed to offset growing Chinese influence and reaffirm their balanced policy in the subcontinent. The record of Soviet military assistance, however, demonstrates their continued commitment to India as their principal client. This case also reveals some of the difficulties which the Soviets confronted in maintaining this balanced approach. It should be added that the shock of the Soviet-Pakistan arms deal in India was only symptomatic of the increasing irritation which characterized Indo-Soviet ties in the post-Khrushchev period.

---

[165] Thus, a *Pravda* article viewed the mass demonstrations protesting the arms deal in front of the Soviet Embassy in New Delhi as "outrages" instigated by the right wing Jana Sangh and Swatantra parties and other avowed enemies of Indo-Soviet friendship. Failing to note what precipitated the protest, the article nevertheless, charged the organizers with trying to distort Soviet foreign policy, and, by contrast, drew attention to that part of Indira Gandhi's Lok Sabha speech in which she stressed that India's ties with the Soviet Union must not be weakened. As if to remind the Indian government of the benefits of their continued friendship, the article also mentioned a long list of 65 industrial projects and facilities which were living proof of Indo-Soviet collaboration. See, V. Maevskii, "Soviet-Indian Friendship is a Great Gain," *Pravda,* July 29, 1968, p. 4, in *CDSP*, XX, No. 30, 18.

[166] This view was expressed by Mohammed Ayoob, writing in the influential *Economic and Political Weekly*. Ayoob noted that since the arms were offered on a commercial basis, they were bound to be limited due to the small volume of Soviet-Pakistani trade. See, Mohammed Ayoob, "Soviet Arms Aid to Pakistan," *Economic and Political Weekly*, October 19, 1968, 1613-14. Ayoob's cool-minded commentary was not typical. A review of the Indian press reveals not only a profound insecurity regarding the future of Indo-Soviet ties but also a sense of frustration that India had lost its maneuverability by becoming too closely aligned with the Soviet Union.

Much of the acrimony in Indo-Soviet relations during the late 1960's centered on their economic ties. As Soviet aid passed the promissory stage, problems relating to production delays, high production costs and large economic losses in most Soviet-assisted public sector projects began to tarnish the Soviet aid record.[167]

Bokaro typified the malaise of Soviet aid to India, for what had started as a propaganda coup soon became something of an albatross. The circumstances surrounding the rejection of Dastur and Co.'s preliminary project report have already been discussed. Yet "l'affaire Dastur" did not end there. Having been given a consolation contract of designing the Indian share of the supportive design work at Bokaro in 1967, three years later it was disclosed that the Central Engineering and Design Bureau would assume this work instead. Moreover, this came immediately after the announcement that a Soviet industrial design organization, GIPROMEZ, had concluded a technical assistance agreement with this state sector design agency—an arrangement which led one Indian journalist to conclude that this was a device enabling the Russians to enter the backdoor for engineering Bokaro's expansion from 1.7 to 4 million tons of output per annum.[168] This revived earlier charges of technological colonialism.[169] Moreover, when the text of this technical assistance agreement was publicized in the Indian press,[170] it proved to be a further embarrassment, since the expense accounts for Soviet personnel were much higher than those of their Indian counterparts. The project was further plagued by high production costs and delays, which by late 1969 were estimated

---

[167] Even the Bhilai plant, on which much of the Soviet reputation in the field of aid was based, was beset by minor problems by the late 1960's. The operation of its sixth blast furnace was delayed for six months due to a lack of power supply. *Economic and Political Weekly*, December 17, 1966, 743-45.

[168] *Economic and Political Weekly*, February 28, 1970, 401-02.

[169] It should be added, herein, that such charges were not entirely accurate, since the Soviets did show some respect for Indian sensitivity in this area. Thus, they have helped to set up a number of state sector engineering consultancy units for designing oil refineries, pipelines and petro-chemical plants in addition to handing the main part of the technical design work for Bhilai's sixth blast furnace over to Indian designers. Their intent may be not so much to check the growth of India's indigenous designing capabilities as to promote its development within the state sector.

[170] *Economic and Political Weekly*, February 28, 1970, 401-02.

to have set Bokaro three years behind schedule.[171]

Bokaro was not the only Soviet project facing serious difficulties. The Soviet-aided pharmaceuticals complex, Indian Drugs and Pharmaceutical Ltd., was plagued by faulty equipment, rising costs and production delays from the outset.[172] It seems that the Soviet preliminary project report had not taken into account the complexities of an Indian market dominated by Western patent rights. As a result, by 1968 the plant was running with a heavy surplus capacity and losses were pegged at 8.9 million rupees.[173] (In fact, most Soviet-aided enterprises already in production were running in the red.)

Having developed a large stake in ensuring the adequate performance of their aid projects, the Soviets could not remain passive in the light of the growing difficulties confronting their aid program. Rather, they took various measures to ensure that their projects would operate as near to full capacity as possible. Thus, during the late 1960's they proceeded to reorient their trade with India to take off the surpluses that had accumulated in Soviet-built projects and other industries which had been suffering from an economic recession. In addition, Soviet aid representatives began to give closer scrutiny to the administration of their aid program. The Heavy Engineering Corporation at Ranchi, which had been incurring very large losses, was particularly noted for its mismanagement. In marked contrast to their previous practice of entrusting the complete administration and operation of a plant to Indian engineers in as short a time as possible, the Soviets dispatched a group

---

[171] R. Thapar, "Follow-up or Mix-up?," *Economic and Political Weekly*, September 27, 1969, 1542. It appears that much of the production delays were the results of poor organization on the Indian side. For example, the Soviets, responding to Indian requests to maximize the use of Indian manufacture in foreign-assisted projects, placed orders for refractory bricks and structural materials with several private Indian firms (and thereby boosting a slumping industry). However, poor quality and production delays from these Indian suppliers induced the Indian government to request Soviet imports of refractory bricks. See, *Statesman Weekly*, May 31, 1969, p. 12; "Bokaro at Last!," *Economic and Political Weekly*, April 20, 1968, 626; "Bokaro Stumbles at First Step," *Economic and Political Weekly*, April 27, 1968, 664-65.

[172] Kapur, *op. cit.*, 213.

[173] "Collaboration, Soviet Brand," *Economic and Political Weekly*, October 5, 1968, 1507.

of forty-two Soviet engineers in 1968 to the Ranchi plant to cope with its chronic management problems.[174] As if to emphasize that Moscow was now going to assume a more active role in its aid program, the head of the State Committee for Foreign Economic Relations (the main Soviet aid organization), S. A. Skachkov, visited India in 1968 for an on-sight inspection of some twenty-seven Soviet projects, after which he made certain recommendations concerning the improvement of their management.[175] Coming in the wake of the Soviet-Pakistan arms deal, Skachkov's visit was unfavorably received in the Indian press, for it was interpreted as indicating that the Soviets no longer felt India's problems could be left to Indians to settle.[176] Moreover, Skachkov was depicted as behaving like a 'viceroy'.[177] Thus, as the Skachkov visit suggests, an increased Soviet role in the supervision of their aid projects has provided an additional irritant in Indo-Soviet relations.

Much of the negative publicity which they received was viewed by the Soviets as inspired by sources hostile to the Soviet Union. From the Soviet viewpoint, Indo-Soviet friendship had become a partisan issue in the post-Nehru period of political instability.

The opening up of protected industries to foreign capital penetration,[178] and the rupee devaluation in 1966 under apparent

---

[174] "Implications of India's Trade with Russia," *Capital*, December 19, 1968, 1137.

[175] *Commerce*, December 21, 1968, 1285.

[176] R. Thapar, "Political Management," *Economic and Political Weekly*, December 21, 1968, 1932.

[177] Cited in Marian P. Kirsch, "Soviet Security Objectives in Asia," *International Organization*, XXIV, No. 3 (Summer, 1970), 462. It appears that this was a particularly poor period for visits by Soviet officials. A visit in September 1968 by Deputy Foreign Minister, N. Firiubin also drew unfavorable comment in the Indian press. Firiubin was criticized for brushing aside queries regarding the Soviet-Pakistan arms deal, the Czech invasion and other sore points in Indo-Soviet relations and for behaving like "an emissary of an Imperial court come to lecture a satrap." See, R. Thapar, "Mobilising Against the Ugly Twins?," *Economic and Political Weekly*, October 5, 1968, 1509.

[178] Permitting Western capital to penetrate the fertilizer industry especially incensed the Soviets. See, A. Maslennikov, "Concessions to Foreign Monopolies," *Pravda*, April 20, 1966, p. 5, in *CDSP*, XVIII, No. 16, 36.

American pressure,[179] all pointed to India's drawing closer to the West. India's economic policy must have reinforced the suspicion that Soviet trade and aid were merely levers to obtain better terms from the West.

Soviet anxiety over the course of India's domestic politics reached a high level in the period before and after the critical February 1967 general elections. The ascendency of Morarji Desai, a man identified as a "representative of big business," to the post of Deputy Prime Minister alarmed Moscow.[180] So too, Krishna Menon's withdrawal as parliamentary candidate, because of pressure from the Bombay Congress organization, caused one *Pravda* commentator to state that this marked a tendency within India to replace "progressive politicians" with right wingers, which would inevitably affect the formation of the future government and its policies.[181] The results of the general election itself, which ended Congress rule in a number of states and ushered in a prolonged period of political instability, were interpreted as reflecting a "process of polarization of forces," with Jana Sangh gains in some north Indian states (viewed as a "cause for concern") offset by Communist-led united front victories in Kerala and West Bengal.[182]

Cast in ideological terms, the growing power of the monopolistic

---

[179] The rupee devaluation brought trade with the Soviet bloc to a halt for two months. Even after adjustments had been made, Indo-Soviet trade declined in value for several years thereafter, and this at a time when Soviet trade with other non-socialist countries was expanding significantly. See, "Rough Weather for Rupee Trade," *Economic and Political Weekly*, October 22, 1966, 396-97.

[180] See, A. Maslennikov, "Indira Gandhi is PM of India," *Pravda*, January 20, 1966, p. 3, in *CDSP*, XVIII, No. 3, 22. The Soviets continued during this period to make their political sympathies known. Over Radio Peace and Progress, Moscow beamed harsh and continuous propaganda against right wing parties, such as the Jana Sangh and Swatantra, and certain Congress leaders. The right wing opposition in Parliament responded by demanding that the government declare the broadcasts an unfriendly act, which the government refused to do. (In response to official inquiries, the Soviets insisted that Radio Peace and Progress was a 'private independent' entity over which they had no authority.) It was only after the domestic political situation changed in Moscow's favor that the frequency and stridency of these broadcasts were toned down. See, *Statesman Weekly*, September 12, 1970, p. 13.

[181] A. Maslennikov, "The Krishna Menon 'Affair'," *Pravda*, December 9, 1966, p. 5, in *CDSP*, XVIII, No. 49, 18.

[182] Iu. Popov, "International Commentary: After the Elections," *Izvestia*, March 2, 1967, p. 2, in *CDSP*, XIX, No. 9, 15.

bourgeoisie and reactionary forces seemed to present an ominous threat. Along with the official line that India was pursuing a course of independent economic development (invariably mentioned in juxtaposition with any reference to Soviet projects in India), increasingly discordant concepts appeared which challenged the very basis of continued Soviet aid to India. In a series of articles in *Pravda*, Professor R. A. Ul'ianovskii, an India specialist who by 1966 had become the deputy director of the International Department of the CPSU Central Committee, expounded an assessment of the national bourgeoisie reminiscent of the Stalinist period. In countries where the national bourgeoisie was in power (e. g., India), he noted that they were sabotaging general democratic transformations such as the state sector and agricultural reforms in pursuit of their own narrow interests; in several countries, the upper strata of the bourgeoisie was openly collaborating with reactionaries.[183] In subsequent articles, Ul'ianovskii was even more critical. While paying lip service to their capacity to struggle against Imperialism, Ul'ianovskii wrote in January 1968[184] that the national bourgeoisie in power constituted the major bloc to further social progress and added that the experience of the past fifteen to twenty years had shown that the national bourgeoisie was inclined to resolve its economic contradictions with foreign capital by coming to terms with the latter and not by uprooting the foundations of their economic power.[185] By pointing to the interdependence of native and foreign capital in such countries as India, Ul'ianovskii was calling into question the validity of the long-accepted official doctrine that India was pursuing a course of economic

---

[183] R. A. Ul'ianovskii, "Aid for the Propagandist: Socialism and the National Liberation Struggle—The Non-Capitalist Path of Development," *Pravda*, April 15, 1966, p. 4, in *CDSP*, XVIII, No. 15, 24.

[184] R. A. Ul'ianovskii, "At New Frontiers—On Some Features of the Present Stage of the National Liberation Movement," *Pravda*, January 3, 1968, pp. 4-5, in *CDSP*, XX, No. 1, 9-11.

[185] This formulation is virtually identical to the concept first enunciated by the Indian Marxist, M. N. Roy, that the colonial bourgeoisie would compromise with Imperialism rather than seek resolution of their objective differences with the latter. This concept constituted the 'left strategy' towards the colonial and dependent countries adopted at the Sixth Comintern Congress in 1928 but revoked seven years later.

independence.[186]

The intent of Ul'ianovskii's articles, which considering his position, appear to have official weight was to forge a new 'national democratic' front that would exclude the pro-Western and monopolistic layers of the bourgeoisie. This was in fact embodied in the resolutions of the Moscow-oriented CPI which called for the political unity of all forces of the left including the CPI(M) in the struggle against the monopolistic bourgeoisie and other reactionary groups.[187]

Although not mentioned in the Soviet press because of its probable negative impact on foreign Communist parties, the growing threat to Indian stability posed by left wing revolutionary radicalism had also become a serious concern. Not only had Peking sought to outflank the Soviets by developing firm ties with Pakistan, but the Chinese had also sought to weaken India by openly supporting separatist movements among the Naga Hill tribes and other paleo-Mongoloid tribes in India's northeast regions. Moreover, Peking's encouragement of Maoist-style guerrilla movements based on the peasantry seemed to materialize with the emergence in West Bengal of the Naxalite movement in 1967, which was soon taken over by a splinter group from the CPI(M).[188]

Thus, Moscow saw its political influence in India jeopardized by growing polarization and subsequent political instability there. Behind their criticism of the rightward drift of the Indian government was the fear that continued governmental ineffectiveness with

---

[186] Incidentally, Ul'ianovskii also charged that the state administrative apparatus in these countries had not been "truly democratized;" rather, many "old colonial functionaries" and others brought up in the colonial traditions still staffed the upper and middle levels of the administrative apparatus. Ul'ianovskii may thus have been venting Soviet suspicions regarding the hostility they had experienced in dealing with the bureaucracies in these countries. With respect to the Indian context, it may be added that Skachkov is reported to have remarked during his visit that certain ministers were in fact discriminating against state sector projects. See, "The Skachkov Mission," *Eastern Economist*, January 10, 1969, 45.

[187] The resolutions are reviewed in A. Maslennikov and I. Serebriakov, "Overcome Dissension," *Pravda*, May 5, 1967, p. 5, in *CDSP*, XIX, No. 18, 15.

[188] For a detailed account of the Naxalite movement and its relation with the Communist Party Marxist-Leninist, India's third CP, consult Marcus Franda, "India's Third Communist Party," *Asian Survey*, IX, No. 11 (November, 1969), 797-817.

respect to pressing needs for social and economic reforms would eventually lead to the adoption of the radical alternative presented by Maoist revolutionary doctrine. The emergence of the Naxalite movement in the late 1960's substantiated Soviet premonitions.

Yet, it was precisely during the post-Tashkent period when the future of Indo-Soviet relations was very much in doubt that Soviet leaders moved to invest these ties with an aura of permanence. Thus, at the Twenty-Third Party Congress in 1966, Brezhnev referred to Indo-Soviet relations in glowing terms as a "traditional friendship...that had withstood the test of time"[189]—an epithet which came into frequent use thereafter. If we assume that this expression was not merely a cover for deep Soviet anxieties, then it may be supposed that Moscow felt that objective conditions dictated continued close ties regardless of the changing political configuration in India. A decade of Soviet political support in the face of Western pressure and Chinese intimidation, underscored by economic and military aid, led them to express confidence in Indo-Soviet ties. The Soviet leadership may have felt that this relationship had reached a stage of trust in which criticism could be tolerated.

It would appear that Moscow was trying to distinguish its ideological predilections from its continuous stake in good relations with India. This is made clear in a speech by Kosygin before the Supreme Soviet,[190] in which he contrasted Soviet policy towards India with its attitudes towards developing countries in general. Having noted that "...we do not conceal that our sympathies are first of all on the side of those peoples who have chosen the path of non-capitalist development" (a list from which Indians were definitely excluded), Kosygin went on to characterize Soviet relations with non-aligned states, such as India, as follows: "In view of the closeness of positions of the Soviet Union and those of the developing countries on many international problems, the Soviet government will maintain close contact with these countries in the interests of peace and the expansion of the anti-Imperialist front." Kosygin was thus seeking to distinguish ideological sympathies from considerations of mutual self-interest.

---

[189] *Pravda*, March 30, 1966, pp. 2-9, in *CDSP*, XVIII, No. 12, 13.
[190] *Pravda*, August 4, 1966, pp. 1, 3-4, in *CDSP*, XVIII, No. 31, 15.

There is little doubt that the solidarity of Soviet-Indian relations depended on the latter criterion.

The dispensation of Soviet aid during the post-Tashkent period also tends to substantiate this point of view. In December 1966 the Soviet Union extended a credit of 300 million rubles in non-project aid which roughly corresponded to repayments due on earlier loans. This represented a departure from the standard Soviet practice of tying all assistance to specific projects and constituted a significant concession to the Indian side. Moreover, the timing of this new aid just prior to the February 1967 general election suggests that Moscow sought to reaffirm its commitment to India regardless of the electoral outcome.[191]

As we have suggested earlier, one of the main areas of mutual self-interest in Soviet-Indian relations was their common hostility towards China, based (more so in the case of India) on disputed territorial claims. Underlying the Soviet desire of putting Indo-Soviet relations on a firmer footing was the growing fear of a Chinese military threat which had reached the point that a preemptive military strike on Chinese nuclear facilities was rumored in the spring of 1969. Certainly, whatever the considerations involved in the decision, large scale Soviet military aid to India was intended to be used against China. Towards the late 1960's the Soviets began to think in terms of including India in a strategy of military defense against China.

An early sign of this was the publication in the September 1967 issue of *Literaturnaia Gazeta* of an article by 'Ernst Henry,'[192] a pseudonym for a Soviet journalist, which warned of Maoist designs for a "superstate" that would eventually encompass, in its second stage of expansion, both the Soviet borderlands in the Far East and Central Asia and the Indian subcontinent. This article, coupled with the publication of an Indian report of renewed fighting along

---

[191] "Fresh Ground in Aid," *Economic and Political Weekly*, December 10, 1966, 695. The absence of new aid in subsequent years does not necessarily indicate a diminished desire to aid India on Moscow's part, for a major problem in Soviet aid to India, as we shall examine in the following section, was to reduce the serious lag that had developed between the extension of aid and the actual drawings on that aid.

[192] Ernst Henry (Pseudonym), "The View from the Pamirs," *Literaturnaia Gazeta*, Nos. 39 and 40 (September 27 and October 4, 1967), 14-15, in *CDSP*, XX, No. 1, 4-5.

the Sino-Indian border,[193] was probably designed to warn India against Chinese aggressive intentions and also to link the defense of India's borders with those of the Soviet Union.

With British withdrawal from Asia and the Americans bogged down in a futile war in Southeast Asia, the Soviets, having strengthened their naval forces, now sought to dramatize their stake in ensuring the security of the area. In the spring of 1968, the Soviet navy showed the flag for the first time in the area by paying goodwill calls on the ports of Bombay, Madras and Karachi. Also, it has been frequently mentioned that the Soviets had been pressing the Indian government for shore facilities in the Indian Ocean—a request which the Indians have refused to this time.[194]

Indian reluctance to grant military facilities to the Soviet Union may be explained by India's objective of becoming the dominant power in the area. Especially after the Soviet-Pakistan arms deal, India had no intention of becoming a Soviet pawn. As we have previously indicated, one of the consequences of that arms arrangement was India's attempt to restore relations with the Chinese.[195]

These overtures to Peking must have been extremely disquieting to Moscow, especially since they coincided with serious military clashes along the Sino-Soviet border. Indeed, the Soviets were reportedly incensed at India's late and subdued response to the engagement on Damanskii Island in March 1969.[196] In a rare overt display of Soviet pique, Kosygin, while attending the funeral of President Husain, remarked: "...not one peace-loving state can remain aloof from active participation in the struggle against

---

[193] *Pravda*, September 13, 1967, p. 5, in *CDSP*, XIX, No. 37, 18.

[194] It has also been reported that Kosygin, in May 1969, offered Soviet assistance in training the Indian armed forces. See *Statesman Weekly*, May 24, 1969, p. 2.

[195] The first hints of Chinese receptivity to Indian overtures came in 1970 when President Giri met with Kuo Mo-Jo in Kathmandu on the occasion of the wedding of the Nepalese Crown Prince. See, *Statesman Weekly*, March 14, 1970, p. 2. In May, Mao was reported to have made a friendly observation to the Indian Charge d'affaires in Peking that India had been a friend of China and that their friendship should be renewed. Inquiries have also been exchanged with the aim of restoring diplomatic relations to the ambassadorial level, and restrictions on Chinese and Indian diplomats, imposed during the Cultural Revolution, have been removed. See, T. Karki Hussain, "Sino-Indian Relations," *Economic and Political Weekly*, September 18, 1971, 2017-22.

[196] *Statesman Weekly*, March 22, 1969, p. 1.

the policies of aggression...."[197]—a statement which may have had the double referent of India's mild stand on Vietnam as well as her belated response to the March Sino-Soviet border clashes.

Soviet concern over Chinese expansion following British and American withdrawal from the area led them to propose a system of collective security in Asia.[198] Although Moscow has soft-peddled the military aspect of the scheme, arguing that it is not directed against any one nation[199] and stressing the economic and political aspects of such a system,[200] reaction to the scheme in South Asia has been negative. Pakistan regarded it as a prelude to a Soviet-led anti-Chinese military bloc. Fearing that any sign of interest would only antagonize China, India was initially cool to the idea, though Moscow may have made some headway following Indian Foreign Minister Dinesh Singh's visit in September 1969.[201] Probably in an attempt to make the scheme more palatable, the Soviets have endorsed an Indian proposal for a nuclear-free zone in the Indian Ocean.[202]

Indian resistance to being drawn into a military alliance is

[197] *Pravda*, May 7, 1969, p. 4, in *CDSP*, XXI, No. 19, 17.

[198] The plan was introduced by Brezhnev at the June 1969 conference of Communist parties. See, *Pravda*, June 8, 1969, pp. 1-4, in *CDSP*, XXI, No. 23, 16.

[199] See Gromyko's rather defensive explanation of the scheme in his July 1969 report to the Supreme Soviet. *Pravda*, July 11, 1969, pp. 2-4, in *CDSP*, XXI, No. 28, 9.

[200] In a review of Chester Bowles' *The View from New Delhi*, the Soviet reviewer, while denigrating the idea of Western-sponsored regionalism, nevertheless suggests that regional collaboration devoid of Western influence could lay the groundwork for a system of regional collective security. V. Skosyrev, "Ambassador's Postscript," *Izvestia*, June 20, 1969, p. 2, in *CDSP*, XXI, No. 25, 22.

[201] Whereas Mr. Singh was reported before his departure for Moscow as having been opposed to any military pact whatsoever (*Statesman Weekly*, September 13, 1969, p. 3), the Soviet press quoted him on his return to India as having said: "India welcomes the proposal of the Soviet Union on the system of collective security in Asia." See, *Pravda*, September 21, 1969, p. 4, in *CDSP*, XXI, No. 38, 16.

[202] The idea was first mentioned in the Soviet press by V. Matveev who noted both Dinesh Singh's and A. Malik's (the Indonesian Foreign Minister) agreement on the desirability of creating a nuclear-free zone in the Indian Ocean "as one measure that could bring nearer the realization of collective security in Asia." V. Matveev, "Southeast Asia: Conflicts or Security?," *Izvestia*, August 9, 1970, p. 2, in *CDSP*, XXII, No. 32, 11. The Soviets have since sponsored this idea at the UN (consult the text of Gromyko's speech there, *Pravda*, October 23, 1970, p. 4. in *CDSP*, XXII, No. 43, 7), and at other forums (see, Brezhnev's speech at the Twenty-Fourth Party Congress reported in *Pravda*, March 31, 1971, pp. 2-10, in *CDSP*, XXIII, No. 12, 13).

rooted in the very concept of non-alignment as espoused by Nehru. Yet, it also illustrates India's long-range desire not to depend on any power outside the area to protect her security interests.

India's determination to remain self-reliant also helps explain her reluctance to sign the nuclear non-proliferation treaty. Having pressed initially for assurances from the United States and the Soviet Union against the threat of nuclear blackmail or attack by the nuclear-'haves' against the nuclear-'have-nots,' the Indians nevertheless refused to sign the treaty even after this demand had been met by the passage of a June 1968 Security Council resolution and simultaneous pledges by the United States, Soviet Union and Great Britain.[203] Yet, despite the comprehensiveness of the resolution's written guarantees, widescale Indian skepticism continued to be expressed concerning their effectiveness against nuclear blackmail or attack.[204] It was generally believed that the treaty would become effective only if China signed it and that, until that time, signing would only serve to antagonize the Chinese. The Indian government has also argued that the treaty only safeguards against 'horizontal' proliferation but does not prevent 'vertical' proliferation, thus enabling the nuclear powers to continue to stockpile, and thereby increasing the distance between the nuclear 'haves' and 'have-nots,' with important political-military advantages accruing to the former. Another argument that has been raised is that the treaty prevents the non-nuclear states from developing atomic energy for peaceful purposes. Yet, probably the basic reason for India's reluctance to sign the treaty is the desire to keep her nuclear options open.

While the Soviets have had little success in coaxing India to affix her signature to the nuclear non-proliferation treaty,[205] they have

[203] For a detailed account of the bargaining leading towards the passage of the treaty, consult, E. L. M. Burns, "The Non-Proliferation Treaty: Its Negotiation and Prospects," *International Organization*, XXIII, No. 4 (Autumn, 1969), 788-807.

[204] See, for example, G. S. Bhargava, "A Non-Policy on Non-Proliferation," *Economic and Political Weekly*, March 23, 1968, 482-83.

[205] India's position has aroused manifest Soviet displeasure, for India's adherence to the treaty was counted upon to place additional pressure on other 'near-nuclear' states to sign the document. In a veiled criticism of the Indian stance, an *Izvestia* commentator warned that "the attempt to overload the treaty with all kinds of conditions going beyond the framework of its basic purpose is a kind of fatalistic reconciliation with the A-bomb." S. Beglov, "Treaty Under Way," *Izvestia*, September 26, 1968, pp. 4-5, in *CDSP*, XX, No. 39, 25-26.

been more successful in restraining India from developing her own nuclear weapons, for here Indian and Soviet interests coincide. Resisting strong domestic pressures to exercise her nuclear option, the Indian government apparently senses that nuclear armament would only force Pakistan to follow suit, thereby adding to the insecurity on the sub-continent—a position which conforms with Soviet desires to defuse tensions there. The prognosis may be added that following the dismemberment of Pakistan in 1971, India might feel less inclined than before to develop her nuclear potential in view of her pronounced military superiority in the region. The true stimulus for an Indian nuclear career, however, remains the Chinese nuclear threat. Continued Chinese belligerency may eventually leave India no choice but to develop a nuclear deterrent.

As in the case of the nuclear non-proliferation treaty, there are a number of other issues upon which Indian and Soviet positions diverge,[206] such as India's reluctance to recognize the Provisional Revolutionary Government of South Vietnam or the German Democratic Republic.[207] Yet, it must be emphasized that such issues are of subsidiary importance in Soviet-Indian relations, for matters relating to the immediate neighbors of Pakistan and China have much greater impact than events in Europe and elsewhere. Thus, for example, while most Indian papers condemned the Soviet intervention in Czechoslovakia, the event did not arouse nearly as sharp a reaction as the announcement a month earlier of the Soviet-Pakistan arms deal. Indeed, the government response seemed somewhat equivocal. Whereas Madame Gandhi, in marked contrast to her father's virtual silence on the subject of Hungary twelve years earlier, did state in a speech before Parliament that the

---

[206] To be sure there are also areas of convergence such as India's support for a European Security Conference, her condemnation of Israel as the aggressor in the June 1967 six-day war and subsequent support for the November 22, 1967 Security Council resolution demanding Israeli withdrawal from occupied territory.

[207] On this latter issue, even though all three Indian Prime Ministers have recognized the existence of two German states, the Indian government, not willing to jeopardize its trade and economic assistance from West Germany, has stopped short of recognizing East Germany. However, in 1969 a trade mission was set up in the GDR with the power to perform consular functions—a step which indicates India is moving in this direction. *Statesman Weekly*, June 14, 1969, p. 3.

principle of non-intervention in the internal affairs of another country had been violated, she nevertheless prefaced her remarks with a statement affirming the value of Indian friendship with the Soviet Union and the other Warsaw Pact countries that had participated in the operation.[208] Moreover, India's abstention on an August 22, 1968 Security Council resolution condemning the armed intervention of the Soviet Union and her allies was rationalized on the grounds that the use of provocative language would not ameliorate the situation in Czechoslovakia.

In retrospect, then, though geo-political considerations augured for continued close ties, Indo-Soviet relations had in the latter half of the 1960's entered a difficult period of strain and tension. From the Indian standpoint, the Soviet overtures towards Pakistan had an unsettling effect which was magnified in the cauldron of domestic political instability. The Soviets, on the other hand, saw the carping criticisms of them as indicative of the growing power of the forces of the political right.

Yet, 1969 marked a watershed in Indian politics which was to have a beneficial impact on Indo-Soviet relations as well. This was the year in which Mrs. Gandhi forced an open split in Congress ranks over the issues of bank nationalization, agrarian reforms and the selection of a new Congress candidate for President. Having nationalized fourteen major commercial banks which were largely in the hands of the major Indian business firms, Indira Gandhi went on to consolidate her power by expelling the conservative members of her government, including Morarji Desai—a move which eventually forced the powerful Congress state leaders, known as the "syndicate," to set up an opposition Congress parliamentary party.

Although the Soviets were well aware of the precariousness of her position (for the first time the central government was not supported by an absolute majority in parliament), they were heartened by Mrs. Gandhi's advocacy of a more leftist course in government policies. The election of her candidate V. V. Giri, as President and the bank nationalization were immediately hailed as a victory of democratic progressive forces over the right wing in India.[209]

---

[208] Cited in Stein, *op. cit.*, p. 267.
[209] S. Vishnevskii, "International Survey: Defeat of Imperialist Policy," *Pravda*, August 24, 1969, pp. 1-4, in *CDSP*, XXI, No. 34, 16.

Sensing that this was the first major opportunity in a decade for them to expand their base of political support in India, the Soviets pressed forth with a strong attack on the political right in India. In September, *Izvestia* informed its readership that the Indian national bourgeoisie, having gained control of "the command posts of the state," considered an alliance with foreign monopolies more advantageous than pursuing the goal of building an independent economy.[210] With the "syndicate" not far from triumph at the critical Bangalore session of the Congress party, all of the social transformations achieved since independence were threatened with complete repudiation. While acknowledging the significance of Giri's victory and bank nationalization, the article stressed that the main task of Indian progressives was to thwart right wing attempts to overthrow Mrs. Gandhi's government and seek new victories over reactionary forces in India. Thus, from the outset, Moscow was throwing its full weight behind Prime Minister Gandhi.

When the formal Congress split crystallized in November, Moscow waxed sanguine over its prospects in India. In an article commemorating Nehru's eightieth birthday, *Pravda* commentator V. Maevskii suggested that the Indian statesman had recognized that India's regeneration could not be achieved along the capitalist path of development and that socialism was the only solution.[211] Having been rather skeptical about such possibilities previously, given the relatively advanced state of development of Indian capitalism, Moscow now held out the possibility of a non-capitalist path for India. This optimism was also reflected in an article by the noted Soviet commentator, V. Kudriavtsev, in which he interpreted these victories as indicating that India was seeking a way out of the impasse of the capitalist path of development, which "would only lead to de facto recolonization by neo-colonialist methods."[212] Kudriavtsev nevertheless added the caveat that the crisis was not over and that the political struggle over India's future would continue to grow. In this struggle, he stated, "India's pro-

---

[210] L. Koriavin, K. Perevoshchikov and A. Ter-Gregorian, "International Survey," *Izvestia*, September 14, 1969, p. 2, in *CDSP*, XXI, No. 37, 13.

[211] V. Maevskii, "On the Eightieth Anniversary of J. Nehru's Birth; Son of India," *Pravda*, November 14, 1969, p. 4, in *CDSP*, XII, No. 46, 15.

[212] V. Kudriavtsev, "Observer's Opinion: A Blow to the Plans of Reaction in India," *Izvestia*, No. 15, 1969, p. 3, in *CDSP*, XXI, No. 46, 15-16.

gressive forces can continue to rely on support from all progressive circles in the world." Indeed, it was Moscow's urgent call for unity among all left forces in India that helped line up CPI members of Parliament behind Mrs. Gandhi's programs.

During the following year, with Mrs. Gandhi more firmly in control, Professor Ul'ianovskii wrote an authoritative evaluation of India's domestic political evolution during the previous decade.[213] According to his interpretation, by the mid-1960's a small group of Indian monopolists had gained considerable strength and, in alliance with foreign capital, had sought to limit the role of the state sector to that of an infrastructural adjunct to private enterprise and also to reduce to a minimum government planning and regulation of the economy. After Nehru's death, these monopolists strengthened their influence within the leadership of the Indian National Congress, finding "obedient servants" in the person of the 'syndicate'— "a group of right wing figures," and were thus able to extract some important concessions between 1965 and 1968. The 1967 elections showed that Congress influence on the "democratic strata" of the population was waning, and, from that point on, there was continuous fighting between left, center and right wing elements within Congress, with the latter group beginning to align openly with the Jana Sangh and Swatantra parties. Ul'ianovskii denies that it was Mrs. Gandhi's promotion of leftist measures that precipitated the split; rather, right wing forces in Congress, seeking posts both in the government and in the Party's highest governing body, launched an offensive in collaboration with the opposition parties on the right. This move was thwarted by the left and center forces within the Congress, and it was only then that Mrs. Gandhi moved ahead with the reforms,[214] which, in turn, led to the open split in November 1969. Ul'ianovskii then stressed the importance of forging a united front of all "left wing and demo-

---

[213] R. A. Ul'ianovskii, "India: The People are Struggling for Democracy and Social Progress," *Pravda*, September 4, 1970, pp. 4-5, in *CDSP*, XXII, No. 36, 12-13.

[214] This interpretation conforms somewhat to that of Western observers who view Mrs. Gandhi's followers as a rather loose collection of left, moderate and even some conservative politicians, who nevertheless saw the need to move slightly to the left if Congress was to hold its own in the upcoming elections. See, Robert L. Hardgrave, Jr., *India: Government and Politics in a Developing Nation* (New York: Harcourt, Brace and World, Inc., 1970), pp. 137-38.

cratic" forces against any threat from the right and took to task "certain democratic parties...(who) occasionally have taken the path of unprincipled collaboration with conservative and right wing forces in the struggle being waged by those forces against the Indian National Congress and the government." Specifically upbraiding the CPI(M) and neo-Maoist splinter groups for taking an obstructionist line, Ul'ianovskii stated that these groups "have refused to see objective allies in the persons of the non-monopolistic petty and middle bourgeoisie, who are battling the monopolists, feudal lords and foreign capital." A major purpose of the article was then to admonish Indian leftists against self-defeating factional in-fighting.

Some important conclusions can be drawn from Ul'ianovskii's article. First, it is evident that the Soviets saw the split as a decisive shift in domestic Indian politics in a direction they found desirable, and one which they were actively encouraging by urging the Communists and other Indian leftist groups to line up in support of the Indian Prime Minister and her party.[215] Given the frank and somber characterization of the period preceding the Congress split, it may also be surmised that the Soviets had profound misgivings regarding India's domestic politics, which were much deeper than they revealed at that time, and that, perhaps, by articulating them now, they felt that the worst was over.

The Soviet strategy of supporting the Indian Prime Minister paid off handsomely. The February 1971 electoral victory of Mrs. Gandhi's party was even more impressive than her father's best efforts. The Congress Party (R) was assured of nearly two-thirds majority in the Lok Sabha[216]—a sufficient majority with

[215] Indeed one month after the publication of this article, the Soviet press focused much attention on discussions of the CPI delegation attending the October Revolution anniversary celebrations with Brezhnev, Suslov, Podgorny and Ul'ianovskii himself. The emphasis in the reporting was on the need to develop a united front strategy of the center-left. See, *Pravda*, November 18, 1970, p. 1, in *CDSP*, XXII, No. 46, 26.

[216] It should also be noted that the pro-Moscow CPI, which had arranged an electoral alliance with Congress (R), was one of the few parties able to improve its position, and as Lloyd Rudolph suggests, its future success seems to be tied to continued support and cooperation with Mrs. Gandhi's party. By contrast, the CPI(M) which shunned any electoral alliance, suffered a serious defeat at the polls, which reduced it to being a regional political force. Thus, it would seem that the Soviet strategy was a glowing success. See, Lloyd Rudolph, "Continuities and Change in Electoral Behavior: The 1971 Parliamentary Election in India," *Asian Survey*, XI, No. 12 (December, 1971), 1131.

which to push through a promised constitutional amendment which would deprive the former princes of their annual privy purses, as well as a number of other important reforms. More significantly, the 1971 election reconstituted a center-left government and reversed the process of growing instability and the directionless leadership that had been the pattern of the 1960's. With Mrs. Gandhi firmly in control, the Soviets were reassured that the political situation in India had stabilized for the near future, and in a way which they found conducive to closer collaboration. With justifiable pride, then, at the Twenty-Fourth Party Congress Brezhnev hailed the "recent nationalization of large banks in India and the inspiring victory over right wing forces in the recent elections to the House of the People of the Indian Parliament."[217]

While Mrs. Gandhi's success gave rise to confidence in the future of Soviet-Indian relations, the December 1970 election results in Pakistan, with their clear manifestation of Bengali sentiment for greater autonomy, caused deep concern in Moscow. President Yahya Khan's decision to use armed force to reverse the verdict of the East Pakistani electorate unhinged Soviet policy towards the subcontinent.

In an unpredictable and dangerous situation the Soviets did not hesitate to impose their influence to bring about a political solution to the problem. Podgorny's letter of April 2, 1971 to Yahya, expressing "alarm" at the military repressions in East Pakistan and urging a political solution to the crisis "as a well-intentioned word from friends" was only one of numerous attempts to defuse this tense situation.[218] It also was a clear rebuke to West Pakistani authorities which indicated that the policy of maintaining good relations with both India and Pakistan was at an end. The Soviets felt that Bengali nationalism was here to stay and could not be suppressed by force of arms. Fearing that continued fighting

---

[217] *Pravda*, March 31, 1971, pp. 2-10, in *CDSP*, XXIII, No. 12, 9. In a section of his speech interrupted frequently by rounds of applause, Brezhnev spoke in glowing terms about the prospects for Indo-Soviet relations: "Our friendly relations with India have received considerable development. The Indian government's pursuit of a peace-loving, independent course in international affairs, the feeling of friendship that traditionally link the peoples of our two countries—all this helps to deepen Soviet-Indian cooperation." See, *Pravda*, March 31, 1971, pp. 2-10, in *CDSP*, XXIII, No. 12, 12.

[218] *Pravda*, April 4, 1971, p. 1, in *CDSP*, XXIII, No. 41, 35-36.

would not only be ruinous for West Pakistan but also play into Chinese hands, with the possibility looming in the distance of an independent pro-Peking Bengali nation perhaps also encompassing the state of West Bengal, which would have accelerated the centrifugal tendencies in India as well, the Soviets pressed for a negotiated political solution to the crisis.[219]

Indeed, it may well have been concern over the Chinese response which stayed Moscow's hand for the next several weeks. The Chinese decision to pass up the opportunity of supporting the Bengalis in a war of national liberation and their denunciation of India, the Soviet Union and the United States for interfering in the internal affairs of Pakistan caused both New Delhi and Moscow considerable anxiety over possible Chinese involvement in the event of an outbreak of Indo-Pakistani hostilities. The fear of such a contingency grew considerably following the revelation in July that Pakistan had opened the channel for Sino-American talks with Henry Kissinger's dramatic trip to Peking. Even had the Nixon administration not shown a partiality towards the Pakistani government (by refusing to halt completely the flow of military aid),[220] any American attempt to establish a new relationship with China at this time would have diminished Indian confidence in strong U.S. support in the event of Chinese intervention in a new war on the subcontinent. Under these circumstances Soviet support was critical.

[219] A hint that the Soviets were prepared for the possibility of dismemberment is suggested by the attendance at the Twenty-Fourth Party Congress (which overlapped in point of time with Podgorny's letter) of a representative of the East Pakistan Communist Party who praised the Soviet role at Tashkent, Soviet aid to Bengali victims of the 1970 cyclone and floods and expressed gratitude for Podgorny's recent letter. *Pravda*, April 8, 1971, pp. 6-7, in *CDSP*, XXIII, No. 15, 33-34.

[220] Despite a formal embargo of arms deliveries to both India and Pakistan following the 1965 Indo-Pakistani conflict, the United States, using Iran and Italy as intermediaries, authorized indirect shipments of military equipment to Pakistan soon thereafter (See above, pp. 56-57). In October 1970, it was reported that the United States had sold B-57 bombers and F-104 fighters to Pakistan. Though arms sales were suspended during the Pakistan civil war, shipments of arms already licensed were allowed to continue until November—a policy which contributed to the sharp deterioration in Indo-American relations at this time. See, Robert H. Donaldson, "India: The Soviet Stake in Stability," *Asian Survey*, XII, No. 6 (June, 1972), 477-78.

In a dramatic move, widely interpreted as designed to stay China's hand and to deter Pakistan from unleashing war on India,[221] a twenty-year Treaty of Peace, Friendship and Cooperation was signed in New Delhi on August 9, 1971. Insofar as this pact had both important short-and long-term consequences, a thorough examination of it is deemed appropriate. In its major paragraphs the treaty reads as follows:

> Article 8. In accordance with the traditional friendship established between the two countries, each of the High Contracting Parties solemnly declares that it will not enter into or participate in any military alliances directed against the other side.
>
> Each of the High Contracting Parties pledges to refrain from any aggression against the other side and not to allow the use of its territory for committing of any act that may be militarily detrimental to the other High Contracting Party.
>
> Article 9. Each of the High Contracting Parties pledges to refrain from giving assistance to any third party taking part in an armed conflict with the other side. In the event that either side is attacked or threatened with attack, the High Contracting Parties will immediately enter into mutual consultations in order to eliminate this threat and take appropriate effective measures to ensure the peace and security of the other countries.
>
> Article 10. Each of the High Contracting Parties solemnly declares that it will not undertake any commitment, secret or open, to a third state or states, incompatible with the present treaty. Each of the High Contracting Parties declares further that it has no commitments to a third state or states and will not make any commitments that may be militarily detrimental to the other side.[222]

---

[221] See, Mohit Sen, "The Indo-Soviet Treaty," *Economic and Political Weekly*, September 25, 1971, 2047-48.

[222] *Pravda*, August 10, 1971, p. 1, in *CDSP*, XXIII, No. 32, 5.

Although the key Article 9 stops short of any military commitments,[223] the pact was nevertheless widely interpreted as a warning to China. It would seem that the Indians were especially eager to drive home this point. Thus, while Gromyko in commenting on the treaty only spoke in general terms of its contribution to "a stronger peace in Asia," Swaran Singh, the Indian Minister of External Affairs, stressed its importance as a "stabilizing factor" in strengthening the security of the region.[224] Certainly, it appears that the Chinese drew the same conclusion since their initial response to the treaty was lowkeyed, and thereafter, they refrained from issuing warnings about likely "Indian aggression" which had characterized their pre-August commentaries.

Furthermore, Article 9 with its provision for mutual consultations in the event of imminent attack also provides a mechanism through which Moscow could urge restraint upon New Delhi. Although the Soviet Union eventually acquiesced to India's military invasion of East Pakistan in December 1971, there is some evidence that the Soviets exercised a moderating influence, urging all parties to resolve the crisis at the negotiating table rather than on the battlefield. Certainly, Moscow's continued reference to "East Pakistan" long after New Delhi had opted for the restoration of the region's colonial name of "East Bengal" as well as the persistent Soviet calls for a political settlement satisfactory to "the entire people" of Pakistan suggest stronger differences as to how to resolve the crisis.[225]

The treaty provided both the Soviet Union and India with more far-reaching mutual assurances. From the Soviet standpoint

---

[223] It is not known whether there were any secret protocols attached to the treaty. The fact that the treaty shuns any firm military agreements also made it easier for Mrs. Gandhi to claim that the treaty is consistent with the traditional Indian foreign policy goals.

[224] *Pravda*, August 10, 1971, p. 4, in *CDSP*, XXIII, No. 32, 6.

[225] Illustratively, while acknowledging the severe burden placed on India because of the growing number of Bengali refugees, the joint communique issued after the signing of the treaty, stated: "Both sides reiterated their firm conviction that there can be no military solution of this problem and consider it necessary that urgent steps be taken in East Pakistan to achieve conditions of safety for the return of the refugees to their homes, which alone will correspond to the interests of the entire people of Pakistan and the cause of the maintenance of peace in the area." *Pravda*, August 12, 1971, p. 4, in *CDSP*, XXIII, No. 32, 9.

the combined effect of Articles 8 and 10 is that India has now legally promised not to permit even such minor clandestine activities as radar monitoring of Soviet Central Asia to be carried out by Western intelligence operatives from Indian territory. It would seem, moreover, that both sides might have had China in mind when they framed Article 10. Considering the long-term perspective, it would appear that both sides have publicly committed themselves not to offer any concessions in future negotiations with the Chinese that would be made at the expense of the other party.

Therefore, the significance of the treaty goes beyond the immediate crisis over Bangladesh. The fact that the treaty had been on the agenda for nearly two years prior to its signing raises the possibility that it evolved as a variant of the Soviet idea of Asian collective security.[226] Before the Soviet Union emerged from the Bangladesh crisis as India's chief benefactor, any move in such a direction would have only fueled the flames of anti-Sovietism in India.[227] It was only the resounding electoral defeat of Mrs. Gandhi's opposition plus the clear demonstration of Soviet support for the Indian position in this crisis that brought about a political climate in which such a measure could be overwhelmingly approved by the Indian public.

The treaty now institutionalizes Soviet-Indian relations and helps to remove them somewhat from the spotlight of partisan politics in India. It would be even more difficult now for any future Indian government to renounce its firm ties with the Soviet Union. In this sense, the pact tends to reduce certain Soviet anxieties that have been present from the beginning of the friendship. At the very least, it ensures that India will not be used in

---

[226] G. P. Deshpande, "The Indo-Soviet Treaty," *Economic and Political Weekly*, August 21, 1971, 1802.

[227] In fact, the criticisms of Soviet policy in India show no sign of abating. In August 1970, for example, the entire anti-Gandhi opposition in the Lok Sabha walked out to protest the publication in the current edition of the Large Soviet Encyclopedia of maps showing large amounts of Indian-claimed territory as Chinese. After demonstrations and government inquiries, the Soviets finally defused the issue by coming out with a new edition of the work in which the disputed areas of the map in question were superimposed by a legend. For Indian press coverage of this matter, see, the following issues of the *Statesman Weekly*: August 15, 1970, p. 1; August 29, 1970, p. 5; December 12, 1970, p. 6; February 20, 1971, p. 1.

any manner as a base of operations by Western powers against the Soviet Union's southern borders, and this, of course, has long remained an important Soviet foreign policy goal in South Asia.

Indeed, it is clear that the Soviets are well aware of these broader implications. Thus, for example, while claiming that the treaty represented an "important landmark" in relations with India, Soviet Foreign Minister Gromyko stressed that "it is difficult to overestimate the importance of this treaty...."[228] Noting that the basis of Indo-Soviet relations had now been made more secure, he observed:

> "We have been together in all times, good and bad. This was so in the past. It is occurring in the present, for the friendship and cooperation between the Soviet Union and India do not rest on transient factors but on the lasting vital interests of our peoples and states and their interest in the maintenance of peace. Our relations are based on mutual trust, equality, respect and non-interference in each other's internal affairs. The conclusion of the Soviet-Indian treaty lays a still stronger political and legal base for these relations."

The Soviet-Indian treaty thus marks a highwater point in Indo-Soviet relations and portends a period of closer cooperation. Certainly events since that time have tended to further strengthen these ties. In the months preceding India's December 1971 military intervention in East Pakistan, the Soviets were reported to have delivered eight shiploads of arms to India.[229] Although the Soviets were publicly urging a peaceful resolution of the crisis, they at the same time had taken steps to ensure that India would be well-armed in the event of war. During India's December rout of West

---

[228] *Pravda*, August 10, 1971, p. 4, in *CDSP*, XXIII, No. 32, 6.

[229] *New York Times*, November 30, 1971, p. 2. Writing from New Delhi, Max Frankel also reported that Gromyko, at the time of the treaty signing in August, promised that, in the event of open hostilities, the Soviets would maneuver their troops along the border with Sinkiang province so as to keep Chinese troops stationary there. While counselling against war, Gromyko was nevertheless supposed to have also promised Indian officials Soviet support regardless of whatever happened.

Pakistani forces in Bangladesh, the Soviet Union was the only country to stand firmly behind India and used its Security Council veto to block cease-fire resolutions, supported by the United States, while the Indians completed their military operations.

This support contrasted even more sharply in India's eyes to China's verbal assault on Indian "expansionists" for allegedly trying to dismember Pakistan and set up a puppet state—a response which was predictable, and to the Nixon administration's partiality towards authoritarian Pakistan over democratic India and its belated display of gun-boat diplomacy with the dispatch of a carrier task force into the Bay of Bengal—responses which, if not totally unforeseen, were nonetheless highly unwelcome. At no point in the last seventeen years then was Soviet prestige higher in India than at the end of 1971.

With the emergence of Bangladesh the balance of power in the subcontinent has altered, perhaps irreversibly, in India's favor. Although the calculations upon which the adoption of a balanced approach to the subcontinent was based have been upset, it should be emphasized that the Soviet Union is still committed to preserving the stability of the area. Along with India, the USSR has had to assume a major burden for restoring Bangladesh to a state of economic health and political viability, for failure to do so would lead only to the search for more radical political and economic solutions. At a time when the Nixon administration appears hesitant to come to the aid of an "international basket case," the Soviet involvement in the region has augmented considerably.

Moreover, although India has emerged from this crisis as the dominant local power, the Soviets are cognizant that future tranquility still rests on the working out of an Indo-Pakistani *modus vivendi*. Even though the Soviets clearly sided with India, they were careful not to burn all their bridges with Pakistan. In view of President Bhutto's trip to the Soviet Union just a few months after the December 1971 war, it would appear that Soviet-Pakistani relations have not been dealt an irreparable blow. As in 1966, the Soviet Union is the only outside power in a position to help mediate the still unresolved issues, such as the repatriation of POW's and war crimes, that grew out of this crisis. Indeed, the possibility that the Soviets may yet work out some *quid pro quo* that could lead to lasting peace in the subcontinent should not be excluded. At present, it seems that the Soviets are content to play a benevolently passive role while President Bhutto and Prime Minister Gandhi attempt resolve their differences themselves.

As far as the future of Indo-Soviet relations is concerned, it would appear that their present basis augurs for continued close ties. To be sure, Moscow still has reservations concerning the domestic course of the present government. As a recent article by *Pravda* commentator V. Shurygin suggests, Moscow recognizes that India is still wedded to the 'capitalist path of development,' that the pace of agrarian reform is very uneven, and that Mrs. Gandhi is still far from being a 'revolutionary democrat.'[230] They most certainly have reservations concerning Mrs. Gandhi's ability to cope with monumental economic problems and social disparities.

As we have repeatedly suggested in the course of this chapter, the solidity of Indo-Soviet ties is based on considerations of mutual self-interest, related particularly to geo-political factors. At present there is a high degree of convergence between Soviet and Indian state interests. Yet these interests may change over time. Certainly, in a period when the configuration of power relations on a world scale is in flux, it is presumptuous to presage the long range pattern of Indo-Soviet relations. However, it can be asserted with assurance that India's present appreciation for Soviet support during the recent Bangladesh crisis may be ephemeral. In this regard, the Soviets could not have felt confident when Mrs. Gandhi, in a reply to C. L. Sulzberger's question of whether India felt obligated to demonstrate her gratitude to the Soviet Union for the latter's support during the crisis, stated that: "We are unable to display gratitude in any tangible sense for anything."[231]

SOVIET ECONOMIC POLICY TOWARDS INDIA

In the preceding sections, we have viewed trade and aid agreements as positive political acts in the development of Indo-Soviet relations. Yet, an examination of the strategy and evolution of Soviet trade and aid practices is instructive, for Soviet economic policy, as a component of overall Soviet policy towards India, tells

---

[230] V. Shurygin, "India: Important Stage," *Pravda*, April 28, 1972, p. 4, in *CDSP*, XXIV, No. 17, 16-17.
[231] *New York Times*, February 17, 1972, p. 14.

us much about Soviet designs and intentions. We are not concerned here with quantitative data, but rather with the qualitative aspects of those economic relations. Suffice it to note that by the end of the 1960's India was the major recipient of Soviet economic aid among non-Communist developing countries.[232] So too, the Soviet Union has become India's second largest foreign trade partner after the United States. Thus, Soviet economic ties with India are considerable and deserving of closer scrutiny.

Although we shall be examining Soviet aid and trade in sequence, it is recognized that the distinction between the two is somewhat artificial, inasmuch as a benevolent trade policy may be of greater benefit to a developing country than a program of economic assistance. So too, it has sometimes been argued that many aid programs are designed to stimulate trade. The distinction is especially tenuous in the case of Soviet aid. With few exceptions, all Soviet assistance to India has come in the form of credits to be paid back at $1\frac{1}{2}\%$ over a twelve-year period by a return flow of Indian exports.[233]

The first major Soviet aid project in the Third World, the Bhilai steel mill, was the product of a convergence of Soviet and Indian aspirations regarding the purposes and objectives of foreign aid. The Indian government had been conducting negotiations with the British and West Germans for assistance in the construction of two steel plants which were to be built in the state sector during

---

[232] A State Department study sets the level of Soviet aid commitments to India up through 1968 at $1.593 billion, some $500 million more than the sum granted to Egypt, the Soviet Union's second largest aid recipient. Of course, this total is far below the volume of American assistance to India during the same period. See, U. S. Dept. of State Research Memorandum, *Communist Governments and Developing Nations: Aid and Trade in 1968*, RSE-65, RSE-65 (September 5, 1969), Table 1, p. 3.

[233] Besides periodic gifts of Soviet wheat to help check severe famines, the only Soviet gifts have been the deliveries of agricultural machinery to the Suratgarh state farm in 1956 and, more recently, to several state seed farms. Also, the Soviets donated the equipment used at the Indian Institute of Technology at Bombay, which had been set up with Soviet aid. See *Eastern Economist*, January 13, 1967, 77. The only exception to the aid terms cited above was the pharmaceuticals and drugs project, built near Madras, which was repayable in seven years.

the Second Five Year Plan.[234] These negotiations had stalled over terms when Moscow stepped in and signed the Bhilai steel plant agreement in February 1955 on favorable terms ($2\frac{1}{2}\%$ interest over a 12-year period), which presumably forced the British and West Germans to ease their negotiating positions.[235] This initial propaganda triumph was soon followed by others, as the Soviets, who spared no efforts in making Bhilai a show case of Soviet aid, were able to put the plant into operation before the British-built Durgapur and West German-built Rourkela factories. Moreover, the Soviet record in the construction phase of the project has been an extremely good one. It has been widely observed for example, that the Soviets made strong efforts to train Indian workers, technicians and engineers both on the site and in the USSR to enable them to take over the operation of the plant as soon as possible. The product of careful planning and good execution, Bhilai has become a model Soviet aid project and a regular part of the itinerary of Soviet tourists in India.

As a heavy industrial project in the state sector, Bhilai typifies most Soviet aid projects.[236] Moscow's predilection for contributing its aid exclusively to state sector projects is determined by a number of factors. In the first place, Khrushchev was most certainly impressed by this institutional emulation of Soviet experience, and

[234] Nehru, an admirer of Soviet economic achievements, had encouraged the emulation of Soviet experience through the organization of a state sector and government planning. These measures did not proceed at the expense of private enterprise. On the contrary, many leading Indian business firms supported the idea of government initiative along these lines. Moreover, the state sector was to be developed by the construction of new enterprises, not by the nationalization of existing ones. As we shall examine in subsequent chapters, the relationship between the state sector and private enterprise has always been a perplexing problem for Soviet analysts.

[235] The softening of Western terms for aid by the mid-1950's has been interpreted by the Soviet press as a consequence of Soviet entry into the field of aid. Khrushchev frequently characterized post-Bhilai Western aid as "indirect" Soviet assistance. Some Indian observers have also taken the view that Soviet assistance serves as a stimulus to increase American aid. See, K. T. Merchant, "Soviet Aid for Economic Development," *Commerce*, May 2, 1970, 928.

[236] The only known exception of Soviet aid to Indian private industry was a small 1954 credit to the Birla-owned Hindustan Gas Co. See, Merchant, *op. cit.*, 927. There were also reports of negotiations for Soviet assistance in producing trucks in the private sector in 1961, but no positive results ensued.

the possibility cannot be excluded that the Soviets believed that encouraging the growth of the state sector would lead to India's selection of the 'non-capitalist path.' However, once these sanguine expectations dissipated the Soviets continued to channel their aid through the state sector in the belief that it could at least serve as a counter-weight to the Indian business community which was becoming increasingly enmeshed with foreign business interests. So too, the Soviets may believe that through the state sector their influence can be more strongly felt. In general, Soviet insistence in limiting its aid to the state sector is the corollary of American determination to steer clear of the state sector in the belief that only by supporting the private sector can private enterprise be encouraged.

These Cold War dichotomies applied to the strategies of economic development as well. Whereas the US concentrated its aid on developing India's economic infrastructure, light industry and agriculture and shunned aid for the development of heavy industry on the grounds of economic rationality, the Soviets viewed American aid as a classic case of a Western attempt to preserve these countries in a state of perpetual economic dependence. Consonant with Indian thinking, the Soviets believed that concentration on the development of heavy industry was the quickest path to industrialization. Moreover, by eliminating foreign imports of producers goods, India would be less dependent on the West. With a manufacturing base of her own, India would be able to overcome the colonial pattern of economic dependence and stand on an equal political footing with the West. This, of course, has been an often-stated long-term Soviet objective.

Whatever additional reasons may be presented (the most obvious one being that heavy industrial projects drew best upon Soviet resources and expertise), Soviet aid strategy was derivative of its own experience. The autarchic model of self-generative development, embodied in the Soviet Five Year Plans, was applied to the post-war Stalinist restructuring of the East European economies as well. It was only natural that the Soviets would utilize this prescription for the development of non-Communist states as well.[237]

---

[237] This approach was later differentiated to account for the limited resources of the USSR's smaller aid recipients. These small countries were encouraged to diversify their export lines and develop semi-manufactures.

Thus, Bhilai was only the center piece of several complementary Soviet projects designed to facilitate India's self-generative industrial growth. Other projects included the heavy machine-building plant at Ranchi, designed to produce three-fourths of India's needs for steel plant machinery, a coal mining machinery plant at Durgapur and other coal mining projects, which would enable India to upgrade the quality and quantity of its coal resources, oil refineries and technical assistance in oil explorations,[238] which would eventually offset India's total dependence on Western suppliers. Soviet aid was thus used to reduce India's dependence on the West in vital areas.

The real test of Soviet aid came in the following decade when a number of projects had already gone into operation. As we have alluded to in the previous section, the Soviet aid program ran into serious difficulties by the mid-1960's. A 1970 Indian study, for example, shows that for the previous four years, eight out of thirteen Soviet-built projects already in operation were running in the red, with the Ranchi heavy machine-building plant incurring the most serious losses, followed by the Bhilai plant, the Indian Drugs and Pharmaceuticals project, and the Durgapur mining machinery plant, respectively.[239] Although the Soviets have explained that such projects normally require long gestation periods before they become profitable concerns,[240] there were additional factors involved.

For one thing, the economic recession which hit India in the mid-1960's, affected the state sector. This meant that several Soviet-built enterprises had surplus production which could not be

---

[238] Important deposits of oil were discovered in the Cambay gulf area in November 1958, at Ankleshwar, Gujarat in 1960, and later at several sites in Assam as well.

[239] "Performance of Soviet-Aided Projects," *Commerce*, May 16, 1970, 1036.

[240] See, particularly the apologia presented in a special edition of *Commerce* on Indo-Soviet economic relations by the Chairman and Deputy Chairman of the Soviet State Committee for Foreign Economic Relations, S. Skachkov and D. Degtiar. Degtiar notes, for example, that the "economic effectiveness of industrial enterprises...is not entirely limited to profitability" but rather to its contribution to the "development of a country's productive resources." S. Skachkov, "Fifteen Years of Economic and Technical Cooperation," *Commerce*, CXX, No. 3075 (April 11, 1970), 20-21. D. Degtiar, "Soviet Assistance to Developing Countries," *Commerce*, CXX, No. 3075 (April 11, 1970), 22-24.

marketed domestically. In fact, Bhilai was producing at only 70% of its rated capacity,[241] and the situation was even worse at the Ranchi and Durgapur plants with both scheduled to run out of orders in the early 1970's.[242]

Moreover, it has been widely acknowledged that the Indian state sector has suffered from chronic mismanagement. The Ranchi plant particularly had a poor reputation in this regard. As the Bokaro project cited earlier suggests, many Soviet projects were behind schedule, often due to delays at the Indian end of the aid pipeline. Indeed, the lag between the amount of aid promised and actually utilized was assuming tremendous proportions. Up through fiscal year 1965/1966, India had drawn on only 50% of the Soviet credits that had been authorized to that point.[243]

Having built these projects, the Soviets had the responsibility to see that they ran as near to full capacity and as efficiently as possible. As the Skachkov mission in late 1968 and the dispatch of Soviet engineers to the Ranchi plant, noted in the previous section, indicate, the post-Khrushchev leadership exercised much closer scrutiny of the administration of their aid program in India.

The Soviets also began to alter their trade to take off the surpluses that had accumulated not only in the Indian state sector, but in the private sector as well. Starting in 1967, the Soviets began to purchase large consignments of Bhilai steel. In 1970, moreover, both the Ranchi and Durgapur plants received a needed boost when aid and trade protocols were signed calling both for the expansion of Bokaro to produce four million tons output per year, which would give additional orders to Ranchi, and for the purchase of products from both plants for marketing in third

---

[241] *Economic and Political Weekly*, May 3, 1969, 742.

[242] "The Skachkov Mission," *Eastern Economist*, January 10, 1969, 45-46.

[243] Merchant, *op. cit.*, Table 1, 928. Soviet compliance with the Indian policy of maximizing import substitutions may also have contributed to the underutilization of Soviet aid, for savings accrued in aid allocation in such manner have not been reallocated for new projects as a rule. The Soviet record on this score is rather good. Bokaro will use only 25% foreign components, whereas previous state sector plants had used 40% (*Statesman Weekly*, May 3, 1969). However, as the case of the switch from domestic private suppliers to Soviet imports of refractory bricks for Bokaro, noted earlier, suggests, this practice may backfire occasionally and result in production delays.

countries—a long-standing Indian request.[244] The Soviet Union has also placed large orders with Indian Drugs and Pharmaceuticals Ltd. to help that project overcome its marketing difficulties (see p. 60).[245] In addition, the Soviets have agreed to purchase large quantities of railway wagons to help relieve that private industry's slump. Although negotiations over this arrangement have been protracted because of differences on prices and specifications,[246] it nevertheless indicates a Soviet willingness to protect Indian industry, both public and private, from the uncertainties of local and international market conditions.

In a basic sense these trade arrangements signify a qualitative change in the nature of Indo-Soviet economic relations. The original development strategy based on the autarchic model of self-generative growth has been definitely discarded in favor of a system of economic integration. To be sure, the emergent pattern bears no resemblance to the colonial pattern of raw materials for finished goods, since India has now emerged as an exporter of industrial products. The professed Soviet aid objective of contributing to India's struggle for economic independence, taken in the literal sense, now becomes extremely suspect, or rather, reveals its anti-Western bias.

Concentrating their efforts on improving the performance of their projects, the Soviets did not proffer new aid credits after 1966. Several other factors also contributed to this. In the first place, it would have been incongruous to authorize new aid when such a large proportion of promised credits had not been utilized. So too, given the fact that the Indian government declared a planning holiday and delayed its Fourth Five Year Plan for several years, it would have been difficult to go ahead with new state sector projects in any event. Thus, there were important practical reasons for the absence of new credits.

Yet, it must also be considered that the curtailment of aid was related to more general considerations. As Western analysts have

[244] *Commerce*, February 28, 1970, 377. For Soviet reportage, see, V. Skosyrev, "Broad Prospects," *Izvestia*, February 22, 1970, p. 2, in *CDSP*, XXII, No. 8, 16.

[245] *Eastern Economist*, April 3, 1970, 655.

[246] *Economic and Political Weekly*, May 31, 1969, 900 and November 29, 1969, 1836. It was last reported that the Indian government may have to subsidize this deal.

observed, the post-Khrushchev Soviet leaders have approached aid with a great deal more caution and have attached more weight to economic criteria, political stability and the ability of a country to absorb aid[247]—all of which criteria were especially relevant to the Indian setting.

Indeed, certain statements in the Soviet press suggest that the grip on the aid purse-strings had tightened. In marked contrast to Khrushchev's bombast that Soviet citizens were prepared to suffer economic deprivations to demonstrate their "international duty" towards developing countries, in recent years the Soviet public has been reminded of the material benefits they receive in return for this aid. Furthermore, whereas as late as 1965 Soviet officials stressed the necessity of external assistance in view of the limited internal resources in developing countries,[248] in later years developing countries were urged to utilize their domestic resources more effectively and not be dependent upon external sources of capital formation.[249]

The Soviets have resisted pressure to increase the amount of its foreign aid. A Soviet commentator rejected the Pearson Commission's recommendation that donor nations set aside 1% of their GNP for foreign aid as a propaganda gimmick and argued instead that a certain percentage of the profits accumulated by foreign-owned companies be deducted for aid as a kind of compensation fund.[250] As in this and other instances when the Soviet Union has been called upon to contribute aid on a scale commensurate with its economic power, the Soviets have rejected such proposals on the grounds that they do not share equal responsibility with other

---

[247] Franklyn D. Holzman, "Soviet Trade and Aid Policies," *Proceedings of the Academy of Political Science*, XIX, No. 3 (1969), 111.

[248] See comments by S. V. Arkhipov, First Vice Chairman of the State Committee for Foreign Economic Relations, *Pravda*, July 28, 1965, p. 5, in *CDSP*, XVII, No. 30, 22-23.

[249] For a typical statement of this kind, see, V. Kudriavtsev, "Problems and Judgments: Real and Fictitious Difficulties," *Izvestia*, November 2, 1968, p. 4, in *CDSP*, XX, No. 44, 21-23.

[250] V. Solodovnikov, "Searching for the Right Path," *Izvestia*, October 31, 1970, p. 1, in *CDSP*, XXII, No. 44, 10. For the full text of the Pearson Commission's report, consult *Partners in Development*: Report of the Commission on International Development chaired by Lester B. Pearson (New York, Washington and London: Praeger Publishers, 1969).

advanced industrial states to assist developing countries, since neither were they a colonial power, nor do they own enterprises in these countries. Such is indeed the substance of the ideological justification Moscow presents to excuse the fact that its appropriations on aid have been less proportionate to its GNP, than those of its major rival.[251]

Finally, after a decade of experience in dealing with aid recipients, there are definite signs that Soviet patience was wearing thin. In his articles on Africa, the noted Soviet commentator, V. Kudriavtsev, warned against the adoption of a "consumer approach", to Soviet assistance on the part of several African leaders.[252] Kudriavtsev was even more outspoken in a 1969 *Izvestia* article,[253] in which he strongly criticized the policy of "prestige industrialization" and the construction of enterprises without considering the available raw materials or marketing outlets. In a rare display of pique, he went so far as to comment on the poor work habits of the Africans (albeit, a product of the colonial past) and called for a radical change in their attitude towards labor. Although Kudriavtsev's commentaries on Africa were not directly related to the Indian aid program, they nevertheless indicate that the post-Khrushchev leadership is more concerned with the economic rationality of new aid projects than with the satisfaction of the grandiose schemes of some Third World leaders. Certainly, this new mood of economic realism helps to explain the increased involvement in the operation of their aid programs.

Underlying the problems concerning Soviet aid to India is the fact that by the mid-1960's India's needs were quite different than they were in the previous decade. Possessing a relatively advanced material-technical base to support such undertakings, India is now in a position to build steel plants on her own. As the Soviets became painfully aware during the 'Bokaro-Dastur' controversy, the days of turn-key foreign assistance projects in India are over. By

---

[251] Holzman estimates that in 1963, a peak year for Soviet aid distribution, aid constituted only 0.2% of the Soviet GNP compared to 0.8% of the American GNP. Holzman, *op. cit.*, 111.

[252] V. Kudriavtsev, "Problems and Judgments: Real and Fictitious Difficulties," *Izvestia*, November 2, 1968, p. 4, in *CDSP*, XX, No. 44, 23.

[253] V. Kudriavtsev, "Problems and Judgments: Work for Yourself," *Izvestia*, January 23, 1969, p. 5, in *CDSP*, XXI, No. 4, 23-24.

the mid-1960's India needed non-project assistance and more specialized types of assistance.

Although the Soviets have been unwilling to untie their aid (the December 1966, 300 million ruble credit being the only example of an extension of non-project aid), they have been more receptive to Indian requests for assistance in new areas. This especially applies to the area of aid for agricultural development.

While Khrushchev's development strategy of full scale industrialization shaped the Soviet aid program in India in its formative phase, by the 1960's, Soviet aid theorists were beginning to have serious misgivings about the general utility of such schemes. Sounding very much like certain 'bourgeois' economists of the 1950's, Kudriavtsev, writing on Africa in 1968,[254] warned against adopting the strategy of "over-industrialization" to the neglect of agricultural development. Kudriavtsev stressed the need for a gradualist approach to industrialization, commencing not with tractors but with improved hoes and with kerosene lanterns instead of electricity. In this instance, it would appear that Soviet aid strategy has come full circle.

Although Kudriavtsev's analyses have little bearing on the Indian case, it should nevertheless be noted that the Soviets in recent years have begun to modify their aid priorities in India to account for the monumental food and population problems there. Thus, the February 1970 protocols provided *inter alia* for the construction of a fertilizer plant in the state sector.[255] Also the Soviets are engaged in a technical assistance project designed to develop an Indian deep sea fishing capacity.[256] Thus, in the food producing areas in which they are technically proficient, they have rendered India assistance. They also seem prepared to assist

[254] V. Kudriavtsev, "Problems and Judgments: Real and Fictitious Difficulties," *Izvestia*, November 2, 1968, p. 4, in *CDSP*, XX, No. 44, 21-23. Kudriavtsev also predicted that a strategy of "over-industrialization" would not lead to the formation of a permanent working class but to an influx of rural migrants, swelling the ranks of declasse elements who often serve as a base of foreign and domestic reaction. This, of course, negates previous Soviet wisdom on this subject.

[255] V. Skosyrev, "Broad Prospects," *Izvestia*, February 22, 1970, p. 2, in *CDSP*, XXII, No. 8, 16.

[256] A. Maslennikov, "Fruitful Cooperation," *Pravda*, February 6, 1970, p. 5, in *CDSP*, XXII, No. 5, 12.

India's program of birth control.²⁵⁷ The manufacture of medical instruments for India's family planning program at the Soviet-built surgical instruments plant near Madras may be a forerunner of more dramatic initiatives in this area.²⁵⁸

On balance, then, the Soviet Union has sought to adjust its aid program to India's urgent needs. Although the pattern of future Soviet assistance is not yet discernible, it shall, as Degtiar noted, be based on "mutual benefit" from an international division of labor.²⁵⁹ This will mean that the closer economic links envisioned will serve to buttress firmer Indo-Soviet political ties as well.

By far the most dynamic sector of Soviet-Indian economic relations is trade. From negligible proportions in the late Stalinist years,²⁶⁰ Indo-Soviet trade has grown dramatically to the point where the Soviet Union by the late 1960's ranked as India's second largest trading partner in terms of total trade turnover. Since the signing of the first five year trade agreement in December 1953, the volume of Soviet Indian trade has risen rather steadily. Whereas the Soviet share of India's foreign trade turnover constituted less than 0.1% in 1953, that figure had risen to 2.2% in 1956 and to approximately 13% by 1969-1970.²⁶¹

Indo-Soviet trade has been conducted on the basis of bilateral agreements, usually five years in duration, which have specified the nomenclature of items available for export from each country.

[257] It should be noted that the Soviets have only recently overcome their longstanding resistance to birth control measures (see below, pp. 258-59).

[258] See F. A. Ahmed, "Indo-Soviet Industrial Collaboration," *Commerce*, April 11, 1970, 6.

[259] Degtiar, *op. cit.*, 24. Degtiar cited the example of the Soviet-Afghan gas pipeline that is being repaid with deliveries of natural gas.

[260] In fact, reflecting the Stalinist phase of hostility to newly independent countries, Indian imports to the USSR fell off between 1948 and 1953 from a volume of $16.2 million to $ 0.7 million; Soviet exports to India declined from $9.8 million to $ 0.9 million over the same time period. See, Stein, *op. cit.*, Appendix B, p. 297.

[261] See, Stein, *op. cit.*, p. 297. The last percentage is recorded by V. I. Smirnov, a Soviet trade representative in India. V. I. Smirnov, "Principles, Prospects and Problems," *Commerce*, April 11, 1970, 44. This last figure may be somewhat inflated, however. Writing in the same issue, the Indian Foreign Trade Minister, B. R. Bhagat, noted that Soviet imports comprise 9.4% of India's total imports and exports to the USSR account for 10.9% of India's exports. B. R. Bhagat, "Promising Prospects Ahead," *Commerce*, April 11, 1970, 15.

Since 1958, rupees have been used as the method of accounting in all bilateral trade agreements between India and the countries of the Soviet bloc—a system which has been advantageous to India since it enables her to economize her reserves of convertible currency.²⁶² Prices, however, are not set down in the agreements but are decided through regular negotiations between the appropriate authorities.

In recent years, there has been growing criticism that prices on Soviet goods have been too high and prices offered on Indian goods too low. As the aforementioned example of the protracted bargaining over the railroad wagon deal indicates, the Soviets have earned the reputation of hard bargainers in the subcontinent. Nevertheless, in a recent analytic study, S. Manoharan, a research economist with the Department of Soviet Studies of the Indian School of International Studies, notes that there is no evidence that the Soviets have been charging higher prices on their products and that in some instances, their prices are, in fact, the lowest.²⁶³ Moreover, Soviet prices have shown a tendency to be stable relative to world market prices. On the question of Soviet prices for Indian goods, however, there remains a good deal of controversy. Manoharan concludes that Soviet prices for Indian goods have been in general slightly better than world market prices.²⁶⁴ Yet, even among the advocates of Soviet Indian trade, there is recognition that Indian products are not competitive on the world market and that the large Soviet orders, in fact, help to reduce production

---

²⁶² Prior to 1958, Indo-Soviet trade was balanced by conversion to pounds sterling.

²⁶³ S. Manoharan, "Indo-Soviet Trade: A Study," *A.I.C.C. Economic Review*, February 1, 1968, 19-22. In a subsequent article, Manoharan, by computing unit value indexes, demonstrates that India's trade expansion with the USSR has not come at the expense of trade on Western markets, since these traditional markets for Indian jute, tea, cashews, etc., had become inelastic in the post-war era. See his "India's Exports to the Soviet Union—Diversion or Expansion?," *A.I.C.C. Economic Review*, February 15, 1969, 19-23. Manoharan's study persuasively disposes of the counter argument that the 'rupee' trade with the Soviet bloc has resulted in a diversion of trade from India's traditional trading partners. For a forthright presentation of this latter point of view, consult J. A. Rosario, "India's Trade with the Socialist Bloc," *Economic and Political Weekly*, October 28, 1967, 1948-51.

²⁶⁴ S. Manoharan, "India's Exports to the Soviet Union," *A.I.C.C. Economic Review*, February 15, 1969, 23.

costs over time.[265] Even Soviet officials have acknowledged that Soviet bargaining positions were designed to reduce the cost price of output by raising Indian labor productivity.[266] Thus, it would seem that much of the controversy over whether the prices Moscow offers are too low or not depends on the perspective one has of the degree of competitiveness of Indian goods on the world market.

In general, it appears that the Soviet Union follows current world market prices in negotiating with India. Attam Parkash, assistant chief of the Indian Institute of Foreign Trade, has noted that "although there is no specific stipulation in the agreements regarding prices, in practice the goods are bought and sold on the basis of world market prices."[267]

The pattern of Soviet Indian trade has generally conformed to India's development needs. Thus, the early post-Stalin years were characterized by a complementary trade pattern, which consisted of Soviet deliveries of machinery, equipment, steel and other structurals in return for traditional Indian exports such as tea, jute, cashews, coffee, etc. Yet, as Indian industry developed, this trade was adjusted, with the Soviet Union serving as a test market for the products of new Indian industries. Whereas the export of Indian manufactures remained practically non-existent until the early 1960's, by the end of the decade the proportion of manufactured goods in the total exports to the Soviet Union stood at 40%, with this percentage expected to rise to 60% by 1975.[268] In most cases, in fact, the USSR is the leading buyer of new Indian industries. According to data provided by V. I. Smirnov, a Soviet trade representative, for 1968-1969 the Soviet share of Indian exports of men's shirts was 55%; of woollen goods—59%; fruit juices—64%; leather footwear—52%; and batteries—60%.[269] The large Soviet orders for these goods, moreover, have helped to ensure the stable development of some of India's small and medium scale industries. This in turn has enabled Indian manufacturers to develop the

[265] See, for example, Manubhai Shah, "Economics of the Rupee Trade—II," *Eastern Economist,* November 10, 1967, 901.

[266] Degtiar, *op. cit.,* 22.

[267] Attam Parkash, "Perspective on Indo-Soviet Trade," *Commerce,* April 11, 1970, 66.

[268] *Commerce,* January 9, 1971, 20.

[269] Smirnov, *op. cit.,* 46.

experience and confidence needed to enter Western markets. In discussing this highly beneficial arrangement, P. L. Tandon, the chairman of the State Trading Corporation (the governmental intermediary for trade with socialist countries), has gone so far as to suggest that India has given the Soviet Union products which did not meet the latter's essential needs.[270] Of course, how much longer the Soviet Union will remain a 'guinea pig' for Indian goods of shoddy quality, especially in light of increased trade with the West, remains an open question.

Whereas the Soviet Union has readily accepted new Indian manufactures as well as industrial surpluses accumulating in their state sector projects, the restructuring of Soviet exports has proceeded with greater difficulty. With India self-sufficient in many of the items imported from the USSR in the 1950's, her import needs have shifted to industrial raw materials, non-ferrous metals such as nickel, copper and zinc, special grade alloy steels, components and parts for her industrial establishment and more sophisticated machine tools. The difficulties that the Soviets have been experiencing in finding suitable exports is illustrated by their unsuccessful bid to sell five TU-134 commercial passenger jets to India as *quid pro quo* for the Soviet purchase of railway wagons.[271] Much of the difficulty stems from Indian preference for Western products, especially those more technologically sophisticated. The 1966 rupee devaluation, which temporarily interrupted trade with the Soviet bloc, and the liberalization of import licenses that ensued made it easier for Indian businessmen to deal with Western companies.

The Indian government's pro-Western policy on economic affairs in the mid-1960's had important negative consequences for Indo-Soviet trade. As may be seen in Table I, even after adjustments were made following rupee devaluation, the volume of Indo-Soviet trade declined for two years thereafter. In part, this

---

[270] P. L. Tandon, "Vital Role of Trade with USSR," *Commerce*, April 11, 1970, 38. This writer can bear witness to the validity of Tandon's statement. During the summer of 1969, the author purchased an Indian wine set that had been on display in a currency shop at Vnukovo airport (Moscow). At the very least this suggests that the Soviets have difficulty in marketing domestically some of their Indian imports.

[271] "Hard Sell by Russians," *Economic and Political Weekly*, June 22, 1968, 924.

was due to the sharp decrease in Soviet shipments of petroleum in 1967 (petroleum exports fell off $28 million in that year). This has been attributed to Soviet reluctance to tie up its tanker capacity on the longer haul to South Asia following the closure of the Suez Canal.[272] The closing of the Suez route doubled the travel time between Odessa and Indian ports, which led the Soviets to seek an overland route through Afghanistan and Pakistan.

TABLE I—SOVIET-INDIAN TRADE

(In Millions of Rubles)

Year	Imports from India	Exports to India
1958	45.8	117.0
1959	54.5	61.2
1960	61.6	42.4
1961	60.2	85.9
1962	64.5	112.3
1963	85.3	199.7
1964	140.3	211.3
1965	169.4	193.5
1966	172.0	174.0
1967	162.7	146.1
1968	164.7	165.0
1969	199.3	154.2
1970	242.6	122.3
1971	255.8	116.3

SOURCES: Ministerstvo Vneshnei Torgovli SSSR, *Vneshniaia Torgovlia SSSR, 1918-1966*, (Moscow, 1967), pp. 208-09; MVT SSSR, *Vneshniaia Torgovlia SSSR za 1967g*, (Moscow, 1968) pp. 229-33; MVT SSSR, *Vneshniaia Torgovlia SSSR za 1969g*, (Moscow, 1970), pp. 216-20; MVT SSSR, *Vneshniaia Torgovlia SSSR za 1971g*, (Moscow, 1972), pp. 231-55.

[272] "Communist Governments and Developing Nations: Aid and Trade in 1968." 9.

While the downward pattern in Indo-Soviet trade reversed itself, what is more significant is that an Indian positive trade balance, which emerged as a definite trend following rupee devaluation, has grown to the point that for the years 1970 and 1971, the annual value of imports from India is approximately double the annual value of Soviet exports to India. Although some Indian economists have argued that India needs a positive trade balance to meet her repayment obligations on economic credits,[273] it has also been recognized that, given the nature of the bilateral trade mechanism, this gap will tend to retard trade growth as a whole, since the Soviets are faced with rupee shortages to pay for Indian imports.[274] Indeed, this may already be happening. While the December 1970 trade agreement projected a 10% increase per annum in total trade turnover, trade volume increased only 3.2% in 1970 and 2.0% in 1971 over preceding years.

Nevertheless, the December 1970 trade agreement, as well as the February 1970 trade and aid protocols which preceded it, stand as landmarks in the development of Indo-Soviet relations. Not only did the trade agreement reflect the structural change in the Indian economy,[275] but the provisions for production collaboration and joint marketing in third countries constituted breakthroughs in long years of negotiations and opened up possibilities for even closer economic ties. In the offing may be agreements on trilateral and multilateral trade arrangements—an idea that had been raised

---

[273] Parkash, *op. cit.*, 64.

[274] It has been argued that bilateralism contains certain inhibiting factors on trade expansion in comparison with multilateral trade arrangements. For a critical analysis of this problem, see S. K. Verghese, "Rupee Payment Arrangements: An Appraisal," *Economic Weekly*, Special Number, July, 1963, 1293-97.

[275] According to the agreement, the Soviet Union will be supplying India with new industrial goods such as helicopters for agricultural use, ships, machine tools with programmed controls and equipment for India's chemical and textile industries. The Soviets will also increase exports of non-ferrous metals, especially platinum, zinc and nickel, components for Soviet-aided projects, rolled steel, refractory bricks, tractors, agricultural machinery, sulphur, fertilizer and newsprint. India shall be supplying the USSR with increasing amounts of manufactured goods, such as electric motors, excavators, machine-made carpets, paints, varnishes, clothing, knitwear, cotton textiles, storage batteries, as well as the traditional exports of tea, jute, footwear and cashews. See *Izvestia*, December 29, 1970, p. 1, in *CDSP*, XXII, No. 52, 31. See also *Commerce*, January 9, 1971, 20.

by countries of the Soviet bloc as early as 1961.[276] Such arrangements would enable the Socialist states to shift their rupee balances, thereby removing obstacles to trade expansion which the present system of bilateralism imposes. The introduction of production collaboration may also herald the emergence of a horizontal division of labor with exchanges of industrial machinery and components, a scheme which the Soviets as well as some Indian advocates of Indo-Soviet trade have favored for a considerable time.[277]

There can be little doubt that the signing of these two important trade documents was itself a by-product of the improved political climate generated by Mrs. Gandhi's consolidation of power. Such trade innovations and prospects would have been highly unlikely a few years before when the Indian government was moving in the direction of closer collaboration with the West. During the mid-1960's, the government was reluctant to engage itself in such long term economic commitments with the Soviet Union, in large part because of the anticipated reaction in the West.[278] So too, considering the state of planning at the time, such joint ventures would have been extremely difficult to coordinate.

Indeed, in order for the new projected trade arrangements to become effective, a major overhaul of planning in India must take place. As Dev Murarka, a Moscow-based Indian journalist,[279] has

---

[276] "Russia Plays Its Trumps," *Economic and Political Weekly*, February 24, 1968, 346. The first trilateral agreement involving India and a socialist country was signed in 1969 with Bulgaria and Tunisia. A sign of Soviet interest in such a scheme came in an article by Soviet economist V. Goriunov, in which he pointed out that the USSR and other socialist countries have never been adverse to any other form of trade ties despite the present formula of bilateralism. V. Goriunov, "World Trade and Economics: Normalization of Trade is a Demand of the Times," *Vneshniaia Torgovlia*, No. 8, (August 1968), 15-19, in *Current Abstracts of the Soviet Press*, I, No. 6, 6-7.

[277] As early as 1965, the Soviets let it be known that they favored a mutually advantageous branch specialization of production. See, for example, the communique marking Shastri's 1965 visit to the Soviet Union. *Pravda*, May 20, 1965, p. 1, in *CDSP*, XVII, No. 20, 11-12. Three years later a visiting Gosplan official reportedly explored with his Indian counterparts the possibilities of new forms of collaboration in shoes, leathergoods and canning of fruit juices. "New Modes of Bilateral Trade," *Economic and Political Weekly*, May 4, 1968, 698.

[278] "Joint Planning," *Economic Weekly*, June 19, 1965, 972.

[279] Dev Murarka, "Testing Time for Indo-Soviet Relations," *Commerce*, April 11, 1970, 52-53.

noted, all talk of dovetailing production plans is useless unless India tightens its planning mechanism, and the general economic performance of her public and private industry improves considerably. The problems involved seem much more basic than mere administrative streamlining. Thus, for example, the Indian business attitude that trade protocols with the USSR are not binding agreements that must be strictly followed may have to change in conformity with Soviet practice. This attitudinal factor points to the presence of problems inherent in trade between countries with different socio-economic systems—a vast and complex subject which is beyond the scope of this essay, however. In any event, it is quite apparent that in forging closer Indo-Soviet economic ties, there lie ahead serious though not insurmountable practical difficulties.

In summation then, Soviet economic policy has adjusted over time to India's needs as an emergent industrializing country. On balance, this policy has been appraised by most Indian analysts as highly beneficial to India. Moreover, it may be seen that even during the troubled period of political uncertainty and economic stagnation of the mid-1960's, the Soviets took the initiative in encouraging new forms of economic collaboration. To be sure, any hesitation on their part, particularly with respect to the aid program, might have redounded to the advantage of the political right wing in India and their allies abroad. Nevertheless, Moscow's assumption of greater responsibilities for Indian economic performance, especially at a time of political instability contrasts sharply with the Soviet general posture of caution regarding the Third World—a consequence not only of the more conservative disposition of the post-Khrushchev leadership, but also of the severe disappointments experienced in the Indonesian countercoup of October 1965 and the fall of Nkrumah during the following year. This, in itself, attests to the importance which the Soviets attach to preserving good relations with India—relations which are founded on the solid bedrock of geo-political self-interests.

Prime Minister Gandhi's consolidation of power has not only stabilized the political environment but will also presumably have a positive effect on the Indian economy as well. Having patiently stood by the present Indian leaders as they navigated through a period of centrifugal strains emanating both from the conservative right and radical left, the Soviets have now broadened the base of their political support in India and can look forward to a period of closer economic and political ties as signalled by the 1970 trade and aid agreements and the 1971 friendship treaty. While Soviet prestige is at an all time high in India in the wake of the Bangladesh crisis, it must be remembered that popularity is a perishable commodity in international relations. The unresolved political problems on the subcontinent may yet lead to renewed strains in Indo-Soviet relations. So too, the monumental problems of agrarian overpopulation and poverty still loom as long-range threats to Indian political stability. Thus, though predictions should be avoided, especially in a period of shifting power relations in South Asia, the Soviets may reasonably be expected to maintain their present support for the Indian government, for it is through this alliance that they have been able to achieve their basic objectives in South Asia.

2.
THE STALINIST BACKGROUND, 1947–1953

THE EMERGENCE OF MODERN SOVIET INDOLOGY

In evaluating the role of Soviet scholars in the formulation of Soviet policy towards India during the post-war Stalin period, preliminary attention must be given to a brief examination of the state of Soviet oriental studies, in general, and research on India, in particular.

While Imperial Russia maintained a strong tradition of oriental studies, its focus was mainly confined to adjacent countries, such as Turkey, Iran, Afghanistan and China, with which there were commercial, cultural and other interests. As a result of mountain barriers which made overland travel virtually impossible as well as British colonial administration which assiduously sought to sanitize India from Russian influence, traditional Russian interest in India, both governmental and academic, was highly limited.[1] What Indological research that existed was confined primarily to fields of ancient and medieval history, religions and languages. Research on contemporary political, economic and social themes remained virtually non-existent in pre-1917 Russia—a situation which was typical for Russian orientology as a whole.

While there were numerous changes in the organization and structure of Russian orientology following the October Revolution,[2] one is nevertheless struck by the basic continuity of specializations and personnel of early post-war Soviet orientology centered in the Institute of Orientology at Leningrad. So faithful to the pre-revolutionary scholarly traditions were the Leningrad-based orientalists that their major organ, *Sovetskoe Vostokovedenie*, published between 1940 and 1949, was accurately criticized for avoiding the publication of anything contemporary or topical.[3]

The origins of present academic expertise on contemporary India may be traced to the 1930's, when a small number of individuals turned to academic pursuits after earlier related careers in party or government service. This handful of experts, which included I. M. Reisner, A. M. D'iakov, V. V. Balabushevich and D. M. Gol'dberg, belonged to the group of Soviet orientalists whom Walter Z. Laquer has characterized as Communists without academic training but with academic ambitions.[4] Situated in Moscow where their expertise was more readily available to the

---

[1] However, the Indian subcontinent far outranked as an area of scholarly interest Africa, Latin America and South East Asia which remained veritable virgin lands as far as Soviet academic inquiry was concerned until after World War II. Separate Institutes of Africa and Latin America were organized in 1959 and 1961, respectively.

[2] On this subject, consult N. A. Kuznetsova and L. M. Kulagina, *Iz Istorii Sovetskogo Vostokovedeniia* (Moscow, 1970), and *Fifty Years of Soviet Oriental Studies: Brief Reviews, 1917-67* (Moscow, 1967).

[3] K. A. Antonova, "Obzor Zhurnala "Sovetskoe Vostokovedenie": Tom IV, 1947, Tom V, 1947," *Vestnik Akademii Nauk SSSR*, No. 12 (1948), 80-84. Another critic, S. P. Tolstov, noted specifically that since its appearance, *Sovetskoe Vostokovedenie* had only published two articles which dealt with the modern Orient (both on the languages of modern India). See S. Tolstov, "For Advanced Soviet Oriental Studies," *Kul'tura i Zhizn'*, August 11, 1950, p. 1, in *CDSP*, II, No. 33, 3-4.

[4] Walter Z. Laquer, "The Shifting Line in Soviet Orientology," *Problems of Communism*, V, No. 2, (March-April 1956), 21.

government ministries, these experts were affiliated either with the Moscow Division of the Institute of Orientology or with the Pacific Institute, the latter having been chartered in the 1930's with the sole function of enabling the USSR to attend sessions of the International Institute of Pacific Relations, but which had begun to sponsor research activity and grant degrees during war years.[5] In contrast to the Institute of Orientology, the Pacific Institute was concerned exclusively with contemporary issues and political problems of the general Pacific Ocean basin area, including South and South East Asia.[6]

Relative to the needs of a Soviet state which had emerged after World War II as a world power, the number of specialists on modern India and Asia in general was strikingly small. On the eve of the major reorganization of the Institute of Orientology which took place in 1950, there were only 36 orientalists affiliated with the Moscow Division of the Institute of Orientology, with half of these being graduate students (aspiranty);[7] still fewer were affiliated with the Pacific Institute.

The numerical shortage of scholars was not the only obstacle to expertise in this area. Soviet capabilities for conducting research on contemporary India were severely circumscribed due, in the first place, to the fact that direct contact with India was extremely limited. It was only in 1952 that a book exchange was established with India,[8] and not until several years later did the political climate had clear to facilitate the regular influx of Indian journals and government documents to Soviet libraries. During the Stalinist

---

[5] Kuznetsova and Kulagina, *op. cit.*, pp. 126-28.

[6] Another institution engaged in research on contemporary world affairs was the Institute of World Economics and World Politics, which concentrated on economic problems, but not those of colonial and dependent countries. In fact, during this period the shortage of economists specializing in this field was especially acute.

[7] *Ibid.*, p. 115. Commenting on the problem of understaffing at that time, the authors note that "the unification in one sector of specialists on Turkey and the Arab countries, Korea and Mongolia, India and Afghanistan spoke for itself." (p. 138).

[8] "Osnovye Itogi Nauchnoi Deiatel'nosti i Vnedreniia Zakonchennykh Nauchnykh Rabot Akademii Nauk SSSR za 1952 god. Doklad Glavnogo Uchenogo Sekretaria Presidiuma Akademii Nauk SSSR Akademika, A. V. Popchieva," *Vestnik Akademii Nauk SSSR*, No. 3 (1953), 99.

period, then, Soviet scholars were dependent upon whatever newspapers and secondary sources were available.

However, with the onset of the Cold War, Soviet scholars were admonished not to depend on "bourgeois" Western sources. At a 1949 conference of Moscow orientalists, "bourgeois cosmopolitanism" was roundly condemned. Delivering the main report, E. M. Zhukov, then Director of the Pacific Institute, warned Soviet orientalists must not cow tow to Western bourgeois orientology and stated that there could be no "world oriental science" as advocated by some representatives of the older generation of Leningrad orientalists.[9] Pointing to the danger of "uncritical uses" of Western sources, Zhukov lauded the writings of Lenin and Stalin as the source of all wisdom in the study of Eastern countries. These remarks were directed more towards the Leningrad orientalists than towards the Moscow specialists on current affairs whose loyalty was less suspect. It is nevertheless evident that the climate of the times was hardly conducive to the assertion of views independent of Party policy. It is no wonder then that the few research articles on contemporary India that appeared in academic journals were often difficult to distinguish from journalistic accounts in the popular press. This is not surprising, since, given the paucity of journalistic expertise in the area, Soviet Indologists, such as A. M. D'iakov and V. V. Balabushevich, were frequently called upon to provide journalistic commentary on current events for the popular press.

Thus, while Soviet orientology did not escape from the general cultural purge of "bourgeois cosmopolitan" influences, it should also be noted that the campaign which unfolded in the late 1940's was directed in large part at modernizing the discipline. There can be no question that Soviet orientology steeped in traditions of research in philology and pre-modern history, was ill-suited to satisfy the intelligence needs of an emergent global power.

Nevertheless the campaign which led to the reorganization of Soviet orientology took the form of an especially severe attack on the Leningrad-based Institute, which was characterized by S. P. Tolstov, in a scathing critique in *Kul'tura i Zhizn'*, as "a sort

---

[9] "Learned Council of the Pacific Institute," *Voprosy Istorii*, No. 3 (1949), 155-59, in *CDSP*, I, No. 39, 12.

of aggregate of feudal principalities, schools of independent scholars, aspiring to monopoly and brooking no criticism."[10] Tolstov was particularly critical of the paucity of research not only on the modern period but also on problems of contemporary significance in studies on the ancient and medieval East. As Tolstov observed in reference to several seemingly trivial subjects of recent articles, "...such pseudo-scientific disquisitions on isolated facts distilled from ancient sources may cover the reluctance of some scholars to engage in genuine Marxist study of the history and culture of the peoples of the East."

Indeed, the reasons for this "internal migration" on the part of Soviet orientalists are quite understandable in the intellectual climate of the late Stalinist period. It should be noted, however, that these pressures affected the Moscow specialists as much as their colleagues in Leningrad. Reisner, D'iakov and others had been in the field long enough to harbor vivid recollections of the fate of many of their teachers and associates who were liquidated during the purges. As a recent Soviet monograph, reviewing the dire consequences of the "cult of Stalin's personality" on the development of orientology, explains:

> "Many orientalists were lost for science as a result of arrests in the second half of the 1930's. Accidental accusations and suspicions led in these years to a significant loss of young and well known scholars. Besides this, repression forced many young orientalists to withdraw from vital contemporary themes and concern themselves with research on "more quiet" problems."[11]

With the revival of repression in the late 1940's and the broad hints which ensued of another major purge, one can but imagine the state of mind of those Moscow scholars who had survived. Indeed, this, among other factors, may explain the low volume of

---

[10] S. Tolstov, "For Advanced Soviet Oriental Studies," *Kul'tura i Zhizn'*, August 11, 1950, 1, in *CDSP*, II, No. 33, 4.

[11] Kuznetsova and Kulagina, *op. cit.*, p. 78. The purges were especially severe among Moscow orientalists. The important quasi-academic journal devoted to contemporary affairs, *Revoliutsionnyi Vostok*, ceased publication in 1937 as its editorial board vanished. See, Laquer, *op. cit.*, 23.

research publications during this period.

In any event, the campaign culminated in the important September 1950 decree of the Presidium of the Akademiia Nauk SSSR which thoroughly restructured Soviet orientology by merging the Pacific Institute into the Institute of Orientology which was now to be centered in Moscow. The first director of the reorganized Institute was the most outspoken critic of the old Institute, S. P. Tolstov. Suggestive that the reorganization was intended to be more than purely administrative and aimed essentially at changing the overall research focus towards contemporary themes, the Institute's affiliation with the Akademiia Nauk was transferred from the Department of Literature and Languages to the Department of History and Philosophy. The description of tasks outlined for the reorganized Institute also stressed such contemporary problems as the national liberation movement and the crisis of the colonial system, agrarian problems and the situation of the peasantry and working class, the nationality question and problems of national formation.[12] The study of ancient and medieval history would not be abandoned, but rather historian-orientalists were exhorted to concentrate on research themes of topical significance.[13]

However, by the time the reorganization effected a substantive increase in scholarly output on contemporary problems, Stalin had passed from the scene. In fact, for several years following the reorganization, there was a marked decline in academic production. A regular journal of Soviet orientologists did not appear until 1955 with the publication of *Sovetskoe Vostokovedenie* (the journal of the same name published in Leningrad ceased publication in 1949). Although two series, *Uchenye Zapiski Instituta Vostokovedeniia* and *Kratkie Soobshcheniia Instituta Vostokovedeniia*, were published in the interim, they could not take up the slack in research publications. Indeed, it would appear that the reorganization itself inhibited research activity at least temporarily. Thus, for example, delays

---

[12] See, "Current Tasks of Historians of the Orient," *Voprosy Istorii*, No. 12 (1950), 3-7, in *CDSP*, III, No. 6, 7-9, and V. I. Avdiev, "New Tasks of Oriental Studies Institute of the USSR Academy of Science," *Vestnik Akademii Nauk SSSR*, No. 2 (1951), 57-60, in *CDSP*, III, No. 21, 10-11.

[13] "Perspektivnyi Plan Raboty Instituta Vostokovedeniia Akademii Nauk SSSR v Blizhaishee Piatiletie," *Kratkie Soobshcheniia Instituta Vostokovedeniia*, Kn. 1 (1951), p. 3.

were reported in the transfer of library funds from Leningrad to Moscow due to lack of space and personnel.[14] So too, the disruption following the reorganization was such that publication plans were far behind schedule. Only seventeen of the twenty-eight books which were to be published in 1952 appeared in print.[15]

It was only in the latter half of the decade that publication activity increased rapidly. In fact, the volume of academic orientological literature more than quadrupled between 1956 and 1960.[16] This was made possible by the opening in 1957 of a separate press for orientological literature, Izdatel'stvo Vostochnoi Literatury, which greatly improved the Institute's publication capabilities.

The geometric increase in publications during the late 1950's was also reflective of the marked strides in overcoming the shortage of Soviet orientologists which was acutely felt during the Stalinist period. Thus, by 1955 there were 220 scientific co-workers at the Institute, of which 105 were historians, 37 were economists, and 75 specialized in the fields of languages and literature.[17] Categorized by country of specialization, India ranked remarkably high with forty-four scholars, just behind China with forty-five, whereas sixty-six scholars concentrated on the countries of the Near and Middle East. However, even this number did not satisfy Soviet needs at that time. Complaints were voiced in the Soviet press that too few well-qualified orientalists were being graduated, that kandidat's dissertations were either not completed on time

---

[14] "O Plane Nauchno-Issledovatel'skikh Rabot Instituta Vostokovedeniia," *Vestnik Akademii Nauk SSSR*, No. 6 (1951), 89.

[15] "O Nauchnoi Deiatel'nosti i Sostoianii Kadrov Instituta Vostokovedeniia," *Vestnik Akademii Nauk SSSR*, No. 4 (1953), 76.

[16] Kuznetsova and Kulagina, *op. cit.*, p. 157.

[17] *Ibid.*, p. 146. Compare these figures with the total of 37 orientologists affiliated with the Moscow Division of the Institute of Orientology in 1950. Although we have no conclusive evidence on this point, it is most probable that this dramatic increase represents an influx of new scholars in the field rather than merely the result of the transfer of scholars from Leningrad to Moscow. Indeed, given the fact that the reorganized Institute became a center for the study of the contemporary East, while Leningrad, which was reconstituted as a Division of the Institute of Orientology, remained a center for research in philology, ancient and medieval history, it seems likely that the transfer of the Institute from Leningrad to Moscow was not accompanied by any major migration of Leningrad orientologists to Moscow.

or were superficial, and that as a result of the continuing shortage, some orientalists were forced to hold several jobs simultaneously.[18]

In subsequent years, steps were taken to upgrade both the quality and quantity of Soviet orientalists. Research trips, which were non-existent in Stalin's lifetime, were encouraged;[19] scholarly ties with foreign research institutions and scholars were established and invitations to twenty scholars from Asian countries were sent for temporary and longer term appointments, with responsibilities in the teaching of oriental languages and the preparation of scholarly works at the Institute of Orientology.[20] These efforts were apparently successful for criticism of the Institute's staff situation abated in the Soviet press. The sharp rise in academic publications by the late 1950's is another indication of positive results in eliminating the general shortage of qualified experts.

Another index of such improvement was the internal restructuring of the Institute in the direction of greater specialization. Whereas in 1955 Indologists were divided into two sectors, one concerned with the history and economy of India and South East Asia and the other devoted to the study of the languages and literatures of this area, by the following year India was elevated to one of six departments within the Institute with three sectors consisting of history and philosophy, economics, and languages and literature.[21] In the year following its name change to the Institute of the Peoples of Asia in 1960,[22] the Institute's structure was again changed with India being grouped with Pakistan, Ceylon and Nepal in one department with sectors in economics and contemporary problems, and history.[23] While subsequent structural

---

[18] "For Further Advance in Soviet Oriental Studies," *Kommunist*, No. 8 (1955), /4-83, in *CDSP*, VII, No. 28, 23.

[19] In 1956, the first group of Soviet Indologists, which included V. V. Balabushevich, A. M. D'iakov, E. N. Komarov, G. G. Kotovskii, V. G. Rastiannikov and others, visited libraries, archives and research institutions in New Delhi, Calcutta and other Indian cities. See, L. S. Gamaiunov and N. M. Gol'dberg, "Sovetsko-Indiiskie Kul'turnye Sviazi," in *Nezavisimaia Indiia: 10 Let Nezavisimosti, 1947-1957* (Moscow, 1958), p. 131.

[20] Kuznetsova and Kulagina, *op. cit.*, p. 247.

[21] *Ibid.*, p. 144.

[22] This resulted from the merger with the short-lived Institute of Sinology. In 1969, the Institute reverted to its former name.

[23] *Ibid.*, p. 161.

changes have occurred, suffice it to note that by the late 1950's, the training and output of qualified Indologists had proceeded far enough to permit functional specialization.

Although we have been discussing exclusively the Institute of Orientology to this point, and for the simple reason that data is available on the organizational development of only this institution, it should be stressed that research on contemporary India has also been conducted at other academic institutions, most prominently at the Institute of World Economy and International Relations, which was established in 1956.[24] However, in contrast to the Institute of Orientology there are few country specialists at the Institute of World Economy and International Relations. Rather, its research structure is organized according to problem areas, such as the sector on problems of socio-economic development of liberated countries, and the character of research produced by the Institute (since 1957 it has had its own organ, *Mirovaia Ekonomika i Mezhdunarodnye Otnosheniia*) has been broadly comparative. Although the research plans of both Institutes have been coordinated, their institutional characters are quite different. While the Institute of Orientology has produced impressively thorough research works on India, the Institute of World Economy and International Relations has more often taken the lead in the expression of innovative and sometimes controversial concepts and formulations.

Besides the substantial institutional growth of Soviet Indological studies in the second half of the 1950's, it is important to note that the political climate of the Khrushchev years provided an academic atmosphere more conducive to scholarly inquiry. Besides the exchange of scholars and establishment of institutional ties, Soviet scholars were no longer bound to display vigilance against "bourgeois cosmopolitan" influences. On the contrary, Soviet orientalists were encouraged to take account of the "latest achievements" of foreign orientological science.[25]

In retrospect then, it is not surprising that a 1967 Soviet review

---

[24] Research on contemporary India has also been conducted at the Institute of Economics and the Institute of International Relations of the Ministry of Foreign Affairs, but the Institute of Orientology and Institute of World Economy and International Relations comprise the main centers of research in this field.

[25] "For Further Advance in Soviet Oriental Studies," *Kommunist*, No. 8 (1955), 74-83, in *CDSP*, VII, No. 28, 23.

establishes the period of the mid-1950's as the beginning of the modern period in the development of Soviet Indology.[26] As far as the Stalinist period is concerned, it is apparent that the conditions were unfavorable for the assertion of any independent influence by scholars on Soviet policy towards India. Given the repressive character of the times, whatever influence there was ran in the opposite direction. Moreover, the very attempt to distinguish an "academic" input becomes problematical, since many scholars doubled as journalists. Thus, the boundary line between academic and popular literature was to some degree effaced. We shall, therefore, employ the procedure of considering all writings by Soviet experts, published in both the academic and the popular press, in evaluating Soviet scholarship on India during this period.

SOVIET SCHOLARSHIP UNDER STALIN

The main focus of Soviet writings on India during the post-war years was the determination of strategy and tactics toward the nationalist movement and specifically towards the Indian National Congress which led it. As we have intimated in the previous chapter, prior to the spring of 1947, there was very little information in the Soviet press that foreshadowed the hostile posture towards the Congress government that followed. On the contrary, in the immediate post-war period, the National Congress won qualified praise from leading Soviet analysts. Thus, for example, the expert on Indian nationality problems, A. M. D'iakov, writing in *Bol'shevik* in 1946,[27] identified the Congress as the "most influential" of the national political organizations in India which was fighting for "full independence." Noting that the Congress constituted an amalgam of ideologically heterogeneous elements, D'iakov in a subsequent article viewed Nehru as something of a progressive, although other members of the provisional government, and especially Sardar Vallabhbhai Patel, were deemed reactionaries.[28] It would seem, however, that as independence approached, the Soviet doubts about the future conduct of the Congress government,

[26] L. B. Alaev and A. K. Vafa, "Indology (History, Economy and Culture)," *Fifty Years of Soviet Oriental Studies: Brief Reviews* (Moscow, 1967), p. 12.

[27] A. M. D'iakov, "Sovremennaia Indiia," *Bol'shevik*, No. 4, 1946, pp. 44-45.

[28] A. D'iakov, "K Sobytiiam v Indii," *Pravda*, October 21, 1946, p. 4.

especially in foreign affairs, increased in intensity. D'iakov, for example, characterized the Indian delegation at the Paris Peace Conference in 1946 as the "loyal vassal of British imperialism" and doubted whether the Indian government would be able to realize Nehru's professed desire of conducting an independent foreign policy.[29]

While the interim Indian government was receiving mixed reviews in the Soviet press, an important work by the Hungarian-born economist, Eugene Varga,[30] laid the theoretical basis for accepting India's independence as an important step forward. Varga argued that during the war, India had accumulated a positive sterling balance in England, making her in fact a creditor of the mother country. After the war, he noted that the British economic position had further been weakened by the fact that British shareholders in Indian enterprises, especially tea plantations, had been selling their interests to native capital. His conclusion was that India's economic dependence on England had been weakened with the implication that political events might soon reflect this changed economic relationship.

Yet, during the spring of 1947 there took place a sharp shift in Soviet policy with the adoption of a hostile posture towards the Nehru government. At a joint session of Moscow economists in May 1974, the views contained in Varga's book were branded heretical and the author was later forced to recant.[31] Varga was taken to task for asserting that colonies could attain freedom through economic evolution and thereby negating the dogma that independence could only be achieved through a successful political revolution against the mother country.[32] With respect to his thesis on the colonial countries Varga's critics held that no qualitative change had taken place and that only the form of exploitation had changed.

At the time when Varga's "decolonization" thesis, as it came to

---

[29] *Ibid.*

[30] E. Varga, *Izmeniia v Ekonomike Kapitalizma v Itoge Vtoroi Mirovoi Voiny* (Moscow, 1946). See, especially, chapter XI which deals with relations between colonial and imperial countries.

[31] See below, pp. 118-19.

[32] See, I. Gladkov, "Ob Izmeneniiakh v Ekonomike Kapitalizma v Rezul'tate Vtoroi Mirovoi Voiny," *Bol'shevik*, No. 17 (1947), p. 63.

be known, was being challenged, E. M. Zhukov, who as head of the Pacific Institute served as a major academic spokesman on the colonies, returned from India[33] with a sharply critical assessment of the political situation there. He found the Indian leaders in a much too conciliatory mood and, for the first time, attacked Nehru for his alleged pro-British sympathies. Moreover, he even went so far as to suggest that India harbored expansionist ambitions of her own in Asia.[34]

An important event in the hardening of the Soviet stance was the conference of Moscow orientalists held in June 1947. The key reports, delivered by Zhukov, D'iakov, V. V. Balabushevich and S. M. Mel'man,[35] all contained sharply negative appraisals of the Indian bourgeoisie and the National Congress. The consensus of opinion was that the Congress had betrayed the liberation movement by accepting the Mountbatten Plan and that the Indian Communists must now assume the leadership of the nationalist struggle. Thus, the "left" strategy, i.e., the attempt to form a united front from below led by the Communists and directed against the leadership of the "bourgeois" parties, received explicit endorsement. However, an important difference of opinion arose in the reports over which layers of the bourgeoisie could be included in the united front. Zhukov and Mel'man mentioned only the big bourgeoisie, which was strongly identified with the leadership of the National Congress, as having joined the camp of reaction,[36] whereas D'iakov and Balabushevich came out against the bourgeoisie as a whole.[37] Thus, although there was unanimity that the Congress

[33] He had attended an unofficial Asian Relations Conference in February at New Delhi and traveled extensively through India before his return.

[34] E. M. Zhukov, "V Indii," *Pravda*, May 12, 1947, p. 3, and *Pravda*, May 16, 1947, p. 3.

[35] Zhukov's report appeared in *Mirovoe Khoziaistvo i Mirovaia Politika*, No. 7 (1947), 3-14, while the papers of D'iakov, Balabushevich and Mel'man appeared two years later in *Uchenye Zapiski Tikhookeanskogo Instituta* Tom II (1949).

[36] E. M. Zhukov, "K Polozheniiu v Indii," *Mirovoe Khoziaistvo i Mirovaia Politika*, No. 7 (1947), 3-14, S. M. Mel'man, "Ekonomicheskie Posledstviia Vtoroi Mirovoi Voiny dlia Indii," *Uchenye Zapiski Tikhookeanskogo Instituta* Tom II (1949), p. 53.

[37] A. M. D'iakov, "Poslevoennye Angliiskie Plany Gosudarstvennogo Ustroistva Indii," *Uchenye Zapiski Tikhookeanskogo Instituta* Tom II (1949), p. 65. V. V. Balabushevich, "Rabochee Klass i Rabochee Dvizhenie v Sovremennoi Indii," *Uchenye Zapiski Tikhookeanskogo Instituta* Tom II (1949), p. 28.

THE STALINIST BACKGROUND

government had betrayed the nationalist movement, there was notable dissension over the precise tactics to be employed at this juncture.[38]

In fact, following the June 1947 conference, there appeared to be a good deal of inconsistency in Soviet writings on India. At a November 1947 session of the Pacific Institute on the subject of the October Revolution's influence on the East, D'iakov delivered a report which viewed positively the Congress's agrarian reform program and economic planning measures,[39] a position which hardly coincided with his flat condemnation of the Congress in his report at the June conference.[40]

Although V. V. Balabushevich in his writings published during the following year condemned the Congress government vehemently for having compromised with British Imperialism, he too retreated from his former militance by singling out only the big bourgeoisie for opprobrium.[41]

By 1949 then, although the tactical line had yet to be given precision, the "left" strategy calling for Communist insurrectionary activity from below had been enunciated. In compliance with this line, the CPI had taken up the call to arms in the Telengana district of Hyderabad State in 1948. At the CPI's Second Congress in Calcutta in February-March 1949, a very militant leftist line was adopted, urging a single stage armed revolution leading to socialism

---

[38] Robert H. Donaldson has recently argued that dissension at the June 1947 conference was more apparent than real and that the reports of D'iakov and Balabushevich were re-written two years later to provide a more scathing denunciation of the Indian bourgeoisie. Donaldson bases his case on the argument that from 1947 to 1949 Soviet scholars were moving towards a more sweeping condemnation of the Indian bourgeoisie, an assertion which, as we shall see below, is not supported by the available evidence. Moreover, the question remains, if D'iakov's and Balabushevich's reports were so revised, why wasn't Mel'man's which appeared in the same volume, revised as well? See, Robert H. Donaldson, "The Soviet Approach to India: Doctrinal Assessment and Operational Strategy." (Unpublished Ph.D. Dissertation, Harvard University, 1968), pp. 171-72.

[39] Reported in "The Great October Revolution and the Countries of the East," *Vestnik Akademii Nauk SSSR*, No. 1 (January 1948) in *Soviet Press Translations*, III, No. 9, 272.

[40] This, of course, tends to support Donaldson's argument.

[41] See V. Balabushevich, "What is Happening in India?" *Trud*, February 18, 1948, in *Soviet Press Translations*, III, No. 11, 328, and V. Balabushevich, "The Anti-Labor Campaign in India and Pakistan," *Trud*, November 21, 1948, in *Soviet Press Translations*, IV, No. 4, 108.

on a path parallel to the East European 'People's Democracies.' Soviet scholars were not detached from this revolutionary enthusiasm and, in fact, encouraged it by exaggerating the political importance of the working class and Communist parties everywhere in Asia. There was even a tendency to overstate the degree of differentiation among the Asian peasantry and to speak of the growing agrarian proletariat.[42] This does not mean that Soviet experts were unaware of the complexities involved in class analyses of Asian societies. In his report to the aforementioned June 1947 conference, Balabushevich noted the continuance of ties between workers and their villages, the effects of caste, religious and ethnic factors in inhibiting the formation of working class consciousness and solidarity. Nevertheless, Balabushevich predicted that the retention of the workers' ties with the village, which were breaking up in any event, would actually have a revolutionary influence on the peasantry. In general, Balabushevich sensed a revolutionary mood amongst the Indian masses.[43]

As revolutionary expectations rose with the success of the Chinese Communists, it was only natural for them to exert a profound influence on other Asian Communists. At a major joint academic conference of the Institute of Economics and the Pacific Institute in June 1949, it was the "neo-Maoist" strategy[44] of a broad Communist-led united front including various elements of the bourgeoisie which gained ascendence. Delivering the major speech at the conference, E. M. Zhukov made this point quite explicit: "In the struggle for People's Democracy in the colonies and semi-colonies are united not only the workers, the peasantry, the urban petty bourgeoisie and the intelligentsia, but even certain sections of the middle bourgeoisie which is interested in saving itself from cut throat foreign competition and from imperialist oppression."[45] By

[42] See, for example, V. Maslennikov, "On the Leading Role of the Working Class in the National Liberation Movement of the Colonial Peoples," *Voprosy Ekonomiki*, No. 9 (1949), 62-75, in *CDSP*, I, No. 49, 7.

[43] V. V. Balabushevich, "Rabochii Klass i Rabochee Dvizhenie v Sovremennoi Indii," pp. 5-28.

[44] This term was coined by John Kautsky, *Moscow and the Communist Party of India* (New York: John Wiley and Sons, Inc., 1956), pp. 8-13.

[45] E. M. Zhukov, "Problems of the National and Colonial Struggle After the Second World War," *Colonial Peoples' Struggle for Liberation* (Bombay: People's Publishing House, 1950), p. 9.

endorsing a broad united front strategy, Zhukov also was calling upon the Indian Communists to desist from pushing revolutionary slogans to the forefront. Thus, he sought to distinguish a People's Democratic revolution in the colonial countries as being primarily anti-Imperialist and anti-feudal in nature and suggested that it would take considerably longer in Asia than in East Europe for such revolutions to pass onto the solution of the social tasks. For the present stage then, Zhukov was urging the inclusion of all forces which could be brought into the anti-Imperialist struggle. This, of course, excluded any form of cooperation with the National Congress which was considered the representative of the big bourgeoisie and landlords. As if to leave no doubt on this point, Zhukov in reference to the Nehru government, villified "national reformists" who insist on neutrality in the Soviet-American conflict. These "national reformists" were considered henchmen of the reactionary bourgeoisie and servitors of the interests of Imperialism.[46]

Of special interest at this conference was the report on India delivered by Balabushevich, who had previously been identified with the "left" strategy which had excluded the bourgeoisie entirely. Here too, we find Balabushevich following Zhukov's lead in endorsing a broad "neo-Maoist" strategy:

> "The complete desertion of the upper Indian bourgeoisie to the camp of Imperialism and reaction does not preclude the possibility of certain groupings of native bourgeoisie still becoming for some time and at some period, fellow-travelers with the democratic forces in their struggle against Imperialism and against its allies in India...i.e., those bourgeois elements particularly affected by foreign capital penetration and those in the most backward parts of India dissatisfied with the prevalence of old monopoly groups on the Indian market but these groups should not be regarded as reliable or permanent members of the anti-Imperialist camp."[47]

Balabushevich, by stressing the unreliability of any bourgeois

---

[46] *Ibid.*, pp. 9-11.

[47] V. Balabushevich, "A New Phase in the National Liberation Struggle of the People of India," *Voprosy Ekonomiki*, No. 8 (1949), 30-48, in *CDSP*, I, No. 49, 10.

elements that might join cause with the Communists, gave a most reluctant endorsement of this line.

Presenting a more precise criterion for determining which bourgeois elements could be included in the united front, Zhukov in his summation of the proceedings stated that "the controversy as to at what stage the colonial bourgeoisie begins to play a reactionary role can be solved only when an answer is given to the main question of its attitude towards the Soviet Union."[48] Thus, the question of the progressiveness of the various strata of the native bourgeoisie was reduced to the transient and superficial factor of current posture towards the USSR, irrespective not only of the domestic role of the bourgeoisie but also of the underlying reasons which orient foreign policy attitudes.

Although the Soviets have turned more than once to such simplistic political criteria,[49] this could hardly be satisfying given the fact that the Soviets have occasionally been burned by nationalists who suddenly turned on them, e.g., Chiang Kai-Shek's *volte face* in 1927 and the consequent massacre of Chinese Communists at Shanghai. Zhukov's disregard of domestic political factors, however, is consistent with the frequent Soviet practice of maintaining good relations with nationalists who were at the same time persecuting their "own" Communists.

The problem of evaluating the bourgeoisie was not resolved at the June 1949 conference, however. In a volume composed of reports submitted to the Pacific Institute in the latter part of 1949, major differences over the role of the bourgeoisie were still evident.

In his introductory remarks, Zhukov reverted to economic criteria in evaluating the bourgeoisie, noting that the "national front" would be wider in the East than in the West and would include those parts of the bourgeoisie which suffered from the

---

[48] E. M. Zhukov, "People's Liberation Struggle in Colonial and Semi-Colonial Countries after the Second World War," in *Colonial Peoples' Struggle for Liberation* (Bombay: People's Publishing House, 1950), p. 98.

[49] In fact, Zhukov's formula was echoed in an article published a few months later by another analyst of colonial affairs, V. Vasil'eva. She too equated the determination of the progressive or reactionary character of one or another party in the national liberation struggle with the attitude of that party towards the Soviet Union. V. Vasil'eva, "Leninsko-Stalinskie Uchenye Natsiiakh i Natsional'no-Kolonial'noi Revoliutsii," *Voprosy Ekonomiki*, No. 12 (1949), 107.

competition of goods from the metropolitan countries.⁵⁰ This, of course, constituted a very broad cross-section which could include even some major Indian industrialists hurt by foreign competition.

Presenting the report on India,⁵¹ D'iakov was compelled to adhere to the revised united front line although at times he lapsed into a more sweeping condemnation of the bourgeoisie.⁵² Nevertheless, his interpretation of the united front approach is much narrower than Zhukov's. In his concluding remarks, he stated: "The struggle against Imperialism for the liberation of India and Pakistan right now is impossible without struggle against Indian feudal princes and landlords, and also against the Indian big bourgeoisie;...without the struggle for national democracy (liquidation of principalities, landlordism, nationalization of large industry, not only owned by foreign capital but also by national capital), full liberation is impossible."⁵³ By pushing to the forefront the more advanced tasks of the national liberation revolution, D'iakov definitely restricts the application of the "neo-Maoist" formula to exclude those sections of the bourgeoisie whose interests might be hurt by foreign competition and who, according to Zhukov, would be candidates for the united front.

The difference is not surprising. As a specialist on nationality problems in the subcontinent, D'iakov had been arguing that the big bourgeoisie in India consisted of Gujaratis, Marwaris, Parsis and Tamils, who not only were exploiting the working classes but also were oppressing the local bourgeoisie of the more backward nationalities of India.⁵⁴ D'iakov viewed the movement for provincial administrative reorganization along linguistic lines and the current nationalist struggles in Telengana, Maharashtra and

---

⁵⁰ E. M. Zhukov, "Obostrenie Krizisa Kolonial'noi Sistemy Posle Vtoroi Mirovoi Voiny," in *Krizis Kolonial'noi Sistemy; Natsional'no—Osvoboditel'naia Bor'ba Narodov Vostochnoi Azii* (Moscow, 1949), p. 23.

⁵¹ A. M. D'iakov, "Krizis Angliiskogo Gospodstva v Indii i Novyi Etap Osvoboditel'noi Bor'by ee Narodov," in *Krizis Kolonial'noi Sistemy* (Moscow, 1949), pp. 87-123.

⁵² Thus, in the introduction, D'iakov stated that full, liberation from Imperialism is impossible without a struggle against the bourgeoisie. *Ibid.*, p. 87.

⁵³ *Ibid.*, p. 121.

⁵⁴ A fuller exposition of his views on this subject may be found in his "Natsional'noe Dvizhenie Na Iuge Indii Posle Vtoroi Mirovoi Voiny," *Uchenye Zapiski Instituta Vostokovedeniia* Tom I (1950), pp. 3-50.

elsewhere as products of the struggles of these local bourgeoisies for larger shares of the regional markets which were dominated by the big Indian capitalists. D'iakov considered these nationalist movements in the Indian states progressive, since they "were directed against the reactionary government of the Indian Union and the governments of the principalities."[55] Yet, D'iakov added that these movements must be approached cautiously, since reactionary elements were trying to use them for their own interests. Indeed, D'iakov seems to purposefully minimize the value of even the bourgeoisie of less-developed nationalities when he argued in his conclusion that their "progressive role...is highly relative and temporal and on no account must it be overestimated."[56]

Thus, while there was general acceptance of the possibility of including at least some bourgeois strata in Communist-led fronts, Soviet scholars were still far apart on determining exactly which groups would be suitable allies, with the Indianists Balabushevich and D'iakov being most reluctant to accept any form of cooperation at all.

While the academic debate over the Indian bourgeoisie continued to preoccupy Soviet scholars during the Stalinist years, a dissonant view of the Indian big bourgeoisie as being something more than passive agents of 'British Imperialism' emerged in the writings of Eugene Varga. Although Varga recanted his earlier views in a 1949 *Voprosy Ekonomiki* article[57] and joined the chorus which viewed India as a semicolony dominated by English capital, he, at the same time, asserted that India was able "to maneuver between England and the United States, utilizing the discord between English and American Imperialism."[58] In a subsequent article in that journal, Varga stated further: "The Indian bourgeoisie, having betrayed the interests of the people, is striving at the same time to strengthen its role by capitalizing upon the contradictions between the British and the USA."[59] This contrasts sharply

[55] D'iakov, "Krizis Angliiskogo Gospodstva v Indii i Novyi Etap Osvoboditel'noi Bor'by ee Narodov," p. 114.

[56] *Ibid.*, p. 122.

[57] E. Varga, "Against the Reformist Tendency in Works on Imperialism," *Voprosy Ekonomiki*, No. 3 (1949), 79-88, in *CDSP*, I, No. 19, 3-9.

[58] *Ibid.*, 8.

[59] E. Varga, "The Decline of British Imperialism," *Voprosy Ekonomiki*, No. 4 (1950), 48-71, in *CDSP*, II, No. 32, 7.

with Zhukov's view, expressed a year earlier, that the Indian "reactionary bourgeois leadership is distinguished by particular servility, not only toward the British but also toward the American imperialists."[60]

Thus, contrary to the popular Soviet image of the Indian government and ruling class as mere docile agents of British capitalism, Varga was hinting that if India could maneuver between England and the United States to extract advantages, then Soviet policy might exploit such differences. Yet, although Soviet state policy towards India in the early 1950's began to change in this direction, Varga's view remained a divergent one. In fact, even after India had displayed her differences with the West over China and the Korean War, Soviet analysts interpreted this as only submission before the growing popular demands in India for peace.[61]

In the declining years of Stalin's rule, the only subsequent modification of the operational code towards India and other Asian countries was made at another important conference held at the Institute of Orientology in November 1951. Delivering the main report, academician Zhukov specifically warned against emulating the Chinese revolution—with its emphasis on peasant-based guerilla warfare—as a "stereotype," since other countries could not necessarily count on acquiring the vitally important advantage of a revolutionary army.[62] Insofar as it was precisely at this time that the Indian Communist Party was abandoning its insurrectionist activity in favor of the peaceful application of the united front strategem through electoral participation, Zhukov's remark constituted an endorsement of this shift.[63]

This message became even clearer in the discussions which followed. V. N. Nikiforov, presenting the counterthesis that conditions for the rise of revolutionary armies were ripe in India and

---

[60] E. M. Zhukov, "Colonial Appetites of the American Monopolies," *Pravda*, July 9, 1949, p. 4, in *CDSP*, I, No. 28, 44.

[61] A typical expression of this position may be found in I. M. Lemin, *Obostrenie Krizisa Britanskoi Imperii Posle Vtoroi Mirovoi Voiny* (Moscow, 1951), pp. 221-23.

[62] "On the Character and Attributes of People's Democracy in Countries of the Orient," *Izvestiia Akademii Nauk SSSR*, No. 1 (1952), 80-87, in *CDSP*, IV, No. 20, 3.

[63] For further detail on CPI activity during this period, consult John Kautsky, *op. cit.*, pp. 130-52.

other Asian countries, was challenged by Iu. P. Nasenko and V. V. Balabushevich, who argued that the Chinese revolution was not an obligatory model for other Asian countries and certainly not for India, "where we have seen the full error of mechanically applying the experience of the Chinese Revolution to Indian circumstances without consideration of India's special features—and, what is more, the interpretation of the Chinese experience applied was incorrect."[64] While Nikiforov, in expressing a dissident opinion, may have been representing a minority viewpoint in Moscow, it is also quite possible that his statement was made merely to have it publicly disavowed. In any event, the session made it quite clear that the view expressed by Zhukov, the most authoritative academic spokesman on Asian affairs, and supported by Balabushevich, an expert on India, was the accepted one. The consequent shift of the CPI to the peaceful application of the united front strategem at the ballot box served as a precondition for the Soviet overtures towards India which soon followed.

In retrospect, the debate over the role of the bourgeoisie and the formulation of Communist operational strategy in Asia were the central concerns of Soviet Asian experts during this period. To be sure, the debates remained largely academic, since in the early 1950's Soviet policy edged towards an accommodation with the Indian government. With the sole exception of Varga's comments, any hint of such overtures could not be detected in the Soviet scholarly literature of the period. To paraphrase the Marxist terminology, in the early 1950's, theory began increasingly to lag behind the practice of Soviet relations with India. The highly negative image of the Congress government as the spokesman for reactionary big bourgeoisie and landlord elements persisted in the academic press until just prior to Nehru's historic 1955 visit.

Thus, one can hardly speak of any academic influence on Soviet state policy during this period. Whatever influence was exerted was on the activities of Asian Communists. The interchange

[64] "On the Character and Attributes of People's Democracy in Countries of the Orient," *Izvestiia Akademii Nauk SSSR*, No. 1 (1952), 80-87, in *CDSP*, IV, No. 20, 6. The reproach to the CPI is in reference to the violent, "neo-Maoist" tactics adopted by the CPI during the summer of 1950, but rescinded shortly before this conference met.

between Moscow and the Communist Party of India during this period has been thoroughly documented in a book of the same name by John Kautsky and need not concern us here since our main concern is academic influence on state policy.[65] Yet, even in this area, one hesitates to speak of any independent initiative on the part of Soviet scholars. Even though Stalin and other high Party officials did not play a visible role, their presence was clearly felt in the orchestration of the denunciation of Varga's views at the May 1947 conference of economists, followed by the dramatic assumption of a hostile posture towards the Indian bourgeoisie and the Congress government at the conference of Moscow orientalists a month later. One cannot agree, therefore, with Charles McLane, who maintains that "the burden of formulating Soviet policy fell on a small band of virtually unknown and politically insignificant scholars—as though the articulation of British or French colonial policy were entrusted to Orientalists at Oxford and the Sorbonne."[66] It would seem that McLane confuses the articulation of policy with the responsibility for formulating that policy. It seems more likely that Soviet scholars in this instance served more as spokesmen for a policy whose basic content had been defined by higher party figures. The official silence on this subject may be explained by the reluctance of ranking Party leaders to become too closely identified with policies whose outcome was highly unpredictable. As Kautsky suggests, it appears rather that the academic conferences served as convenient platforms from which to broadcast the latest Party pronouncements to foreign Communists. In this sense, the very distinction between an official and an academic point of view becomes tenuous.

If Soviet scholars on the whole did not elicit any clues to the forthcoming changes in Soviet policy in the early 1950's, then at least they provided a good deal of insight into the broader Soviet

[65] Kautsky explains that much of the differences among Soviet experts and the subsequent confusion among the ranks of Indian Communists was the result basically of inattention and ignorance, since Soviet attention was riveted elsewhere. The strategies which emerged, therefore, did not take into account Indian conditions but were determined by Moscow's dominant foreign policy needs which, at least until 1949, were regarded primarily in view of the situation in the West. See, Kautsky, *op. cit.*, p. 196.

[66] Charles B. McLane, *Soviet Strategies in Southeast Asia* (Princeton, N. J.: Princeton University Press, 1966), pp. 348-49.

perspective of the tumultuous events which gripped the subcontinent at the time.

In a different context, we have noted A. M. D'iakov's qualified support to nationalist movements within India. While suspicious of the nationalist organizations themselves, D'iakov nevertheless strongly urged Indian Communists to exploit and take over the leadership of the nationalist movements whose "revolutionary possibilities" were still "far from exhausted."[67] D'iakov specifically endorsed the Communist-led insurrection in the Telengana district, which, in his view, not only constituted a peasant uprising but was also a part of the Telugu national movement for the formation of a Telugu-speaking Andhra state.[68]

Soviet support for regional nationalism in India, as enunciated by D'iakov, was designed to subvert the Indian Congress government by undermining the structure of Indian federalism. By so doing, the Soviets were also trying to prevent India's becoming the bulwark of Anglo-American plans to contain Chinese Communism.[69]

Underlying the practical significance of Moscow's encouragement of national separatism in India were certain well-formulated theoretical arguments advanced by D'iakov on the eve of Indian independence. In a lengthy, scholarly article published in 1947, D'iakov presented a detailed analysis of the state of national formation in India in which he implicitly suggested the possible "Balkanization" of the Indian subcontinent.[70] Thus, at the outset, he dispelled the widely held view popularized by the British-Indian Communist R. Palme Dutt (in his *India Today*) that India was becoming a unified nation with one tongue. Rather, as D'iakov

[67] A. M. D'iakov, "Natsional'noe Dvizhenie Na Iuge Indii Posle Vtoroi Mirovoi Voiny," *Uchenye Zapiski Instituta Vostokovedeniia* Tom I (1950), p. 49.

[68] *Ibid.*, pp. 24-25.

[69] The Soviets were well aware of India's potential usefulness in any scheme to contain China. Writing soon after the installation of the Communist regime in Peking, D'iakov wrote: "...The imperialist camp would wish to place upon India the heavy and shameful burden of the champion of Anglo-American aggressive plans in Asia. The choice of India is determined not only by the fact that after China, India is the largest Asian country; the main reason is that the political regime is very similar to the reactionary regime directed against the people which existed in Kuomintang China." A. M. D'iakov, "Anglo-American Plans in India," *Pravda*, November 25, 1949, p. 3, in *CDSP*, I, No. 48, 33.

[70] A. M. D'iakov, "K Voprosu o Natsional'nom Sostave Naseleniia Indii," *Uchenye Zapiski Tikhookeanskogo Instituta* Tom I (1947), pp. 223-330.

THE STALINIST BACKGROUND

observed, India was a multi-national state whose constituent nationalities were as diverse as those of Europe,[71] and that while most of the population belonged to a comparatively few large nations, there was no indication of any merger.[72] Proceeding from the Marxist tenet that a national community was a product of the growth of capitalism, D'iakov stated that the various nationalities of India were to be found at diverse stages of development, determined primarily by their degree of contact with British rule.[73] Thus, the movements for national autonomy in some Indian provinces and princely states and the general movement for administrative reorganization along linguistic lines reflected the aspirations of the bourgeoisie of the less-developed nationalities to increase their share of the local markets then dominated by the Indian big bourgeoisie—which, in D'iakov's view, was composed of representatives of a few smaller ethnic groups and religious sects, that had benefited from early commercial dealings with the British. Hence, the nationalist stirrings among the various nationalities were deemed to be progressive and worthy of support.

What was retrogressive, in D'iakov's view, was the partition of India which satisfied Muslim League demands for the establishment of a Muslim state. Indeed, the League's identification of a nation with religion was antithetical to the concept of national identity as defined by the Soviet Marxists' leading authority on nationalities, J. V. Stalin.[74] It was not that D'iakov ignored the severe communal tensions in the Punjab, Kashmir, Bengal and elsewhere, although he did stress that communalism was often aggravated by class factors (e.g., Hindu landlords and usurers exploiting Muslim tenants in East Bengal and Kashmir, etc.). Rather, he stated that communalism was an obstacle to national formation,[75] and that the partition along communal lines of Bengal and the Punjab, which constituted two integral nations, could hardly be seen as a solution to India's nationality problems.

---

[71] *Ibid.*, pp. 234-38.
[72] *Ibid.*, p. 243.
[73] *Ibid.*, pp. 291-92.
[74] See his *Marxism and the National Question* (New York, 1942) in which the four attributes of national identity were defined as common language, common territory, common psychological make-up and a common economic life.
[75] *Ibid.*, p. 289.

In his subsequent articles, D'iakov became even more critical of the partition, noting that it would neither solve religious problems, since millions of Muslims remained in India, nor was it economically rational, since normal trade channels in the Punjab and Bengal had been disrupted.[76] Having challenged the grounds for the formation of a separate Islamic state, D'iakov went on to a more sweeping denunciation of the Muslim League as an agent of pressure used by the British to force concessions from the Congress leadership,[77] and characterized Pakistan, whose government had a "very narrow social base," as "the most artificial state in the world," which "could hardly survive without the help of English Imperialism."[78]

Thus, while encouraging separatist tendencies in India, the Soviets at the same time questioned Pakistan's capability of survival. Indeed, one gets the impression from Soviet commentators in this period that Pakistan was a less legitimate enterprise than the Indian Union, for at least the "democratic forces" (i.e., CPI) were more active on the latter's territory. Although it would be perhaps more accurate to say that Soviet analysts displayed equanimity in their hostility towards both governments, nevertheless on specific issues a slight pro-Indian bias is discernible.

This is especially apparent in the Soviet assessment of the first Indo-Pakistani war over Kashmir. In the first major Soviet article on the subject, Z. Petrunicheva set forth the view that Kashmir represented a separate nation,[79] whose predominantly Muslim peasants, exploited by Hindu landlords and rulers, were suffering a double yoke of national discrimination and feudal oppression.[80] While acknowledging that the nationalist movement in Kashmir

[76] A. M. D'iakov, "The English Plan for the Partition of India," *Izvestia*, July 5, 1947, in *Soviet Press Translations*, II, No. 18, 202.

[77] A. M. D'iakov, "Poslevoennye Angliiskie Plany Gosudarstvennogo Ustroistva Indii," *Uchenye Zapiski Tikhookeanskogo Instituta* Tom II (1949), pp. 60-61.

[78] A. M. D'iakov, "Natsional'nye Dvizhenie Na Iuge Indii Posle Vtoroi Mirovoi Voiny," *Uchenye Zapiski Instituta Vostokovedeniia* Tom I (1950), p. 8.

[79] The maps of the period show Kashmir and Jammu as separate entities, neither part of India nor Pakistan. See, for example, V. A. Maslennikov, ed., *Ugublenie Krizisa Kolonial'noi Sistemy Imperializma (Posle Vtoroi Mirovoi Voiny)* (Moscow, 1953), map, pp. 280-81.

[80] Z. Petrunicheva, "Natsional'no—Osvoboditel'noe Dvizhenie v Kniazhestve Kashmira," *Uchenye Zapiski Instituta Vostokovedeniia* Tom I (1950), p. 163.

had at its inception a religious hue, Petrunicheva stressed that the movement had nevertheless become a nationalist one aimed at Kashmiri independence.[81] The Kashmiri National Conference, headed by Sheikh Abdullah was given qualified support for spearheading the movement for national autonomy. However, Petrunicheva interpreted the acquiescence of Sheikh Abdullah, then head of the provisional Kashmiri government, to the Indian government's offer to dispatch troops to defend Kashmir against invading Pakistani-supported Pathan tribesmen in return for Kashmir's entry into the Indian Union as a betrayal of the Kashmiri movement for national autonomy—a move which paralleled Nehru's transition to the camp of reaction.[82] Thus, it is apparent that the Soviets preferred an independent Kashmir.

Yet, the intervention of the United States and Great Britain into the Kashmir dispute elicited Soviet tacit approval for India's annexation of Kashmir. Indeed, according to Petrunicheva, England had in fact been using Kashmir to aggravate relations between India and Pakistan, in order to preserve her influence. Britain's support of Pakistan's claims to Kashmir reflected her calculation that Pakistan would be more dependent on Great Britain than India. The United States' efforts to set in motion UN mediation of the dispute was interpreted as an American attempt to get in the back door and establish their influence in the strategic area.[83] In any event, both Western powers did not want Kashmir to join the Indian Union, since the stronger "mass movement" there would eventually threaten the principality's reactionary ruling regime.[84] Thus there is a strong inference that Kashmir's union with India was preferable to either a UN trusteeship or Pakistani administration. Petrunicheva provides oblique confirmation of this when she stressed that Kashmir is strategically and economically important to India, serving as a food granary and as a source of industrial raw materials.[85]

While the Soviets approached the contending claims to Kashmir with studied silence, their reaction to Western initiatives led them

[81] *Ibid.*, p. 170.
[82] *Ibid.*, pp. 220-21.
[83] *Ibid.*, pp. 214-17.
[84] *Ibid.*, p. 218.
[85] *Ibid.*, p. 219.

to lean towards India's position in the dispute. Thus, it is evident that although Stalin ostensibly maintained a balanced policy in the subcontinent, i.e., balanced hostility towards both governments, one can nevertheless discern from D'iakov's denigration of Pakistan and Petrunicheva's assessment of the Kashmir conflict the outline of a pro-India policy. Yet, as long as the Soviets were committed to the subversion of the established governments, such considerations remained irrelevant. It was only once the Soviet attitudes towards the "bourgeois" leadership of the newly independent states had shifted, that this initial predisposition became effective. Although we do not suggest that Soviet scholars had much effect in influencing Khrushchev's behavior, it should nevertheless be noted that his 1955 declaration of support for India on the Kashmir issue was preceded by years of Soviet reflection which was conducive towards the adoption of a pro-India position on this question.

3.
THE EARLY KHRUSHCHEV YEARS.
1953-1959

THE POST-STALIN INTERIM, 1953-1955

As we have observed in the first chapter, Stalin's demise served as a catalyst to the improvement of relations with India. The change in the diplomatic atmosphere following his death was quite noticeable. Yet, Stalin's passing had no tangible effect on Soviet academic perceptions of India. Until virtually the eve of Nehru's historic visit to the Soviet Union, Soviet state policy and academic analysis of India grew further apart.

In the two year interim between Stalin's death and the announcement of the positive reappraisal of the Nehru government, the Stalinist view of India as a semi-colony, governed by a reactionary regime representing the interests of the big monopolist bourgeoisie who were themselves in league with foreign capital and tied to feudal landlords, persisted.[1] The task of forging a Communist-led united front that would include the petty and middle bourgeoisie, i.e., those bourgeois layers whose interests were infringed by foreign and domestic monopoly capital—remained the order of the day.

Inasmuch as Soviet research was directed towards the elaboration and elucidation of the current tactical line, much of the published research in this interim period concerned the situation amongst the Indian working class and peasantry. In contrast to the rather sanguine expectations of Communist victories in Asia at the time of the Chinese revolution, Soviet experts on the Indian social structure presented rather pessimistic assessments of revolutionary prospects in India. Thus, for example, reviewing the problems of organizing the Indian workers, V. V. Balabushevich noted that the CPI confronted such serious difficulties as reunifying a fragmented trade union movement and overcoming strong "bourgeois reformist" as well as "reactionary Gandhian" influences among the working classes.[2] This bleak appraisal of the class consciousness and solidarity of Indian workers augured for a rather protracted period of CPI organizational activity before a revolutionary situation could emerge.

In a more penetrating article on the industrial workers of Bengal E. N. Komarov cited their extreme poverty as the basic factor which forced them to maintain close ties with the village, thereby checking the differentiation of the workers from the peasants and obstructing the formation of an industrial proletariat.[3] Any improvement in the position of industrial workers, he concluded, depended on the development of a national industry, which was "impossible without the conquest of real national independence" and the liquidation of the "rule of feudal vestiges" in the village.[4]

In view of Soviet analyses of the situation of the Indian peasantry, the prospects for agrarian revolution seemed no brighter.

---

[1] See, for example, V. V. Balabushevich, "Natsional'no-Osvoboditel'naia Bor'ba Narodov Indii," in *Ugublenie Krizisa Kolonial'noi Sistemy Imperializma*, ed. by V. A. Maslennikov (Moscow, 1953), pp. 265-342.

[2] *Ibid.*, pp. 305-06.

[3] E. N. Komarov, "Material'noe Polozhenie Promyshlennogo Proletariata Bengalii i Nekotorye Voprosy ego Formirovaniia," *Uchenye Zapiski Instituta Vostokovedeniia* Tom V (Moscow, 1953), 21.

[4] *Ibid.*, 73-74.

Thus, G. G. Kotovskii, the leading Soviet specialist on social relations in rural India, viewed the caste system and untouchability, which were generated and preserved by the continued dominance of feudal land relations, as major obstacles to the unification of the peasantry in the anti-feudal struggle.[5] Moreover, insofar as caste divisions carried over into industrial occupations, with untouchables predominating among the unskilled categories, caste obstructed the consolidation of the working class as well.[6] However, Kotovskii added rather optimistically that with the development of capitalism several signs of untouchability were gradually being effaced and sometimes disappeared completely.[7]

If Soviet scholars suggested that the revolutionary awakening of the Indian toiling masses was not a near prospect, they nevertheless continued to think in terms of maximal and not partial solutions to India's acute economic and social problems. Thus, for example, Kotovskii explained the critical problem of 'relative' agrarian overpopulation as a consequence of the dominance of feudal agrarian relations in combination with the presence of trade-usurer forms of capital circulation.[8] Presenting the standard Soviet response of the period, Kotovskii stated that the solution to this crisis depended not on the 'neo-Malthusian' proposals of birth control, but on greatly increasing agricultural production. This, in turn, depended on the elimination of 'feudal remnants' in agriculture. Although Soviet analysts were reticent to say what mode of agrarian relations would replace the 'feudal' ones, there is nevertheless a broad indication that capitalism offered no solution to India's poverty. O. Klesmet, writing in *Voprosy Ekonomiki*, for example, drew attention to the resistance of Indian monopolists to invest the sums necessary for land irrigation since the financial returns from such a venture were insufficient.[9] Hence, it may be inferred that socialist

---

[5] G. G. Kotovskii, "Sotsial'no-Ekonomicheskoe Soderzhanie Problemy 'Neprikasaemykh'," *Uchenye Zapiski Instituta Vostokovedeniia* Tom V (Moscow, 1953), 85.

[6] *Ibid.*, 146-47.

[7] *Ibid.*, 85.

[8] G. G. Kotovskii, "Sistema Ekspluatatsii Plantatsionnykh Rabochikh Iuzhnoi Indii," *Uchenye Zapiski Instituta Vostokovedeniia* Tom X (Moscow, 1954), 90-91.

[9] O. Klesmet, "Upadok Sel'skogo Khoziaistva v Kolonial'nykh i Zavisimykh Stranakh," *Voprosy Ekonomiki*, No. 6 (1954), 69.

forms of the organization of production would be necessary to stimulate agricultural and, for that matter, industrial production. In general, then, one must view Soviet scholarship published during this interim period as but an extension of the preceding period.

REAPPRAISAL AND RESISTANCE

The first major indication of a positive reappraisal of the Nehru government came in the form of a programmatic article by A. M. D'iakov, heretofore not known as an admirer of the Congress leadership.[10] Published in the very first issue of the new journal of the Institute of Orientology, it praised India's contribution to the cause of peace in Asia and the world. In a sharp departure from previous pronouncements on the subject, D'iakov stated that:

> "The peace-loving policy of the Indian government is supported even by certain circles of the Indian bourgeoisie, including the big bourgeoisie, for this policy not only guarantees India's not being dragged into war, but also secures the possibility of smashing out of the grip of economic dependence on the Imperialist powers."[11]

Thus, not only had the Congress government been rehabilitated in Soviet eyes, but India could no longer be considered as a semi-colony. India suddenly became the leading example of a sovereign country struggling to attain economic independence. What underlying shifts in the relations between the Indian bourgeoisie and foreign capital had taken place to support this new line was not explained. Indeed important questions that had been raised by the dramatic reappraisal of the Nehru government, such as the character of the Indian bourgeoisie and its economic programs, and the role of foreign capital in India, were left for other scholars to analyze in the next few years. By restricting his commentary to Nehru's foreign policy, D'iakov skirted these issues.

Judging from subsequent scholarly articles, there was widespread resistance to the new line within academic circles. A good illustra-

---

[10] A. M. D'iakov "Indiia v Bor'be Za Mir," *Sovetskoe Vostokovedenie*, No. 1 (1955), 36-43.

[11] *Ibid.*, 42.

tion of this was a report delivered by the Sinologist, V. A. Maslennikov at the Institute of Orientology on February 25, 1955 and the discussion which followed.[12] While paying lip service to the new line that India had "entered the path of independent sovereign development," Maslennikov added the caveat that "in certain conditions, the proclamation of independence does not change the essence of the rule of Imperialism."[13] Moreover, with respect to the Indian ruling classes, he reiterated the familiar Stalinist view that the bourgeoisie displayed contradictory tendencies, between those elements interested in independent economic development and those tied to foreign capital, and feudal land holding.[14] Hence, the Indian bourgeoisie could not be counted as a firm fighter against Imperialism and feudalism. Rather, Maslennikov emphasized the role of the working class and peasantry as the most consistent fighters in this struggle, and in conclusion, advocated the Maoist model of the anti-Imperialist four-class united front, "led by the working class and its vanguard."[15]

In the discussion of Maslennikov's report which followed, divergent views on the degree of subordination of the Indian economy to foreign monopolies were expressed. Thus, while Iu. N. Rosaliev emphasized the incompatibility of interests of the native and foreign monopolies, R. T. Akhramovich challenged the new line by stating that even in those countries on the independent path of development the rule of foreign capital had not ended—clearly meant as a contradiction in terms.[16] Indeed, if foreign capital continued to dominate these countries, then they could be independent only in a formal sense.

An authoritative opinion on this controversy was soon forthcoming. In the same issue in which the discussion of Maslennikov's report appeared, an editorial stated explicitly that foreign capital could no longer be considered to have "uncontrollable rule" in

---

[12] V. A. Maslennikov, "Nekotorye Osobennosti Ekonomicheskogo Razvitiia Kolonial'nykh i Zavisimykh Stran v Epokhu Imperializma," *Sovetskoe Vostokovedenie*, No. 4 (1955), 31-42. This is a revision of the original report.

[13] *Ibid.*, 42.

[14] *Ibid.*, 40.

[15] *Ibid.*, 42.

[16] "Diskussiia ob Ekonomicheskom Razvitii Kolonial'nykh i Zavisimykh Stran v Epokhu Imperializma," *Sovetskoe Vostokovedenie*, No. 4 (1955), 6.

countries embarked on the path of independent development.[17] The editorial also criticized Soviet scholars for not noting the strengthening of capitalist elements in the countryside. However, the editorial did not check the undercurrent of scholarly criticism of the new Party policy.

In the very same issue of *Sovetskoe Vostokovedenie*, for example, I. M. Lemin stated that there had been as yet no social transformations in the countries now considered to be traveling on the path of independent development (i.e., India, Indonesia and Burma), and that they remained as before within the world capitalist economy.[18] Contrary to the popular view that India had made rapid economic strides since independence, Lemin noted that her economic growth was still very low and that she would continue to be dependent on foreign capital for a considerable period of time.[19] Characteristically, Lemin did not share the enthusiasm of the Soviet popular press for such aspects of Indian economic policy as planning: "This plan is neither a directive, nor a law. It foresees definite measures for financing and stimulating the development of these and other branches of the economy."[20] Thus, at a time when the popular press was filled with uncritical encomiums of praise for the Nehru government, Lemin was evidently seeking to dampen the excessive optimism that had been generated by Nehru's reception.

A more detailed account of India's economic development was presented by M. Rubinshtein in *Voprosy Ekonomiki* towards the end of the year.[21] Noting the progressive role of the state in promoting heavy industrial development in the state sector, a program which was meeting resistance from foreign capital, Rubinshtein drew attention to the fact that the administrative apparatus inherited from the period of British rule would have to be adapted to the tasks of economic management for these government economic

[17] "Ob Izuchenii Ekonomiki Stran Vostoka," *Sovetskoe Vostokovedenie*, No. 4 (1955), 6.

[18] I. M. Lemin, "Politicheskie i Ekonomicheskie Izmeniia Na Dal'nem Vostoke Posle Vtoroi Mirovoi Voiny," *Sovetskoe Vostokovedenie*, No. 4 (1955), 17.

[19] *Ibid.*, 25-26.

[20] *Ibid.*, 25.

[21] M. Rubinshtein, "Ob Ekonomicheskom Razvitii Sovremennoi Indii," *Voprosy Ekonomiki*, No. 10 (1955), 108-25.

programs to become effective.[22] More significantly, Rubinshtein drew attention to the fact that even with the low level of industrial production, India was having large sales difficulties—a fact which was attributed to her extremely narrow domestic market.[23] Nor did he find evidence of any change in agriculture that would have led to an expansion of the market for industrial products. Indeed, Rubinshtein was one of the first to note that the agrarian reforms being implemented in several states were on the whole half-hearted measures, which were not accompanied by any basic change in the predominant semi-feudal mode of agrarian relations.[24] At a time when news items and analyses in the popular press virtually omitted reference to the class struggle within India, Rubinshtein stressed the exploitative character of Indian capitalism, pointing to the vast scale of unemployment that had created an unlimited labor reservoir which capitalists had used to maintain extremely poor working conditions and low wage scales. Moreover, he noted that unemployment was not confined to unskilled workers, but affected teachers, engineers and doctors as well.[25] Thus, while the Soviet public was being furnished with an unblemished account of the Indian government's accomplishments in the field of foreign and domestic affairs, more sober assessments of India's economic problems continued to appear in the academic press.

The resistance to the official line among Soviet scholars did not go unchallenged for long. At the Twentieth Party Congress which formally sanctioned the new Party policy towards newly sovereign states, Anastas I. Mikoyan chastized Soviet orientalists thus: "There is in the system of the Akademiia Nauk an institute studying the problems of the Orient, but about it one can say that if the entire East has awakened in our time, then this institute slumbers to this day (animation in the hall, laughter)."[26]

Interpreting the official line, a major editorial in *Sovetskoe Vostokovedenie* took Soviet orientalists to task for still committing errors of

---

[22] *Ibid.*, 120. Rubinshtein explained that the Indian government had assumed the burden of constructing heavy industry because the Indian bourgeoisie did not possess sufficient funds for such a vast undertaking.

[23] *Ibid.*, 113.

[24] *Ibid.*

[25] *Ibid.*, 116.

[26] *Pravda*, February 18, 1956, p. 6.

the past.[27] Economists, for example, were criticized for being too often concerned with the activity of foreign capital in these countries and not giving needed attention to objective tendencies towards independent capitalist development. The editorial emphasized that Soviet economists had forgotten the Leninist precept that in the era of Imperialism the general tendency towards decay did not exclude the possibility of the rapid growth of capitalism in individual countries.[28] On the perplexing question of the role of foreign capital, the editorial stated that the dominant economic position of foreign capital in these countries did not mean that Imperialism ruled their political life as well. Hence, not only could genuine political independence be achieved without substantive changes in the economic relations between former metropolitan and colonial countries, but political independence itself was viewed as a prerequisite for achieving economic independence.[29] Indeed, Soviet Indologists were chided for interpreting Indian independence as a "final deal" between the Indian big bourgeoisie and Imperialism which had led to an underestimation of the contradictions between the national bourgeoisie and Imperialism. They had been wrong in not acknowledging the fact that the Indian national bourgeoisie and its party, the National Congress, had led the victorious struggle for independence; they had erred in considering Gandhi a reactionary representative of the feudal landlords and also in characterizing the domestic and foreign policy of the Congress government as an exercise in demagoguery. In short, a whole

[27] "XX C"ezd Kommunisticheskoi Partii Sovetskogo Soiuza i Zadachi Izucheniia Sovremennogo Vostoka," *Sovetskoe Vostokovedenie*, No. 1 (1956), 3-12.

[28] This information which virtually endorses the capitalist path of development for developing countries constitutes something of a high water mark of Soviet acceptance of India's economic development. By the middle of 1957 the view that capitalism could answer the economic development needs of the new states began to be challenged.

[29] A fuller elaboration of this thesis may be found in V. Semenov, "The Disintegration of the Colonial System of Imperialism and Questions of International Relations." *Kommunist*, December, 1956, p. 97, in *CDSP*, IX, No. 10, 3. On this question, Semenov forcefully states: "To assert that the winning of state independence by the countries of the East in the conditions of Imperialism does not substantially change their status is theoretically wrong and politically harmful." Yet at the same time he warns that without the achievement of economic independence these countries face the danger of relapsing into a situation of political dependence.

series of Stalinist positions on India were now authoritatively refuted, although blame for the commission of these shortcomings was focused exclusively upon the Soviet Indologists.[30] Finally, Soviet specialists on Indian agriculture were chided for exaggerating the role of feudal vestiges and minimizing the development of capitalism in the Indian countryside.

The *Sovetskoe Vostokovedenie* editorial heralded the emergence of the post-Stalinist perspective on the 'Third World.' Yet, with respect to the procedural aspects of the relationship of Soviet research to policy formation, it represented a continuation of the old habits. Didactic in tone, the editorial not only redirected the research emphases of Soviet orientalists but also informed them which conclusions they should draw from their research. Scholarly research was as before to substantiate the preconceived positions of the Party leadership. As we shall see later, however, in practice concrete research occasionally challenged the official line. At the same time, however, the editorial had an immediate impact on the Soviet academic community. Scholarly assessments of India during 1956 reflected on the whole the uncritical euphoria that had already infected the popular press the year before.

The general theoretical articles appearing in academic journals, for example, displayed a tendency to accept the Congress government's slogan of building a society on the socialist model at face value. In an authoritative article in *Sovetskoe Vostokovedenie*, A. A. Guber noted that the popularity of socialist ideas in the newly independent states was so great that the national bourgeoisies of India and Burma were officially advancing the tasks of creating an economy of the socialist type[31]—an observation that would have been merely a statement of fact had it been accompanied by the rejoinder that these 'bourgeois' concepts of socialism departed sharply from the Marxist-Leninist view. By not including this

---

[30] In an article rehabilitating Gandhi as a progressive leader of the Indian nationalist movement and as a spokesman of the national bourgeoisie, the noted Soviet Indologists, A. M. D'iakov and I. M. Reisner place the shoe on the right foot by holding Stalin responsible for all the erroneous views of India in the past. A. M D'iakov and I. M. Reisner, "Rol' Gandi v Natsional'no-Osvoboditel'noi Bor'be Narodov Indii," *Sovetskoe Vostokovedenie*, No. 5 (1956), 21-34.

[31] A. A. Guber, "Gluboko i Vsestoronne Izuchat' Krizis i Raspad Kolonial'noi Sistemy Imperializma," *Sovetskoe Vostokovedenie*, No. 3 (1956), 13.

rejoinder, Guber left his readers with the impression that Nehru's economic policies had something in common with socialism.

A similar line of thought may be found in an article by A. Azizian appearing later in the year in *Voprosy Ekonomiki*.[32] Commenting on the progressive aspects of the economic policies of India and other newly independent states, such as planning and the creation of a heavy industrial base within the state sector, Azizian observed that "...this in turn secures more favorable conditions for the further progress of these countries on the path of socialism."[33]

It would seem then that Indian state capitalism, if not actually being socialism was nevertheless a step towards it. In by far the most provocative article of this genre, M. I. Rubinshtein explained that state capitalism in the developmental context was a step towards socialism, but that further steps which would change the ownership of the means of production would be required.[34] Yet, he suggestively added that "...in India, which is advancing along the road of independent political and economic development, the objective possibilities exist for obviating the continued growth of monopoly capital and by peaceful methods, in conformity with the will of the majority of the people, taking the socialist path."[35] Very clearly then, the idea that the continued development of state capitalism in India could lead to socialism gained a certain amount of support among Soviet scholars at this time.

The sanguine expectations expressed in Rubinshtein's *New Times* article, however, seem quite uncharacteristic of this author who, as we have noted earlier (see pp. 132-33), had written a realistic account of India's economic development problems in a 1955 issue of *Voprosy Ekonomiki*. Indeed, in an assessment of India's Second Five Year Plan, published in *Sovetskoe Vostokovedenie* at virtually the same time as the *New Times* piece,[36] Rubinshtein drew

---

[32] A. Azizian, 'Raspad Kolonial'noi Sistemy Imperializma i Novye Otnosheniia Mezhdu Stranami," *Voprosy Ekonomiki*, No. 10 (1956), 3-23.

[33] *Ibid.*, 22.

[34] M. I. Rubinshtein, "A Non-Capitalist Path for Underdeveloped Countries." *New Times*, No. 28 (1956), 6.

[35] *Ibid.*, 4.

[36] M. I. Rubinshtein, "Vtoroi Piatiletnyi Plan Respubliki Indii," *Sovetskoe Vostokovedenie*, No. 4 (1956), 28-44.

attention to the class character of Nehru's economic programs and this at a time when a virtual moratorium on analyses of class conflicts in India had been called. With respect to financing India's five year plans, Rubinshtein noted that the burden fell on the shoulders of the working classes, while potentially significant sources of accumulation such as the profits of foreign companies and the incomes of the big bourgeoisie and former princes remained untapped.[37] Rubinshtein saved his sharpest barbs for the agrarian reform measures then being conducted. While noting certain positive aspects of the community development program in the fields of sanitation, education and the implementation of simple technical improvements, he cited Indian press commentary that these communal projects were insufficient since they were not tied to long overdue socio-economic reforms and that as a result, the benefits of these programs, such as eased credit terms, extension of mineral fertilizers, etc., were going to the rich land owners. Although agrarian reforms in several states were eliminating the middleman, curtailing the multiplicity of types of land rent and establishing ceilings on land ownership, almost nothing had been done to give land to the landless peasants.[38] Furthermore, he noted that the reforms were quite timid and indefinite and gave the landlords the possibility of evading the measures on land ceilings by evicting tenants and dividing their estates among their relatives.[39]

The temporal juxtaposition of this highly critical assessment with the rose-colored *New Times* evaluation is highly unusual and enigmatic. In the absence of additional evidence, one may only speculate that the *New Times* piece constituted something of a diversion from his highly critical commentary and that it might have been the price he paid for continued publication of his critical research on India. In any event, Rubinshtein's sober evaluation

---

[37] *Ibid.*, 38.

[38] Compare this with the statement made a few months earlier by V. A. Maslennikov in a general, semi-official article in *Sovetskoe Vostokovedenie* that agrarian reforms, while not solving the agrarian question as a whole, were nevertheless alleviating the life of the peasant population of India. V.A. Maslennikov, "Velikie Istoricheskie Sobytiia v Stranakh Vostoka," *Sovetskoe Vostokovedenie*, No. 1 (1956), 16.

[39] M. I. Rubinshtein, "Vtoroi Piatiletnyi Plan Respubliki Indii," 36.

of India's Second Five Year Plan was exceptional for this period.[40]

A more typical research article which clearly shows the influence of the official constraints operative at that time is a study of Indian industrial and agricultural production by leading experts in the fields, V. I. Pavlov and G. G. Kotovskii.[41] Discussing India's industrial development, the authors stressed the rapid strides that had been made since independence, while drawing attention to government measures in limiting the role of foreign capital and protecting weak economic branches from foreign competition through tariff controls.[42] The authors also spoke approvingly of government measures to alleviate the serious food problem and to improve the situation in agriculture through the introduction of Japanese methods of rice growing, the installation of credit and sales cooperatives, irrigation works, road construction, etc. Nevertheless, the authors observed that the general level of consumption was still too low to increase purchasing power, which would in turn expand India's domestic market for industrial production. Pavlov and Kotovskii stressed, however, that the success of the various measures to increase food production would depend on the solution of the agrarian question around which "goes on a serious struggle."[43] In sharp contrast to Rubinshtein's evaluation of agrarian reforms, this is as far as the authors came to noting the presence of a class struggle in India. Commenting favorably on India's agricultural programs, Kotovskii and Pavlov made no effort to determine which groups were benefiting from these programs and which ones weren't. Here then is an example of Party

---

[40] In only one other work published in that year, can criticism of Indian government reforms be discerned. L. I. Frei, in a monographic study of Indian finances, warned that government restrictions on the activity of management agencies through which foreign and domestic capital operated in a wide sphere of economic activities in India, could easily be avoided. L. I. Frei, *Denezhno-Kreditnaia Sistema i Mezhdunarodnye Raschety Respubliki Indii* (Moscow, 1956), pp. 207-08.

[41] G. G. Kotovskii and V. I. Pavlov, "Sel'skokhoziaistvennoe i Promyshlennoe Proizvodstvo v Respublike Indii," *Sovetskoe Vostokovedenie*, No. 1 (1956), 129-44.

[42] The technical problem of India's weak coal reserves was noted, but the authors suggested peaceful utilization of atomic energy through collaboration with the Soviet Union as a potential remedy to India's energy deficits.

[43] Kotovskii and Pavlov, *op. cit.*, 136.

pressures operating to limit academic analysis to the presentation of relatively untarnished images of the Indian government's domestic programs.

Another article bearing the imprint of official expectations regarding the development of agrarian capitalism was authored by M. A. Maksimov and V. G. Rastiannikov and appeared in *Sovetskoe Vostokovedenie* at the end of the year.[44] In it, the authors argued that entrepreneurial capital in Indian agriculture was still at very rudimentary stages of development and marked by an extremely low organic composition of capital (i.e., a low technical base).[45] While acknowledging that capitalism was developing more in breadth than in depth, Maksimov and Rastiannikov nevertheless saw signs, such as irrigation, the use of mineral fertilizers and introduction of tractors, that pointed to a rise in the technical level of agriculture. As in the previous article, the authors viewed agrarian reforms positively, noting that the liquidation of feudal intermediaries, the lowering of land rents and the limitation of land ownership "objectively assists the development of capitalism in agriculture."[46]

DEFINING THE NATIONAL BOURGEOISIE

While the Nehru government received highly favorable treatment on the whole in the months following the Twentieth Party Congress, doubts concerning the degree of progressiveness of the national bourgeoisie of India and other developing countries persisted in the academic community. Part of the confusion rested with the fact that the term national bourgeoisie had never been given a precise definition in the post-war period. It had been invariably used as a normative concept to delineate that section of the bourgeoisie which was deemed at the moment to be playing an "historically progressive" role as contrasted to the "compradore bourgeoisie" who were seen as lackeys of Imperialism.

---

[44] M. A. Maksimov and V. G. Rastiannikov, "Nekotorye Osobennosti Formirovaniia i Ekspluatatsii Sel'skokhoziaistvennogo Proletariata v Kolonial'noi Indii," *Sovetskoe Vostokovedenie*, No. 6 (1956), 42-55.

[45] This could, of course, be interpreted as something of a rebuff to the official line since it posits the development of capitalism in agriculture at such a low level.

[46] Maksimov and Rastiannikov, *op. cit.*, 46.

With the major shift in the post-Stalinist perspective towards developing countries, an attempt was made to add some degree of precision to the concept of the national bourgeoisie at a conference on this subject held towards the end of 1956 at the Institute of Orientology.[47] Delivering the report on the Indian national bourgeoisie, A. I. Levkovskii gave the term an economic definition stating that it referred to local industrial capital in the wide sense of the word. Consisting of three groups—the big, middle and petty bourgeoisie—the national bourgeoisie, despite the presence of internal contradictions which were complicated by caste, religious and national features, stood as a class against Imperialism and feudalism since both fettered their activity. Attempting to reconcile this assertion with the fact that the national bourgeoisie maintained close ties with both foreign capital and native landlords, Levkovskii advanced the dialectical explanation that serious contradictions with these two groups emerged as local capital developed. Positing the Indian monopolists as a subgroup of the big national bourgeoisie, Levkovskii clearly placed them in the anti-Imperialist progressive camp.[48] In contrast to the national bourgeoisie was a much smaller group, the compradore bourgeoisie, who, Levkovskii explained, were not simply that part of the bourgeoisie involved in foreign trade operations but rather those who were tied to the exploitation of India as a colonial market, i.e., in those operations that tended to freeze the independent economic development of the country. In response to A. A. Guber's comment that the national bourgeoisie should be defined as a political category—a position reminiscent of E. M. Zhukov's definition proposed at a similar session five years earlier—Levkovskii insisted that the national bourgeoisie constituted a class with its own clearly defined class interests that were as much economic as political and did not represent "some kind of temporary tendencies."[49] In short, Levkovskii considered the national bourgeoisie a durable entity whose composition could be determined by analyzing the socio-economic structure of a country.

Levkovskii's classification did not, however, still persistent doubts

---

[47] Coverage of the proceedings of this session are contained in G. S., "Diskussiia ob Ekonomicheskikh i Politicheskikh Pozitsiiakh Natsional'noi Burzhuazii v Stranakh Vostoka," *Sovetskoe Vostokovedenie*, No. 1 (1957), 174-84.

[48] *Ibid.*, 175.

[49] *Ibid.*, 183.

concerning the degree of progressiveness of the national bourgeoisie. Indeed, the discussion of his report is notable in that not only were echoes of Stalinist hostility to the Congress government aired for the last time, but also more critical evaluations of the role of the Indian bourgeoisie began to surface. Judging from the manner in which both types of criticisms were reported, it is apparent that only the latter variety acquired official approbation. Thus, in his summation of the proceedings, V. V. Balabushevich recorded that "Schmidt and Shastitko had stubbornly tried to prove that in India power was still in the hands of the monopolies and landlords and that the Indian National Congress was a party of monopolies and landlords. Such expressions received sharp rebuff in the discussions."[50] It should be added that these two advocates of the Stalinist position were not even given the courtesy of having their opinions recorded in the summaries of the discussions. More moderate criticisms were given appropriate attention.

For example, strong challenges to Levkovskii's characterization of the national bourgeoisie were expressed by L. Gordon and G. G. Kotovskii. Stressing the ties between the lower layers of national bourgeoisie and rural money lenders and traders, Gordon argued that although the national bourgeoisie could participate in the anti-Imperialist struggle, "because of its nature it did not become and cannot become consistent fighters against feudal landlord ownership."[51] The agrarian specialist, G. G. Kotovskii, further elaborated upon this theme, noting that the big bourgeoisie was tied more to usurer capital than to landlord elements, whereas the latter maintained close connections with the middle and petty bourgeoisie, who often invested their capital in land; this explained why the petty bourgeoisie was not always more radical than the big bourgeoisie when it came to questions of abolishing landlordism. Expressing a view that would gain currency in subsequent years, Kotovskii observed that the current agrarian reforms had been conducted to preserve the land ownership of those landlords who had entered the capitalist path of development. Inasmuch as the national bourgeoisie as a whole maintained wide ties with both landlord and usurers, the Indian National Congress could not come

[50] *Ibid.*, 183-84.
[51] *Ibid.*, 178.

out for the liquidation of feudal landlordism. While struggling against Imperialism, the Indian bourgeoisie had sought to prevent this struggle from developing into an anti-feudal revolution.[52]

Criticism of Indian monopolies, which had been muted in preceding months, also surfaced in the discussions. Thus, for example, A. A. Guber stressed the fundamental divergence of interests between Indian monopolies, which contained within them elements of decay, and the rest of the national bourgeoisie. Although he did not specify the nature of these differences, he asserted that the strengthening of the state sector reflected the process of struggle between the big, middle and even petty bourgeoisie with the monopolists, with the inference clearly being that the latter sought to check the development of the state sector.[53]

E. N. Komarov went even further in questioning the anti-Imperialist credentials of the national bourgeoisie. Reproaching Levkovskii for not giving sufficient attention to the forms of linkage between the Indian monopolies and Imperialism, he asserted that the sharpening of contradictions between the national bourgeoisie and Imperialism did not develop along a straight line, and thereby gave the impression that instances of retreat or withdrawal from the anti-Imperialist struggle could be attributed to the influence of the Indian monopolies.[54]

While these critical perceptions gained widescale support among Soviet scholars in subsequent years, the consensus of opinion among the participants at this conference, as Balabushevich recorded, was that the national bourgeoisie was a progressive force and that the monopoly layer was part of it. Indeed, Balabushevich clearly affirmed the progressive character of the Indian National Congress by formulating that it represented the national bourgeoisie and that part of the landlords interested in capitalist development.

In his concluding remarks, Balabushevich addressed himself to a question that had not been clearly articulated at the conference but which nevertheless lay at the root of academic resistance to accepting the new Party line—i.e., "Is the affirmation of the progressiveness of the bourgeoisie of these countries in the era of the general crisis of capitalism in the period of its decay a departure

[52] *Ibid.*, 180.
[53] *Ibid.*, 181.
[54] *Ibid.*

from Marxist-Leninism?"[55] Echoing the formulation first enunciated in the major *Sovetskoe Vostokovedenie* editorial published at the time of the Twentieth Party Congress, Balabushevich asserted that while capitalism as a world system was in the period of eclipse, it did not follow that capitalism could not develop in separate countries, such as India and other developing states. As we have noted in an earlier context, this formulation suggests Soviet acceptance of a rather prolonged period of capitalist development in India. This certainly must have been a difficult pill for Indian Communists to swallow. As we shall see below, this rather embarrassing thesis was soon dropped. Indeed, towards the close of the decade, despite continued official approval of the Indian national bourgeoisie, the undercurrents of academic skepticism, first articulated at the 1956 conference on the national bourgeoisie, gathered considerable momentum.

THE REASSESSMENT OF INDIAN STATE CAPITALISM

With the examination of the national bourgeoisie out of the way, the next major target of academic scrutiny was the role and character of state capitalism in the newly independent states—a subject which we have noted had led to some rather bold speculation concerning the prospects for a "peaceful transition to socialism" in these countries. Given the fact that Soviet aid was channeled exclusively through the state sector, this topic was an especially sensitive one.

The first major research article on the subject of state capitalism in India appeared in the No. 4, 1957 issue of *Sovetskoe Vostokovedenie*, and was written by R. A. Ul'ianovskii, who had recently completed his kandidat's dissertation on this problem.[56] According to Ul'ianovskii, state capitalism in India arose from the necessity of

---

[55] *Ibid.*, 183.

[56] R. A. Ul'ianovskii, "Indiia v Bor'be za Ekonomicheskuiu Nezavisimost' (O Gosudarstvennom Sektore v Ekonomike Indii)," *Sovetskoe Vostokovedenie*, No. 4 (1957), 9-26. Despite his acquisition of the kandidat's degree, Ul'ianovskii was not a neophyte in the field. He had contributed a number of articles on India to academic journals in the 1930's under the pseudonym O. Roslavlev, but was interned in a prison camp during the purges and released presumably after Stalin's death.

industrialization. By channeling large scale capital investments, especially into the creation of a modern heavy industrial base, which Ul'ianovskii affirmed was the key to industrialization, the state was shortening the primary forms of capital accumulation. Hence, although state capitalism did not replace the predominate capitalist mode of production in India, it was nevertheless an historically more progressive form of bourgeois ownership, in that it accelerated the rates of economic growth.[57] Yet, economic criteria were not the sole base of evaluating the nature of state capitalism. As Ul'ianovskii explained, overcoming economic backwardness was not purely a technical matter, since India's quest for industrialization and national independence was thwarted by foreign capital. He interpreted recent aid commitments by Western states to public sector projects as the result of several factors, such as intra-Imperialist competition, the influence of Soviet aid and the fact that these states could no longer check India's industrialization program; yet, Ul'ianovskii insisted that foreign capital was fundamentally opposed to the industrialization of developing states. Therefore, state capitalism also represented an anti-Imperialist force, since its goal was the attainment of economic and political independence, which only industrialization could secure. While attracting foreign aid and foreign capital investments, the Indian government at the same time sought to limit and channel the activities of foreign capital into areas which assisted India's economic development. Indeed, Ul'ianovskii characterized Indian state capitalism as a most important means of political and economic self-defense from the penetration of foreign capital. Thus, state capitalism was identified with Nehru's foreign as well as domestic policies. Its progressiveness was determined by both political and economic factors.

In contrast to the unblemished approbations of previous years, Ul'ianovskii qualified his positive appraisal with a number of critical notations. For example, he drew attention for the first time to the pressure exerted by Indian monopolies to limit or subordinate the state sector to their own interests. Moreover, he also noted the close personal unions of several government leaders with Indian business magnates and recorded instances of state financial favoritism accorded the latter. Yet, Ul'ianovskii asserted that Indian mono-

[57] *Ibid.*, 16.

polists did not dominate the state sector, for state capitalism in India could not be equated with state monopoly capitalism of the West. The author also drew attention to additional problems, such as the use of deficit financing that had generated strong inflationary pressures, the government's reluctance to attract additional sources of internal capital accumulation by taxing more heavily the propertied classes, and the fact that the hastened tempos of capitalist industrial development since independence had not been accompanied by any substantive increase in the number of the industrial workers.[58]

In his conclusion, Ul'ianovskii endorsed a number of concrete proposals that had been advanced by Indian Communists, such as further limitations on the activity of foreign monopolies, strict controls on the export of profits abroad and government regulation of foreign trade.[59]

Despite its strong ideological bias towards a positive assessment, Ul'ianovskii's article represents a shift towards a more realistic evaluation of the Indian economy. Yet, it did not apparently dispel some of the sanguine expectations that continued to be attached to state capitalism in developing countries such as India. Reviewing the results of the 1957 Moscow meeting of Communist party-states, an editorial in *Sovetskoe Vostokovedenie* called attention to the mistaken tendency among some orientalists of considering the progressive economic transformations in several young, independent states as socialist by nature.[60]

In an effort to resolve such confusion regarding the problem of state capitalism in underdeveloped countries an important conference was held at the Institute of Orientology in February 1958.[61]

---

[58] Indeed, the problem of employment, hardly mentioned in the 1950's, would be given major attention by Soviet scholars in the late 1960's (see below, pp. 259-63).

[59] In advocating this last measure, Ul'ianovskii at the same time cautioned that state control of domestic trade would be difficult to achieve. This represents one of the earliest instances of Soviet respect for the criterion of economic viability—a trend which would gain considerable force in the post-Khrushchev era.

[60] "Dokumenty Vsemirno-Istoricheskogo Znacheniia," *Sovetskoe Vostokovedenie*, No. 1 (1957), 8.

[61] "Problemy Gosudarstvennogo Kapitalizma v Slaborazvitykh Stranakh Vostoka," *Sovetskoe Vostokovedenie*, No. 4 (1958), 213-25.

The proceedings deserve considerable attention since they revealed much heated controversy over the criteria to be employed in evaluating state capitalism in various countries.

Delivering the report on Indian state capitalism, A. I. Levkovskii followed Ul'ianovskii's lead in stating that state capitalism could be evaluated only by analyzing internal economic conditions with due account to the international situation in which it arose. State capitalism developed as a consequence of India's need to liquidate her economic backwardness through independent economic and political development—hence, its progressive anti-Imperialist direction. Taking into account the fact that the state sector in India had originated under the British, Levkovskii argued that this colonial state sector was an extension of state monopoly capitalism, aimed at the colonial exploitation of the country in the interests of the metropolitan country. It was only after the acquisition of political independence that India had the opportunity to pursue an economic policy aimed at national independence.

In the remainder of his report, Levkovskii stressed domestic socio-economic aspects of Indian economic policy, noting that Indian state capitalism had a definite class content conforming to the interests of the national bourgeoisie, which thereby explained its contradictoriness and indecisiveness especially in respect to foreign capital and landlord ownership. Rejecting speculation that Indian state capitalism constituted a transitional step towards socialism, Levkovskii argued that both the state and private sectors were part of the same capitalist mode of production relations and that whatever contradictions appeared between them were of a non-antagonistic nature. In his estimation, "state capitalism seeks to resolve its internal conflicts on the paths of capitalist development."[62] In the final analysis, the rapporteur stated that the development of state capitalism in India depended not only on the struggle amongst various strata of the national bourgeoisie, but also to a large degree was determined by the broader class struggle within India.

By emphasizing domestic socio-economic factors in evaluating Indian state capitalism, Levkovskii opened the door for a more negative appraisal of it. Indeed, in the discussion which followed,

---

[62] *Ibid.*, 214.

sharply divergent views emerged depending on whether internal or external factors were stressed as the main determinants of Indian state capitalism. Emphasizing the significance of the indigenous class struggle, A. M. D'iakov, V. I. Pavlov, G. G. Kotovskii and V. M. Fedorenko all warned about the dangers of monopolist penetration of the state sector. Kotovskii even raised the possibility of the conversion of state capitalism into state monopoly capitalism.[63]

In rebuttal to these skeptics, R. A. Ul'ianovskii argued that it was the anti-Imperialist character of state capitalism in India, its commitment to the defense of national independence, which accounted for its progressiveness. Ul'ianovskii inaccurately charged Levkovskii with having given disproportionate weight to economic criteria in evaluating state capitalism.[64] In his view, material contributions to the development of a country's productive forces should not be considered the major index of progressivity of state capitalism, for if this were the case, both Israel and the Philippines, whose tempos of capital accumulation were higher than India's, would have to be considered more progressive. Yet, this was not the case, because in these "dependent" countries, state capitalism had been adopted to the needs of the Imperialists, whereas Indian state capitalism was directed to the attainment of national independence. Inasmuch as this goal met resistance from foreign capital, state capitalism in India was anti-Imperialist in character.[65] Thus echoing the views expressed by E. M. Zhukov and A. A. Guber at previous conferences, Ul'ianovskii was claiming the primacy of international politics in assessing the role of state capitalism. The identification of state capitalism and foreign policy was made even more explicit by B. M. Dantsig, who categorically stated that state capitalism was "progressive only where it bore an anti-Imperialist character, and where the country, which conducted it, conducted a peace-loving foreign policy, and did not participate in aggressive blocs, etc."[66]

---

[63] *Ibid.*, 218.

[64] Levkovskii attached as much weight to the international context as Ul'ianovskii had. This suggests that Ul'ianovskii may have been setting up Levkovskii as a straw man to contrast his thesis more sharply to the pessimistic views of the participants who preceded him.

[65] "Problemy Gosudarstvennogo Kapitalizma v Slaborazvitykh Stranakh Vostoka," 218.

[66] *Ibid.*, 217.

The formulation advanced by Ul'ianovskii, Dantsig and others, met with sharp criticism, especially from economists affiliated with the newly-established Institute of World Economy and International Relations. A. A. Poliak, a research worker there, argued that the development of state capitalism did not depend on foreign political conditions but on the domestic class struggle. Articulating the fundamental inconsistency which had troubled Soviet scholars ever since the Party leadership's *volte face* on India, Poliak argued that Ul'ianovskii had erroneously proceeded from the position that the political superstructure had a determinant influence on the economic base.[67]

Further elaborating this line of criticism, another Institute of World Economy and International Relations associate, M. A. Maksimov, attacked Ul'ianovskii for not recognizing that state capitalism was above all an economic and not a political category. Posing the basic dilemma which affected all Soviet scholars, Maksimov forcefully argued that it would be "impossible to objectively investigate problems of state capitalism on the basis of the study of such transient and to a certain degree circumstantial factors as participation or non-participation of one or another country or group of countries in different Imperialist blocs, or whether or not the national bourgeoisie of a certain country conducted an anti-Imperialist policy."[68] Reiterating Poliak's point, Maksimov argued that state capitalism arose in response to the needs of the ruling class to resolve internal political and economic contradictions and that in the final analysis, it must be evaluated within the context of the domestic class struggle.

Although Ul'ianovskii was given the opportunity to reply to these charges,[69] neither his response nor those of other speakers which followed effectively bridged the gap.[70] No satisfactory con-

[67] *Ibid.*, 218-19.

[68] *Ibid.*, 220.

[69] Ul'ianovskii rather unconvincingly argued that the problem of the struggle against Imperialism was not an external problem, but "the most internal of all external problems," *Ibid.*, 222.

[70] There were various unsuccessful attempts to find a compromise formula. For example, having first stated that internal socio-economic conditions and the domestic class struggle determined the character of state capitalism, G. G. Kotovskii then remarked that "the sole criterion for judging state capitalism was the degree to which in a given country it assisted or didn't assist the weakening of World Imperialism," *Ibid.*, 223.

sensus on how to evaluate state capitalism emerged. Summarizing the results of the proceedings, S. M. Mel'man merely observed that in some areas there was agreement, while in others disagreement.[71]

On balance, it appears that the discussions generated more heat than light. The failure to come up with a consistent set of criteria with which to evaluate state capitalism pointed to a continuing dilemma. At stake in the dialogue between Ul'ianovskii and his critics was the question of whether research was to proceed deductively on the basis of current Party directives (which, of course, would preclude the possibility of an independent input by Soviet scholars into the decision-making process), or inductively with conclusions drawn from concrete research. In practice, as we shall see below, Soviet researchers tried to resolve this problem by paying lip service to the official line and allowing their data to speak for itself—with the result that occasional discrepancies appeared.

With no common ground reached on the nature of state capitalism during the February 1958 conference, the expression of divergent assessments continued to be aired in the academic literature. In an article appearing in a 1958 anthology on India,[72] R. A. Ul'ianovskii, in fact, distanced himself even further from his critics. While reiterating most of the points made in his 1957 article, Ul'ianovskii categorically denied that Nehru's economic policy was determined by monopolist pressures. Rejecting the view that the Indian state sector served only as a base for the development of a capitalist economy, Ul'ianovskii stated that "to consider the significance of the state sector as playing only a subservient, auxiliary role, presupposes the rule of monopolies in India."[73] While acknowledging that state ownership in India was not distinct in principle from private capitalist ownership, albeit a higher form of bourgeois ownership, Ul'ianovskii held that its further development depended on the strength of the national liberation, anti-Imperialist struggle. Leaving little doubt of his belief in the progressive direction of the Indian economy, he concluded, "In conditions of bourgeois democracy, the implementation of the Indian

---

[71] *Ibid.*, 225.

[72] R. A. Ul'ianovskii, "Indiia v Bor'be za Ekonomicheskuiu Nezavisimost' (Voprosy Goskapitalizma)," in *Nezavisimaia Indiia: 10 let Nezavisimosti, 1947-1957* (Moscow, 1958), pp. 61-80.

[73] *Ibid.*, p. 43.

government's economic policy is a step towards socialism, but it still is not socialism and not a preparatory point of departure for the non-capitalist path of development...."[74]

THE ROLE OF FOREIGN PRIVATE CAPITAL

Ul'ianovskii's apparent shift to an even stronger endorsement of Nehru's economic policy was not, however, typical of Soviet research scholarship towards the close of the decade. Indeed, with the publication of concrete research, the pristine positive images of the anti-Imperialist bourgeoisie gave way to more realistic views of the complex relations between Indian and foreign capital.

Writing in the journal of the Institute of World Economy and International Relations,[75] V. Kondrat'ev challenged the official dogma regarding the anti-Imperialist character of the national bourgeoisie by noting that Indian capitalism was not growing at the expense of foreign capital, which continued to hold strong positions in the economy. On the contrary, Kondrat'ev drew attention to the government's policy of encouraging foreign capital investment.[76]

Kondrat'ev's article also suggests a growing disenchantment with the progress of India's economy. Despite notable state capitalist tendencies, the author noted that industrial development proceeded slowly within the limits of private capitalism, and suggested that the reason for these slow growth tempos was the dominant influence of monopolist groups.[77] Kondrat'ev went even further in pointing to the preponderant role of Indian monopolies in the Indian economy, by calling for the limitation of the activity of both foreign and native monopoly capital and the nationalization of a number of branches of industry. While warnings regarding the potential dangers of monopolist pressures had been sounded in previous years, Kondrat'ev's article marked the beginning of a trend towards viewing Indian big business as a class enemy along with foreign capital.

---

[74] *Ibid.*, p. 44.

[75] V. Kondrat'ev, "Natsional'naia Burzhuaziia i Promyshlennoe Razvitie Sovremennoi Indii," *Mirovaia Ekonomika i Mezhdunarodnye Onosheniia*, No. 8 (1959), 61-72.

[76] *Ibid.*, 64.

[77] *Ibid.*, 72.

Kondrat'ev's analysis was further corroborated by a major research work examining in depth for the first time the relations of foreign and native capital in India.[78] The author, L. I. Reisner, on the basis of data for the state of Uttar Pradesh, observed that foreign-controlled private electrical companies in that state were extracting benefits from the state government which boosted their profits enormously. In fact, the state government was creating favorable conditions for the penetration of foreign monopolies into the heavy electro-equipment industry. Nor were foreign interests the sole recipients of such benefits. The state had also offered large rebates and other advantages to large manufacturers. Indian monopoly capital, which for the most part was not tied to manufacturing industry in Uttar Pradesh, had refrained from making large capital investments which had contributed to the stagnation of industrial development in the state. Where expansion of production had taken place, it had occurred mainly through an increase in the number of small factories owned by members of the small and middle bourgeoisie. Reisner discerned a clear and growing conflict between the small and middle entrepreneurs interested in economic growth and Indian monopolies whose ties with foreign capital had strengthened in recent years and who constituted a parasitical obstacle to industrial growth in Uttar Pradesh. Not only are the battle lines clearly drawn between the various layers of the Indian bourgeoisie, but in Reisner's work, the state government is clearly implicated by abetting the concentration of economic power in the hands of a small number of monopolists and at the same time strengthening the positions of foreign capital in various manufacturing branches. Obliquely challenging the official line on the subject, Reisner in his concluding remarks stated that the example of industrial development in Uttar Pradesh since independence indicated that the "development of national industry and the liberation of the local economy from the domination of foreign monopoly capital occurs rather slowly with zigzags and even with reverse movements."[79]

Although Reisner's research suffers from the limitations of a

---

[78] L. I. Reisner, *Inostrannyi i Natsional'nyi Kapital v Promyshlennosti Indii (Shtat Uttar-Pradesh, 1947-1957)* (Moscow, 1959).

[79] *Ibid.*, p. 167.

case study, this major work nevertheless calls into question several tenets of Party policy on developing countries. In the first place, what did India's path of independent economic development mean when the positions of foreign capital were not only strengthening but its interests interlocking with native monopoly capital? Secondly, how anti-Imperialistic was Indian state capitalism when it not only encouraged foreign private capital investment but also helped boost the profits of foreign-controlled electric companies that were not contributing to the country's industrial expansion? Finally, to what extent could it be said that government economic policy answered the interests of broad layers of the "national bourgeoisie" when the Uttar Pradesh government, at least, operated as a servitor of monopoly capital? In retrospect, it appears that the weight of academic research towards the close of the decade increasingly favored more negative assessments of India's socio-economic development.

THE IMPACT OF AGRARIAN REFORMS

This wave of criticism encompassed not only the Indian government's industrial policies. Soviet scholars also became disenchanted with the agrarian reforms that had been conducted in India since independence.

In a major article on the subject,[80] G. G. Kotovskii elaborated upon his view expressed at the 1956 scholarly conference on the national bourgeoisie that the reforms had pushed landlords onto the path of capitalist entrepreneurship. Kotovskii explained that while the reforms had been aimed at fostering agrarian capitalism, they at the same time had preserved conditions for the preservation, in somewhat modified form, of feudal landlord ownership and the system of semi-feudal exploitation based upon it. To be sure, some landlords had transferred to capitalist farming methods with the application of machines. So too, the reforms had assisted the conversion of the richer peasants (i.e., those capable of affording the redemption payments to landlords for the purchase of land) into capitalist entrepreneurs. Yet, albeit progressive, the reforms had not eliminated the predominant semi-feudal system of exploitation in rural India. What differentiation had taken place among the

[80] G. G. Kotovskii, "Indiia," in *Agrarnye Otnosheniia v Stranakh Vostoka* (Moscow, 1958), pp. 7-133.

peasantry had occurred in convoluted forms. Thus, the poorest strata of the peasantry, who had not profited at all from the reforms, had not yet been transformed into free agricultural workers but rather were driven further into subtenancy which "represented an intermediate stage in the process of their proletarianization." The basic reason for this phenomenon was India's high "relative" agrarian overpopulation,[81] which, according to Kotovskii, was the product of the "deformed nature" of the development of trade-usurer capital in agriculture. Agrarian overpopulation made the maintenance of feudal rent and usurer practices more profitable in most instances than the introduction of machinery and other capital-intensive methods of farming. Even the rich peasant entrepreneurs, whom Kotovskii identified as Kulaks, often employed feudal methods of exploitation, renting their lands to tenants. Moreover, the author noted that capitalist forms of land rent arose only sporadically, and when it arose, it was often difficult to distinguish capitalist from pre-capitalist rent.[82] In general, Kotovskii concluded that capitalism was growing at a very slow rate, and that when it appeared, it was often interconnected with pre-capitalist agricultural methods.

Kotovskii's interpretation of the reforms as giving an impetus to the slow transformation of landlords and the upper strata of the peasantry into an agrarian bourgeoisie while not on the whole eliminating conditions for the continued predominance of pre-capitalist land relations was subsequently confirmed at a December 1958 joint conference of the Institutes of Orientology and World Economy and International Relations on agrarian reforms in the countries of the East.[83] Delivering the report on India, Kotovskii argued that the reforms had been conducted in the interests of the national bourgeoisie, including the agrarian bourgeoisie and to a certain extent the landlord class at the expense of the overwhelming majority of the peasants. Kotovskii also noted that the differentiation of the upper strata of the peasantry had proceeded, as a result of the reforms, to the degree where a Kulak class had been formed,

---

[81] It was not until the mid-1960's that the anti-Malthusian ideological barrier was lowered to permit Soviet writers to drop the epithet "relative" (to the state of economic productivity) when describing agrarian overpopulation.

[82] Kotovskii, "Indiia," pp. 54-55.

[83] A summary of the proceedings may be found in "Agrarnye Reformy v Stranakh Zarubezhnogo Vostoka," *Problemy Vostokovedeniia*, No. 4 (1959), 207-16.

which on a number of basic economic and political questions stood closer to the landlords than to the rest of the peasantry. The concomitant desertion of the Kulaks from the anti-feudal struggle had led to a decline in the activity of the peasant movement in India, which however was temporary since the agrarian question had not yet been solved.[84]

In contrast to the heated session on state capitalism a few months earlier, a consensus on the character of agrarian reforms was not difficult to achieve. There were two areas of disagreement, however: a minor one, involving the utility of employing the term landlord or "Prussian" path of the development of capitalism in agriculture and a more substantive one, concerning whose interests had benefited most from the reforms.

In both instances, R. A. Ul'ianovskii, who had by now clearly become a Party spokesman within the academic community, was the chief protagonist.[85] Ul'ianovskii objected to the widespread practice of employing the concept of the "Prussian" path of capitalist development, formulated by Lenin at the turn of the century, to describe the situation in such countries as India, with its agrarian overpopulation and complex system of land tenancy—a unique situation, not analogous in the least to conditions in Prussia at that time. Moreover, Ul'ianovskii questioned whether the reforms were of a purely landlord type; and suggested rather that the national bourgeoisie, to preserve their influence over the peasantry, had been forced to conduct reforms which, while not destroying the landlord class, limited their landownership and to a degree infringed their interests.[86] This point was echoed by N. I. Lazarev who stated that in conducting agrarian reforms the national bourgeoisie had to consider the interests of the peasantry to a greater extent than

---

[84] *Ibid.*, 208-09.

[85] Dissatisfied with the negative conclusions that emanated from the reports, Ul'ianovskii chastized the rapporteurs for over-emphasizing the significance of the struggle with feudalism as a criterion for evaluating the role of the national bourgeoisie, which led to the underestimation of the anti-Imperialist factor, which, in his view, constituted the major test of the degree of progressiveness of the national bourgeoisie. As we have noted previously, for Ul'ianovskii, all domestic considerations reflecting on the character of the bourgeoisie were subordinate to its foreign policy role; to put it simply, everything revolved around the question of relations with the Soviet Union.

[86] "Agrarnye Reformy v Stranakh Zarubezhnogo Vostoka," 214-15.

the interests of the landlords.[87]

While Ul'ianovskii and Lazarev equivocated in assessing the character of agrarian reforms, other participants were quite forthright in underscoring the landlord character of the reforms. A. A. Poliak, for example, stated that as long as the bourgeoisie remained in power, the agrarian question would be solved only in the interests of the landlords. Just as the bourgeois democratic revolution could not liquidate the economic dominance of foreign capital, so it could not resolve the agrarian question in the interests of the peasants, i. e., through the nationalization of land, for this could be accomplished only during the national democratic revolution that would follow.[88]

Although Poliak seems far to the left of Ul'ianovskii and Lazarev in his evaluation of land reforms, there was nevertheless a sufficient consensus of opinion for M. I. Lukianova, who summarized the results of the conference, to conclude that agrarian reforms in the newly independent states bore a landlord character.[89]

In retrospect then, by the end of the decade, Soviet scholars, on the whole, had become disillusioned with the performance of the Indian bourgeoisie not only with respect to land reforms, but with regard to its other economic policies as well. Their participation in the anti-Imperialist, anti-feudal struggle was clearly circumspect.

What is more significant is that a strong note of pessimism concerning the prospects for Indian economic development among its current lines pervaded the writings of Soviet specialists. Industrialization was impeded in large part because of the narrow domestic market for industrial products. Yet, the entry of the peasant population into market relations was checked by precapitalist agrarian relations, which continued to dominate rural India because of the enormous weight of agrarian overpopulation. Yet, as anti-Malthusians, Soviet scholars at this time maintained that this problem would be resolved only through industrialization which would absorb the surplus rural population. Having thus delineated this vicious circle, Soviet analysts increasingly pointed to the necessity of a revolutionary break of the existing production

[87] *Ibid.*, 212.
[88] *Ibid.*, 216.
[89] *Ibid.*

relations as the solution to this crisis. Virtually no consideration was given to either partial solutions to immediate problems or to what would happen on the day after the revolution.[90] In short, the Soviets were still thinking about developing countries within the traditional Marxist categories of the stages of revolutionary metamorphosis. Indian reality was viewed through the prism of the rather simplistic Marxist lexicon that had been based largely on European development. As the criticism of the term the "Prussian path of landlord capitalism" expressed at the December 1958 conference on agrarian reforms indicates, however, Soviet scholars were becoming aware of the unique problems posed by the Asian developmental context.

In short, Soviet scholars during this period were concerned with the description of phenomena in developing countries. No consideration was given to the concrete elaboration and resolution of problems arising in the process of economic development. Or rather, to put it more accurately, whatever problems arose were thought to be endemic to the prevailing mode of production relations. It was assumed that these problems would be resolved in the course of the revolutionary transformation of these societies. Thus, any attempt at solving such problems seemed premature. This was deferred to the post-revolutionary future.

THE REFINEMENT OF ECONOMIC DEVELOPMENT STRATEGIES

Although Soviet scholars focused their attention on evaluating the character of the Indian regime largely in terms of its economic programs, other issues, such as economic development strategies

---

[90] A singular exception to this is the attempt by the Leningrad-based scholar S. I. Tiul'panov to consider the practical aspects of the problem of increasing food production. In contrast to the advocates of land nationalization, Tiul'panov noted that redistribution of the land to the tillers would not necessarily lead to increased production of foodstuffs for the market, but only to greater consumption. Increasing the number of peasant allotments would also impede the introduction of contemporary technology. Instead, Tiul'panov advocated the development of peasant cooperatives. See, S. I. Tiul'panov, "K Voprosu o Perspektivakh Razvitiia Slaborazvitykh Stran," *Vestnik Leningradskogo Universiteta*, Seriia Ekonomiki, Filosofii i Prava, vyp. 3, No. 17 (1959), 15.

and foreign aid, were considered as a consequence of the post-Stalin reassessment of developing countries. However, Soviet academic thinking on these and other peripheral areas of inquiry departed much less from official policy than Soviet research on Indian socio-economic development.

As we have noted in chapter one, the development model which guided initial Soviet ventures into the field of foreign aid was based on their own experience with priority attached to the development of heavy industry. Following the announcement of the Soviet credit for constructing the Bhilai steel mill, this development strategy was endorsed in the academic literature as necessary for the securance of fast growth tempos[91] and as the sole means for achieving economic independence.[92] Yet, as the Soviets expanded their aid program to smaller countries less well endowed with the material prerequisites for industrialization, they began to adopt a differentiated approach to the problem of development strategies.

A landmark work in the refinement of Soviet perspectives on the development process was the 1958 publication of the first monograph by the innovative young research workers of the Institute of World Economy and International Relations, G. I. Mirskii and L. V. Stepanov.[93] Published as a stimulant to discussion and further research,[94] the authors basically advocate the development of regional economic collaboration as an alternative to an autarchic model of economic development, inasmuch as most smaller developing countries were incapable of self-generative industrial development. Industrialization would thus come about through specialization of manufacturing and other industrial branches and

---

[91] M. I. Rubinshtein, "Ob Ekonomicheskom Razvitii Sovremennoi Indii," *Voprosy Ekonomiki*, No. 10 (1955), 124.

[92] V. Kollontai, "Burzhuaznaia Politekonomiia o Problemakh Ekonomicheskogo Razvitiia Slaborazvitykh Stran," *Voprosy Ekonomiki*, No. 3 (1956), 127.

[93] G. I. Mirskii and L. V. Stepanov, *O Perspektivakh Ekonomicheskogo Sotrudnichestva Stran Azii i Afriki* (Moscow, 1958). This work was later translated into English under the title, *Asia and Africa: A New Era* (Moscow: Foreign Languages Publishing House, n. d.).

[94] This is explicitly stated in the preface by A. A. Arzumanian, who also notes the presence of many debatable points in the text. *Ibid.*, p. 2.

a general expansion of economic ties.[95] Although this strategy was more applicable to smaller countries than to larger states such as India, Mirskii and Stepanov held out the possibility that India would be included in such a scheme by citing as a precedent India's imports of industrial raw materials from other developing countries.[96]

Concomitant with their sponsorship of regional economic cooperation, the authors also expressed some divergent views on the strategy of economic development, in general, and the character of Soviet foreign aid, in particular. Mirskii and Stepanov stressed that industrialization did not mean exclusive emphasis on the development of heavy industry, but rather asserted that all-sided economic development was necessary. Industrialization should not be counterposed to the development of agriculture, mining and other branches, since industrialization presupposed significant increases in marketed foodstuffs, industrial crops and raw materials.[97]

With respect to foreign assistance programs, the authors warned that aid funds "would be completely ineffective if dispensed on the construction of projects not having decisive significance for these countries, or in other words, on the construction of objects which seem more like models propagandizing the achievements of advanced countries than being of practical use."[98] Although the authors cited the example of an American model cowbarn in Lebanon, their observation was just as applicable to Soviet projects and might have been intended as an oblique reminder to Soviet planners to scale foreign aid projects to the needs of recipient countries.

Although Mirskii's and Stepanov's recommendations and observations were presented tentatively, by the close of the decade their views gained additional adherents. Thus, for example,

---

[95] The authors also suggested that developing countries coordinate a "collective defense" against foreign monopolies and specifically try to alter the "non-equivalent exchange" that characterized trade relations between industrialized capitalist countries and developing states by raising prices on their exports while seeking to prevent corresponding increases in world prices on imported industrial goods. *Ibid.*, p. 71.

[96] *Ibid.*, p. 68.

[97] *Ibid.*, pp. 21-22.

[98] *Ibid.*, p. 44.

A. K. Kakharov and G. M. Prokhorov in a 1959 study of Soviet aid specifically endorsed the strategy of regional economic cooperation as a method of maximizing the rational utilization of these countries' natural resources.[99]

This trend towards a differentiated approach in the selection of development strategies still met with resistance from some representatives of the older generation of scholars. Writing in a 1959 issue of *Problemy Vostokovedeniia*, I. M. Lemin continued to attach priority to the development of heavy industry and specifically characterized as a "false formula of bourgeois authors" the view that equal weight should be given to the development of industry and agriculture—a direct challenge to the pronouncements of Mirskii and Stepanov on this subject.[100] Nevertheless, given the fact that the editors of the journal prefaced his article with the request that readers express their opinions on the views presented by Lemin, it would seem that such formulations no longer received official backing. It may be concluded then that Lemin's statements represented a minority viewpoint.

THE PERSPECTIVE ON FOREIGN AID

The slight shift in the academic perspective of the development process was not accompanied by an innovative analysis with respect to foreign aid, both Soviet and Western. Indeed, with the possible exception of Mirskii and Stepanov's subtle caveat noted above, academic statements on Soviet foreign aid followed the official line very closely and consisted for the most part of propagandistic paeans extolling the virtues of Soviet aid while denigrating the aims and motives of Western aid. Characteristic of Khrushchevian generosity, these accounts stressed the benefits accruing to the recipient countries from Soviet aid while remaining silent with respect to any possible advantages the Soviets might have received in return.

With respect to India, there was no attempt to evaluate the

---

[99] A. K. Kakharov and G. M. Prokhorov, *Druzheskaia Pomoshch' i Vzaimovygodnoe Sotrudnichestvo* (*Ekonomicheskie Sviazi SSSR s Promyshlenno-Slaborazvitymi Stranami Vostoka* (Moscow, 1959), p. 12.

[100] I. M. Lemin, "Ekonomicheskaia Sushchnost' Sovremennogo Kolonializma," *Problemy Vostokovedeniia*, No. 4 (1959), 19.

effectiveness of any Soviet aid project. To be sure, some highly technical and descriptive accounts of the Bhilai steel mill were published, but these did little more than point out that the decision to build a steel factory in Madhya Pradesh was based not so much on economic criteria as on the government's desire to decentralize Indian metallurgy.[101] Yet, it should be added that the Soviets fully endorsed the Indian government's program of decentralizing industry to lessen the disparities of the levels of economic development among the various regions that had resulted from the colonial heritage.[102] Although Soviet writers expressed some concern about the scarcity of coal deposits in India, this was seen as something of a technical problem which could be resolved by utilizing alternative sources of energy. V. Vladimirov, in an article on this subject,[103] estimated India's stores of raw materials necessary for atomic energy as thirty times greater than her coal potential, thus hinting at possible Soviet collaboration in the peaceful utilization of atomic energy.[104] In general, however, the lacuna of critical commentary in academic journals is indicative of how highly sensitive the subject of Soviet aid was at the time.

The treatment of Western aid policies fared little better. Whereas during the Stalinist period Western aid was disparaged as an exploitative weapon in the arsenal of "neo-colonialism," by the close of the 1950's the Soviets had revised their perceptions in response to improvement in the terms of aid offered to developing countries by the major Western states, and perhaps more significantly as a consequence of the realization of these countries'

[101] V. M. Shtein, "Chernaia Metallurgiia Indii i Proektiruemyi Zavod v Madkhiia Pradesh," *Izvestiia Vsesoiuznogo Geograficheskogo Obshchestva* Tom 88, vyp. 1 (January-February 1956), 16-29. Shtein notes that the area around Calcutta (where the Tata Iron and Steel Works are located) was actually one of the cheapest steel-producing areas of the world.

[102] For a favorable appraisal of this program, see, L. I. Bonafat'eva, "O Formirovanii Ekonomicheskikh Raionov Indii," *Izvestiia Vsesoiuznogo Geograficheskogo Obshchestva* Tom 90, vyp. 5 (September-October 1958), 453-66.

[103] V. Vladimirov, "Indiia i Problema Ispol'zovaniia Atomnoi Energii," *Mirovaia Ekonomika i Mezhdunarodnye Otnosheniia*, No. 3 (1959), 118-19.

[104] Bulganin, it will be remembered, had raised such a possibility during the 1955 tour of India. After years of subsequent discussions, it was announced in February 1961 that the Soviets would build a reactor in India. Cited in Arthur Stein, *op. cit.*, p. 181.

enormous need for foreign capital investment and technical assistance. The fact that many industrialized capitalist states had begun to extend credits at eased rates and even subsidies for the construction of heavy industrial projects in the state sectors of India and other developing countries forced the Soviets to modify their interpretation of the Western aid and development strategy. As a 1958 *Sovetskoe Vostokovedenie* editorial recognized, the Western countries had partially weakened their traditional anti-industrialization policy and had made certain concessions to the developing countries.[105] These improvements were attributed not to any change of heart, but to several external factors, such as the impact of Soviet aid, intra-Imperialist economic competition, the realization that industrial development in the state sector could no longer be prevented,[106] and by the general desire to keep these countries within the world capitalist economy.[107] In the case of increased American aid to India, the latter's weight in international affairs was acknowledged as an additional factor.[108] Indeed, writing on this topic, R. A. Ul'ianovskii spoke in rather positive terms of American aid, noting that "...India can under certain conditions draw out economic advantages from the competitive struggle between private and state foreign capital."[109] In fact, Ul'ianovskii for the first time deleted the usual brackets in reference to Western aid—a practice that had suggested it was a misnomer.

Nevertheless, these acknowledgments of the changes in Western aid did not alter Soviet hostility towards Western economic policies. To the Soviet viewpoint, Imperialism had not suddenly changed its stripes, but had only adjusted to new conditions. Soviet writers argued that the exploitative essence of Western economic policies

[105] "Kolonializm-Zleishii Vrag Narodov Vostoka," *Sovetskoe Vostokovedenie*, No. 2 (1958), 8.

[106] See, R. A. Ul'ianovskii, "Indiia v Bor'be za Ekonomicheskuiu Nezavisimost'," *Sovetskoe Vostokovedenie*, No. 4 (1957), 16-19.

[107] V. Tiagunenko, "Nekotorye Problemy Bor'by Narodov Slaborazvitykh Stran za Nezavisimost'," *Mirovaia Ekonomika i Mezhdunarodnye Otnosheniia*, No. 3 (1959), 93.

[108] S. I. Tiul'panov, "K Voprosu o Perspektivakh Razvitiia Slaborazvitykh Stran," *Vestnik Leningradskogo Universiteta*, Seriia Ekonomiki, Filosofii i Prava, vyp. 3, No. 17 (1959), 9.

[109] R. A. Ul'ianovskii, "SShA i Industrializatsiia Indii," *Sovetskoe Vostokovedenie*, No. 4 (1958), 42.

remained and warned, therefore, that capitalist countries might try to use their aid to gain control of the new branches of industry,[110] or to extract long-run economic privileges and other concessions.[111]

Generally speaking, Soviet scholars encouraged the developing states to make use of the more favorable terms of Western aid and, at the same time, scored propaganda points by questioning the motives underlying the extension of that aid. The most forthright statement of the Soviet position may be found in Mirskii and Stepanov's 1958 book, in which the authors stress that "the underdeveloped countries need assistance and economic collaboration not only with socialist but also with capitalist countries, but the main thing is on *what basis* [emphasis in the original] the relations with the capitalist countries will be built."[112] In any event, it is evident that the Soviets were not willing to shoulder the entire burden of aid by encouraging developing countries to sever their economic ties with the West.

THE REASSESSMENT OF NATIONALITY PROBLEMS IN INDIA

The awakening of Indo-Soviet friendship also generated a new perspective of Indian national integration. As a logical consequence of the recognition of the Congress government as a progressive force, movements for national autonomy were now deemed to be little more than Imperialist ploys to weaken India. A good case in point is the separatist movement among the Naga hill tribes along the Burmese border. While Soviet scholars showed sympathy for the plight of these and other tribes,[113] the Nagas' separatist movement was seen as an Imperialist plot to complicate Indo-Burman relations.[114]

---

[110] G. G. Kotovskii and V. I. Pavlov, "Sel'skokhoziaistvennoe i Promyshlennoe Proizvodstvo v Respublike Indii," *Sovetskoe Vostokovedenie*, No. 1 (1956), 140.

[111] Tiul'panov, *op. cit.*, p. 7.

[112] Mirskii and Stepanov, *op. cit.*, p. 74.

[113] I. D. Levin and V. A. Mamaev in a 1957 study of the Indian state structure admit that errors were made in administering the region which led to the Naga uprising, but add that the situation has been improving with the introduction of government economic and cultural reforms in the tribal regions. I. D. Levin and V. A. Mamaev, *Gosudarstvennyi Stroi Indii* (Moscow, 1957), p. 119.

[114] This is suggested in V. P. Nikhamin, *Ocherki Vneshnei Politiki Indii, 1947-1957gg* (Moscow, 1959), p. 204.

In a similar vein, previous expressions of support for Kashmiri independence during the Stalinist period were discarded as Soviet writers, adhering to the Khrushchev line that the Kashmir issue had already been decided by the people of Kashmir themselves, portrayed unification with India as a positive act and took note of the substantial agrarian and other democratic reforms that had been conducted there since annexation.[115]

A contributory factor in this reassessment of local nationalism in India was the implementation in 1956 of the long-awaited States Reorganization Act, which at one stroke redrew existing state boundaries in greater conformity with linguistic divisions, eliminated the remaining political powers of the Indian princes and abolished previous administrative distinctions among the states. This was hailed as a major domestic achievement by the Nehru government. In an article on this subject, L. V. Shaposhnikova praised the reforms in the following words: "Considering the aspiration of the national masses for the creation of separate national areas, the government basically supported the linguistic principle for the reorganization of states. This is one of the most important manifestations of the progressive policy of the Indian government headed by Nehru."[116]

While the States Reorganization Act was acknowledged as an important contribution to the solution of the national question in India, its deficiencies were also recognized. Specifically, the decision to leave Bombay and Maharashtra as separate states ran counter to Marathi national sentiment and was interpreted as a concession to monopolist groups consisting of Parsis and Gujaratis centered in the Western metropolis.[117] In addition, as A. M. D'iakov and T. F. Deviatkina noted, the reforms had left out large number of peoples and tribes, each with their own languages and customs, such as the Santhals of Bihar who desired greater autonomy and the

---

[115] S. A. Mikoyan, "Indiiskie Kniazhestva v Period Krizisa Britanskogo Gospodstva v Indii," *Sovetskoe Vostokovedenie*, No. 5 (1956), 104.

[116] L. V. Shaposhnikova, "Bor'ba Narodov Indii za Natsional'noe Samoopredelenie i Reorganizatsiia Shtatov (1950-1956)," in *Indiia i Afganistan: Ocherki Istorii i Ekonomiki* (Moscow, 1958), p. 268.

[117] See, L. A. Kniazhinskaia, *Zapadnaia Indiia: Ekonomiko-Geograficheskaia Kharakteristika* (Moscow, 1959), p. 113.

introduction of their native language.[118] Nevertheless, these two specialists on Indian nationalities concluded that the creation of linguistic states and the liquidation of principalities would hasten the economic and cultural development of India, strengthen her unity and ultimately assist the growth of her international authority.[119]

Just as Stalin had encouraged separatism to erode India's stature, now the Soviets were strongly committed to her unification in the full knowledge that India's presence could be felt in world politics only with domestic political stability secured. Soviet authors were quite explicit in their support of a strong central government in India. S. I. Rusinova, for example, writing on the state structures of newly independent states, viewed the centralist tendencies of Indian federalism as a positive means of merging her various peoples and enhancing unification.[120]

However, it would seem that the Soviets had second thoughts concerning the powers of the central government over the states, particularly after the election of the Communist-led government in Kerala. Whereas the only article on the Kerala Communist government to appear in the academic literature was a journalistic account, parroting the official line in emphasizing that the reform program being conducted in that state did not go beyond the legal limits of the Indian Constitution,[121] another article by L. P. Ul'ianova on the subject of finance legislation in India implied

[118] T. F. Deviatkina and A. M. D'iakov, "Sozdanie Shtatov po Lingvisticheskomu Printsipu i Likvidatsiia Kniazhestv," in *Nezavisimaia Indiia: 10 Let Nezavisimosti, 1947-1957* (Moscow, 1958), pp. 99-100.

[119] *Ibid.*, p. 100.

[120] S. I. Rusinova, "Formy Gosudarstvennogo Ustroistva Stran Osvobodivshikhsia ot Kolonializma," *Vestnik Leningradskogo Universiteta*, Seriia Ekonomiki, Filosofii i Prava, vyp. 4, No. 23 (1959), 128.

[121] A. Maslennikov, "V Kerale Likvidiruetsia Pomeshchich'e Zemlevladenie," *Mirovaia Ekonomika i Mezhdunarodnye Otnosheniia*, No. 9 (1958), 99-101. The reaction to the dissolution of the Communist Kerala government in 1959 was extremely sharp in the academic literature. V. Sukhanova, writing on this topic, bluntly chastized the Nehru leadership in the following words: "Not having the support of the broad, popular masses, this 'struggle' would have ended with the defeat of the reaction if not for the political and moral support of the central government and the leadership the National Congress had shown it." V. Sukhanova, "K Sobytiiam v Shtate Kerala," *Mirovaia Ekonomika i Mezhdunarodnye Otnosheniia*, No. 11 (1959), 107.

that the powers of the central government in any event prevented this from happening.¹²² Ul'ianova specifically interpreted the Indian President's power to review state bills on compulsory alienation of property as a guarantee against any possible nationalization measures by the states which were not desired by the ruling groups at the center.¹²³ The author rather plaintively concluded that the center's finance controls over the states meant that the states were economically and politically defenseless before the power of the central government. On balance, however, the anti-centrist slant of this article did not alter the pronounced Soviet proclivity to favor a strong Indian national government.

THE REEVALUATION OF INDIAN FOREIGN POLICY

The rapprochement with India also led to a sweeping reinterpretation of Indian foreign policy. However, in the first few years after the exchange of historic visits, Soviet writing on Indian foreign policy consisted for the most part of non-analytic journalistic accounts, whitewashing India's "peace-loving" foreign policy even to the extent of deleting embarrassing factual details.¹²⁴

By the close of the decade, however, the aura surrounding India had dissipated sufficiently to enable the publication of a more realistic and balanced scholarly account of Indian foreign policy.¹²⁵ Even though its author, V. P. Nikhamin, at the outset disclaims any detailed analysis of the internal political determinants of Indian foreign policy, the work is nevertheless notable in that it marks the first time that the evolution of Indian foreign policy was related to the domestic class struggle. Specifically, Nikhamin views the Indian government's wavering attitude towards the West as

---

¹²² L. P. Ul'ianova, "Finansovye Prava i Polozhenie Shtatov v Indiiskom Soiuze," *Kratkie Soobshcheniia Instituta Vostokovedeniia*, Kn. 31 (1959), 3-15.

¹²³ *Ibid.*, 15.

¹²⁴ For an excellent example of this genre, consult T. Giiasov, *Indiia i Bor'ba za Oslablenie Napriazhennosti v Iugo-Vostochnoi Azii i Na Dal'nem Vostoke*, Trudy, Sredneaziatskii Gosudarstvennyi Universitet, Novaia Seriia, vyp. 105, Kn. 23 (Tashkent, 1957). Giiasov, for example, omits any reference to India's support for the June 1950 UN Resolution condemning Communist aggression in South Korea and states only that India was for peace from the beginning of the Korean conflict (p. 23).

¹²⁵ V. P. Nikhamin, *Ocherki Vneshnei Politiki Indii, 1947-1957gg* (Moscow, 1959).

a consequence of the basic duplicity of the Indian bourgeoisie, i.e., on the one hand, its basic economic contradictions with Imperialism lead it to adopt anti-Western positions, while on the other hand, its fear of the masses drives it to seek Western economic and political support.[126] This, of course, is not a novel idea and constitutes only a throw back to the old image of the double nature of the colonial bourgeoisie. This in itself, however, is indicative of how far the perceptual pendulum had recoiled from the euphoria of preceding years. Nikhamin is even less generous with respect to the Indian monopolies, noting that being tied to foreign capital, they desired a basic revision of the government's anti-Imperialist foreign policy. Illustratively, the author states that it was a combination of Western and Indian monopolies which tried to prevent the Bhilai agreement,[127] and also records subsequent efforts by right wing monopolies to use issues such as the Hungarian crisis to torpedo Indo-Soviet friendship.[128]

Nikhamin's work is also noteworthy in that it sheds light on Soviet perspectives of Indian foreign policy during the pre-1955 period and, in so doing, touches upon a number of sensitive issues. Thus, noting that India did not fully take an independent foreign policy course in the first few years following independence, Nikhamin explains that this was partly the consequence of illusions concerning the readiness of Great Britain and the United States to assist India's economic development on acceptable terms which led to her making political concessions to the Western powers, such as attending a 1949 conference of non-Communist Asian states to discuss a crisis in Indonesia.[129]

[126] *Ibid.*, p. 17.

[127] *Ibid.*, p. 186. This is not the only instance of such criticism. M. A. Kocharian, in a work on Indo-Soviet relations published at this time, notes various attempts by the Indian big bourgeoisie and landlords to delay or prevent implementation of measures connected with the development of Indo-Soviet economic relations. He cites, as an example, the attempt of an Indian firm, connected with American capital, to prolong negotiations on an agreement for Soviet assistance in the construction of a pharmaceuticals plant. M. A. Kocharian, *Druzhba i Sotrudnichestvo SSSR i Indii* (Moscow, 1959), p. 45.

[128] Nikhamin, *op. cit.* p. 200. Nikhamin appreciatively takes note of Nehru's refusal to support the Western-sponsored UN resolution calling for the dispatch of UN troops to Hungary.

[129] *Ibid.*, p. 17.

On the subject of the Indo-Pakistani imbroglio over Kashmir, Nikhamin skirts the issue itself, but suggests that initially both sides were interested in wide economic and trade ties but that these relations became poisoned by Western interference and intervention on Pakistan's side in the Kashmir dispute. The author suggests, moreover, that Indo-Pakistani problems could be worked out without big power interference.[130] This view not only contrasts markedly with the pro-India bias on this issue then current in Soviet literature,[131] but also adumbrates by several years the balanced policy Moscow would later employ to resolve this conflict.

According to Nikhamin's periodization, the second state of the evolution of India's foreign policy commenced in 1950 and was marked by the increasing assertion of an independent position which manifested itself in India's efforts to achieve a peaceful resolution of the Korean War,[132] her refusal to sign the 1951 Japanese Peace Treaty and her mediatory role in Indochina. Yet, in discussing this period, Nikhamin raises the sensitive issue of India's Himalayan policy. Specifically, Nikhamin records that Indian monopoly circles, desirous of retaining the economic and extra-territorial privileges the British had extracted in Tibet, urged the government soon after the Communist consolidation of power in China to take military measures along the border.[133] Nehru, however, refused to submit to such pressures and was able to conclude an agreement with the Chinese on Tibet in 1954, which Nikhamin considers "an example of how just solutions of any international problems can be achieved."[134] These conservative forces were apparently more influential with respect to the Himalayan states. Although they failed to prevent the establishment of diplo-

---

[130] *Ibid.*, pp. 123-24.

[131] During this as in the Stalinist period, the Soviets continued to view Pakistan as a tool of Imperialist pressure on India. See, for example, T. M. Ershov, "Indiiskaia Respublika-Vashnyi Faktor Mira," in *Nezavisimaia Indiia: 10 Let Nezavisimosti, 1947-1957* (Moscow, 1958), p. 140.

[132] Unlike Giiasov, Nikhamin did not gloss over India's initial approval of the 1950 UN resolution calling for intervention to check Communist aggression in Korea. Interestingly, Nikhamin explains that Nehru was not fully aware of the facts and was deliberately misled by Indian officials at the UN. Nikhamin, *op. cit.*, p. 82.

[133] *Ibid.*, p. 166.

[134] *Ibid.*, p. 170.

matic relations between Nepal and China, Nikhamin intimates that these circles were behind India's intervention on the side of the Nepalese King against the Rana clan, since consequentially, the July 1950 Indo-Nepalese friendship and trade treaties gave Indian entrepreneurs significant advantages over the weaker Nepalese middle classes. Nevertheless, although India's intervention also resulted in the demise of leftist democratic forces in Nepal, Nikhamin justifies India's action on the basis that it precluded the intervention of Western powers in this sensitive region. In the same manner, India's treaties with Bhutan and Sikkim, which made both states Indian protectorates, are also rationalized as depriving the Western powers of the possibility to use these territories for provocative purposes.[135] Thus, it seems the Soviets were content to let India play an "Imperial" role along the Himalayan border, as long as these strategic areas were thereby denied to the West.

Although Nikhamin does not consider the tensions on the Sino-Indian border which erupted in the fall of 1959, his analysis of the Tibetan problem and the situation in the Himalayan border states in the early 1950's indicates at the very least that Indian monopoly circles were proponents of a more hostile posture towards the Chinese in this region. On this point, the Chinese would not have disagreed. Their fundamental point of difference, however, was in their assessment of the Nehru government. Nehru's alleged indirect assistance to the Tibetan rebels and India's provision of a political sanctuary to the Dalai Lama convinced the Chinese that the Congress government had finally gone over to the side of reaction. Yet, despite his admission that differences of a "non-irreconcilable" character existed on separate aspects of India's relations with socialist countries,[136] Nikhamin, on the contrary, concludes that India continued to conduct a "peace-loving" policy.

In the broader perspective, Nikhamin's suggestive references to the reactionary foreign policy role of the Indian monopolies is entirely consistent with the negative assessment of Indian big business which constituted a veritable leitmotif in the academic literature at this time. Although Soviet analysts seemed to be moving on a course parallel to their Chinese counterparts, they

[135] *Ibid.*, pp. 206-08.
[136] *Ibid.*, p. 201.

evidently exerted a negligible impact on official policy. Certainly, the Soviet leadership's major decision to continue their support of India despite the outbreak of open hostilities along the Sino-Indian border, a commitment which determined much of Soviet policy towards India during the next decade, bore no imprint of any academic input and must be explained exclusively in terms of the broader foreign policy goals of East-West detente that Khrushchev was pursuing at that time. Indeed, the fact that this momentous commitment to India was made against the background of disillusion with the reform program of the Nehru government and increasing anxieties over the power and influence of the Indian monopolies strongly suggests how little weight was attached to the specifics of the Indian context in reaching this decision.

* * *

In retrospect then, even though the volume of academic literature and the number of Soviet specialists in this area sharply increased during the period, it appears that the influence which Soviet scholars exerted on foreign policy-making was imperceptible. If any influence was exerted, it was certainly unsolicited. Editorials in *Sovetskoe Vostokovedenie*, and its successor, for example, not only directed Soviet orientalists as to which topics to investigate but also informed them as to the conclusions their research should yield.[137] Thus, if Soviet scholars were encouraged to study the foreign policy of non-aligned states, they were simultaneously instructed that these policies were progressive and peace-loving. In analyzing the economic development of these countries, economists were directed to reveal their exploitation by foreign capital or to show the progressiveness of their state sectors. In short, Soviet scholars were not called upon to exercise any independent judgments, but rather were expected to merely substantiate and document in a mechanistic fashion the latest Party pronouncements.

In general, with the notable exception of Mirskii and Stepanov's 1958 monograph, this was not an innovative period. Furthermore, although there were a few solid pieces of research such as

---

[137] For a typical example of this genre, see, "Put' k Prochnomu Miru vo Vsem Mire," *Problemy Vostokovedeniia*, No. 6 (1959), 3-8.

L. I. Reisner's Uttar Pradesh study, there was a great deal of repetition of standard positions. So too, the main journal of Soviet orientalists, *Sovetskoe Vostokovedenie*, often published non-scholarly propaganda pieces alongside research articles.[138] In fact, at a meeting of members of the Leningrad division of the Institute of Orientology with the editor of the journal, I. S. Braginskii, this practice was scored by the noted orientalist N. V. Pigulevskaia, who noted that the journal too often included "popular" materials "intended for mass readers" and argued that the journal be reoriented towards academic specialists.[139] A survey of articles published in *Sovetskoe Vostokovedenie* and its successor during the later 1950's corroborates this bold and frank criticism, for under the new leadership of the Institute of Orientology,[140] the journal had degenerated into something of a semi-official propaganda organ.

In retrospect, the pervasive timidity displayed by most Soviet scholars at this time may be explained by the retention of behavioral patterns learned during an earlier era. On balance, the Soviet scholars had yet to exert an independent influence on the policy-making process.

---

[138] An excellent example of the former is B. G. Gafurov, "Kolonial'naia Politika SShA v Stranakh Azii i Afriki pod Maskoi Ekonomicheskoi 'Pomoshch' '', " *Problemy Vostokovedeniia*, No. 1 (1959), 26-36. A diatribe against American aid, the article contains no footnotes.

[139] "Khronika-Konferentsiia Chitatelei Zhurnala," *Problemy Vostokovedeniia*, No. 6 (1959), 224.

[140] In 1956, B. G. Gafurov, a Central Asian who had mixed party work with journalism before becoming the First Secretary of the Communist Party of Tadzhikistan, was appointed director of the Institute of Orientology. I. S. Braginskii, a long time associate of Gafurov's, became the editor of the Institute's main journal. For further biographical data on Gafurov, consult, Iu. V. Gankovskii, "60-Letie Akademika B. G. Gafurova," *Voprosy Istorii*, No. 4 (1969), 148-50.

4.
THE LATE KHRUSHCHEV YEARS, 1960-1964

THE EFFECT OF THE SINO-INDIAN BORDER DISPUTE

Perhaps the most remarkable aspect of Soviet academic literature on India during the early 1960's was the veritable lacuna of commentary on what is generally regarded as the major complicating factor in Indo-Soviet relations in that decade— i.e., the eruption of hostilities along the Sino-Indian border and the concomitant Sino-Indian enmity. This, in itself, attests to the sensitivity of the issue.

What commentary appeared on the Sino-Indian border conflict in the scholarly literature constituted a faithful and perfunctory reproduction of the official line. Thus, an editorial in *Problemy Vostokovedeniia*, which appeared soon after the border clashes in 1959, stated that the Imperialists were trying to use the border conflict to activize right wing forces in India and thereby alter Nehru's foreign policy of non-alignment.[1] The causes of the dispute as well as its consequences for Indo-Soviet relations were studiously ignored. Undoubtedly, the Soviets felt that public scrutiny of the dispute would not only be embarrassing, but would further complicate the problem.

The response was similar following the more serious October 1962 border war. An article written by S. Nesterov, almost a year later, accused the British and Americans of exploiting the crisis to tie India with military "aid" and warned that the situation had, in fact, strengthened reactionary forces in India with the resultant repression of the CPI and the dismissal from the government of such friendly political figures as K. D. Malaviya and Krishna Menon.[2] Reflecting the tone of the public anti-Chinese diatribes of that year, the article placed responsibility with the Chinese for expanding the scales of the conflict, but did not mention India's role. So too, on the subject of the Soviet response to the Sino-Indian conflict, and specifically, the decision to continue the flow of military aid, the Soviets were silent.[3] Obviously, the Soviet role in the Sino-Indian imbroglio—a topic which attracted much attention in the West—was too sensitive to be aired publicly.

This does not mean that the Soviets were unconcerned about the impact of the Sino-Indian border dispute on India. On the contrary, strong fears were expressed, especially following the 1962 border conflict, that right wing forces in India might succeed in diverting India from her traditional policy of non-alignment. As O. V. Maev observed, Indian monopolies were using the Sino-Indian conflict to subvert Nehru's policy of non-participation in military blocs.[4] While the possibility of a formal departure from

[1] "Osnovye Problemy Sovremennogo Razvitiia Stran Vostoka," *Problemy Vostokovedeniia*, No. 1 (1960), 5.

[2] S. Nesterov, "Manevry Amerikanskogo Imperializma v Iugo-Vostochnoi Azii," *Mirovaia Ekonomika i Mezhdunarodnye Otnosheniia*, No. 10 (1963), 73.

[3] The Soviets pointedly avoided mentioning their military aid to India, even when the opportunity arose. Thus, in a 1964 book on the Indian economy, G. I. Mamrykin referred to the production of British-designed HF-24 jets without mentioning the construction of the MIG plant in India. G. I. Mamrykin, *Stroitel'stvo Natsional'noi Ekonomiki Indii (Problemy, Itogi, Perspektivy)* (Moscow, 1964), p. 238.

[4] O. V. Maev, "Indiiskii Monopolisticheskii Kapital," *Narody Azii i Afriki*, No. 1 (1964), 35.

India's non-aligned foreign policy became more remote, more perceptive Soviet analysts speculated that India might nevertheless establish firmer economic, political and military ties with the West while formally preserving a neutralist posture. This scenario was elaborated by Ia. Etinger during a discussion of underdeveloped countries organized by the editors of *Mirovaia Ekonomika i Mezhdunarodnye Otnosheniia* in 1964; he supported his prognosis by referring to a recent statement by Zbigniew Brzezinski in an article in *Foreign Affairs* to the effect that it would be illusory to think that India would, at present, sign any pact of the Seato-type.[5] Thus, the Soviets were attuned to the danger that a substantive change in Indian foreign policy might not be accompanied by any formal indications.

The chief beneficiary of any change in Indian foreign policy would, of course, be the West and, more specifically, the United States. Yet, while the Soviets stressed this point frequently, they were less certain of the precise objectives of American policy in the region. Tracing American aims through the activities of the World Bank, which the Soviets deemed an instrument of American foreign policy, M. A. Aleksandrov noted that the United States was seeking to improve Indo-Pakistani relations in order to include India in a system of common defense against socialist countries.[6] R. A. Ul'ianovskii, in an article which appeared in *Narody Azii i Afriki* in 1963, however, argued that the United States wanted to embroil India in a conflict with both China and Pakistan.[7]

THE GROWING INFLUENCE OF INDIAN MONOPOLIES

Yet, whatever the precise contours of American policy in the subcontinent, the Soviets viewed the growing American influence

---

[5] For Etinger's comments, see, "Sotsializm, Kapitalizm, Slaborazvitye Strany," *Mirovaia Ekonomika i Mezhdunarodnye Otnosheniia*, No. 6 (1964), 68. Brzezinski's statement is contained in his article, "Threat and Opportunity in the Communist Schism," *Foreign Affairs*, XLI, No. 3 (April, 1963), 523-24.

[6] M. A. Aleksandrov, "Ispol'zovanie Soedinennymi Shtatami Mezhdunarodnogo Banka Rekonstruktsii i Razvitiia v Indii," *Kratkie Soobshcheniia Instituta Narodov Azii*, Kn. 51 (Moscow, 1962), 91.

[7] R. A. Ul'ianovskii, "Amerikanskaia Politika 'Pomoshchi' i Neitralizm Indii," *Narody Azii i Afriki*, No. 3 (1963), 23.

there as a threat to their own position. Indeed, a thorough examination of the scholarly literature of the early 1960's reveals a pervasive fear that India was succumbing to Western pressures and gradually drawing closer to the Western orbit. This is seen most vividly in the Soviet analysis of the course of Indian economic development, in general, and their perception of the growing influence of Indian monopolies and their strengthening ties with foreign capital, in particular.

The perception of this threat contained in the growing power of Indian monopolies was not something new, for, as was noted in the previous chapter, a significant number of Soviet Indologists had by the late 1950's already raised this problem. In the early 1960's this analytic tendency was further elaborated and gained additional adherents.

One indication of this broadening consensus was the 1960 publication of a major article on state capitalism in India by R. A. Ul'ianovskii, who had earlier been noted for his rather positive appraisal of the Indian government and its economic policy, but who now drew attention to the increasing threat posed by powerful Indian monopolies.[8] Ul'ianovskii commenced by stating that in general the development of state capitalism in India "at present" bore an anti-Imperialist character and was directed to the goal of attaining economic independence,[9] thus leaving the impression that this was subject to change. This hint was made more explicit in his ensuing discussion of the role of the Indian monopolist bourgeoisie. While Ul'ianovskii held that the monopolist circles in India had not yet succeeded in privatizing the more prosperous state

---

[8] R. A. Ul'ianovskii, "Ob Osobennostiakh Razvitiia i Kharaktere Gosudarstvennoi Kapitalizma v Nezavisimoi Indii," *Problemy Vostokovedeniia*, No. 3 (1960), 23-41.

[9] *Ibid.*, p. 26. For Ul'ianovskii, it was this anti-Western content which determined the progressiveness of Indian state capitalism. The preeminence of political over economic criteria in Ul'ianovskii's perspective is clearly evidenced in his challenge to the view held by many Soviet scholars that state capitalism should be judged solely by economic considerations: "The attitude towards Imperialism, as historic experience shows, serves as the most important and surest criterion for determining the degree of progressiveness of state capitalism in the economically underdeveloped countries. The condition that a given state capitalism develops productive forces is still not the decisive criterion of its progressiveness." *Ibid.*, 37.

enterprises or subordinating the state apparatus to its own interest, he acknowledged that they had clearly gained some important concessions from the government, such as the renunciation of nationalization and the removal of barriers to foreign capital penetration of certain new branches of industry that had earlier been forbidden to it.[10] Although Indian state capitalism had not yet become state monopoly capitalism (which would signify the total domination of the economy by the monopolies), Ul'ianovskii raised an apparition of how this might come about, by noting that the monopolist bourgeoisie was seeking to enlist officials in the government apparatus and dissatisfied political leaders in parliament and the state ministries in their efforts to subordinate state capitalism to their interests.[11] Thus, Ul'ianovskii was attuned to the possibility that the conversion of Indian state capitalism could be effected even without such visible signposts as electoral victories by either of the two major conservative political parties (i.e., the Swatantra and Jana Sangh).

Other scholars presented additional data pointing to the growing influence of Indian monopolies. Having documented the personal ties between public corporations and big business in India, A. I. Levkovskii concluded that Indian monopolies exerted a great deal of influence on the economic and political life of the country.[12] A. L. Batalov, in a study of Indian transportation, described the ways in which monopolies used their representation on government railway boards to receive preferential freight rates and high prices for equipment sold to the government railroads.[13] Additional examples of private companies selling products at inflated prices to state sector enterprises were cited in an article by S. I. Tiul'panov.[14]

Soviet scholars also pointed out that, with the activation of Indian monopolies, the Congress government had shifted to the

[10] *Ibid.*, 34-35.
[11] *Ibid.*, 36.
[12] A. I. Levkovskii, "Osnovye Problemy Razvitiia Gosudarstvennogo Kapitalizma v Sovremmennoi Indii," in *Gosudarstvennyi Kapitalizm v Stranakh Vostoka* (Moscow, 1960), pp. 74-75.
[13] A. L. Batalov, *Transport v Sovremennoi Indii* (Moscow, 1961), pp. 124-26.
[14] S. I. Tiul'panov, "O Nekotorykh Osobennostiakh Gosudarstvennogo Kapitalizma Slaborazvitykh Stran," *Vestnik Leningradskogo Universiteta*, Seriia Ekonomiki, Filosofii i Prava, vyp. 2, No. 11 (1961), 11.

right in both domestic and foreign policies.[15] They were especially alarmed that the Indian government, courting foreign capital, had offered important concessions, such as guarantees against nationalization, the right to repatriate profits and the suspension of controls on foreign participation in joint stock companies. This trend, they felt, was bound to increase the effectiveness of Western pressure on Indian foreign policy.[16]

Reviewing the progress of Indian state capitalism in a significant article published at the time of the October 1962 border conflict, S. A. Bessonov drew an even more alarmist picture of the influence of Indian monopolies than Ul'ianovskii had done two years earlier, by emphasizing the statement of the late CPI leader Ajoy Ghosh at the Sixth CPI Congress in 1961 to the effect that the ties between monopolists and influential representatives in Congress and the government were strengthening, and that, as this process continued, the danger arose that state capitalism would gradually acquire the features of state monopoly capitalism.[17] Bessonov observed that in recent years the government had become all the more subordinate to the big monopolist bourgeoisie. Instead of waging a consistent struggle against Imperialism, the ruling circles in India had shown a great amount of indecisiveness and had departed more and more from a consistent anti-Imperialist course. This conservative trend in the government's domestic and foreign policies, Bessonov explained, was rooted in the growing class struggle within the country which forced the ruling circles to seek the assistance of the Imperialists in the struggle to suppress the toiling masses.[18] The Indian bourgeoisie had subordinated their basic economic interest of achieving economic independence to the political necessity of maintaining their power. Thus, India's economic dependence on the West had

[15] L. N. Chernov, "Kommunisty Stran Azii i Afriki—v Avangarde Bor'by za Svobodu i Natsional'nuiu Nezavisimost'," *Narody Azii i Afriki,* No. 5 (1961), 21.

[16] See, especially, V. Kondrat'ev, "Novye Tendentsii v Strukture Ekonomiki Sovremennoi Indii," *Mirovaia Ekonomika i Mezhdunarodnye Otnosheniia,* No. 7 (1961), 54, and E. I. Mironova, "Nekotorye Formy Sotrudnichestva Indiiskikh i Inostrannykh Monopolii," *Kratkie Soobshcheniia Instituta Narodov Azii,* Kn. 81 (1964), 30-31.

[17] S. A. Bessonov, "O Roli Gosudarstvennogo Kapitalizma v Ekonomicheskom Razvitii Sovremennoi Indii," *Vestnik Moskovskogo Universiteta,* Seriia VIII: Ekonomika, Filosofiia, No. 6 (1962), 65-66.

[18] *Ibid.,* 66.

actually grown since independence; the level of foreign capital investment had more than doubled since World War II. Therefore, he concluded that the contradictoriness of Indian state capitalism consisted in the fact that the government was employing methods to hasten economic progress which objectively strengthened her economic dependence on Imperialism.[19]

Such pessimistic soundings as those contained in Bessonov's article increased in intensity after the Sino-Indian border war. As we have noted at the outset of this chapter, the repression of the CPI, the dismissal of leftist political figures from the cabinet and the accompanying demands for a reassessment of India's foreign policy contained the ominous threat of the ascendence of the monopolist bourgeoisie. Indeed, at a conference on the problems of economic development of underdeveloped countries held at Leningrad University in April 1963, A. I. Nikitin, delivering the report on India, again pointed to the present danger of state capitalism being converted into state monopoly capitalism.[20] These anxieties intensified following Nehru's death, when the direction of political leadership in India was at stake. Indeed, at that time Soviet writers began to speak openly of a right wing in Congress, identified with such figures as Morarji Desai and S. K. Patil who were personally linked with those monopoly interests which actively opposed further socio-economic reforms.[21] Thus, the Soviets were

---

[19] *Ibid.*, 67. It is interesting to note that Bessonov, in paying the perfunctory lip service to the official positive line on Indian state capitalism, inserted the following paragraph at the end of his article which directly contradicted his earlier remarks: "Nevertheless, state capitalism in India is progressive since it assists the strengthening of the national sovereignty of the country. It is progressive also because in conjunction with the peace-loving and on the whole anti-colonial foreign policy of the government, it hastens the decline of the colonial system, and consequently, weakens world Imperialism." *Ibid.*, 67.

[20] His statement is contained in M. A. Skliar and G. I. Chufrin, "Nauchnaia Konferentsiia Po Problemam Ekonomicheskogo Razvitiia Slaborazvitykh Stran," *Vestnik Leningradskogo Universiteta*, Seriia Ekonomiki, Filosofii i Prava, vyp. 2, No. 11 (1963), 165.

[21] See, A. M. Mel'nikov, "Bor'ba Indiiskogo Krest'ianstva za Radikal'nye Agrarnye Reformy (1957-1962)," *Narody Azii i Afriki*, No. 5 (1964), 83, and L. I. Seleznev, "O Nekotorykh Osobennostiakh Monopolisticheskogo Kapitala Indii," *Vestnik Leningradskogo Universiteta*, Seriia Ekonomiki, Filosofii i Prava, vyp. 4, No. 23 (1964), 34-35. Seleznev noted that Nehru's death gave reactionary forces "new hopes" of successfully dominating the government.

beginning to play an openly partisan role in the leadership succession following Nehru's death.

Despite these alarmist presentiments, it should not be inferred that the Soviets had given up hope on Indian state capitalism and concluded that government policy was now dictated by monopoly interests. Here we are not referring to the ritualistic formularies acknowledging the progressive character of Indian state capitalism that invariably introduced and concluded discussions of the subject, for these were most probably sops to the censor.[22] Rather, it would seem that the Soviets genuinely viewed state capitalism and the state sector as arenas of struggle between progressive and reactionary tendencies, with the outcome of this struggle still undetermined. As V. Cheprakov concluded in a 1963 article in *Voprosy Ekonomiki*, state capitalism in India "...will either be used by developing big capital and converted into state monopoly capitalism or will be used for the struggle against monopolies, for the progressive path of development."[23]

Even at a time of heightened anxieties following the Sino-Indian border war, Ul'ianovskii advised his colleagues that "it would be a mistake to assume that preparedness for concessions to foreign capital dominated the policy of the ruling circles of India."[24] While Ul'ianovskii admitted that the Indian monopolies had gained certain objectives regarding government economic policy, they had not won others; specifically, they had not succeeded to transfer the Bokaro steel mill project to the private sector, nor had they inter-

---

[22] An example of such practice has been cited in the discussion of Bessonov's article above (see Fn. 17, page 176). For an additional example, see A. I. Levkovskii, "Osnovye Problemy Razvitiia Gosudarstvennogo Kapitalizma v Sovremennoi Indii," in *Gosudarstvennyi Kapitalizm v Stranakh Vostoka* (Moscow, 1960), pp. 161ff. That Soviet authors have occasionally inserted traditional formulations to make innovative concepts more palatable has been publicly acknowledged by Iu. Ostrovitianov, at a 1968 symposium discussing the three volume work, *Klassy i Klassovaia Bor'ba v Razvivaiushchikhsia Stranakh* (3 vols., Moscow, 1967-1968). See his comments in "Sotsial'nye Sily i Perspektivy "Tret'ego Mira"," *Mirovaia Ekonomika i Mezhdunarodnye Otnosheniia*, No. 5 (1968), 92.

[23] V. Cheprakov, "Sotsializm, Imperializm i Osvobodivshiesia Strany," *Voprosy Ekonomiki*, No. 12 (1963), 99.

[24] R. A. Ul'ianovskii, "Amerikanskaia Strategiia v Indii," *Mirovaia Ekonomika i Mezhdunarodnye Otonosheniia*, No. 5 (1963), 36.

rupted the expansion of collaboration with the Soviet Union and other socialist countries.[25]

The Indian state sector was seen as the last line of defense against the establishment of the monopolists' economic rule in India.[26] Although, to be sure, private capital extracted certain advantages from the state sector, they were on the whole hostile towards it. If, at present, the state sector's progressiveness was limited by the degree of influence of Indian big business, then, in the future, under more favorable socio-political conditions, the state sector could begin to curb big native and foreign capital and eventually serve as a "material base for the transition to the non-capitalist path of development."[27] As Ul'ianovskii explained at a 1964 conference on underdeveloped countries, in order to "democratize" the state sector, it would be necessary to remove from the state apparatus the advocates of compromise with foreign capital and the bearers of pro-Imperialist capitalist tendencies.[28] Thus, while cognizant of its present deficiencies,[29] the Soviets still found ample reasons to come to the defense of the Indian state sector which went beyond mere rationalizations for the large amount of forcign aid that the Soviets had already invested in it.

From the above, it is apparent that the Soviets had moved almost full circle in placing the monopolist bourgeoisie squarely in the camp of reaction where they had been in Stalinist times. Nevertheless, although scholarly commentary frequently referred to Indian monopolists as reactionaries, more concrete analysis of the Indian bourgeoisie revealed considerable difficulties specifically with respect to the determination of which strata were the most pro-Imperialist.

Thus, for example, N. A. Savel'ev, a specialist on the Indian

---

[25] *Ibid.*, 37.

[26] This point is made by O. V. Maev, "Indiiskii Monopolisticheskii Kapital," *Narody Azii i Afriki*, No. 1 (1964), 32.

[27] Iu. A. Krasin and V. F. Li, "O Zakonomernostiakh Nekapitalisticheskikh Razvitiia Osvobodivshikhsia Stran," *Voprosy Filosofii*, No. 8 (1964), 35.

[28] For Ul'ianovskii's comments, see, "Sotsializm, Kapitalizm, Slaborazvitye Strany," *Mirovaia Ekonomika i Mezhdunarodnye Otnosheniia*, No. 6 (1964), 73.

[29] For further evidence of Soviet awareness of the administrative defects of the Indian state sectors' operation, see below, pp. 207-12.

bourgeoisie, in a series of articles on this subject,[30] sought to distinguish the older industrial-trade bourgeoisie, which maintained firm ties with landlords, usurers and foreign monopolies, from the younger industrial bourgeoisie, which was only slightly tied with feudal landlords and more independent of foreign capital. While on certain questions, this latter segment of the big bourgeoisie could support the more radical anti-Imperialist and anti-feudal positions of the petty and middle bourgeoisie, it did not forego collaboration with foreign capital and therefore, on some questions joined forces with the bloc of right wing forces. While calling for a differentiated approach towards the bourgeoisie which would take into account the positions of its various strata on specific questions, Savel'ev set forth a set of criteria for evaluating the bourgeoisie which conspicuously deleted any reference to its relation to foreign capital,[31] thus totally bypassing this thorny question.

Soviet authors were beginning to understand that attitudes towards foreign capital were not only subject to change but could not be ascribed to one specific stratum of the bourgeoisie. In his 1963 article on American aid strategy towards India, Ul'ianovskii observed that the two tendencies of struggling with Imperialism on the one hand, and collaborating with it for the sake of aid on the other, were always found intermingled and often represented by the same social layer of the national bourgeoisie.[32]

---

[30] See, his chapter in *Problemy Industrializatsii Suverennykh Slaborazvitykh Stran Azii* (*Indiia, Indoneziia, Birma*) (Moscow, 1960), ch. 5, and his articles: "O Natsional'noi Burzhuazii v Stranakh Iugo-Vostochnoi Azii," *Mirovaia Ekonomika i Mezhdunarodnye Otnosheniia*, No. 4 (1961), 38-51, and "Role of the Bourgeoisie in the National Liberation Movement," *Mirovaia Ekonomika i Mezhdunarodnye Otnosheniia*, No. 5 (1962), 97-102, as translated in *Joint Publications Research Service*, (hereinafter *JPRS*), No. 14, 552.

[31] N. Savel'ev, "Role of the Bourgeoisie in the National Liberation Movement," *Mirovaia Ekonomika i Mezhdunarodnye Otnosheniia*, No. 5 (1962), in *JPRS*, No. 14, 552,67. The criteria Savel'ev includes are consistency on agrarian and other domestic reforms and attitudes toward the Soviet Union and other socialist countries.

[32] R. A. Ul'ianovskii, "Amerikanskaia Politika "Pomoshchi" i Neitralizm Indii," *Narody Azii i Afriki*, No. 3 (1963), 36. Ul'ianovskii's observations echoed the views of R. Avakov and G. Mirskii at a conference held a year earlier on the problems of the national liberation movement and the socio-economic development of liberated countries, organized by the Institute of World Economy and International Relations. Avakov and Mirskii specifically noted that the national and pro-Imperialist bourgeoisies were not two stagnant, stable entities separated from each other by a "Chinese Wall." See, R. Avakov and G. Mirskii, "The Class Structure in the Underdeveloped Countries," *Mirovaia Ekonomika i Mezhdunarodnye Otnosheniia*, No. 4 (1962), translated in *JPRS*, No. 14, 607, 39.

Yet, perhaps the most striking illustration of the perplexity surrounding this problem was revealed at a conference on private foreign investments in Asia held at the Institute of the Peoples of Asia in March 1963. Delivering the main report, G. P. Kolykhalova asserted that the contradictions between big native and foreign capital, so central to Soviet thinking in the mid-1950's, were now of secondary importance as compared to the deepening contradictions between the progressive democratic national forces, which included the working class, peasantry and the bulk of the national bourgeoisie on the one hand, and the Imperialists in league with the upper layer of the big local bourgeoisie on the other.[33] While this formulation seems quite typical of the period, her definition of the monopolist bourgeoisie as the group most closely tied with foreign capital was taken to task by the noted Indologist, G. K. Shirokov. Shirokov remarked that Indian monopolies could conclude agreements with foreign firms on more or less equal terms; this collaboration, while desirable, was not unavoidable for them. On the other hand, the non-monopolist big and even middle bourgeoisie, not possessing such capital resources, could realize expanded reproduction only with the assistance of foreign capital. Hence, Shirokov noted, most of the 1300 agreements on economic collaboration between Western and Indian firms signed between 1959 and 1962 were actually concluded not with Indian monopolies but with representatives of the middle and non-monopolist big bourgeoisie. Therefore, Shirokov argued that the division in the Indian bourgeoisie with respect to its relationship to foreign capital, which Kolykhalova had alluded to in her report, had not yet occurred.[34] Indeed, one might add that Shirokov implied that it was the non-monopolist segments of the Indian bourgeoisie which were more susceptible to Imperialist pressures—a view which certainly contravened contemporary thinking on the subject.

THE CHANGING PERSPECTIVE OF FOREIGN CAPITAL INVESTMENT

Perhaps, one of the main reasons for Soviet reluctance to regard

---

[33] See, "Nauchnaia Diskussiia, Posviashchennaia Roli Chastnykh Inostrannykh Investitsii v Ekonomike Stran Azii," *Narody Azii i Afriki*, No. 1 (1964), 224.
[34] *Ibid.*, 225-26.

attitudes toward foreign capital as a determinant of progressiveness of the Indian bourgeoisie can be traced to a gradual reevaluation of the role of foreign capital investment that took place during this period.

In the first place, it should be stressed that the Soviets never urged a cessation of the influx of private foreign capital to underdeveloped countries. As V. Ia. Arkhipov stated in a 1960 study of foreign capital in South East Asia, "... it would be incorrect to deny any possibility of the utilization by economically underdeveloped countries of foreign capital for accelerating the development of their economies. However, the question of the possibility of its attraction, the degree and forms of its utilization cannot be decided without regard to the economic and political conditions of a given country...."[35] The problem then was of ensuring that private foreign capital be subject to strict government controls so that it would contribute to economic development without threatening the national sovereignty of the recipient country.[36] Where foreign capital already commanded strong economic positions, the task was one of eliminating the "dominance" of foreign capital by placing limitations on it and even, when the preparatory groundwork had been laid, of undertaking measures of nationalization.[37] Otherwise, the unchecked penetration by foreign monopoly capital could become the basis of neocolonialism, as G. I. Mamrykin warned in his 1964 study of the Indian economy.[38] Yet, however advantageously Western foreign capital could be employed, Soviet analysts always attributed base motives to the 'Imperialistic' policies which generated it. As we have noted in the previous chapter (consult pp. 160-61), improvements in the terms of foreign aid and private capital investment were explicable in terms of such transient factors as the impact of Soviet aid and the desire to keep these countries within the world capitalist economy; they did not connote any

---

[35] V. Ia. Arkhipov, *Inostrannyi Kapital v Ekonomike Stran Iugo-Vostochnoi Azii* (Moscow, 1960), p. 30.

[36] This point is concisely stated in R. Ul'ianovskii, "SShA i Problemy Industrializatsii Slaborazvitykh Stran," *Mirovaia Ekonomika i Mezhdunarodnye Otnosheniia*, No. 9 (1962), 51.

[37] For a fuller discussion of the Soviet viewpoint on nationalization, see below, pp. 204-05.

[38] G. I. Mamrykin, *op. cit.*, p. 248.

basic change in Western economic policy which remained exploitative in essence and fundamentally antithetic to the process of industrialization.

Nevertheless, by the early 1960's, some faint challenges to the doctrinaire assumptions regarding the anti-industrialization policy of the West began to appear. Thus, for example, R. A. Ul'ianovskii in a 1962 article in *Mirovaia Ekonomika i Mezhdunarodnye Otnosheniia* observed that the advanced capitalist states, due to surplus production of the products of heavy industry, now had an economic interest in furnishing capital goods to the underdeveloped countries on a competitive basis—a situation obviously beneficial to the recipient states.[39] Hence, there arose a certain possibility of agreement between the native and Imperialist bourgeoisie on the basis of this confluence of economic interest. However, Ul'ianovskii stopped short of drawing the implication that this portended a revision of the West's anti-industrialization policy. Ul'ianovskii argued that this did not signify that the developed capitalist states now had a vested economic interest in the industrialization of underdeveloped countries but rather that it was temporarily expedient for them to engage in economic trade and aid which would "objectively weaken their own monopolist positions in the world capitalist economy."[40]

In a more forthright exposition, G. P. Kolykhalova, at the 1963 academic conference on private foreign investments in Asia, asserted that the capitalist states were encouraging economic development among the underdeveloped countries since they felt that a certain modicum of industrial development would not threaten their economic interests. From this she concluded that the exploitation of underdeveloped countries as agrarian raw material appendages was evanescing as the operational strategy of Western economic policy— a conclusion, however, which was widely criticized.[41]

While Soviet scholars were beginning to acknowledge that the West did not oppose the industrialization of the underdeveloped

---

[39] R. A. Ul'ianovskii, "SShA i Problemy Industrializatsii Slaborazvitykh Stran." *Mirovaia Ekonomika i Mezhdunarodnye Otnosheniia*, No. 9 (1962), 52.

[40] *Ibid.*, 53-54.

[41] For her report and the discussion of it, see, "Nauchnaia Diskussiia, Posviashchennaia Roli Chastnykh Inostrannykh Investsii v Ekonomike Stran Azii," *Narody Azii i Afriki*, No. 1 (1964), 223-26.

countries, they were at the same time becoming aware that the industrialization process itself did not lead directly to economic self-sufficiency but was accompanied by some measure of growing interdependence between native and foreign capital. Research on the industrialization of India conducted by G. K. Shirokov showed, for example, that India was in fact becoming more and more dependent on the deliveries of industrial equipment, components and semi-finished goods and consequently, had yet to realize a full reproduction cycle of social capital in industry on a national basis.[42] In fact, so essential had these industrial imports become that recent government efforts to limit them, due to foreign exchange deficits, had created significant production standstills and increased overall production costs.[43] Shirokov found that the present dependence on Western industrial imports was profitable for both Indian and foreign capital, a fact which not only strengthened the community of their economic interest but also augured for the long-term continuation of close economic ties.[44]

While thus acknowledging the durability of Indian and Western economic ties, Soviet analysts were also beginning to recognize that they were not necessarily nefarious or detrimental to India's economic development. An apparently sympathetic treatment of the role of collaboration of native and foreign capital in India was presented in a 1964 article on this subject by E. I. Mironova.[45] She observed, for example, that joint stock companies removed a number of serious problems which accompanied the extremely limited production of capital equipment, the insufficiency of several types of industrial raw materials and parts, scant technical

[42] G. K. Shirokov, "Nekotorye Osobennosti Lomki Kolonial'noi Struktury Indiiskoi Promyshlennosti," *Narody Azii i Afriki*, No. 4 (1964), 12-21.

[43] *Ibid.*, 19.

[44] *Ibid.*, 20. In addition, Shirokov detected an even longer range trend towards economic dependence in Indian industry's reliance on Western scientific technology, due to the fact that the Indian business community was not interested in developing its own scientific research base to compete with the West. As a result, he predicted that India's dependence on imports of capital equipment and industrial components would be eliminated much earlier than her reliance on foreign technological experience.

[45] E. I. Mironova, "Nekotorye Formy Sotrudnichestva Indiiskikh i Inostrannykh Monopolii," *Kratkie Soobshcheniia Instituta Narodov Azii*, Kn. 81 (1964), 29-34.

experience and the shortage of foreign currency reserves. This form of collaboration also promoted sales within India due to the popularity of Western brand names. While the foreign partners had certainly derived definite advantages through this collaboration by economizing on investment funds, Mironova nevertheless stressed that many benefits accrued to the Indian participants who had been able to extract favorable contract terms by playin on the competition among Western concerns. She observed, in fact, that "Often a foreign firm, not wishing to lose its Indian partner, is forced to make concessions with the conclusion of agreements, sometimes even to its own detriment."[46] Although Mironova paid the perfunctory lip service to the ideologically enshrined dogma that serious contradictions between Indian and foreign capital still pertained, one nevertheless gets the strong impression that Mironova actually, viewed relations between native and foreign capital not as adversary ones, but based on genuine collaboration with mutual advantages accruing to both, and that furthermore, the fruits of this collaboration were promoting India's economic development.

Reviewing the research of these Soviet Indologists, then, one senses some movement towards a reconciliation with the more or less permanent role of foreign capital in India which was accompanied by a growing awareness that on the whole new foreign investments were making a useful contribution towards India's economic development. It is for this reason most probably that the Soviets treated the subject of the Indian bourgeoisie's attitude towards foreign capital most gingerly, since private foreign capital could no longer be considered the same nemesis as it had been in the past.

THE ASSESSMENT OF INDIA'S CURRENT
REVOLUTIONARY POTENTIAL

In the broader perspective, it is apparent that Moscow was compelled to maintain its level of support to India mainly because of the practical realities of the Sino-Soviet-Indian triangle and despite mounting fears of the growing influence of Indian monopolies and the strengthening bonds with foreign capital, which augured for continued economic dependence on the West. Yet, if their influence

---

[46] *Ibid.*, 34.

on the course of Indian development was secondary to that of the West, the Soviets were nonetheless determined to maintain their foothold in India. Certainly, as we have discussed extensively in the first chapter, it is hard to conceive of their doing anything to jeopardize Indo-Soviet relations. In practical terms, their policy was one of maintaining general support for the established government, while using the CPI to pressure the government to resist concessions to the forces on the right and to continue domestic reforms.[47] Moreover, the CPI was also called upon to support the government when, for example, the latter's candidates faced serious electoral challenges from right wing political candidates.[48]

Certainly, a contributing but by no means major factor in Moscow's decision to use the CPI in this essentially auxiliary role was the calculation that the Indian Communists were not capable of posing any serious political challenge to the present regime in India. Although the official line for reasons of morale still spoke of the important role which the working class would assume as the national liberation movement progressed,[49] published research on the situation of the Indian working class showed just the opposite findings.

As we have seen in the preceding chapters, scholarly analysis of the working class of India, following a brief wave of euphoria in the late 1940's, was generally pessimistic with respect to their revolutionary potential. Their small number, the retention of ties with the village, the divisive influence of caste, religious, national

---

[47] This approach was sanctioned by G. F. Kim in a semi-official article in *Narody Azii i Afriki* in which he asserted that the working class in underdeveloped countries could and must weaken or paralyze the compromising tendencies of the national bourgeoisie and activate its remaining anti-Imperialist potentialities. See, G. F. Kim, "Soiuz Rabochego Klassa i Krest'ianstva v Natsional'no-Osvoboditel'nykh Revoliutsiiakh," *Narody Azii i Afriki*, No. 5 (1962), 11.

[48] Instances of CPI support for the Congress against right wing parties in a number of electoral constituencies during the 1962 general elections are recorded by Bessonov, *op. cit.*, 67.

[49] For typical formulations, consult the following semi-official editorials: "Velichestvennaia Postup' Kommunizma," *Mirovaia Ekonomika i Mezhdunarodnye Otnosheniia*, No. 12 (1960), 15, (published on the occasion of the 1960 Moscow Conference of 81 Communist Parties) and "Velikaia Programma Stroitel'stva Kommunizma," *Narody Azii i Afriki*, No. 4 (1961), 6 (commemorating the publication of the 1961 CPSU program).

and other factors obstructed working class solidarity. Nor did the trade union schism in India contribute to the organizational unity of the proletariat. The publication of even more sophisticated research during the early 1960's buttressed these gloomy observations.

By far the most impressive analysis of the Indian working class was presented in a study by L. A. Gordon and L. A. Fridman, which was based on data for both India and Egypt.[50] Therein, the authors drew a sharp distinction between manual laborers—i.e., those involved in small scale production—and the smaller core of the industrial proletariat, who were highly concentrated in the few geographic pockets of industrialization in India.[51] The highly imbalanced quantitative ratio of proletariat to manual workers was such that despite the fact that the number of proletarians had doubled in both India and Egypt in the previous twenty years, this had not resulted in any basic proportionate shift. For the industrial proletariat to become prominent would require a five- to ten-fold increase in their number—an eventuality which the authors did not anticipate since the increase of industrial workers per unit of capital investment was substantially less in these two countries than in the industrialized states of North America and Western Europe.[52] Rather, it was the urban unemployed and semi-proletarian strata occupied with small crafts production whose numbers were expanding fastest.[53] Urbanization was in fact outstripping industrialization and was to be considered an extension of agrarian overpopulation.

---

[50] L. A. Gordon and L. A. Fridman, "Distinctive Aspects of the Composition and Structure of the Working Class in the Economically Underdeveloped Countries of Asia and Africa (Based on Data for India and the UAR)," *Narody Azii i Afriki*, No. 2 (1963), translated in *Soviet Sociology*, II, No. 3, 46-63.

[51] *Ibid.*, 48-50.

[52] In an earlier study, T. Pokataeva found that an increase in labor productivity associated with industrial modernization was accompanied by a net decrease in the number of employed, and thence concluded that the opportunities for expanding the levels of employment were more limited in the underdeveloped countries than in the industrialized capitalist states. See, T. Pokataeva, "Urgent Problems of Employment in Underdeveloped Countries," *Mirovaia Ekonomika i Mezhdunarodnye Otnosheniia*, No. 5 (1962), 78-79, translated in *JPRS* No. 14, 552.

[53] *Ibid.*, 54-55.

Insofar as the needs of modern industry demanded a literate, skilled work force, the authors noted that the industrial workers were being separated from other workers and beginning to constitute a skilled group with higher wages and better working conditions. In short, the authors suggested that the industrial proletariat was beginning to constitute something of a labor aristocracy in relation to the much broader strata of manual workers and craftsmen.[54] In point of fact, industrial workers had found common cause with office workers, government employees and other non-manual professional and technical personnel that constituted the most active force in the trade union movement.[55] The importance then of the distinction between the industrial working class and other strata associated with a modern economy, on the one hand, and the much larger circle of laborers engaged in small scale production, on the other, had significant policy implications.[56] The authors cautioned that underestimating these distinctions and thence grouping all laboring strata into one undifferentiated whole might result in inflating the size of the proletariat and thereby exaggerating the degree of capitalist development.[57] Even in the more industrially advanced developing countries of Egypt and India, the authors argued that it would be premature to speak of the attainment of proletarian hegemony in the national liberation movement.

Furthermore, Gordon and Fridman stressed that the industrial workers were not yet liberated from petty bourgeois and reformist illusions. In the first place, they noted that a hereditary cadre proletariat had not yet been formed, since not only were most of the new workers recruited from amongst impoverished peasants and craftsmen, but also because the industrial workers still maintained close ties with the village—a fact which helped to explain

---

[54] *Ibid.*, 60.

[55] *Ibid.*, 56.

[56] That research on the working class was designed to have such policy relevance is substantiated by A. A. Iskenderov, who, in reviewing some recent books on this subject, observed that research on the material situation of the working class was not an end in itself, but served to help the proletariat better recognize "its historic role in social life." See, A. A. Iskenderov, "Issledovaniia Sovetskikh Uchenykh O Rabochem Klasse Azii i Afriki," *Narody Azii i Afriki*, No. 3 (1963), 116.

[57] *Ibid.*, 58.

why strikes could be of such a long duration (since strikers could find employment in their native villages).[58] In an earlier article on this subject, Gordon had elaborated upon the paradoxical situation according to which second and even third generation workers spent their childhoods in the village, then left for the city factory while leaving their wives in the village and returned there in their old age.[59] This contact with the village, it was explained, left a strong imprint on the mentality of industrial workers and strengthened their "lag of consciousness behind the conditions of their material existence."[60] In brief, they considered themselves more village peasants than urban workers—a state of mind which opened wide possibilities for the penetration of petty bourgeois illusions among them.

Besides being subject to the petty bourgeois influence of the village, industrial workers were also susceptible to the demagogic appeals of the Congress government. It was observed that the Congress and its trade union auxiliary, the Indian National Trade Union Congress (INTUC), still enjoyed such prestige and authority not only on account of its leadership of the independence movement, but also because of its experience in practical work among the masses. So too, the reform program of the Congress government, for all its inconsistency, enabled the bourgeoisie to channel worker dissatisfaction along reformist lines. In addition, the prominent role of the government in the economy, with its occasional entry even against representatives of the business community, had given the Indian bourgeoisie possibilities of maintaining a strong influence over the workers and obscured the opposition of the interests of capital and labor.[61]

Yet, the maintenance of close ties by the industrial workers with their native villages could also be a two-way street. If it led, on the one hand, to the retention of petty bourgeois illusions among the industrial workers, on the other, it gave the class con-

---

[58] *Ibid.*, 54.
[59] L. A. Gordon, "Polozhenie Promyshlennogo Proletariata Indii i Nekotorye Osobennosti Bor'by Rabochego Klassa," in *Polozhenie Rabochego Klassa i Rabochee Dvizhenie v Stranakh Azii i Afriki (1959-1961)* (Moscow, 1962), p. 77.
[60] *Ibid.*, p. 78.
[61] *Ibid.*, p. 76.

scious workers additional opportunities to penetrate the peasant milieu and organize them. Gordon and Fridman observed that, while the potential for revolutionary leadership by the vanguard of the proletariat was there, in order for it to be realized careful consideration had to be given to the contradictory social nature of the peasants, craftsmen and small production manual laborers.[62] On this point, however, the authors were not very optimistic. In a subsequent article, they warned that where the working class was young and closely tied to the non-proletarian masses, and where nationalistic impulses had an enormous influence on their social consciousness, such influences could be highly dangerous for the proletariat and could create "additional difficulties in the path of socialist construction."[63] Although the Chinese Communist Party is not mentioned by name, its implication seems obvious. Certainly, the suggestion that the Chinese 'petty bourgeois' schismatic divergence might be rooted in the Asian development context itself hardly constitutes an endorsement for other Asian Communists to seek power. Thus, the research conducted by Gordon and Fridman would seem to have left Soviet policy leaders little choice but to continue to seek their objectives in India by working through the existent political regime.

INDIA AND THE THIRD WORLD

In a comparative perspective, it is important to recognize that the pervasive pessimism among Soviet analysts with respect to India's course of development came against a background of ebullient optimism in regard to other Afro-Asian states in the early 1960's. The Soviet image of India, which had been held up as a model of progressiveness for newly independent states in the 1950's, began to tarnish as the Soviets waxed enthusiastically at the radical domestic and foreign policies being conducted in Egypt, Burma, Ghana, Guinea and other developing countries. While at the beginning of the decade India ranked among the most progressive

---

[62] Gordon and Fridman, *op. cit.*, 58.
[63] L. A. Gordon and L. A. Fridman, "Nekotorye Osobennosti Sotsial'noi Struktury Razvivaiushchikhsia Stran," *Narody Azii i Afriki*, No. 6 (1964), 18.

THE LATE KHRUSHCHEV YEARS

developing countries,[64] by 1962 she was already being relegated to a secondary category in the hierarchy of progressive underdeveloped countries.[65] This was not so much a consequence of the diminished regard for India as much as a result of a surge of expectations sparked by radical reforms in other developing states. To appreciate the waning prestige of India, it would be worthwhile, herein, to review the evolution of Soviet expectations with respect to developing countries during this period.

It will be remembered from the discussion in chapter one (see p. 32) that the communique of the November 1960 Moscow Conference of 81 Communist Parties formulated the goal for underdeveloped states of establishing a national democratic state as a transitional form on the "non-capitalist path of development" leading towards socialism. According to that document, the state of national democracy was one which "consistently upholds its political and economic independence, fights against Imperialism..., rejects dictatorial and despotic methods of government... [and ensures people] broad and democratic rights and freedoms, the opportunity to work for the enactment of agrarian reform and other social changes and for participation in shaping government policy."[66] This statement represents a rather modest set of expectations which were largely derivative of the broader goals of national sovereignty

---

[64] As compared to such pro-Imperialist countries as Turkey, Iran, Pakistan and the Philippines, India was considered along with Indonesia, Egypt, Burma, Ceylon, Ghana and Guinea as states which refused to join military blocs and maintained independent foreign policies. This typology, based purely on foreign policy considerations, remained operative through 1961 and occasionally reappeared thereafter. For examples of its use, consult G. Mirskii and V. Tiagunenko, "Tendentsii i Perspektivy Natsional'no-Osvoboditel'nykh Revoliutsii," *Mirovaia Ekonomika i Mezhdunarodnye Otnosheniia*, No. 11 (1961), 25-26, and L. V. Stepanov and G. I. Mirskii, *Aziia i Afrika—Kontinenty v Dvizhenii* (Moscow, 1963), p. 59.

[65] V. Ia. Avarin in a 1962 article in *Narody Azii i Afriki* placed Guinea, Ghana and Mali in the forefront of those countries seeking "real" independence. V. Ia. Avarin, "O Glavnykh Chertakh Zavershchaiushchego Etapa Raspada Kolonial'noi Sistemy," *Narody Azii i Afriki*, No. 1 (1962), 21. However, it was only during the following year that a typology based on domestic transformations began to be widely employed which posited India in a category below such progressive countries as Egypt, Burma, Guinea, Ghana, Mali, etc.

[66] *Communique on the Meeting of Representatives of 81 Communist and Workers' Parties, Moscow, November 1960*, in John Gittings, ed., *Survey of the Sino-Soviet Dispute* (Oxford University Press: London, 1968), Appendix Q, p. 363.

and economic independence. It is apparent that India was not moving in this direction, since she failed to meet some important requirements (e.g., her open door policy towards foreign capital). Yet, inasmuch as the document did not go beyond advocating broad democratic liberties and the "opportunity" for conducting socio-economic reforms, the national democratic state as defined therein seems well-suited on the whole to India's form of democracy. It should be noted, herein, that although the document stressed that Communist parties were the most consistent fighters for the establishment of this state, it did not specify that a Communist party would have to achieve political hegemony for this state to be consummated; indeed, the entire question of political leadership remained ambiguous. Suffice it to note that the academic literature at the time merely reiterated this official line with but minor elaborations.[67]

Yet, by early 1962, the concept of the national democratic state was given a more radical definition in an article by M. S. Dzhunusov in *Voprosy Filosofii*.[68] Therein, the state of national democracy was viewed as a means of struggle against "anti-patriotic" forces, feudal landlord groups and the reactionary wing of the national bourgeoisie, and whose economic tasks were defined as the destruction of feudal land relations, the limitation of capitalism and the creation of a new socialist layer.[69] The more radical tenor of Dzhunusov's formulation was but a preview of the sanguine expectations which surfaced in the last two years of Khrushchev's tenure.

In a dialogue conducted over the pages of *Mirovaia Ekonomika i Mezhdunarodnye Otnosheniia* in 1963, it was acknowledged that the reforms being conducted in such countries as Egypt, Algeria, Burma and Ghana, etc., went beyond the limits of traditional state capitalist measures though they were not yet to be equated with

---

[67] M. G. Kirichenko in an article on this subject raised the criterion of national integration as an additional characteristic of the national democratic state. See, M. G. Kirichenko, "O Nezavisimom Gosudarstve Natsional'noi Demokratii," *Sovetskoe Gosudarstvo i Pravo*, No. 11 (1961), 112.

[68] M. S. Dzhunusov, "O Zakonomernostiakh Nekapitalisticheskogo Puti Razitiia Otstalykh Stran K Sotsializmu," *Voprosy Filosofii*, No. 2 (1962), 15-24.

[69] *Ibid.*, 22-23.

socialist measures.[70] It was also asserted that certain "intermediate" social strata such as the intelligentsia and army officers could become bearers of "non-capitalist" tendencies. Moreover, the socialist slogans propagated by these "revolutionary democratic" leaders were seen as containing elements of scientific socialism and were not merely examples of bourgeois demagoguery.[71] Indeed, the idea that these revolutionary democrats, for all the inconsistency of their socialist ideas and programs, could be won over to positions of scientific socialism and the working class, following the Cuban example, was raised by V. Cheprakov in an article in *Voprosy Ekonomiki* at the end of 1963.[72] Indicative of the revisionist assertions espoused at the time, Cheprakov argued that "revolutionary democrats" could lead the advance along the non-capitalist path towards socialism even in those countries lacking a proletariat (e.g., Africa). According to him, the fact that several states under the leadership of revolutionary democratic forces had already entered the non-capitalist path was to be explained by the presence of the world socialist system which could "execute the function for them of a dictatorship of the proletariat."[73] It would seem that for Cheprakov, the primary requisite for the evolution of these countries on the non-capitalist path was strong links with socialist countries, which indeed represented a very bold and ambitious claim for the powers of Soviet aid.

[70] This is advanced by R. Avakov and L. Stepanov, "Sotsial'nye Problemy Natsional'no-Osvoboditel'noi Revoliutsii," *Mirovaia Ekonomika i Mezhdunarodnye Otnosheniia*, No. 5 (1963), 49.

[71] See, G. I. Mirskii, "Creative Marxism and the Problems of the National Liberation Revolution," *Mirovaia Ekonomika i Mezhdunarodnye Otnosheniia*, No. 2 (1963), translated in *JPRS*, No. 19, 821, 63-64. However, skepticism regarding the value of such socialist slogans continued to be voiced. In a rejoinder to Mirskii, V. Kiselev argued that the doctrines of socialism of a national type mouthed by "petty bourgeois nationalists," albeit progressive, did not serve socialist ends and were only used to confuse the working class and maintain influence over them. V. Kiselev, "Rabochii Klass i Natsional'no-Osvoboditel'nye Revoliutsii," *Mirovaia Ekonomika i Mezhdunarodnye Otnosheniia*, No. 10 (1963), 96-97. For an earlier typical denunciation of such socialist appeals as sheer exercises in bourgeois demagoguery, see, "Dal'neishee Razvitie Marksistsko-Leninskogo Ucheniia O Natsional'no-Kolonial'nom Voprose," *Problemy Vostokovedeniia*, No. 1 (1961), 9.

[72] V. Cheprakov, "Sotsializm, Imperializm, i Osvobodivshiesia Strany," *Voprosy Ekonomiki*, No. 12 (1963), 92-104.

[73] *Ibid.*, 102.

While much discussion was generated over whether or not revolutionary democrats could succeed in carrying out radical measures leading towards socialism without at some point in time political leadership being assumed by the "vanguard of the working class,"[74] and also over precisely how the socialist doctrines of these radical leaders should be evaluated,[75] the more revisionist views prevailed by the end of the Khrushchev era. A good illustration may be found in a general theoretical article by A. Arzumanian, which although published in *Mirovaia Ekonomika i Mezhdunarodnye Otnosheniia* just a few months after Khrushchev's ouster, seems to mark the apogee of the revisionist tendencies that characterized his last months in power.[76] Therein, revolutionary democrats were viewed as nothing less than a proxy for a Communist party. According to the author, these revolutionary democrats were beginning to essentially carry out the same historically necessary activities which would have been performed by the proletarian vanguard had it been sufficiently strong. Moreover, Arzumanian clearly identified

[74] For a presentation of the view that working class hegemony was necessary for the successful passage on the non-capitalist path, see, Ia. Guzevatyi, " 'Third' Way or Genuine Freedom?: Prospects for Social Development of Newly Independent Countries," *International Affairs*, No. 4 (1963) 48.

[75] V. Tiagunenko, in his concluding remarks at the aforementioned 1964 discussion on developing countries conducted by the journal, *Mirovaia Ekonomika i Mezhdunarodnye Otnosheniia*, cautioned against interpreting 'objectively' progressive programs and events in these countries as reactionary solely because they were initiated by representatives of non-proletarian elements. He argued that evaluating doctrines of socialism in underdeveloped countries only on the basis of the class origin of their proponents and thereby not taking into account the possibility that petty bourgeois and even bourgeois figures could be won over, under the influence of the world socialist system, to positions of the working class was an "incorrect dogmatic approach." See his comments in "Sotsializm, Kapitalizm, Slaborazvitye Strany," *Mirovaia Ekonomika i Mezhdunarodnye Otnosheniia*, No. 6 (1964), 81. However, Tiagunenko's formulary might have led Soviet scholars to accept any manifestation of a socialist doctrine at face value. This defect was noted by Iu. Ostrovitianov in a rejoinder in which he insisted on the more familiar criterion of class interest as the surest method of evaluating socialist doctrines in underdeveloped countries. See, Iu. Ostrovitianov, "Sotsialisticheskie Doktriny Razvivaiushchikhsia Stran: Formy, Sotsial'noe Soderzhanie," *Mirovaia Ekonomika i Mezhdunarodnye Otnosheniia*, No. 6 (1964), 84.

[76] A. Arzumanian, "Itogi Mirovogo Razvitiia za 100 Let i Aktual'nye Problemy Mezhdunarodnogo Revoliutsionno-Osvoboditel'nogo Dvizheniia," *Mirovaia Ekonomika i Mezhdunarodnye Otnosheniia*, No. 12 (1964), 74-97.

the non-capitalist path of development with socialism—a practice which had come into vogue with Khrushchev's trip to Egypt in June 1964.[77]

Soviet revisionist thinking on developing countries also elicited a reappraisal of the concept of the national democratic state. Now Soviet analysts were no longer satisfied with the execution of "general national" tasks but levied the additional demand that the national democratic state solve certain tasks of the social revolution.[78] Another departure from the "bourgeois democratic" state upon which the national democratic state was patterned was the acceptance of one party regimes in the progressive underdeveloped countries. In an article on this topic, G. V. Ignatenko asserted that Western political institutions did not answer popular needs and that opposition parties could easily become agents of neo-colonialism.[79] In fact, Ignatenko went so far as to justify the suspension of civil liberties and the use of coercion to meet resistance to the implementation of revolutionary measures by redefining the national democratic state as the "democratic dictatorship of a bloc of all anti-Imperialist classes and layers."[80] Finally, further evidence of the change in Soviet thinking on this subject is provided in an article by Iu. A. Krasin and V. F. Li in which the tasks of the national democratic state are redefined as the conduct of deep agrarian reform, nationalization of foreign monopolies, the establishment of an independent foreign policy with a "firm union" with the world socialist system and the mobilization of private national capital under strict state control for the solution of primary tasks of economic development.[81] This, of course, went well beyond the tasks initially outlined in the November 1960 communique.

While these revisionist tendencies magnified the divergence

[77] *Ibid.*, 95. It should be noted that earlier formulations had spoken only of a non-capitalist path leading towards socialism. See, R. Avakov and L. Stepanov, *op. cit.*, 49-50.

[78] For further elucidation of this point, consult, V. Tiagunenko, "Aktual'nye Voprosy Nekapitalisticheskogo Puti Razvitiia," *Mirovaia Ekonomika i Mezhdunarodnye Otnosheniia*, No. 10 (1964), 15-16.

[79] G. V. Ignatenko, "Gosudarstvenno-Pravovye Aspekty Natsional'no-Osvoboditel'nogo Dvizheniia," *Sovetskoe Gosudarstvo i Pravo*, No. 11 (1963), 28-29.

[80] *Ibid.*, 30.

[81] Iu. A. Krasin and V. F. Li, "O Zakonomernostiakh Nekapitalisticheskikh Razvitiia Osvobodivshikhsia Stran," *Voprosy Filosofii*, No. 8 (1964), 37.

between the more progressive Afro-Asian states and India in Soviet eyes, it may be well to ask the additional question of whether such concepts as revolutionary democrats and the non-capitalist path were at all relevant to the Indian context. By and large it would seem that this was not the case. We do not suggest that the non-capitalist path was totally inappropriate for India. As G. I. Mirskii noted, in a major article in *Mirovaia Ekonomika i Mezhdunarodnye Otnosheniia*, even where the national bourgeoisie prevailed a mechanical repetition of the traditional capitalist path of development was not likely to occur.[82] Rather, with the ascendence to political leadership of the progressive bloc of workers, peasants, urban petty bourgeoisie and patriotic elements of the national bourgeoisie, a transition to the non-capitalist path could commence, signalled by the limitation and gradual subversion of the private capitalist sector.[83]

Nevertheless, it must be remembered that India was viewed as a developing country with a relatively advanced capitalist structure where the national bourgeoisie and working class had already formed as distinct classes. On the other hand, the potentialities of revolutionary democrats were seen to be realized only in such areas as Africa where class relations had not yet crystallized. Thus, for example, in drawing attention for the first time in Soviet literature to the independent political role played by army officers, the "bureaucratic bourgeoisie,"[84] students and the intelligentsia, Mirskii qualified his remarks by noting that in such countries as India where the national bourgeoisie was unquestionably in power, these social layers did not play an independent role since they were already enmeshed in the social layers of a class stratified society.[85]

---

[82] G. I. Mirskii, "Creative Marxism and Problems of the National Liberation Movement," *Mirovaia Ekonomika i Mezhdunarodnye Otnosheniia*, No. 2 (1963), in *JPRS* No. 19, 821, 64.

[83] This point must be credited to V. I. Pavlov and I. B. Red'ko, "Leninskii Soiuz Mirovogo Sotsializma s Natsional'no-Osvoboditel'nym Dvizheniem," *Narody Azii i Afriki*, No. 5 (1963), 21.

[84] This term referred to conservative bureaucrats whose life style was bourgeois, but who did not own any means of production, nor exploit hired labor; being dependent for their income on the state sector, they supported it but largely for their own personal enrichment.

[85] See, G. I. Mirskii's remarks at the aforementioned 1964 conference on developing countries in "Sotsializm, Kapitalizm, Slaborazvitye Strany," *Mirovaia Ekonomika i Mezhdunarodnye Otnosheniia*, No. 6 (1964), 62-63.

It would appear then, that revolutionary democrats, who came from the ranks of these independent social strata, had little chance of establishing their authority. The traditional formula of working class hegemony as a prerequisite for fundamental socio-economic transformations would seem to apply.[86]

Furthermore, while there was a marked difference of opinion on how to evaluate the socialist doctrines emergent from the "Third World," there was not such discord with respect to Nehru's dictum of constructing "a society on the socialist model"—which was clearly seen as a slogan utilized by the national bourgeoisie to preserve their influence. Indeed, the most charitable treatment of this Indian variant of socialism appeared in a 1964 article by Iu. Ostrovitianov, in which he identified it with the struggle for independent capitalist development with a strong state sector and elements of national planning.[87] Ostrovitianov added, however, that Nehru's brand of socialism, which was akin to West European democratic socialism, could give way, as present circumstances indicated, to anti-Communist hysteria.

In answer to the question of whether India was qualified for the non-capitalist path of development, from the above it seems clear that while she was eligible, her transition was predicted to take place in much more traditional forms. In contrast to other Afro-Asian countries, importance continued to be attached to the Indian Communist Party's central role in the national liberation revolution. However, it would be judicious to add the following proviso: Prior to its elevation to the ranks of a country "on the socialist path of construction," Egypt was considered, along with India, as an underdeveloped country with a highly developed

---

[86] This is advanced by V. I. Pavlov and I. B. Red'ko, "Gosudarstvo Natsional'noi Demokratii i Perekhod K Nekapitalisticheskomu Razvitiiu," *Narody Azii i Afriki*, No. 1 (1963), 34. In this regard, it is interesting that A. M. Mel'nikov, in an article on the movement for agrarian reform in India, identified revolutionary democratic tendencies with the CPI and its peasant affiliate, the All-India Kisan Sabha, and cited the Communist-led government in Kerala in 1957 as an example of a revolutionary democratic regime. See, A. M. Mel'nikov, "Bor'ba Indiiskogo Krest'ianstva za Radikal'nye Agrarnye Reformy," *Narody Azii i Afriki*, No. 5 (1964), 84-85. Obviously then, revolutionary democrats had not only not supplanted Communists in India but were in fact equated with Communist rule there.

[87] Iu. Ostrovitianov, *op. cit.*, 84.

capitalist structure. Thus, one cannot rule out the possibility that given the ascendence of a radical non-Communist leadership in India, the Soviets might also confer on it the appellation "revolutionary democrat" and thereby doom the Indian Communists to historical insignificance. Such a turnabout, to be sure, would require some theoretical gymnastics, but then again this is a service Soviet scholars have often rendered in the past.

TOWARDS A REALISTIC PERSPECTIVE OF ECONOMIC DEVELOPMENT

While revisionist thought on the "non-capitalist path of development" reached its peak in Khrushchev's last year of power, there emerged at the same time a contrapuntal tendency towards greater realism which gradually permeated Soviet thinking on the strategy of economic development. As we have recorded in previous chapters, the Soviets attached main priority to the development of heavy industry in their strategy of economic development with allowance made for the capabilities of various underdeveloped countries to undertake such a program. Possessing most of the natural resources and a potentially wide internal market, India was seen as one of several Afro-Asian countries suited to such an endeavor. It should be stressed that priority on heavy industrial growth was engendered by a strong ideological bias. However, in the 1960's this doctrinaire insistence on the development of heavy industry gradually gave way under the influence of economic realism, towards a more differentiated approach.

However, at the beginning of the decade, the commitment to heavy industrialization remained as strong as ever. Indeed, V. A. Kondrat'ev in his chapter in the 1960 work, *Problems of Industrialization of the Sovereign Underdeveloped Countries of Asia*, maintained the traditional view that production of the means of production was the very essence of the process of industrialization.[88] Other Soviet analysts added that heavy industrialization was the key to the fast growth of productive

---

[88] *Problemy Industrializatsii Suverennykh Slaborazvitykh Stran Azii (Indiia, Indoneziia, Birma)* (Moscow, 1960), p. 318.

forces,[89] provided the highest norms of labor productivity,[90] ensured the largest output of production per unit of capital investment and labor expenditure,[91] and gave the best prospects for the growth of capital accumulation.[92]

This is not to say that Soviet authors ignored the need for the development of an economic infrastructure. Indeed, the development of a modern communication and transportation network and an energy base was recognized as important adjuncts to the process of industrialization. However, it was felt that Western emphasis on its development was derivative from the needs of their own operations in these countries. In an article polemicizing with Western economists, N. Shmelev argued that the process of industrialization would itself generate the construction of infrastructural supports and interpreted Western priority to its development as but a thinly veiled attempt to obstruct the industrialization of underdeveloped countries.[93]

While the Soviets continued to show strong support for the development of a capital goods sector, one senses that below the surface doubts existed even then. This may be deduced from the facts that while in the early 1960's Soviet scholars levelled sharp and highly defensive criticisms of Western economic development strategies, as the decade wore on they began to adopt many of the same positions which had earlier been condemned as "false, bourgeois" concepts. To be sure, the full expression of these new views did not take place until after Khrushchev's ouster, and therefore, full consideration of this transition will be undertaken in the next chapter. For the moment, however, it would be useful to set

[89] V. A. Shchetinin, "Pomoshch' Stran Sotsialisticheskogo Lageria-Vazhnyi Faktor Nezavisimogo Natsional'nogo Razvitiia Osvobodivshikhsia Narodov," *Voprosy Ekonomiki*, No. 6 (1961), 78.

[90] V. Tiagunenko, "Principal Structural Changes in the Economies of Underdeveloped Countries," *Mirovaia Ekonomika i Mezhdunarodnye Otnosheniia*, No. 3 (1960), in *Problems of Economics*, III, No. 8, 59-61.

[91] V. D. Shchetinin, "Rol' Pomoshchi Stran Mirovoi Sotsialisticheskoi Sistemy v Razvitii Ekonomiki Molodykh Natsional'nykh Gosudarstv," *Institut Mezhdunarodnykh Otnoshenii, Uchenie Zapiski*, Seriia Ekonomicheskaia, vyp. 6 (1961), 12.

[92] N. Shmelev, "O Nekapitalisticheskom Puti Razvitiia Ekonomicheski Otstalykh Stran," *Voprosy Ekonomiki*, No. 5 (1962), 76.

[93] N. Shmelev, "Burzhuaznye Teorii Konservatsii Otstalosti Slaborazvitykh Stran," *Voprosy Ekonomiki*, No. 7 (1961), 105.

forth some of the initial critiques as a basis for further comparison.

Initiating this barrage of criticism, V. Tiagunenko in a 1960 article on Western "aid" programs, castigated Western concern that trade with underdeveloped countries be based on the principle of comparative costs, since such considerations meant continued emphasis on export specializations which would condemn these countries to remain agrarian raw material appendages of the West.[94] In addition, he argued that the Western concept of staged economic growth, with priority attached first to the creation of an economic infrastructure, followed by the construction of enterprises processing raw materials, then by the development of light industry and only after an indefinite period by the production of the means of productions, was in fact designed to prevent industrialization and to maintain these countries' backwardness and dependence on the West.

Underlying Tiagunenko's criticism was the widely shared view that economic independence was the chief goal of the process of economic development. By this was meant the liberation of underdeveloped countries from the binding ties of trade and aid with the West and the elimination of the dominance of foreign private capital in their economies. The most effective path towards this goal was seen to be forced industrialization patterned as close to the Soviet experience as resources would allow. Indeed, it seemed at this time that the concept of industrialization became inextricably linked with the task of attaining economic independence. In a 1961 study of development aid, for example, L. A. Fituni and V. D. Shchetinin argued that only that type of industrialization which led to the construction of an independent national economy could be considered economic development.[95] Those Western economists who based their recommendations on economic considerations of raising income per unit of capital, the authors warned, were proposing only the modernization of the existent iniquitous economic system which bound these countries to the world market on the basis of non-equivalent exchange of high-priced industrial imports for low-priced raw material exports. The authors further

---

[94] V. Tiagunenko, "Reaktsionnaia Sushchnost' Imperialisticheskikh Programm 'Pomoshch' ' Slaborazvitym Stranam," *Voprosy Ekonomiki*, No. 12 (1960), 65.

[95] L. A. Fituni and V. D. Shchetinin, *Problemy Pomoshchi Ekonomicheski Slaborazvitym Stranam* (Moscow, 1961), p. 30.

argued that such prescriptions would not generate any essential structural change which was of vital importance for the economic development of these countries.⁹⁶ Adding to this line of thought, N. Shmelev, at a 1962 conference organized by the Institute of World Economy and International Relations, stated that it would be "non-sensical to apply the concept of profitability in its narrow private-capitalist meaning to processes which in truth touch upon the structure of the economy as a whole,...."⁹⁷ The crux of these arguments, then, was that considerations of economic cost must be subordinate to the basic need for structural change in the economies of developing countries.

In general then, Soviet economists appeared quite defensive in criticizing their Western counterparts for emphasizing economic criteria. In the light of subsequent important changes in Soviet thinking on these problems, it would appear that such disputations were not merely propaganda exercises, but also intended to stifle the articulation of similar views among Soviet scholars. These efforts went for nought, however, since there soon appeared in the Soviet scholarly literature ideas which echoed those of Western economists in heeding the principle of cost effectiveness in the determination of development strategies.

This theoretical transition towards economic realism was set in motion by R. A. Andreasian and A. El'ianov in an article on monoculture specialization in underdeveloped countries.⁹⁸ Therein, the authors reversed the earlier Soviet position by expressing support for the continued development of export branches on the grounds that they exhibited a higher degree of labor productivity and boosted levels of employment.⁹⁹ By stressing economic criteria, the authors exhibited this inceptive proclivity towards economic

⁹⁶ *Ibid.*, p. 51.

⁹⁷ N. Shmelev, "Bourgeois Economists on the Role of the State in the Economy of the Underdeveloped Countries," *Mirovaia Ekonomika i Mezhdunarodnye Otnosheniia*, No. 4 (1962), in *JPRS*, No. 14, 607.

⁹⁸ R. Andreasian and A. El'ianov, "Monotovarnaia Spetsializatsiia i Ekonomicheskaia Nezavisimost'," *Mirovaia Ekonomika i Mezhdunarodnye Otnosheniia*, No. 6 (1962), 85-97, in *JPRS* No. 14, 870.

⁹⁹ *Ibid.*, 86. For a lucid presentation of the previous argument against the development of export specializations, see, V. D. Shchetinin, "Pomoshch' Stran Sotsialisticheskogo Lageria—Vazhnyi Faktor Nezavisimogo Natsional'nogo Razvitiia Osvobodivshikhsia Narodov," *Voprosy Ekonomiki*, No. 6 (1961), 74.

realism which contained an implicit reconciliation with the existent economic relationships of the world capitalist market.

Another landmark in this theoretical transformation was the publication a year later of an article in *International Affairs* by V. Rymalov, in which this specialist on foreign aid and trade defined economic development not as the quest for economic independence but as the steady growth of labor productivity—a purely economic category.[100]

Rymalov left ideological considerations even further behind by enumerating a list of basic problems which all underdeveloped countries, regardless of whether they were pursuing a capitalist or non-capitalist path, must face. These were: the solution of the agrarian problem, the most rational direction of industrial development, the growth of labor productivity, educational and cultural advancement and the solution of the problem of unemployment (which, he felt, could be done only through the development of manufacturing industry).[101] The very posing of these common problems, which cut across the standard Soviet typology based on degrees of progressiveness, suggests a certain hardheaded, common sense approach to the perennial problems confronting all underdeveloped countries.

A major breakthrough in the advance towards economic realism took place at the above-mentioned 1964 conference organized by the editors of *Mirovaia Ekonomika i Mezhdunarodnye Otnosheniia*, at which problems of economic development were discussed by leading Soviet experts in the field. G. I. Mirskii began the discussion by expressly criticizing the "recently widespread" view that economic development had to begin for any developing country with the creation of heavy industry. He pointed out that where natural and socio-economic conditions were unfavorable, attempts to create a heavy industrial base might prove so ineffective as to discredit the very idea of industrialization.[102] In this same iconoclastic spirit, R. A. Ul'ianovskii refuted earlier formulations on the question of economic development priorities by stating that the industrialization

---

[100] V. Rymalov, "The Social Preconditions for Economic Independence," *International Affairs*, No. 6 (1963), 23.

[101] *Ibid.*, 19.

[102] For his comments, see, "Sotsializm, Kapitalizm, Slaborazvitye Strany," *Mirovaia Ekonomika i Mezhdunarodnye Otnosheniia*, No. 4 (1964), 122.

process might not necessarily commence with the construction of heavy industry, but might begin with the creation of an economic infrastructure even before the construction of large scale industry. What was important, Ul'ianovskii noted, was that foreign monopolies not be permitted to harness the economic infrastructure for their own interests. For good measure, he added that it was "not necessary to copy the economic experience of the USSR everywhere."[103] With Mirskii and Ul'ianovskii leading the way, Soviet scholars were beginning to gravitate towards the perspective of their Western counterparts on the problems of economic development.

The conference was also significant in that it touched upon the problem of employment and its relation to development strategies. As we have noted above (see p. 187), Soviet analysts were cognizant that the experience of industrialization in developing countries, while raising labor productivity, had not appreciably reduced widescale unemployment produced by agrarian overpopulation. On the other hand, traditional labor-intensive economic branches, such as the crafts industry, were not regarded favorably since they did not generate fast economic growth.[104] Yet, while opting for industrialization, Soviet scholars maintained a discreet silence on this latent problem.

Although the conference did not elicit a solution to this dilemma, it did bring the problem more clearly into focus. In his commentary at the proceedings, V. Rymalov posed the problem thus: "How can the hundreds of millions of people be included in highly productive labor?"[105] Following Rymalov's lead, V. Kollontai argued that if the criterion of employment became the determinant factor in devising strategies of industrialization, then it would be necessary to commence with the development of light industry and only gradually shift to the construction of heavy industry, since light industry afforded better opportunities to absorb surplus labor than heavy industry. Yet, while tracing this problem through to

[103] *Ibid.*, 122.

[104] For a more detailed elaboration of the Soviet view on this point, see, L. B. Alaev, "Kustarnye Promysly i Melkaia Promyshlennost'," in *Ekonomika Sovremennoi Indii* (Moscow, 1960), pp. 319-22.

[105] "Sotsializm, Kapitalizm, Slaborazvitye Strany," *Mirovaia Ekonomika i Mezhdunarodnye Otnosheniia*, No. 4 (1964), 126.

its logical conclusion, Kollontai stopped short of embracing this formula which had earlier been proposed by Western economists. Rather, he rejected the use of any one set of criteria, such as employment, for the determination of industrial priorities and opted instead for a program of balanced growth with the construction of an industrial complex of mutually supporting enterprises.[106] Despite his timorous backtracking, however, Kollontai had made a significant contribution in bringing the problem of unemployment and its relation to economic development strategies into the open.

As a whole, the conference served as a stimulant to the questioning of the established positions on development strategies. Yet, the fruits of this discussion became manifest only after the departure of Khrushchev and the installation in power of a leadership more attentive to considerations of economic effectiveness.

However, it should be noted that a practical indication of Soviet respect for the principle of economic efficiency was evident, even at this time, in the consideration of the problem of nationalization of foreign property. During the early 1960's, Soviet writers warned that sweeping programs of nationalization might prove economically disastrous,[107] and that nationalization of foreign-owned enterprises must be preceded by thorough economic and socio-political preparations with due considerations given to the international and domestic political situations.[108] In an especially cautious posture, G. V. Ignatenko stated that compensation for nationalized property was justified on both political and economic grounds, but added that the amount and conditions of compensation must be determined by the states concerned.[109]

This circumspect approach towards nationalization was especially in evidence with respect to India. The major targets for nationalization there were foreign-owned tea plantations, coal mines, oil

---

[106] *Ibid.*, 127.

[107] See, G. I. Mirskii, "Creative Marxism and Problems of the National Liberation Revolution," *Mirovaia Ekonomika i Mezhdunarodnye Otnosheniia*, No. 2 (1963), in *JPRS*, No. 19, 821.

[108] V. Tiagunenko, "Aktual'nye Voprosy Nekapitalisticheskogo Puti Razvitiia," *Mirovaia Ekonomika i Mezhdunarodnye Otnosheniia*, No. 11 (1964), 16.

[109] G. V. Ignatenko, *op. cit.*, 16.

refineries, management agencies and the large national banks.[110] While the chief aim here was to undermine the positions of foreign (and particularly English) capital and the Indian monopolies, certain practical economic considerations were operative as well. Specifically, it was felt that a major reason for the low productivity of Indian coal mines was the fact that English capital, which owned many of the mines, refused to invest needed capital for their modernization since they feared nationalization in any event.[111] Government intervention was needed here especially since scarce coal resources remained a basic problem in India's industrialization program.[112] Hence, India represented a typical case of Soviet respect for the principle of economic effectiveness when it came to the question of nationalization.

SOVIET AID TO INDIA

The perceptual shift towards economic realism in the determination of development strategies, that has been observed above, could obviously be expected to have a far-reaching impact on the character and direction of the Soviet aid program. However, this impact could be felt more readily in programs to smaller and more recent aid recipients who were not suited to the Soviet pattern of industrialization. On the other hand, Soviet aid to India, which was deemed capable of engaging in a broad scale program of industrialization, had started in the 1950's and subsequent Soviet aid projects there were designed to secure the maximum effectiveness of earlier ones. Changes in the Soviet aid program to India were therefore likely to be incremental. Given the continued stability

---

[110] This list is derived from the following works: V. Ia. Arkhipov, *op. cit.*, p. 107, and *Problemy Industrializatsii Suverennykh Slaboravitykh Stran Azii (Indiia, Indoneziia, Birma)* (Moscow, 1960), pp. 115 and 433.

[111] See, V. Kondrat'ev, "Novye Tendentsii v Strukture Ekonomiki Sovremennoi Indii," *Mirovaia Ekonmika i Mezhdunarodnye Otnosheniia*, No. 7 (1961), 55, and G. I. Mamrykin, *op. cit.*, p. 195.

[112] For evidence that the Soviets were well aware of this deficiency, consult P. S. Oraevskii, "Obshchie Voprosy Organizatsii Nauki v Indii," *Kratkie Soobshcheniia Instituta Narodov Azii*, Kn. 51 (1962), 211; R. N. Dolnykova, "Metallurgicheskaia Promyshlennost' v Gosudarstvennom Sektore Indii," *Kratkie Soobshcheniia Instituta Narodov Azii*, Kn. 75 (1964), 20, and G. I. Mamrykin, *op. cit.*, p. 181.

of Indo-Soviet ties, a major alteration was really out of the question.

It is not surprising, therefore, that Soviet writing on Soviet aid did not offer any prescriptions for new programs, especially in the case of India.[113] Unblemished propagandistic accounts of Soviet aid programs continued to exemplify Soviet writing in this sensitive area.[114]

The only perceptible criticism of Soviet aid in India was a rather obscure one which affected but a minor aspect of the program. It will be remembered from the first chapter that the Soviet contract to build the Bokaro steel mill on a turn-key basis without the participation of the private engineering design firm of Dastur and Co., elicited a sharp protest in the Indian press (see above, p. 44). At the time of this agreement, Mamrykin's book on the Indian economy appeared, in which Dastur's preliminary project report, recommending the utilization of several Soviet techniques in ferrous metallurgy, was favorably mentioned.[115] It would seem that Mamrykin was in effect seeking to disarm internal suspicions over dealing with a private designing firm by drawing attention to the fact that their report called for close Soviet collaboration. Although this point is admittedly speculative, it may be inferred that Mamrykin's observations constitute an oblique criticism of the Soviet Bokaro agreement. The Soviet refusal for political reasons to submit their aid program to critical public scrutiny did not prevent mounting criticism that their aid was not being put to proper use. R. S. Gorchakov, in an article on Indian state capitalism, for example, referred to sharp criticism in the Indian Communist press regarding an alleged shift on the part of the government towards "restrained relations" in dealing with aid

---

[113] In their 1961 work on aid, Fituni and Shchetinin did however remark that the development of atomic energy in India would be more expensive than the development of other forms of energy. Fituni and Shchetinin, *op. cit.*, p. 90. This may be interpreted as a clue to a Soviet decision to downplay assistance in this field, even though they had just signed an agreement to build a nuclear reactor in India. (See above, Fn. 104, p. 160).

[114] For a typical example of this genre, see, E. K. Semenov, "Ekonomicheskoe Sotrudnichestvo Sovetskogo Soiuza i Drugikh Sotsialisticheskikh Stran s Indiei," *Narody Azii i Afriki*, No. 1 (1964), 53-60.

[115] G. I. Mamrykin, *op. cit.*, p. 192.

from socialist countries.[116] This was manifest in instances of failure on the part of the Indian government to comply with the concrete terms of aid agreements, in the propensity to employ Western instead of Soviet technicians, even though the maintenance costs of the former were higher, and finally in the tendency to consider negotiations with socialist countries only as a bargaining tool to gain concessions from the industrialized capitalist states. Thus, although the Soviets continued to justify their aid partially on the grounds that it forced the West to concede better terms of aid, they, at the same time, were beginning to resent the fact that their aid was often used exclusively for this purpose.

EVALUATING THE PERFORMANCE OF THE INDIAN STATE SECTOR

A more pressing concern, however, was the poor performance of the Indian public sector in which the Soviets had made such a large investment of foreign aid.[117] With increasing difficulties in the operation of the state sector which generated demands from the political right in India for a major overhaul or for dismantling it entirely, the Soviets were put on the defensive and forced to acknowledge that the performance of state sector had been far from satisfactory. The Soviet writers explained that India's weak financial situation had forced her to limit imports which had resulted in delays in the construction of several state sector projects.[118] These production delays in turn had lowered projected capacities of the industrial plants.[119] Symptomatic of these delays was the fact that India was absorbing the aid already extended to her at a

[116] R. S. Gorchakov, "Nekotorye Voprosy Razvitiia Gosudarstvennogo Kapitalizma v Indii v Sviazi s Tret'im Piatiletnim Planom," *Vestnik Leningradskogo Universiteta*, Seriia Ekonomiki, Filosofii i Prava, vyp. 4, No. 23 (1961), 45.

[117] Indeed so large was the Soviet stake in the state sector that some writers equated the progressiveness of any aid program with its attitude towards the state sector. See, Fituni and Shchetinin, *op. cit.*, p. 53.

[118] V. A. Shchetinin, "Economic Assistance of Socialist Countries to Young National States," *Voprosy Ekonomiki*, No. 6. (1960), in *Problems of Economics*, III, No. 4, 38.

[119] V. A. Shchetinin, "Economic Assistance of Socialist Countries to Young National States," *Voprosy Ekonomiki*, No. 6, (1960), in *Problems of Economics*, III, No. 4, 38.

very low rate—a problem that was attributed partially to the failure of Western donors to observe time schedules for the delivery of credits and to errors in planning on the Indian side.[120]

Yet, production delays were only a minor aspect of a more serious problem—i.e., the lack of profitability of the state sector as a whole. Here the Soviets could not fail to respond to criticism in India that government-run enterprises were incurring large losses. Yet, their response was far from uniform. When the problem was first raised at the beginning of the decade, Soviet writers acknowledged that the Indian state enterprises were bringing insufficient returns, but argued that this was due to the fact that the production process itself was just being mastered and that the branches of the economy which the state was developing were either backward or totally new and therefore could not be expected to bring fast returns.[121] The problem of unprofitability was thus seen as a temporary one which would be overcome as production techniques were mastered. Yet, as we have seen above in a different context (see p. 201), there was also attendant a tendency to tolerate low norms of profit. N. Shmelev's interesting statement quoted above, was in effect an apologia for the unprofitability of state enterprises, which, according to him, were running in the red only "from the private capitalist standpoint."[122]

However, it should be noted that Shmelev's opinions were not generally shared by his colleagues. With the trend towards economic realism emergent in Khrushchev's last years, Soviet scholars paid increasing attention to the importance of profitability in evaluating the state sector. M. A. Skliar, for example, argued that the functions of state capitalism could be considered completed only when state enterprises became a basic source of revenue in

[120] I. I. Egorov, "Finansirovanie Piatiletnykh Planov Indii (1951-1962)," *Kratkie Soobshcheniia Instituta Narodov Azii*, Kn. 75 (1964), 8.

[121] See, *Problemy Industrializatsii Suverennykh Slaborazvitykh Stran Azii (Indiia, Indoneziia, Birma)* (Moscow, 1960), p. 189, and E. Bragina and O. Ul'rikh, *Gosudarstvennyi Kapitalizm v Promyshlennosti Stran Vostoka* (Moscow, 1961), pp. 54-55.

[122] N. Shmelev, *loc. cit.* In an earlier article, Shmelev defended the non-profitability of state enterprises by arguing that "the concept of profitability in the process of development of a backward economy loses the narrow practical content with which the defenders of Imperialism invest it." N. Shmelev, "Burzhuaznye Teorii Konservatsii Otstalosti Slaborazvitykh Stran," *Voprosy Ekonomiki*, No. 7 (1961), 108.

the state budget.[123]

Although the Soviets became more concerned with the economic performance of state sector projects, there were differences of opinion over just how unprofitable was the Indian state sector. There were some analysts who, in fact, felt that the Indian state enterprises were marginally profitable. Having earlier supported the view that the Indian state sector was unprofitable, E. A. Bragina in a 1963 article produced some Indian data which showed profits ranging from 1 to 10% on capital invested in 24 of 35 public enterprises, which, she believed, proved the effectiveness of their operations.[124] Providing supportive evidence, B. N. Brodovich later found that 19 state enterprises in India between 1956 and 1959 registered profits, and further argued that the growth of income of government enterprises after mastering the production process was fully regular—a fact which he felt exposed the "myth" circulated by Indian capitalists that state enterprises were organically unprofitable.[125] Nevertheless, other scholars found profit levels to be much lower.[126] By and large, most Soviet analysts were not nearly as optimistic as Bragina and Brodovich, and the problem of low profitability continued to draw attention. This problem was deemed serious not only because profits from state enterprises could become a firm source of revenue for the state sector as a whole and thereby lessen India's strong dependence on foreign aid,[127] but

---

[123] M. A. Skliar, "O Vnutrennikh Istochnikakh Gosudarstvennykh Nakoplennii v Molodykh Politicheski Nezavisimykh Gosudarstvakh," *Vestnik Leningradskogo Universiteta,* Seriia Ekonomiki, Filosofii i Prava, vyp. 1, No. 5 (1964), 34. Skliar even suggested that the study of Soviet experience in obtaining cost effectiveness be undertaken to raise the profitability of state enterprises.

[124] E. A. Bragina, "Tretii Piatiletnii Plan i Ekonomika Indii," *Narody Azii i Afriki,* No. 2 (1963), 38.

[125] B. N. Brodovich, "Rol' Kredita v Razvitii Gosudarstvennogo Sektora Ekonomiki Indii," *Kratkie Soobshcheniia Instituta Narodov Azii,* Kn. 79 (1964), 12.

[126] I. I. Egorov, for example, found that Indian state enterprises on the whole registered only a 0.3% return on investment capital. I. I. Egorov, *op. cit.,* 6.

[127] I. I. Egorov criticized Indian planners for placing excessive reliance on foreign aid sources in planning the budget for the Third Five Year Plan. He added that potential internal sources of income, such as profits from private corporations and non-productive consumption by propertied classes, had not yet been tapped but could contribute significant budgetary revenues. See, I. I. Egorov, *op. cit.,* 17.

also, and perhaps mainly, because it was tarnishing the reputation of the state sector with which so much Soviet prestige was involved.

To be sure, the Soviets were not at a loss to explain the poor performance. Besides the aforementioned construction delays, much attention was also focused on the problem of administrative incompetence in the Indian state sector. Thus, for example, S. I. Tiul'panov and G. I. Chufrin in a 1962 article probing problems of the Indian state sector, warned against bureaucratic methods of management, administrative delays, poorly trained personnel and cited several scandalous cases of corruption in the management of these enterprises—all of which was being used by right wing elements in India in a dangerous campaign to remove parliamentary control over the state sector under the slogan "abolish bureaucratic control by politicians."[128] Another aspect of the administrative problem was the extremely high overhead costs. The Soviets felt that too large a proportion of the budget was being spent merely on maintenance of a government apparatus that had doubled in size in the previous decade.[129]

Exemplary of these administrative problems was the Indian State Trading Corporation which had been set up in 1956 to handle trade with socialist countries. L. A. Vladimirskii, writing on this institution in a 1964 article, found that despite India's emphasis on expanding the nomenclature of her exports to socialist countries, very little progress had been made in this direction, largely because the State Trading Corporation had very few officials knowledgeable in the problems of foreign trade and in the import needs of socialist countries—this despite an

---

[128] S. I. Tiul'panov and G. I. Chufrin, "Nekotorye Voprosy Razvitiia Gosudarstvennogo Sektora Promyshlennosti Indii v Period Tret'ego Piatiletnego Plana," *Vestnik Leningradskogo Universiteta,* Seriia Ekonomiki, Filosofii i Prava, vyp 3, No. 17 (1962), 12-13. Tiul'panov and Chufrin were not the first to point out this problem of administrative cadres. A. I. Levkovskii in a 1960 article noted that incompetent officials in a number of cases were running state enterprises and added that there was a basic lack of coordination on important problems of economic development because of disagreements among several ministers. See, A. I. Levkovskii, "Osnovye Problemy Razvitiia Gosudarstvennogo Kapitalizma v Sovremennoi Indii," in *Gosudarstvennyi Kapitalizm v Stranakh Vostoka* (Moscow, 1960), p. 28.

[129] M. A. Skliar, *op. cit.,* 29.

THE LATE KHRUSHCHEV YEARS

enormous staff of over 500 in New Delhi.[130]

The Soviets were not at a loss, however, to prescribe remedial measures for this set of problems. Specifically, they recommended that steps be taken to economize on overhead costs for the administrative apparatus of the state sector,[131] and that the management of state enterprises be "democratized" by including workers' representatives in positions of managerial responsibility and by setting up workers' councils to maximize their participation.[132] Thus, the solution to the administrative problem was visualized in political terms.[133]

Besides the administrative problem, there were other contributing factors to the poor performance of the state sector, such as problems of planning in a capitalist market economy,[134] underutilization of existing capacities because of shortages of raw materials and insufficient transport and energy bases, and also the diversion of funds for food imports and military purposes.[135] But perhaps

[130] L. A. Vladimirskii, "Nekotorye Voprosy Razvitiia Gosudarstvennogo Sektora vo Vneshnei Torgovle Indii," *Kratkie Soobshcheniia Instituta Narodov Azii*, Kn. 75 (1964), 67-68. Vladimirskii also articulated Soviet dissatisfaction with their trade relations with India by pointing to the need for India to improve the quality of their exports to the Soviet Union. Further elaborating upon this problem, A. S. Baskin, in an article on Indo-West German trade, asserted that an obstacle to Indian trade expansion was the comparatively high costs of her exports. This was especially true of textiles, since manufacturers, reliant on the home market, refused to raise the quality of their products and lower production costs by modernizing their factories. See, A. S. Baskin, "O Torgovlykh Otnosheniiakh Indii s FRG," *Vestnik Leningradskogo Universiteta*, Seriia Ekonomiki, Filosofii i Prava, vyp. 1, No. 5 (1964), 156.

[131] I. I. Egorov, *op. cit.*, 18.

[132] S. I. Tiul'panov and G. I. Chufrin, *op. cit.*, 13. Tiul'panov and Chufrin, whose article is very extensive on this subject, also recommended that a sliding pay scale geared to changes in living costs be introduced at state enterprises—a measure which they felt would remove some of the reasons for strikes in the state sector. *Ibid.*, 17.

[133] Indeed, in an interview granted to this writer at the Institute of Orientology (the Institute of the Peoples of Asia reverted to its old title in 1969), G. G. Kotovskii, the noted specialist on Indian agrarian relations, acknowledged that administrative difficulties in India were viewed mainly as a political problem. The interview was conducted in August 1969 during a visit to the USSR.

[134] L. A. Fituni, "Problems of Planning in the Underdeveloped Sovereign Countries of Asia," *Mirovaia Ekonomika i Mezhdunarodnye Otnosheniia*, No. 6 (1962), in *JPRS*, No. 14, 870, 97-100.

[135] E. A. Bragina, *op. cit.*, 48.

the most basic reason was the fact that the state sector was rooted in the wider capitalist economy and, as such, played an auxiliary role. As we have noted earlier, the state sector benefited the private sector through a favorable price structure for its goods and services by absorbing losses in unprofitable but essential branches of the economy and in a number of other ways. In short, the Soviets recognized that the state sector constituted a form of government subsidization of the private capitalist economy. As such, it was not necessarily expected to show profitable returns.[136] Paralleling the trend towards economic realism noted above with reference to Soviet thinking on development strategies, tolerant attitudes towards the financial difficulties of the Indian state sector gave way to a more "businesslike" concern for cost effectiveness. The Soviets were obviously becoming more sensitive to the problem of how their aid was being utilized. An important indication of this tendency was the attempt by the aid expert, G. Prokhorov, to elaborate a set of criteria which would measure the effectiveness of Soviet aid mainly in terms of its contribution to economic development.[137] The Soviets were thus seeking ways of maximizing the return for their foreign aid.

PERCEPTIONS OF THE AGRARIAN QUESTION IN INDIA

A full consideration of Soviet views of India at this point could not be considered complete without an examination of Soviet perceptions of the agrarian question. Agrarian overpopulation and the food problem, after all, lay at the heart of India's economic problems.

To the Soviet viewpoint, food imports not only increased India's dependence on the United States but also diverted financial

---

[136] Making this very point at the 1964 conference organized by *Mirovaia Ekonomika i Mezhdunarodnye Otnosheniia*, V. Kollontai strongly criticized the view held by many Indian economists that state enterprises should be run according to the principle of neither profit nor loss. See his comments in "Sotsializm, Kapitalizm, Slaborazvitye Strany," *Mirovaia Ekonomika i Mezhdunarodnye Otnosheniia*, No. 4 (1964), 125.

[137] G. Prokhorov, "Sotrudnichestvo Mirovoi Sotsialisticheskoi Sistemy So Slaborazvitymi Stranami," *Voprosy Ekonomiki*, No. 11 (1962), 84.

resources from her pressing needs for industrial development.[138] India's food deficits attracted much Soviet attention, as evidenced, for example, by the publication in 1961 of a small book by A. L. Batalov and R. P. Gurvich, entitled *Can India Feed Herself?* The authors, having examined the state of Indian agriculture, came to the conclusion that India had "enormous potential possibilities to feed herself, but all those resources... could be used only on the condition of a radical solution of the agrarian question."[139] As in the previous decade, Soviet scholars looked to agrarian reform as the key to increased agricultural productivity.

Even more than in the preceding decade, Soviet scholars displayed greater sensitivity to the question of just which type of agrarian reforms would meet this problem. As Avakov and Mirskii advised their colleagues in 1962, it was now not enough to merely criticize reforms and then make general statements on the need for more radical ones: "The moot point is just what concretely radical reform is desired."[140] In contrast to earlier views which put forth as the immediate goal a general redistribution of land to the peasantry, Soviet analysts now became increasingly aware that this would not substantially augment marketed agricultural commodities, since any increases in food production among the small and middle peasantry were usually immediately consumed.[141] Moreover, it was recognized that small parcels of land were unsuitable for modern agro-technical measures.[142] As R. A. Ul'ianovskii

---

[138] R. P. Gurvich, *Sel'skoe Khoziaistvo Indii i Polozhenie Krest'ianstva* (Moscow, 1960), p. 212. The Soviets did not, however, urge cessation of these food imports, but saw them rather as temporary means of alleviating food crises.

[139] A. L. Batalov and R. P. Gurvich, *Mozhet-li Indiia Prokormit' Sebia?* (Moscow, 1961), p. 94. Characteristically, the reasons for the aggravation of India's food problems were seen as social and not demographic. The anti-Malthusian ideological shackle specifically ruled out birth control measures as a method of alleviating the problem. In fact, R. P. Gurvich, while recognizing the severity of the food crisis, stated that a large population was not a liability but rather an "enormous potential source for the creation of significant material values, for the accumulation of national wealth." R. P. Gurvich, *Sel'skoe Khoziaistvo Indii i Polozhenie Krest'ianstva* (Moscow, 1960), p. 213.

[140] R. Avakov and G. Mirskii, "The Class Structure in the Underdeveloped Countries," *Mirovaia Ekonomika i Mezhdunarodnye Otnosheniia*, No. 4 (1962), in *JPRS*, No. 14, 607, 38.

[141] A. L. Batalov and R. P. Gurvich, *op. cit.*, p. 41.

[142] On this point, consult E. Bragina and O. Ul'rikh, *op. cit.*, p. 57.

in a 1960 collection of articles on the Indian economy noted, the transition to large scale farming was unavoidable if India's food crisis were to be resolved.[143] Agricultural cooperatives were clearly seen to be the answer. Cooperative agriculture would substantially raise agricultural production through the application of more rational forms of labor organization and the introduction of machines, fertilizers and irrigation works—tasks which were beyond the capabilities of individual small peasant farms. Cooperatives were also seen as offering real possibilities for the solution of agrarian overpopulation.[144] Indeed, producers cooperatives "in the hands of progressive forces" were deemed nothing less than a point of departure for the non-capitalist path of development.[145]

The Soviets were also cognizant that just as the institutional machinery of state capitalism by itself offered no short cut to socialism, cooperative forms of agriculture were rooted in and reflective of existent socio-political conditions. India, with her comparatively extensive experience in agricultural cooperatives and the community development program, provided empirical evidence demonstrating this connection.

In the Soviet perspective, Indian cooperatives did not constitute a model worthy of emulation. Separate Soviet studies revealed that production and sales cooperatives in India were of diverse forms which reflected by and large the state of agrarian relations there.[146] First of all, there were 'pseudo-cooperatives' which were set up by landlords merely to accommodate themselves to the new reforms in India, but which represented nothing more than a masked form of previous feudal landlord relations. There were

---

[143] R. A. Ul'ianovskii, "Reformy Agrarnogo Stroia," in *Ekonomika Sovremennoi Indii* (Moscow, 1960), p. 108.

[144] N. Shmelev, "O Nekapitalisticheskom Puti Razvitiia Ekonomicheski Otstalykh Stran," *Voprosy Ekonomiki*, No. 5 (1962), 77.

[145] See, the remarks made by V. A. Popov at a conference on the agrarian and peasant questions held at the Institute of the Peoples of Asia in April 1964, summarized in Iu. G. Aleksandrov, "The Agrarian and Peasant Question in the Developing Countries of Asia and Africa at the Present Stage," *Narody Azii i Afriki*, No. 5 (1964), in *Soviet Anthropology and Archeology*, IV, No. 1 (Summer 1965), 61-62.

[146] Much of the information related above is extracted from L. K. Orleanskaia, "K Voprosu o Razvitii Proizvodstvennykh Zemledel'cheskikh Kooperativov v Indii," *Kratkie Soobshcheniia Instituta Narodov Azii*, Kn. 51 (1962), 49-59.

also cooperatives organized by Kulaks and landlords interested in capitalist development who took advantage of government credit to be free of usurer exploitation.[147] These cooperatives were marked by a relatively high organic composition of capital and a significant amount of productive reinvestment. Cooperatives of this type assisted the transition of agriculture to the course of capitalist development. While these cooperatives could be considered progressive in the sense that they limited usurer operations and enhanced agricultural productivity, they, at the same time, exploited the poorer peasant strata by often hiring them as field hands.[148] Hence, they were accelerating class differentiation in the village and hastening the progressive ruination of the poor peasantry.

Even with respect to the third type of agricultural cooperatives which grouped together the poor and landless peasants, Soviet agrarianists, though supportive, were not very optimistic regarding their present state. R. P. Gurvich did find, nevertheless, that a few of these poor peasant cooperatives showed good production results, even without modern equipment, largely as a result of a more rational organization of labor.[149] This had definitely improved the lot of their members. However, she added that positive results were attained by very few of these cooperatives and that some of them had in fact been ruined by excessive local taxation.[150] Further elaborating on this subject, L. K. Orleanskaia found that these cooperatives could develop and realize expanded reproduction only with constant and multi-sided government assistance.[151] In general their financial situation was much worse than the cooperatives composed of richer landowning peasants. She explained that the government promoted poor peasant cooperatives to develop fallow land and more significantly to reduce agrarian unemployment.

[147] However, R. P. Gurvich also noted that occasionally rich peasants had used cooperative credit to set up usurer operations on their own. See, Gurvich, *op. cit.*, p. 196.

[148] R. P. Gurvich, "Nekotorye Voprosy Razvitiia Sel'skogo Khoziaistva," in *Ekonomika Sovremennoi Indii* (Moscow, 1960), pp. 244ff.

[149] R. P. Gurvich, *Sel'skoe Khoziaistvo Indii i Polozhenie Krest'ianstva* (Moscow, 1960), p. 137.

[150] *Ibid.*, p. 140.

[151] L. K. Orleanskaia, *op. cit.*, 57.

The implication here was that these cooperatives were being subsidized and were likely to continue to depend on government support. Orleanskaia pessimistically concluded that these poor peasant cooperatives could not be considered a means of basic transformation of Indian agriculture, which would be impossible without far-reaching land reforms.[152]

Therefore, agricultural cooperatives with all their variety and complexity basically reflected the underlying agrarian structure. While they assisted the development of agrarian capitalism, they did not significantly affect pre-capitalist land relations. Where they had not been successful in obstructing the cooperative movement,[153] both landlords and usurers had accommodated themselves to the situation and even exploited cooperatives to their own advantage.[154] At best, the more productive cooperatives of rich peasants and former landlords were making a material contribution to India's needs for marketed foodstuffs, but at the social cost of further ruination of the masses of poor peasants. The cooperative movement, as it existed in India, then clearly did not meet Soviet expectations. Its conversion to a "point of departure for the non-capitalist path of development" depended on accompanying radical agrarian reforms.

With respect to agrarian reforms and the general evolution of agriculture in India, Soviet analysts were even less satisfied in the early 1960's than they were in the previous decade, due to the heightened expectations which accompanied the obsession with the non-capitalist path of development. The development of agrarian capitalism, which would have been seen as progressive in the 1950's, lost its former salience as the Soviets set their sight on socialized forms of agriculture. Nevertheless, it was not an inconsequential matter since widespread disagreement over the character of agrarian reforms in India and the degree of development of agrarian

---

[152] *Ibid.*, 59.

[153] Gurvich observed that some usurer groups who were actively opposed to state credit and cooperatives were able to limit government activities in this area in some states. See, R. P. Gurvich, *Sel'skoe Khoziaistvo Indii i Polozhenie Krest'ianstva* (Moscow, 1960), p. 127.

[154] For further elucidation, consult, L. K. Orleanskaia, "Sel'skokhoziaistvennye Sbytovye Kooperativy Indii," *Kratkie Soobshcheniia Instituta Narodov Azii*, Kn. 75 1964), 55.

capitalism continued to appear in the scholarly literature.[155]

As we have recorded in the previous chapter, divergent opinions over whether or not the reforms had benefited the peasantry were expressed at the December 1958 conference on agrarian reforms (see above, pp. 154-55). The general consensus there was that the reforms were purely of a landlord character. Nevertheless, the conference did not still debate on this subject.

As he had during the 1958 discussion, R. A. Ul'ianovskii continued to be the main spokesman for the view that the reforms had promoted agrarian capitalism and to some degree benefited the Indian peasantry. In an article on agrarian reform, published in the *Economy of Contemporary India*, he argued that while feudal vestiges had not disappeared, the agrarian reforms had nonetheless accelerated the formation of capitalist relations in the countryside with the crystallization of capitalist landlords and the separation of a rich Kulak layer from the rest of the peasantry.[156] Admittedly, the bourgeois evolution of the landlords and Kulaks was a complex and contradictory process with old methods of exploitation often found in combination with new ones. Far from exclusively favoring the landlords, the reforms had benefited not only the rich peasants, who received the possibility of land ownership through redemption payments to former landlords, but also the middle peasants, who were now becoming defended tenants with future prospects of land ownership. The poor peasants, however, had suffered insofar as they were subjected to mass eviction where the landlords, consonant with the new agrarian legislation, had opted to farm their lands themselves.[157] Although Ul'ianovskii believed that the reforms

---

[155] It should be noted that these differences of viewpoint were openly acknowledged. For a frank admission of this, see, V. G. Rastiannikov and M. A. Maksimov, "K Voprosu o Tempakh Rosta Proizvoditel'nykh Sil v Sel'skom Khoziaistve Poreformennoi Indii," *Kratkie Soobshcheniia Instituta Narodov Azii*, Kn. 51 (1962), 37.

[156] R. A. Ul'ianovskii, "Reforma Agrarnogo Stroia," in *Ekonomika Sovremennoi Indii* (Moscow, 1960), pp. 92-95.

[157] *Ibid.*, p. 123. In a subsequent article, Ul'ianovskii adduced a political rationale for the reforms. He explained that while trying to keep the landlords as allies against peasant radicalism, the national bourgeoisie at the same time was forced to consider the interests of the peasantry, if only to preserve their influence over them and isolate them from the working class. He felt that they had partly succeeded in this, as evidenced by the decline of the peasant movement in India in the 1950's. See, R. A. Ul'ianovskii, "Agrarnye Reformy v Stranakh Blizhnego

had given a definite impetus to agrarian capitalism, he did not feel that this constituted real progress. In his estimation, the controversy over which type of agrarian capitalism (the "Prussian"- landlord and "American"-peasant variants) was taking form in India had lost its salience given the presence of opportunities for socialist development. The order of the day in the Indian countryside consisted no longer in determining which variants of capitalist development should be encouraged but in advancing the non-capitalist as opposed to the capitalist development model.[158]

In contrast to Ul'ianovskii's assessment, there was expressed another viewpoint, advocated by a group of younger scholars, that the reforms had brought about no basic change in production relations in Indian villages. In a 1961 article, for example, the noted agrarianists M. A. Maksimov and A. A. Maslennikov asserted that agrarian reforms had not led to a real increase in the amount of land utilized by the peasantry and that, in fact, land utilization had decreased somewhat with tenant evictions.[159] In their estimation, the reforms had not brought about any cardinal change in the agrarian structure of India. In an apparent rebuttal of Ul'ianovskii, the authors argued that it would be incorrect to equate the removal of the Zamindari landlord system that had occurred after independence with the liquidation or even change in the character of landlord ownership, since even under British rule the odious Zamindari system had become marked for extinction.[160] It is important to add, however, that their differences with Ul'ianovskii were limited. They conceded the fact that the peasant movement had declined in the 1950's due to certain changes in the attitudes of the rich peasants who received definite benefits from the agricultural policy of the government.[161]

Another expression of skepticism regarding the progress of agrarian capitalism in India appeared in a 1962 article co-authored by M. A. Maksimov and V. G. Rastiannikov.[162] In their assessment,

i Srednego Vostoka, Indii i Iugo-Vostochnoi Azii," *Narody Azii i Afriki*, No. 2 (1961), 15-16.

[158] Ul'ianovskii, "Reforma Agrarnogo Stroia," p. 130.

[159] M. A. Maksimov and A. A. Maslennikov, "Puti Resheniia Agrarnogo Voprosa v Indii," *Mirovaia Ekonomika i Mezhdunarodnye Otnosheniia*, No. 12 (1961), 56.

[160] *Ibid.*, 57.

[161] *Ibid.*, 64-65.

[162] V. G. Rastiannikov and M. A. Maksimov, "K Voprosu o Tempakh Rosta

agrarian capitalism was developing at such slow tempos that it didn't show any tangible influence on the internal market. Changes in the technical base of agriculture in connection with the reforms were either unnoticeable or only beginning to appear. Because of their limitedness, the reforms did not stimulate the domestic demand for agricultural equipment.[163]

In an apparent effort to resolve these persistent differences of opinion regarding Indian agricultural development, another conference on agrarian reforms was organized by the Institute of the Peoples of Asia in April 1964.[164] In contrast to the previous conference, the majority viewpoint there agreed with Ul'ianovskii in adjudging that the reforms had benefited the peasantry and accelerated the formation of capitalist relations in the village. In the major report delivered by G. G. Kotovskii, V. A. Popov and P. P. Moiseev, the view advanced earlier, in the above-mentioned 1961 article by Maksimov and Maslennikov to the effect that no improvement in the position of the peasantry, in terms of increased land utilization, had resulted from the reforms, was specifically challenged. On the contrary, the authors claimed that land redistribution between the landlords and peasants had taken place. As a result of the reforms, the authors asserted that the contradictions between the rich peasants and the remainder of the peasantry were intensifying while those between the rich peasants and landlords were diminishing as agrarian relations changed.[165]

Further elaborating this point of view, A. M. Mel'nikov, in a report on India, criticized those Soviet analysts who viewed agrarian policy in India as wholly anti-peasant and stated that the reforms were directed at both the elimination of the landlord class as an independent social force and the replacement of semi-feudal production relations with capitalist relations. Mel'nikov went so far as to assert that capitalism already occupied a

Proizvoditel'nykh Sil v Sel'skom Khoziaistve Poreformennoi Indii," *Kratkie Soobshcheniia Instituta Narodov Azii*, Kn. 51 (1962), 37-48.

[163] *Ibid.*, 46.

[164] The proceedings of the conference were summarized in Iu. G. Aleksandrov, "The Agrarian and Peasant Questions in the Developing Countries of Asia and Africa at the Present Stage," *Narody Azii i Afriki*, No. 5 (1964), in *Soviet Anthropology and Archeology*, IV, No. 1 (Summer 1965), 46-53.

[165] *Ibid.*, 47-48.

dominant position in Indian agriculture.[166]

Nevertheless, dissident views continued to be aired at the conference. A. A. Maslennikov, for example, maintained that the bourgeois nationalist ruling class needed an alliance with the landlords against the mass struggle for the non-capitalist path, and hence, stopped short of supporting the peasants' demands for the complete and final elimination of the landlord class. He hastened to add, however, that the bourgeoisie had at the same time certain common interests with the peasantry against feudal exploitation, and, for that reason, their agrarian policy reflected not only an alliance with the landlords who had taken on capitalist characteristics, but also embodied the joint struggle with the peasantry against those landlords who preserved their pre-capitalist methods of exploitation.[167] Yet, even this rather balanced and moderate formulation was criticized during the discussion by Ul'ianovskii, who objected to Maslennikov's assertion that the national bourgeoisie could resolve the agrarian question only in alliance with the landlords.[168]

The consensus of opinion then was that bourgeois agrarian reforms had led to significant changes from which the peasantry had benefited to a certain degree. Nevertheless, the participants were far from satisfied with the progress that had been made in such countries as India. Indicative of the shift that had taken place in Soviet thinking on the agrarian question in the 1960's G. G. Kotovskii in his summation stated that the solution of the agrarian question in favor of the peasantry was possible only via the non-capitalist path of development, for the development of capitalism in the countryside had proven its inability to resolve the basic economic, social and political problems that arose there.[169] In a basic sense then, the debate over the extent to which land reforms

---

[166] *Ibid.*, 51. It should be noted that this position was not widely accepted. While sharing the view that the reforms had reduced semi-feudal exploitation, Mamrykin, in his 1964 work, agreed with the American expert Daniel Thorner that capitalism had not yet become the dominant form of production relations in Indian agriculture. See, Mamrykin, *op. cit.*, p. 98.

[167] Iu. G. Aleksandrov, "The Agrarian and Peasant Questions in the Developing Countries of Asia and Africa at the Present Stage," 58-59.

[168] *Ibid.*, 59.

[169] *Ibid.*, 62.

had promoted agrarian capitalism in India and other developing countries was largely academic, since progress was now measured only along the "non-capitalist path of development." This, of course, provides additional confirmation of India's demotion in the Soviet hierarchy of progressive developing countries during Khrushchev's last years in power.

* * *

In retrospect then, Soviet literature on India during this period is perhaps more revealing for what was left unsaid than said. The Sino-Soviet dispute, which had such an important bearing on the conduct of Soviet-Indian relations at this time, was not once discussed in relation to India. This fact, in itself, bears eloquent testimony to the sensitivity of this issue. Nor were any reliable clues to the evolution of a balanced policy towards India and Pakistan forthcoming. The Pakistani regime continued to be characterized as pro-Imperialist and "ultra-reactionary" in the scholarly literature.[170] Perhaps the only remote hint of a forthcoming shift was the fact that after 1960 (the year of the U-2 incident) the Kashmir issue was muted in the scholarly press.[171]

This does not mean, however, that the scholarly literature provided no guide at all to Soviet policy towards India. Inasmuch as it may be assumed that academic analysis to some degree reflected official thinking, it is evident that the Soviets were very much troubled by India's gravitation towards the West—an anxiety

---

[170] See, for example, Guzevaty, *op. cit.,* 45, and Stepanov and Mirskii, *op. cit.,* p. 105. It is interesting to note, however, that Mirskii in an article he co-authored in 1962 suggested that the foreign policy of Pakistan was to be explained largely by "historical factors," e.g., enmity towards India. This at least suggests that Moscow was aware that the key to Pakistani foreign policy was India and that despite the conservative leanings of its ruling elite, Pakistani foreign policy was flexible. See, R. Avakov and G. Mirskii, "The Class Structure in the Underdeveloped Countries," *Mirovaia Ekonomika i Mezhdunarodnye Otnosheniia,* No. 4 (1962), in *JPRS,* No. 14, 607, 40.

[171] The last separate study on Kashmir was a 1960 book written by the Uzbek scholar U. A. Rustamov, in which the author reiterated Khrushchev's 1955 commitment to the effect that the fate of Kashmir had been decided *de jure* and *de facto* by her full unification with India in 1956. See, U. A. Rustamov, *Sovremennyi Kashmir,* Tashkent (1960), p. 31.

which was perhaps equal to their unstated concern over the Chinese threat. Indeed, the Soviets may have felt themselves being wedged out of India. It is in this context that their continued economic and political support for India makes sense.

If the academic literature is of limited value in discerning the broader dimensions of Soviet policy towards India, then it provides a much more accurate forecast of their trade and aid programs for India and other developing countries. Perhaps the most significant change in this period was the growing tendency towards economic realism in the determination of development strategies and the evaluation of foreign aid. The days when Khrushchev could exhort Soviet citizens to make material sacrifices for the peoples of the Third World as part of their "international duty" were clearly numbered. Yet, it was only after Khrushchev's departure that this tendency towards economic realism became regnant, with far-reaching implications for the very character of Soviet relations with India and other developing countries; but these became clear only by the latter part of the decade.

5.
THE POST-KHRUSHCHEV PERIOD, 1965-1971

*THE SHIFTING VIEW OF THE
INDIAN POLITICAL SCENE*

Since Khrushchev's fall from power, Soviet scholarship on developing countries has undergone profound change. In the broad temporal perspective, if the transition between the Stalin and Khrushchev eras was marked more by a change in the substance of policy than the mode of analysis, then the post-Khrushchev period may be noted more for sweeping changes in the conduct of inquiry and the role of scholarship, which has affected the substance of thought as well.

The catalyst of change was the confluence of two factors: the presence of a cautious leadership more attuned to practical realities both at home and abroad, and a series of setbacks which the Soviets suffered in the Third World, starting with the overthrow of Nkrumah in Ghana in 1966. In the late 1960's then, the expectations that had been inflated during Khrushchev's last years of power rapidly dissipated and gave way to a more realistic assessment of the potentialities and prospects for development in the Third World.

While the official euphoria over the "revolutionary democratic" regimes evanesced, Prime Minister Gandhi's consolidation of power brought about a partial rehabilitation of India in Soviet eyes. It should be stressed, however, that prior to the Congress split in 1969, anxieties over the growing power and influence of monopoly capital in India, which were clearly seen during the Khrushchev years, continued to mount. Soviet authors interpreted government measures which seemed to infringe or challenge the interests of the business community, such as the limitations and controls placed upon the management agencies and the establishment of a commission to investigate Indian monopolies, as either ineffectual[1] or mere attempts to assuage public discontent.[2] On the contrary, Soviet analysts accused the Indian government of creating "hot-house" conditions for the maturation of monopoly capital.[3] Raising the possibility of government capitulation to monopoly interests, A. Maslennikov, writing from New Delhi in 1966, noted that in response to Indian big business's demands for full freedom for foreign and native private capital in India, the government had abolished state control over cement production in January 1966, then followed suit by granting foreign capital the right to set up under its control joint companies in fertilizer production and, in May 1966, abolished both licensing controls on parallel industrial branches in the state and private sectors, including the steel, machine-building, construction and

[1] A. Medovoi, in fact, maintained that government measures had liquidated only the smaller management agencies, allowing the larger ones connected with monopoly interests to strengthen their position. See, A. Medovoi, "Osobennosti Kontsentratsii Proizvodstva i Kapitala v Indii," *Mirovaia Ekonomika i Mezhdunarodnye Otnosheniia*, No. 6 (1965), 44.

[2] O. V. Maev, "Rekomendatsii Komissii Po Monopoliiam i ikh Znachenie." *Narody Azii i Afriki*, No. 3 (1967), 139. Maev asserts that the recommendations of the commission, contained in *Report of the Monopolies Inquiry Commission* (New Delhi, 1967), did not seriously threaten the interests of the Indian monopolies at all. *Ibid.*, 145.

[3] N. Savel'ev, "Monopoly Drive in India," *International Affairs*, No. 4 (1967), 36.

chemical industries, and limitations on imports of industrial raw materials and industrial components.[4] There was little doubt then of the subordinate role of Indian state capitalism to the interests of big business. As A. Medovoi observed, "There is thus occurring the formation of a layer of businessmen and politicians, officials and managers, a unique ruling elite, whose significance and influence permanently grows and whose activity on domestic and foreign policies strengthens."[5]

Thus, Soviet dissatisfaction over the growing influence of the monopolist bourgeoisie was, in part, related to their broader concern for the future direction of Indian foreign policy. While in the past Soviet scholars had intimated that India's conservative domestic course was affecting her foreign policy as well, they now progressed to a more pointed criticism of the pro-Western drift of Indian foreign policy. In an important article in *Narody Azii i Afriki* at the end of 1968, Iu. P. Nasenko, a specialist on the foreign policies of developing countries, observed that the policy of non-alignment, professed by many emerging nations, had degenerated into a policy of neutralism.[6] According to Nasenko, the policy of non-alignment, which, as originally designed by Nehru, not only promoted disarmament and condemned colonialism but also was directed against military blocs and those who forged them, had begun to lose its anti-Imperialist content, for several states which adhered to this policy now displayed the tendency to abstain in big power disputes and to denounce aggression but not the aggressor.[7] Intimating that the Soviet Union might no longer respond passively to further departures from the "anti-Imperialist" course, Nasenko stressed that non-alignment was unthinkable without the support of the Soviet Union and other socialist countries.[8] Further developing this line of thought, Nasenko criticized those Indian

---

[4] A. Maslennikov, "Indiia: Bor'ba Vokrug Ekonomicheskoi Politiki," *Mirovaia Ekonomika i Mezhdunarodnye Otnosheniia*, No. 11 (1966), 106.

[5] Medovoi, *op. cit.*, 49.

[6] Iu. P. Nasenko, "Indiia: Evoliutsiia Politiki Neprisoedineniia," *Narody Azii i Afriki*, No. 6 (1968), 22.

[7] *Ibid.*, 16-18. Nasenko was referring to India's reticence to issue a condemnation of American escalation of the war in Vietnam and not to the invasion of Czechoslovakia.

[8] *Ibid.*, 20.

political figures who, while accepting Soviet aid and urging continuous economic callaboration with the socialist countries, reviled the USSR on other occasions and advocated entry into the Western bloc.[9] Implicit in this statement is the admonition that the Soviets would not tolerate such duplicity. Yet, the author also extended a "carrot" to offset this veiled "stick." Nasenko concluded with an appeal to the political self-interest of the Indian ruling circles by citing approvingly the statement of the Indian Ambassador to France, S. Jha, made at a diplomatic seminar at Salzburg in August 1967, to the effect that non-alignment promoted domestic stability, averted the polarization of left and right forces within India and served as a symbol of national unity.[10] Thus, in the light of such recent events as India's critical response to the invasion of Czechoslovakia and the anti-Soviet demonstrations which followed the announcement of the Soviet-Pakistani arms deal, it would appear that Soviet patience was beginning to wear thin. Through this and other articles which appeared on the subject of non-alignment at this time,[11] the Soviets might have been serving advance notice that a further shift to the West might have serious repercussions for Indo-Soviet relations.

In addition to the conservative domestic and foreign policy course of the Indian government, the Soviets were also deeply disturbed by the growing threat to stability in the sub-continent posed by the resurgence of right-wing religious-communalist political organizations and parties such as the Rashtriya Swayamsevak Sangh and the Jana Sangh, both of which were seen as playing on the frustrations and discontent of the urban poor and unemployed to organize demonstrations that were aggravating communal tensions—a situation that was certainly not contributing to the

[9] *Ibid.*, 23.
[10] *Ibid.*, 24.
[11] See, especially I. Shatalov, "The Leninist Foreign Policy and the National Liberation Movement," *International Affairs*, No. 1 (1969), 70-76 and A. Klimov and V. Laptev, "On the Policy of Non-Alignment," *International Affairs*, No. 3 (1969), 14-19. Shatalov stressed that non-alignment was incompatible with "playing on the contradictions" between the two world systems, nor did it mean neutrality or passivity "where the destinies of the national liberation movement in a certain area or the destinies of world peace and security are at stake." *Ibid.*, 74-75. This last remark might be interpreted as criticism of India's overtures to China at a time of mounting tensions along the Sino-Soviet border.

normalization of Indo-Pakistani relations.[12] Indeed, Soviet enmity towards these communalist organizations became so intense that one Soviet writer equated the Jana Sangh's appeals to racial Aryan purity with Hitlerite fascism.[13]

While the Soviets sharply castigated religious-communalist groups, they were more circumspect regarding the emergence of regional autonomy movements. The Soviets were indeed quite sensitive to the complexities of the nationality problem in India and eschewed the categorically negative or positive appraisals that had typified the Stalin and Khrushchev periods. A good illustration of this approach is L. P. Ul'ianova's "State-Legal Forms of the Solution of the National Question in India," which appeared in *Sovetskoe Gosudarstvo i Pravo*, No. 10 (1967),[14] in which greater national autonomy was advocated but within the federal framework of the Indian republic. Specifically, the author felt that the 1956 states' reorganization had not gone far enough in satisfying the legitimate aspirations to self-determination of several small nationalities such as the Nagas and other peoples.[15] With respect to the movements for national autonomy among the larger Indian nationalities, Ul'ianova asserted that they were being supported by bourgeois elements tied to regional markets and desirous of fortifying their own economic positions.[16] Their efforts, which in her

---

[12] A. G. Bel'skii, "Kontseptsiia "Istinnogo Natsionalizma" i ee Reaktsionnaia Sushchnost' (O Nekotorykh Osobennostiakh Politicheskoi Ideologii Induiskogo Kommunalizma)," *Narody Azii i Afriki*, No. 4 (1966), 16-26.

[13] A. Azarkh, "Aktivizatsiia Ul'trapravykh v Indii." *Mirovaia Ekonomika i Mezhdunarodnye Otnosheniia*, No. 10 (1970), 71.

[14] L. P. Ul'ianova, "Gosudarstvenno-Pravovye Formy Resheniia Natsional'nogo Voprosa v Indii," *Sovetskoe Gosudarstvo i Pravo*, No. 10 (1967), 119-24.

[15] It should be noted, herein, that the Soviets considered many "registered tribes" as nationalities which were entitled to opportunities for further development and consolidation into formed nations. See, on this point, N. N. Cheboksarov, "Materials and Research on the Ethnography and Anthropology of Asian Countries" *Sovetskaia Etnografiia*, No. 2 (March-April 1966), 50-58, translated in *JPRS*, No. 35, 983.

[16] In a subsequent article on this subject, Iu. V. Gankovskii, the noted specialist on nationality problems in Pakistan, added that frequently these regional bourgeois groups were joined by feudal and semi-feudal elements intent on regaining lost positions and privileges. Gankovskii adjudged, however, that this alliance was temporary and extremely unstable since the bourgeois supporters of these regional movements also sought to push forward democratic socio-economic reforms. See, Iu. V. Gankovskii, "Ob Avtonomistskikh Dvizheniiakh v Stranakh Iuzhnoi Azii," *Mirovaia Ekonomika i Mezhdunarodnye Otnosheniia*, No. 8 (1970), 55-56.

estimation coincided with the interests of the broad masses for a democratic solution of the national question, were resisted by the monopolists and other elements of the big bourgeoisie whose interests were tied to the all-India market and who, consequently, viewed such movements as a threat to state unity.[17] While this interpretation of the socio-economic base of regional movements is reminiscent of the Stalinist period, it is important to delineate some essential differences. In the first place, Ul'ianova wished to distinguish these movements for greater national autonomy within the multinational federal structure, which were worthy of support, from separatist movements sponsored largely by feudal elements and tribal groups which would lead to the formation of small states, independent of India but dependent upon some external power.[18] Secondly, while encouraging regional autonomy, Ul'ianova was not desirous of undermining Indian political unity. Rather, she was in favor of further reforms of the Indian federal structure, which in her opinion was already a flexible one permitting significant legislative and administrative autonomy to the states, in order to make it more responsive to the legitimate aspirations of the national minorities.[19] Moreover, she did not feel that the ruling classes had been wholly negligent in this regard. For example, in supporting the CPI position on language policy, according to which English would be gradually replaced by Hindi as an all-India language, but not to the detriment of other Indian languages, and, in addition, the languages of the smaller nationalities would be utilized to a wider degree in all spheres of social and public life, she approvingly acknowledged that the ruling class had displayed a certain flexibility on this question.[20] Ul'ianova's analysis suggests then that while the Soviets clearly desired the preservation of the

---

[17] *Ibid.*, 120-21.

[18] Although the Soviets continued to be reluctant to discuss the Chinese factor in the subcontinent, they were not unaware or indifferent to Chinese efforts to exploit separatist movements for their own aims. Gankovskii, for example, cited "foreign interference" enabling extremist elements to gain the upper hand among the smaller peoples of Assam—a probable allusion to Chinese activities in the area, which included the training and equipping of Naga rebels. See, Gankovskii, "Ob Avtonomistskikh Dvizheniiakh v Stranakh Iuzhnoi Azii," 58.

[19] *Ibid.*, 122-23.

[20] *Ibid.*, 124.

unity of the multi-national Indian state, they realized that this could best be achieved only through accommodation of various national minority groups in the form of a more flexible, responsive federal structure.

By the late 1960's the Soviets were cognizant that these divisive social, communal and national tensions had brought about a situation of political instability. The landmark 1967 general elections, which saw non-Congress coalitions take power in 9 of the 17 states, were interpreted as indicative of the growing polarization of political forces in India.[21] While taking note of the victories of the Communist-led united front governments in West Bengal and Kerala, one Soviet analyst, alarmed at the successes of the Jana Sangh and Swatantra parties and the political consolidation of conservative elements within the Congress party, was led to pose the question of whether the electoral victory was not one of triumph for big monopoly capital.[22]

Cognizant of the growing political polarization in India, the Soviets could not have been very much surprised at the open Congress split in 1969. They had, of course, pointed to political divisions within the Congress leadership since Nehru's demise (see above p. 177). In fact, in an article written on the eve of the 1967 general elections, N. Andreev provided a preview of the policy positions of the left wing of Congress, such as the nationalization of major commercial banks, foreign trade and other anti-monopolist measures, some of which would be implemented two years later.[23]

While the 1969 Congress split over the issue of bank nationalization marked the first reversal of the conservative direction of Indian governmental policy in the 1960's, the Soviets reacted to these events with profound caution and considerable trepidation over the future. In the first place, it is important to note that Indira Gandhi

[21] See, P. Kutsobin, "Voprosy, Volnuiushchie Indiiu," *Mirovaia Ekonomika i Mezhdunarodnye Otnosheniia*, No. 3 (1968), 113. Kutsobin, a *Pravda* correspondent, noted that the elections broke the 20-year monopoly of Congress in power. Sharing this opinion, E. N. Komarov, at a March 1969 symposium at the Institute of Orientology, noted that the Congress monopoly at the state level was being replaced by a multi-party system. See his remarks in "Reisnerovskie Chteniia," *Narody Azii i Afriki*, No. 6 (1969), 229.

[22] Savel'ev, "Monopoly Drive in India," 40.

[23] N. Andreev, "India's State Structure and Political Parties," *International Affairs*, No. 1 (1967), 113.

and her supporters were far from being received as "revolutionary democrats." Rather, the new Congress party that emerged under her leadership was viewed as a "center-left" coalition, in which Mrs. Gandhi and many of her top aides such as Jagjivan Ram, C. Subramaniam and Fakhruddin Ali Ahmed were identified as members of the center, flanked on the left by a group of younger political figures, such as Chandra Sekhar and Mohan Dharia, who were pressing for the realization of the democratic reform measures passed at the Congress's July 1969 Bangalore session, which included bank nationalization, land reforms, ceilings on urban income and property, and curbs on industrial monopolies.[24] In fact, it was revealed that some of her most important supporters, such as Y. B. Chavan and K. Kamaraj, had formerly been associated with the "syndicate" but had nevertheless joined Mrs. Gandhi, largely because they had publicly committed themselves to the idea of bank nationalization and were compelled to come to her side in the dispute.[25] It was also asserted that many centrist supporters of Mrs. Gandhi did not consider it efficacious to undertake bolder anti-monopolist measures and had vetoed the idea of Congress entering a center-left coalition with political parties on the left—a programmatic line which the Soviets were vigorously pursuing at the time.[26] Writing in early 1971, P. V. Kutsobin added in this regard that there were still within the newly reconstituted Congress (R) many "reactionary elements" who did everything in their power to freeze the further radicalization of government policy and who flatly refused to collaborate with the Communists and other left wing forces.[27] While, on the one hand, Kutsobin explained that many farsighted Congress political leaders, cognizant of the sharp decline in the party's prestige in the 1967 elections, sensed the need for a more progressive posture to reverse this decline of

[24] A. Iverov, "Slozhnaia Obstanovka v Indii," *Mirovaia Ekonomika i Mezhdunarodnye Otnosheniia*, No. 10 (1969), 95.

[25] *Ibid.*, 96.

[26] In fact, at a December 1970 conference of Soviet Indologists, the prospects for restructuring the party system of India and creating a union of democratic parties were discussed. See, "Konferentsiia Sovetskikh Indologov," *Narody Azii i Afriki*, No. 3 (1971), 221.

[27] P. V. Kutsobin, "Pravye Sily v Indii: Tseli i Metody Bor'by," *Narody Azii i Afriki*, No. 2 (1971), 28.

the Party's influence, he, at the same time, asserted that the Congress split had brought about a major regrouping of class and political forces in India and argued that Mrs. Gandhi's reform program provided objective conditions for unity of action on the part of all left democratic forces against attacks from the right-wing forces. In fact, he went so far as to castigate the leadership of both the United Socialist Party for pursuing a policy of "blind anti-Congressism" and the "parallel" Communist party for erroneously claiming that no demarcation of forces within the national bourgeoisie had yet occurred and that between the "syndicate" and the ruling Gandhian wing no essential differences existed.[28]

Not only did Soviet scholars display considerable realism in analyzing the Congress split, but they also greeted Mrs. Gandhi's victories in a cautious mood. Thus, A. Iverov warned that despite the victory of Mrs. Gandhi's Presidential candidate, V. V. Giri, the right-wing had suffered only a temporary defeat and predicted that new political battles were yet to come, which only intensified the need for a united front of left democratic forces.[29] Echoing this viewpoint, O. Maev cautioned that despite bank nationalization and Giri's victory, monopoly capital still retained strong positions in India's economic and social life.[30]

Furthermore, Soviet scholars eschewed the propensity characteristic of the Khrushchev era to become overly impressed with the institutional manifestations of socio-economic reform and lose sight of the character of the reform itself, by reserving praise until the meaning of the bank nationalization became known. Thus, for example, while expressing the hope that the banks would now extend needed credit to the agricultural sector and especially to the poorer and middle peasants and artisans, as well as to small-scale industry, O. Maev stressed that the real significance of the nationalization of the 14 major commercial banks would depend on the

---

[28] *Ibid.*, 27-28. It is interesting to note that the analyses of Kutsobin and Iverov of the diverse political tendencies within the Congress (R) leadership lend support to the CPI(M)'s position that no real demarcation had yet taken place. The possibility cannot be ruled out that Soviet commentators were in this instance taking the desirable for the real in a concerted effort to help forge a viable coalition of the center-left.

[29] A. Iverov, "Slozhnaia Obstanovka v Indii," 97.

[30] O. Maev, "Blow at the Monopolies," *International Affairs*, No. 10 (1969), 98.

character and direction of future fiscal and credit policies and warned that if these banks continued their former policy of financing mainly the enterprises of the monopolies, the fact of nationalization would have changed very little.[31] Writing on the same subject, M. Stasov drew attention to the fact that nationalization had not affected foreign banks in India, but found encouragement in the fact that the government had acceded to proposals advanced by the Communist and United Socialist parties by setting up advisory bank boards whose officers included bank employees, peasants, workers and artisans.[32]

Thus, while Soviet hopes have on the whole been rewarded with respect to Mrs. Gandhi's impressive victories in recent years, it should be noted that these hopes were moderate and devoid of the inflated expectations of the Khrushchev era. The Soviets have approached the ascendance of Mrs. Gandhi and the decline of right-wing influence in India with a prudent measure of restraint. Their cautious response was determined not exclusively by their sensitivity to Indian political instability and social unrest in the 1960's. To some extent, their views were influenced by their disappointment in other areas of the Third World.

TOWARDS A REALISTIC ASSESSMENT OF THE "NON-CAPITALIST PATH OF DEVELOPMENT"

Towards the end of his rule, it will be remembered, Khrushchev had generated his own "revolution of rising expectations," identifying the radical measures being conducted by several Afro-Asian states with revolutionary socialism. The post-Khrushchev leadership, however, soon began to recoil from some of the bolder statements of Khrushchev and to reevaluate their policy towards these radical regimes although it took two years before a consistent position on the significance of the "non-capitalist path" of development emerged. A striking illustration of this inconsistency was the publication in the same month in *Pravda* of a joint communique of the CPSU and the Algerian FLN, which acknowledged that

---

[31] O. Maev, "Monopolii, Banki i Politika," *Mirovaia Ekonomika i Mezhdunarodnye Otnosheniia*, No. 11 (1969), 59-61.

[32] M. Stasov, "Nationalization of the Big Commercial Banks in India," *International Affairs*, No. 11 (1969), 125-26.

"Algeria had made an irreversible choice in favor of socialism,"[33] and an article by A. Sevastianov appropriately commemorating the 45th anniversary of Lenin's "Left-Wing Communism," in which it was stated that in Algeria, Mali, the UAR, Burma, Ghana and Guinea only the groundwork was being prepared for the non-capitalist path of development.[34]

In the academic literature, doubts soon appeared regarding the prospects for the national liberation movement and the non-capitalist path of development. Professor G. A. Dadashev of Azerbaidzhan University, in an article approving the creation of a new subdivision in Marxist political economy for the study of developing countries,[35] argued that the national liberation revolution should not be viewed as a unilinear process, but constituted an entire historical epoch with many struggles ahead.[36] In subsequent months, this viewpoint was further elaborated first by G. Mirskii, who, at a conference on the post-colonial advanced capitalist states, observed that the non-capitalist path of development had met with only variable success,[37] and later by K. Brutents, who, in an article in *International Affairs*, asserted that the anti-capitalist direction of many Afro-Asian states as yet represented only a

---

[33] "Joint Communique of the CPSU and the National Liberation Front Party of the Algerian People's Democratic Republic," *Pravda*, May 22, 1965, p. 3, translated in *CDSP*, XVII, No. 21, 24. It should be noted that the Soviets at this time began to assiduously cultivate direct relations with the governing political parties and national fronts of these "revolutionary democratic" regimes. Illustratively, a visiting delegation of officials of the Sudanese Union party of Mali was referred to in *Pravda* as the "Mali comrades"—an appellation previously reserved for Communists. See "Group of Mali Party Officials Has Completed Studies," *Pravda*, April 8, 1965, p. 3, translated in *CDSP*, XVII, No. 14, 22.

[34] A. Sevastianov, "Model of Internationalism and Creative Marxism—45th Anniversary of V. I. Lenin's book "Left-Wing Communism: an Infantile Disorder," *Pravda*, May 27, 1965, pp. 2-3, translated in *CDSP*, XVII, No. 21, 13.

[35] The prime sponsor of this proposal was S. I. Tiul'panov, the head of the Chair of Modern Capitalism at Leningrad University, who has been offering a course on the political economy of developing countries since 1964. See, S. Tiul'panov, "Osnovye Problemy Politekonomii Razvivaiushchikhsia Stran," *Mirovaia Ekonomika i Mezhdunarodnye Otnosheniia*, No. 9 (1965), 70.

[36] G. A. Dadashev, "Marksistskaia Politicheskaia Ekonomiia i Razvivaiush-chiesia Strany," *Mirovaia Ekonomika i Mezhdunarodnye Otnosheniia*, No. 2 (1965), 89.

[37] Mirskii's comments may be found in "Metropolii bez Kolonii," *Mirovaia Ekonomika i Mezhdunarodnye Otnosheniia*, No. 10 (1965), 107.

tendency whose victory was not predetermined.³⁸

If the first year following Khrushchev's ouster witnessed a retreat from some of his more adventuristic ideas, the series of reverses the Soviets suffered in Asia and Africa, most acutely felt in the case of Nkrumah's overthrow in Ghana in 1966, triggered something of a shockwave which had on the whole a sobering effect on the Soviet perception of the process of change in the Third World. The immediate impact was to broaden the discussion of the national liberation movement for the expression of widely divergent views. One reaction to these events was the reinforcement of the doubts and pessimism exhibited earlier. Reflecting this attitude, K. Ivanov, in an article in *International Affairs* in early 1966, warned of "zig-zags and retreats" in the national liberation movement and frankly admitted that the

> "...problems of the underdeveloped countries' progress towards socialism, avoiding the capitalist stage, are today practically much more involved than they seemed a short time ago. To people who live only by past concepts and experience they might even appear insoluble inasmuch as many of the conditions which existed, say, after the revolution in Russia or in Mongolia are absent."³⁹

Another variant of this pessimistic response was to deny the socialist character of the reforms being conducted by these radical regimes. Polemicizing with V. L. Tiagunenko on this point, N. A. Simoniia argued that the national liberation revolution had not yet advanced beyond the bourgeois-democratic phase and, at its present stage, was analogous to the early period of capitalist development in Europe when varieties of petty bourgeois socialism appeared on the base of immature material conditions.⁴⁰ These

---

³⁸ Karen Brutents, "Developing Countries and the Breakup of the Colonial System," *International Affairs*, No. 1 (1966), 68.

³⁹ K. Ivanov, "The National Liberation Movement and the Non-Capitalist Path of Development," *International Affairs*, No. 2 (1966), 19.

⁴⁰ N. A. Simoniia, "O Kharaktere Natsional'no-Osvoboditel'nykh Revoliutsii," *Narody Azii i Afriki*, No. 6 (1966), 6-8. Simoniia was taking issue with Tiagunenko's assertion that the non-capitalist path of development combined features of the democratic and socialist revolutions. See, V. L. Tiagunenko, *Problemy Sovremennykh Natsional'no-Osvoboditel'nykh Revoliutsii* (Moscow, 1966), p. 26.

national democratic revolutions were not a "new type" but were rather occurring in new historical conditions in which international factors, such as the World Socialist System, could influence the direction of "national socialism" towards "scientific socialism."

A diametrically opposite viewpoint appeared in an article in *Narody Azii i Afriki*, No. 4, 1966, written by A. K. Bochagov, who was identified as an "active participant... in the socialist construction of Kazakhstan." In a statement reminiscent of the Khrushchev line, Bochagov asserted,

> "If in countries which have entered the non-capitalist path of development, there are already being conducted measures bearing a socialist character, this testifies to the fact that these countries are already moving on the path of socialism."[41]

Yet, the formulation which became the accepted one viewed the non-capitalist path not as identical with socialism, but as a transitional, intermediate stage of acute class struggle, which, depending on the correlation of class forces, would either lead towards socialism or be subverted by bourgeois elements onto the capitalist path of development.[42] It was affirmed that the non-capitalist path would neither automatically nor quickly secure socialism, but represented a long contradictory process.[43] Estimates of the length of time needed before the process of the transition towards socialism became irreversible ranged from 10 to 15 years.[44] Indeed, the non-capitalist path of development, while desirable,

---

[41] A. K. Bochagov, "O Teoreticheskikh Osnovakh Nekapitalisticheskogo Puti Razvitiia," *Narody Azii i Afriki*, No. 4 (1966), 65. The appearance of this article, which reiterated the Khrushchevian identification of the non-capitalist path with socialism, is puzzling, since its viewpoint found no reflection in the popular press at this time nor was it repeated in subsequent scholarly articles.

[42] For an early exposition of this formulation, see, V. A. Pechenev, "O Gosudarstve Natsional'noi Demokratii," *Vestnik Moskovskogo Universiteta*, Seriia VIII: Ekonomika, Filosofiia, No. 4 (1965), 56.

[43] For authoritative affirmation of this view, see, "Velikii Oktiabr' i Istoricheskie Sud'by Narodov Vostoka," *Narody Azii i Afriki*, No. 1 (1967), 15.

[44] R. Ul'ianovskii, "At New Frontiers—On Some Features of the Present Stage of the National Liberation Movement," *Pravda*, January 3, 1968, pp. 4-5, translated in *CDSP*, XX, No. 1, 9.

was no longer visualized as the painless panacea for the plight of developing countries. As V. Kudriavtsev aptly stated in an article on Africa, "it would be wrong to close one's eyes to the fact that the countries on the non-capitalist path of development have to solve the same problems that countries on the capitalist path of development have."[45]

The realization that the non-capitalist path was strewn with obstacles engendered a more realistic assessment of the situation in the Third World. Enunciating this perceptual transition, Academician E. M. Zhukov, speaking before a March 1967 conference on the problems of the national liberation movement, advised that there were no "one-act solutions" for the achievement of economic independence and berated those "impatient men" who were in a hurry to qualify progressive changes as socialist. He added that progress along the non-capitalist path was neither easy nor automatic, that, in fact, there were some instances of an economic slowdown or a decline in levels of mass consumption, and finally that it would be utopian to expect rapid changes in the economy, living standards and cultural levels.[46]

Speaking in a similar vein before a special jubilee session at the Institute of World Economics and International Relations commemorating the 50th anniversary of the October Revolution, V.Tiagunenko acknowledged that there had existed the inclination among Soviet scholars until recently to adorn the successes of countries traveling on the non-capitalist path, to depict democratic transformations as socialist and to take the "desired for the real"—with the consequent expectations of immoderately fast results, "forgetting what great labor must be done for the victory of socialism."[47] Tiagunenko's concern was that the overevaluation of the gains made by these countries had created false hopes which were easily shattered and followed by deep disappointments; this had led in turn to the very questioning of the utility of the term "non-capitalist path"—the

---

[45] V. Kudriavtsev, "Problems and Judgments: Real and Fictitious Difficulties," *Izvestia*, November 2, 1968, p. 4, translated in *CDSP*, XX, No. 44, 22.

[46] E. M. Zhukov, "The Contemporary Pace of Development of National Liberation Revolutions," *International Affairs*, No. 5 (1967), 52-53.

[47] A summary of his report is contained in "Iubileinoe Zasedanie Uchenogo Soveta IMEMO, Posviashchennoe 50-letiiu Velikoi Oktiabr'skoi Sotsialisticheskoi Revoliutsii," *Mirovaia Ekonomika i Mezhdunarodnye Otnosheniia*, No. 1 (1968), 132.

renunciation of which, Tiagunenko admonished, would be tantamount to accepting the Maoist viewpoint.[48] Thus, while the concept of the "non-capitalist path of development" has been retained, there is now general acceptance of the view that it contains no short-cut to socialism.[49]

From their setbacks in Ghana and other countries, the Soviets drew some basic lessons. In the first place, they began to attach much importance to the development of a vanguard party guided by the precepts of Marxism-Leninism which would integrate the society and mobilize the population for progressive socio-economic goals. Indeed, the ease with which Nkrumah was overthrown was explained to be partially the result of a lack of involvement by the broad popular masses in political and state life.[50] In the scholarly literature, the importance of the vanguard party was emphasized in a 1966 article co-authored by N. K. Vaintsvaig, L. M. Gataullina, G. F. Kim and F. I. Kulikova, in which they asserted that the decisive criteria for determining whether national democratic states were entering the socialist phase would be the conversion of

---

[48] *Ibid.*, 132. At the same session, the director of the Institute, N. N. Inozemtsev also cautioned against "unjustified nihilism" engendered by separate failures among the Afro-Asian states. See, *Ibid.*, 121.

[49] It should be noted, however, that there have been various attempts, as yet unsuccessful, to replace the term "non-capitalist path." For example, G. Starushenko, at a 1968 conference organized by the editorial board of *Mirovaia Ekonomika i Mezhdunarodnye Otnosheniia*, opted for the term "countries of a socialist orientation" instead of "countries on the non-capitalist path," arguing that the former was more precise. Moreover, he questioned the validity of calling most developing countries "capitalist," insofar as the direction of their future economic development had in most cases not yet been determined. See, his remarks in "Sotsial'nye Sily i Perspektivy "Tret'ego Mira"," *Mirovaia Ekonomika i Mezhdunarodnye Otnosheniia*, No. 5 (1968), 89.

[50] V. Kudriavtsev, "Problems and Judgments: Intense Heat of Struggle in Africa," *Izvestia*, March 6, 1966, p. 3, translated in *CDSP*, XVIII, No. 10, 22. It should be noted, however, that the idea of promoting the development of a vanguard party pre-dates the Ghanaian coup. Several months earlier a *Pravda* article, in which economic and political difficulties in many of the progressive Afro-Asian states were discussed, called attention to the need for building a mass-based political party with socialist goals. See, F. Burlatskii, "The Liberation Movement and Scientific Socialism," *Pravda*, August 15, 1965, pp. 3-4, translated in *CDSP*, XVII, No. 33, 5. The cultivation of closer relations with the ruling parties in these states may well have been part of this strategy. (See above p. 46.)

revolutionary democratic parties into parties expressing the ideology of scientific socialism.[51] Yet, it was acknowledged that these parties still had a long way to go in this direction. V. L. Tiagunenko, in an important article in *Mirovaia Ekonomika i Mezhdunarodnye Otnosheniia*, No. 1 (1967), observed that the political organizations which existed in these countries were not really political parties but more in the nature of mass organizations of the national front type. He added that only the first steps were being taken towards the creation of a vanguard party, based on Marxist-Leninist theory.[52]

Another lesson which the Soviets drew from the experience of these setbacks was the realization that the objective material conditions in these countries were not ripe for the conduct of rapid socio-economic transformations and that ambitious efforts in this direction had only created additional economic difficulties and summoned widescale discontent and disaffection from these regimes. The Soviet academic literature was replete with warnings about ill-prepared and hasty nationalization,[53] premature government measures to assume control of medium, small and even cottage industries, transportation and commercial enterprises,[54] and also untimely state interference in food production and distribution.[55] With respect to Africa, V. Kudriavtsev noted that: "It is easy to destroy an existing distribution apparatus, but very difficult to get one going in the absence of experienced cadres and funds." As A. Iskenderov and G. Starushenko stressed in a 1966 *Pravda* article, rational economic management was based on a consideration of objective conditions and was incompatible with skipping intermediate stages of development or copying forms and methods typical of the more

---

[51] N. K. Vaintsvaig, L. M. Gataullina, G. F. Kim and F. I. Kulikova, "Teoriia i Praktika Nekapitalisticheskogo Puti Razvitiia," *Narody Azii i Afriki*, No. 4 (1966), 57.

[52] V. L. Tiagunenko, "Oktiabr' i Sovremennaia Natsional'no-Osvoboditel'naia Revoliutsiia," *Mirovaia Ekonomika i Mezhdunarodnye Otnosheniia*, No. 1 (1967), 17.

[53] See, for example, V. Kollontai, "Osvobodivshiesia Strany: Vybor Puti Razvitiia," *Mirovaia Ekonomika i Mezhdunarodnye Otnosheniia*, No. 10 (1965), 34.

[54] See, Tiagunenko, "Oktiabr' i Sovremennaia Natsional'no-Osvoboditel'naia Revoliutsiia," 15.

[55] See, G. Kim and A. Kaufman, "Non-Capitalist Development: Achievements and Prospects," *International Affairs*, No. 12 (1967), 74.

advanced states (which would include, of course, the USSR).[56] As K. Brutents added in this regard, the success of revolutionary forces would largely be determined by their ability to manage the economy.[57]

Reflecting a new climate of thought on the problems of economic development (which shall be explored more extensively below), the Soviets frankly admitted that they were in no position to satisfy all requests for foreign aid,[58] and, in fact, advised the "non-capitalist" states to encourage the participation, through joint enterprises and other forms of collaboration, of foreign and local capital in the tasks of economic development.[59] To be sure, they added the caveat that private foreign capital must not be allowed to subvert the progressive socio-economic course of these countries. At the same time, however, one Soviet writer acknowledged that the developing countries would have to extend various concessions and guarantees to invite the participation of foreign capital in economic development programs.[60] On the theoretical level, then, a severance of economic ties with the advanced capitalist states was no longer viewed as a prerequisite for the non-capitalist path of development.[61]

In the light of a more realistic assessment of the economic situation of developing countries, it would appear that some of the differences between the capitalist and non-capitalist path were beginning to be effaced. Yet, while the euphoria surrounding the

---

[56] A. Iskenderov and G. Starushenko, "On International Themes: Intrigues of Imperialism in Africa," *Pravda*, August 14, 1966, p. 4, translated in *CDSP*, XVIII, No. 33, 19.

[57] Brutents, *op. cit.*, 69.

[58] Tiagunenko, "Oktiabr' i Sovremennaia Natsional'no-Osvoboditel'naia Revoliutsiia," 16.

[59] Kollontai, "Osvobodivshiesia Strany: Vybor Puti Razvitiia," 33. For another endorsement of the utilization of joint enterprises, consult, S. I. Tiul'panov, "Smeshannye Predpriatiia kak Perekhodnaia Forma Proizvodstvennykh Otnoshenii," *Vestnik Leningradskogo Universiteta*. Seriia Ekonomiki, Filosofii i Prava. vyp. 1, No. 5 (1966), 133-34.

[60] L. M. Entin, "Natsional'noe Demokraticheskoe Gosudarstvo i Ekonomicheskoe Razvitie," *Sovetskoe Gosudarstvo i Pravo*, No. 1 (1968), 89.

[61] For further elaboration of this point, consult, L. Zevin, "Vneshneekonomicheskie Problemy Nekapitalisticheskogo Razvitiia Osvobodivshikhsia Stran," *Voprosy Ekonomiki*, No. 3 (1966), 89-90.

prospects for the non-capitalist path definitely had been deflated by the late 1960's, the Soviets had not abandoned the typology of capitalist and non-capitalist development. While, in the comparative perspective, India's standing in Soviet eyes had definitely improved, she was not restored to the front ranks of progressive developing countries—a position which she had occupied until the early 1960's.

Moreover, as the decade of the 1970's began, there were new signs that the Soviets were growing less tolerant of countries developing along the capitalist path. Thus, in a major theoretical article in *Mirovaia Ekonomika i Mezhdunarodnye Otnosheniia*, No. 5 (1970), V. Tiagunenko challenged the long held dogma (which has continued to rationalize Soviet aid to India) that capitalist development was compatible with economic independence.[62] According to Tiagunenko, by virtue of the necessity of attracting foreign capital, capitalist development would only strengthen a country's ties with the World Capitalist System and would lead eventually towards the emergence of neo-colonial dependence on Imperialism. The struggle for economic independence, on the other hand, would lead inexorably to the struggle against native capitalism which could not be successfully developed without the support of Imperialist monopolies.

Tiagunenko's more critical posture towards the capitalist path of development is reflective of an important shift, which appeared at this time, in the official perspective of the national liberation movement. As General Secretary, Brezhnev announced at the Lenin centennial celebration in 1970,

> "Now when the destruction of the colonial empire of the capitalist countries has been largely completed, the former colonial world has entered a new period: *The struggle no longer solely for national liberation but also—and this is now the main thing—for social liberation is more and more clearly coming into the forefront.*"[63]

[62] V. Tiagunenko, "Nekotorye Problemy Natsional'no-Osvoboditel'nykh Revoliutsii v Svete Leninizma," *Mirovaia Ekonomika i Mezhdunarodnye Otnosheniia*, No. 5 (1970), 29.

[63] "Lenin's Cause Lives and Triumphs—Report by Comrade L. I. Brezhnev

However, while the present leadership has elevated its criteria for evaluating the progressiveness of developing countries by announcing that the tasks of national liberation had largely been completed and had thereby outlived their "historical progressiveness," this posture has little in common with Khrushchev's simplistic, unilinear view of progress. Thus, for example, in his speech before the 24th Party Congress in 1971, Brezhnev, while hailing the nationalization of foreign property and agrarian reform in Egypt, Burma, Algeria and other countries, admonished that "...the radical reconstruction of backward social relations on a non-capitalist basis, and in an atmosphere of incessant attacks by neo-colonialists and domestic reaction, is not an easy matter."[64] It is fortunate for India that Mrs. Gandhi's redirection of Indian domestic and foreign policy on a more leftward course has stood India in Soviet good graces.[65] Yet, it should also be noted that, insofar as the Soviets have raised their theoretical demands for the Third World, it would prove difficult for them to accept a reversion to the conservative policies that characterized India's development in the 1960's.

NEW DIRECTIONS IN THE SOVIET VIEW OF ECONOMIC DEVELOPMENT

In the broader perspective, the sense of disillusionment over the prospects for the national liberation movement deeply affected Soviet thinking on the problems of economic development as well. As the simplistic, ideological exhortations for sweeping reform proved either ineffectual or disastrous when put into practice, the Soviets became more attuned to the economic realities of the Third World. If no magical formularies were forthcoming, the

---

at the Joint Ceremonial Session of the CPSU Central Committee, the USSR Supreme Soviet and the Russian Republic Supreme Soviet on April 21, 1970, dedicated to the 100th Anniversary of the Birth of Vladimir Il'ich Lenin," *Pravda*, April 22, 1970, pp. 2-5, translated in *CDSP*, XXII, No. 16, 16.

[64] "The Report of the CPSU Central Committee to the 24th Congress of the Communist Party of the Soviet Union—Report by Comrade L. I. Brezhnev, General Secretary of the Central Committee, on March 30, 1971," *Pravda*, March 31, 1971, pp. 2-10, translated in *CDSP*, XXIII, No. 12, 9.

[65] In his speech, Brezhnev lauded the bank nationalization and Mrs. Gandhi's impressive victory in the 1971 Parliamentary elections. *Ibid.*, 9-10.

Soviets began to think in terms of short-range and partial solutions to the economic problems of developing countries.

Yet, it should be noted that the tendency towards economic realism was apparent even in Khrushchev's last years (see above, pp. 201-03) and received an important boost forward with his passing from power. Indeed, his departure had a liberating influence upon the entire field of Soviet research on developing countries. Illustratively, a 1966 editorial in *Narody Azii i Afriki*, which called for more creative discussions and the free expression of different opinions on complex, unclear problems, linked such negative phenomena as "subjectivism and voluntarism" (both associated with Khrushchev's leadership) with "dogmatic distortions" of Leninism and the reduction of complex problems to "sociological simplifications."[66]

In promoting a freer environment for scholarly inquiry, the Soviet leadership finally acknowledged that social scientists could play a more useful role than merely being official apologists. In fact, a subsequent *Narody Azii i Afriki* editorial excoriated the "still existant view" that social science had only propaganda significance and stressed its importance in the solution of basic problems of social theory and the elaboration of practical recommendations derivative of this undertaking. The editorial also recognized that Soviet orientologists would have to transcend the behavioral constraints imposed in the past in order to perform this role. In this regard, the editorial stated that there

> "...must be overcome such negative phenomena, still often appearing in our research, as timidity and indecisiveness in the posing of sharp problems of contemporary development and fear of responsibility in the formulation of scientific conclusions, substitutions of independent conclusions by mechanically done citations, often no longer reflecting the real situation...."[67]

---

[66] "O Nauchnoi Polemike v Oblasti Vostokovedeniia," *Narody Azii i Afriki*, No. 1 (1966), 3-6. Not surprisingly, the number of discussions of problems of developing countries increased in the post-Khrushchev period, but, as in the past, most of the more interesting ones were held at the Institute of World Economy and International Relations.

[67] "Pod Znamenem Leninskikh Idei," *Narody Azii i Afriki*, No. 3 (1966), 6.

Of major significance in the Party's efforts to revitalize Soviet social science was the promulgation of the August 1967 CPSU Central Committee resolution which enhanced the role of the social sciences and urged a more "creative atmosphere" for scholarly inquiry.[68] A *Narody Azii i Afriki* editorial, interpreting the resolution's significance for Soviet orientologists, stressed the important role of the social sciences in the solution of "international tasks." Redefining the Party-scholar relationship, the editorial stated that the "Party puts before scholars questions determining the direction of research and expects from scholars scientifically based, precise answers not bound to prepared solutions...."[69]

The official expectation then was that Soviet scholars would begin to generate policy-oriented recommendations. Reflecting this perspective, the director of the Institute of the Peoples of Asia, in an article commemorating the 50th anniversary of Soviet orientology, asserted that orientologists were expected not only to explain the facts but to a certain extent give a prognosis of the future.[70]

Whether scholars have, in fact, exerted such an influence on Soviet policy towards the Third World is a question that will be considered later. Suffice it to note at present that the leadership itself has encouraged new directions in Soviet thinking on the problems of economic development.

Whereas, in the past, economic development was viewed as a process of industrialization leading towards greater economic independence (see above, p. 200), both concepts were so substantially overhauled as to give a new meaning to the Soviet view of economic development. At a 1967 conference on the problems of industrialization of developing countries, the industrialization process itself was redefined in the broad sense of restructuring and modernization of the economic and social structure with the

---

[68] Consult, "On Measures for Further Developing Social Sciences and Heightening their Role in Communist Construction," *Pravda*, August 22, 1967, pp. 1-2 in *CDSP*, XIX, No. 34, 7-10.

[69] "Neotlozhnye Zadachi Dal'neishego Razvitiia Obshchestvennykh Nauk," *Narody Azii i Afriki*, No. 6 (1967), 9.

[70] B. G. Gafurov, "50 let Sovetskogo Vostokovedeniia," *Voprosy Istorii*, No. 1 (1968), 63.

concomitant growth of the social productivity of labor.[71] While industrialization was expected to bring about eventual economic parity in the world community, it was no longer inextricably identified with economic independence.

Indeed, the very concept of economic independence was turned upside down. This important change in the Soviet perspective on economic development was articulated in an important article by L. Zevin, in which he argued that a policy of autarchical economic development would deprive the developing countries of "the advantages offered by the international division of labor and of the disinterested aid and technical and scientific experience of the socialist countries."[72] Thus, it would seem that the Soviets had abandoned the goal of economic independence, which had been associated with the political aim of undermining Western economic and political influence, in favor of a strategy of participation by the developing countries in the international division of labor.[73] To be sure, this was not the first instance of Soviet support for utilizing the international division of labor in foreign trade. At the 20th Party Congress in 1956, Anastas Mikoyan had endorsed it as a basis for trade expansion between socialist and capitalist countries.[74] However, Zevin's article represents the first specific application of this principle to trade between socialist and developing countries. The earlier Soviet reluctance to adopt this approach to trade with developing countries may be related to Khrushchev's penchant for

---

[71] See, especially the comments of O. Ul'rikh and V. Tiagunenko contained in "Problemy Industrializatsii Razvivaiushchikhsia Stran," *Mirovaia Ekonomika i Mezhdunarodnye Otnosheniia*, No. 4 (1967), 113 and No. 5 (1967), 105, respectively.

[72] L. Zevin, "The Mutual Advantage of Economic Cooperation between the Socialist and Developing Countries," *Voprosy Ekonomiki*, No. 2 (1965), translated in *The American Review of Soviet and East European Foreign Trade*, I, No. 4 (July-August 1965), 32. In criticizing autarchical economic development, Zevin most probably had the Chinese defense of this Stalinist strategy in mind.

[73] It should be noted that the Soviets continued to use the term economic independence, but substantially reinterprted its meaning. Illustratively, N. Simoniia, at a June 1969 conference organized by the Institute of Orientology, stated: "Economic independence presumes...the obligation of participation of each country in the international division of labor...." See, "Konferentsiia po Problemam Bor'by za Ekonomicheskuiu Samostoiatel'nost' Razvivaiushchikhsia Stran," *Narody Azii i Afriki*, No. 2 (1970), 227.

[74] *Pravda*, February 18, 1956, pp. 4-6, in *CDSP*, VIII, No. 8, 6.

stressing the political aims and minimizing the economic returns from Soviet economic collaboration with the Third World.

If Soviet economists had earlier displayed a certain tolerance of efforts to bring about major economic structural change irrespective of costs (see above p. 201), they now affirmed that economic development should begin by taking advantage of the international division of labor (which had, of course, been shaped in the colonial pattern of economic relations). Developing countries were encouraged to make use of existing export branch specializations in order to finance their economic development programs.[75] Yet, the acceptance of the "bourgeois" economic theory of comparative advantage did not mean that Soviet scholars had reconciled themselves to the long term preservation of the colonial economic structures of developing countries.

In fact, Soviet economists recognized that this was no longer feasible given the impact of the scientific technical revolution on world trade. It was acknowledged that the production of synthetic substitutes had generated a sharp reduction in the demand for traditional raw material exports such as rubber, natural fibers, jute and lacquer, etc., although, to be sure, the market had expanded for oil and, to a lesser degree, for rare metals and certain minerals.[76] This meant that the industrialized capitalist states were now less dependent on the underdeveloped countries than in the past. Arguing this point against the Chinese view that Imperialism could not survive a revolutionary upheaval in the Third World, E. Arab-Ogly substantiated his case by noting that exports to underdeveloped countries accounted for only 2% of the total trade turnover of the advanced capitalist states.[77] Moreover, it was acknowledged that the scientific technical revolution had raised the technological requirements for large capital investment in developing countries. The Third World had for the most part ceased to be a profitable

---

[75] L. Zevin, "Vneshneekonomicheskie Problemy Nekapitalisticheskogo Razvitiia Osvobodivshikhsia Stran," *Voprosy Ekonomiki*, No. 3 (1966), 90.

[76] For a pessimistic account of the effects of the scientific technical revolution on the trade of developing countries, consult, A. Iu. Shpirt, "Nauchno-Tekhnicheskaia Revoliutsiia i Ekonomika 'Tret'ego Mira'," *Mirovaia Ekonomika i Mezhdunarodnye Otnosheniia*, No. 3 (1969), 100.

[77] E. Arab-Ogly, "Mif o "Natsiiakh-Burzhua" i "Natsiiakh-Proletariakh"," *Mirovaia Ekonomika i Mezhdunarodnye Otnosheniia*, No. 6 (1966), 53.

source of investment, as verified by the fact the most private export capital was now circulating among the advanced capitalist countries themselves.[78] The Soviets now began to accept the view that Western aid was being used to raise the economic levels of developing countries to the point at which profitable private foreign investment and economic relations could begin to take place. Indeed, the old dogma that the capitalist states were seeking to preserve the agrarian raw material status of the developing countries was laid to rest at a 1965 discussion on the theme "Metropoles without Colonies."[79]

In view of the unfavorable trade situation brought about by technological advances, underdeveloped countries were encouraged to upgrade the quality of their traditional exports in order to make them more competitive and to raise the degree of manufacture of their export commodities by engaging in preliminary processing of food and raw material exports and by expanding the export of finished and industrial products.[80] The achievements of India and Pakistan in this regard were cited as exemplary.[81] To offset the problem of a narrow domestic market, underdeveloped countries were now advised to encourage and even initially subsidize, through short and long term credits, the development of branches oriented

---

[78] V. Rymalov, "New Phenomena in the Export of Capital from the Imperialist Countries," *Mirovaia Ekonomika i Mezhdunarodnye Otnosheniia*, No. 7 (1965), translated in *The Soviet Review*, VII. No. 2 (Summer 1966), 31.

[79] The post-mortem was performed by G. Mirskii and V. Pavlov. See, their comments in "Metropolii bez Kolonii," *Mirovaia Ekonomika i Mezhdunarodnye Otnosheniia*, No. 10 (1965), 106-07. When the need has arisen, however, the Soviets have revived this outmoded dogma to denigrate Western economic policy towards developing countries. See, for example, Iu. Potemkin, "Aktual'nye Voprosy Sotsial'no-Ekonomicheskogo Razvitiia Osvobodivshikhsia Stran," *Mirovaia Ekonomika i Mezhdunarodnye Otnosheniia*, No. 11 (1965), 61-63, and Ia. El'iutin and M. Petrov, "American 'Aid': New Trends?" *International Affairs*, No. 6 (1966), 54-55.

[80] Iu. Ol'sevich, "Problems of Reproduction in the Developing Countries and the Structural Crisis of the World Capitalist Economy," *Mirovaia Ekonomika i Mezhdunarodnye Otnosheniia*, No. 11 (1965), translated in *Problems of Economics*, IX, No. 4, 33.

[81] V. Kondrat'ev, "Razvivaiushchiesia Strany: Bor'ba za Preobrazovanie Vneshnei Torgovli," *Mirovaia Ekonomika i Mezhdunarodnye Otnosheniia*, No. 10 (1966), 38.

for export.⁸² Yet, the selection of these new export branches would be guided by strictly economic criteria, such as considerations of the real and potential market for a given commodity, requisite technical experience and qualified cadres and the capacity for financing such ventures.⁸³ Indeed, so attuned had Soviet economists become to the criteria of comparative advantage that they began to recommend that developing countries discontinue 'anti-import' production, on the grounds that this policy of import substitution had led to the creation of economically inefficient enterprises with high production costs which depended upon continuous government subsidization.⁸⁴

Not only did Soviet economists endorse the concept of comparative advantage offered through the international division of labor, but they embraced as well the formerly discredited "bourgeois" theory of staged economic growth, according to which, in the initial stages of development, most countries would experience the quantitative growth and technological renovation of their existant economic structures, to be followed, in the second stage, by qualitative structural changes with the development of modern large scale industry.⁸⁵ In this regard, India, Egypt and a few other

---

[82] V. I. Pavlov, " "Netraditsionnyi" Eksport Razvivaiushchikhsia Stran," *Narody Azii i Afriki*, No. 3 (1966), 25.

[83] V. Pavlov, "Promyshlennyi Eksport Razvivaiushchikhsia Stran: Problemy i Perspektivy," *Mirovaia Ekonomika i Mezhdunarodnye Otnosheniia*, No. 7 (1967), 61-62.

[84] See, I. Aleshina's recommendation to this effect at the important 1967 conference on problems of industrialization of developing countries contained in "Problemy Industrializatsii Razvivaiushchikhsia Stran," *Mirovaia Ekonomika i Mezhdunarodnye Otnosheniia*, No. 4 (1967), 117. Although V. Tiagunenko in his introductory remarks at this conference expressed a divergent view supportive of import substitution on the basis that it helped liquidate the deficit balance of payments of these countries (*Ibid.*, 107), later considerations of this policy viewed it as being economically ineffective and costly. See especially on this point, R. Andreasian and A. El'ianov, "Razvivaiushchiesia Strany: Diversifikatsiia Ekonomiki i Strategiia Promyshlennogo Razvitiia," *Mirovaia Ekonomika i Mezhdunarodnye Otnosheniia*, No. 1 (1968), 36.

[85] This strategy was first presented at the 1967 conference on problems of industrialization of developing countries by O. Ul'rikh and V. Tiagunenko. See their comments, in "Problemy Industrializatsii Razvivaiushchikhsia Stran," *Mirovaia Ekonomika i Mezhdunarodnye Otnosheniia*, No. 4 (1967), 113, and No. 5 (1967), 107, respectively.

countries represented something of an exception in that they possessed more or less sufficient financial resources, a skilled work force and qualified technical cadres, and a potentially capacious domestic market, all of which enabled them to undertake a program of complex industrialization at this time.[86] For most developing countries, however, industrialization would commence with the expansion of export branches and especially with the development of food and light industries. Indeed, light industry was especially attractive in that it did not require relatively large capital investment and could be profitable even with limited markets. Moreover, light industry did not demand a highly qualified work force, and, because of the labor intensive character of its production, it effectively assisted the growth of employment.[87] Yet, it was also acknowledged that light industry could not secure at the same time a fast rise in labor productivity, which Soviet scholars now viewed as the essence of the industrialization process (see above, pp. 243-44). Only large scale heavy industry could provide a steady growth of labor productivity.[88]

Insofar as most developing countries were incapable of undertaking such ambitious programs of large scale industrialization on their own, regional economic cooperation and integration were offered as potential solutions. As the foremost Soviet expert in this field, A. Kodachenko, explained, regional economic collaboration, which would eventually include joint economic planning and coordinated investment policies, would be necessary for the development

---

[86] See, Tiagunenko's concluding remarks at the 1967 conference in "Problemy Industrializatsii Razvivaiushchikhsia Stran," *Mirovaia Ekonomika i Mezhdunarodnye Otnosheniia*, No. 5 (1967), 107. In his introductory remarks, however, Tiagunenko shed some doubt over India's capabilities for such an undertaking by citing India as a case in which the construction of large scale industrial projects with a weakly developed internal market for these products had led to a chronic underloading of the rated capacities of these newly built enterprises. This, of course, suggests an oblique criticism of the Soviet decision to help underwrite India's program of large scale industrial construction in the first place. See, "Problemy Industrializatsii Razvivaiushchikhsia Stran," *Mirovaia Ekonomika i Mezhdunarodnye Otnosheniia*, No. 4 (1967), 108.

[87] See, O. Klesmet's comments in "Problemy Industrializatsii Razvivaiushchikhsia Stran," *Mirovaia Ekonomika i Mezhdunarodnye Otnosheniia*, No. 4 (1967), 121.

[88] Andreasian and El'ianov, *op. cit.*, 33.

of heavy industrial branches, requiring large capital investment and a wide market of sale. Kodachenko was, however, cognizant that given their present state of economic development, economic integration was still a long way off. For the present, only partial measures in arranging economic collaboration, starting with individual joint projects and then advancing towards the formation of free trade markets, were feasible. Yet, he also recognized that even these initial steps had met obstacles derivative from the essentially competitive economic structures of these countries as well as from their different political orientations and political disputes carried over from colonial days.[89]

Whereas past discussion of regional economic cooperation had focused on Africa, the Soviets now began to think that Asia, which already possessed relatively high levels of intra-regional trade, was somewhat more promising in this regard. This meant that regional economic cooperation was relevant to India's development, despite her capabilities for undertaking a broad program of industrialization.[90] Thus, for example, A. Kodachenko, writing on economic collaboration in Asia, noted positively India's expanding trade ties with the countries of South and South East Asia.[91]

---

[89] See, Kodachenko's comments in "Problemy Industrializatsii Razvivaiushchikhsia Stran," *Mirovaia Ekonomika i Mezhdunarodnye Otnosheniia*, No. 5 (1967), 96. In a later article, Kodachenko expressed some additional reservations over the free trade associations that had been formed, arguing that, as presently structured, they would only lead to the intensification of uneven economic development among the trade partners. See, A. Kodachenko, "An International Development Strategy for the Third World," *International Affairs*, No. 3 (1969), 51. Another economist, V. Pavlov, was even less optimistic than Kodachenko over the prospects for economic integration. Writing soon after the 1967 conference on industrialization, he argued that for a long time to come, most developing countries would continue to lack the economic base necessary for the realization of mutual collaboration in trade and economic development. See, Pavlov, "Promyshlennyi Eksport Razvivaiushchikhsia Stran: Problemy i Perspektivy," 66.

[90] In arguing that autarchic development was unsuitable even for India, V. I. Pavlov noted that India did not possess all the prerequisite minerals and raw materials for industrialization. See his chapter, in *Natsional'no-Osvoboditel'noe Dvizhenie v Azii i Afrike*, Vol. III: *Na Novom Puti* (Moscow, 1968), p. 202.

[91] A. S. Kodachenko, "Problemy Khoziaistvennogo Sotrudnichestva Razvivaiushchikhsia Stran Azii," *Narody Azii i Afriki*, No. 6 (1967), 20.

THE REEVALUATION OF SOCIALIST ECONOMIC RELATIONS WITH DEVELOPING COUNTRIES

While regional economic integration represented a long term goal, the Soviets held out much better prospects for the development of trade ties with the socialist countries. Indeed, it may be asserted that the immediate beneficiary of the application of the doctrine of comparative advantage was the development of trade between the socialist and developing countries. It may well be that one of the prime determinants of this change was the consideration of the economic self-interest that it would be more efficacious for East European countries to import raw materials, minerals and fuels from the developing countries than from the Soviet Union. Indeed, it will be remembered that, in raising the idea in the first place, L. Zevin had spoken of the international division of labor within the context of broadening and deepening economic ties between socialist and developing countries. As Zevin revealed, this strengthening of economic ties might take the form of production cooperation whereby Soviet bloc aid would be earmarked for the construction of enterprises manufacturing products for the socialist market.[92] To be sure, production cooperation was not designed exclusively to benefit the socialist states. Underdeveloped states would be able to utilize these ties to combine advancement of their traditional branches with the creation of new industries, thereby contributing to their programs of industrialization. Yet, there can be little doubt that the economic interests of socialist countries out-weighed all other considerations. In his article, Zevin referred to estimates, conducted by the sector of economic relations of socialist countries with capitalist and underdeveloped countries of the Institute of Economics, which indicated that it would be economically expedient to organize production cooperation for importing oil, iron ore, cotton, several non-ferrous metals and other commodities which would partially replace Soviet exports of these items to East Europe.[93]

The rather sudden acceptance of the idea of production cooperation so soon after Khrushchev's ouster may not be

---

[92] Zevin, "The Mutual Advantage of Economic Cooperation between the Socialist and Developing Countries," 37.

[93] *Ibid.*, 45-46.

coincidental. As I. Dudinskii later revealed,

> "One important aspect in solving the raw material problem in the CMEA countries is to attract the resources of the developing countries. Until recently, due to a series of objective and, in part, also subjective reasons, the CMEA countries imported a relatively small amount of raw materials from the non-socialist world."[94]

Although the removal of Khrushchev was apparently a condition for its acceptance, the idea of production cooperation was warmly endorsed in a manner reminiscent of the Khrushchevian style as a means of bringing underdeveloped countries into the international socialist division of labor.[95] In subsequent years, the idea of production collaboration was further elaborated with suggestions for bilateral and multi-lateral "industrial branch agreements" among government trade organizations, state and private enterprises.[96] Enterprises based on the principle of "progressive assemblage," according to which the share of participation of the host country in the joint output of production would continuously rise to the point of mastering the entire production process on its own, were also envisioned.[97] Necessitating adjustments in the economic plans of the participant countries, it was believed that cooperation in the sphere of production would also stabilize and strengthen the economic relations of socialist

---

[94] I. Dudinskii, "The Problem of Fuels and Raw Materials in the Comecon Countries and the Ways to Solve It," *Voprosy Ekonomiki*, No. 4 (1966), translated in *The American Review of Soviet and East European Foreign Trade*, II, No. 5 (Sept.-Oct. 1966), 37.

[95] G. Prokhorov, "Mirovaia Sistema Sotsializma i Osvobodivshiesia Strany," *Voprosy Ekonomiki*, No. 11 (1965), 87.

[96] Pavlov, "Promyshlenny Eksport Razvivaiushchikhsia Stran: Problemy i Perspektivy," 67.

[97] L. Zevin, "Nekotorye Tendentsii v Razdelenii Truda Mezhdu Sotsialisticheskimi i Razvivaiushchimisia Stranami," *Voprosy Ekonomiki*, No. 8 (1967), 90. In a later article, Zevin mentioned such new forms of economic relations as the development of trade with patents and import licenses, and the organization of commissions on economic and scientific technical collaboration. See, L. Zevin, "Ekonomicheskoe Sotrudnichestvo Sotsialisticheskikh i Razvivaiushchikhsia Stran." *Voprosy Ekonomiki*, No. 9 (1970), 82.

and underdeveloped countries.

Towards the close of the decade, however, doubts began to be expressed regarding the practicality of such ambitious schemes. In an article frankly discussing problems of economic collaboration between socialist and developing countries, Iu. F. Shamrai noted the presence of several obstacles on the path towards closer economic relations.[98] Specifically, he drew attention to the problem of unstable and sometimes discontinuous trade turnover generated by such factors as political instability and the retention of protectionist and, sometimes, inconsistent foreign trade policies—all of which tended to lessen trust and confidence in the established economic ties which would be essential for the successful implementation of more advanced forms of collaboration.[99] As far as production cooperation was concerned, Shamrai raised the possibility that the socialist countries might not be ready to undertake such projects because of deficit capital. So too, he stated that many complex decisions had to be made regarding prices and the distribution of surplus product between the partners in such joint ventures. Shamrai noted in this regard that distribution must be arranged so that developing countries will prefer socialist countries as partners. Therefore, the profit for socialist countries from such enterprises must be significantly less than what competing Western firms would demand, but, at the same time should not be less than

---

[98] Iu. F. Shamrai, "Problemy Sovershenstvovaniia Ekonomicheskogo Sotrudnichestva Sotsialisticheskikh i Razvivaiushchikhsia Stran," *Narody Azii i Afriki*, No. 4 (1968), 9-10.

[99] The Soviets became particularly vexed by the discriminatory trade policies conducted by several countries in relation to trade with the socialist countries. V. P. Goriunov, for example, noted that developing countries often refused to sell socialist countries products in wide demand on the world market or expanded exports but limited imports from the socialist countries, which they viewed as but a secondary market. V. P. Goriunov, "Torgovye i Ekonomicheskie Otnosheniia SSSR s Razvivaiushchimisia Stranami Azii i Afriki," *Narody Azii i Afriki*, No. 2 (1969), 5-6. In order to place trade on a more regular basis, the Soviets recommended the conclusion of international price stabilization agreements which would cover not only traditional raw material exports but also the newer industrial and semi-finished products being exported by the developing countries. See; N. N. Shmigol', "Mirovaia Sistema Sotsializma i Razvivaiushchiesia Strany," *Vestnik Moskovskogo Universiteta*, Seriia VII, Ekonomika, No. 3 (1969), 62.

to the "independent, progressive" path. At a subsequent academic conference, B. N. Brodovich further elaborated this position by pointing to the need to study the social consequences of Soviet aid.[118] In light of the abundant evidence gathered by Soviet Indologists suggestive of the subordinate role of the Indian state sector (Soviet-built factories included) to Indian big business, the publication of research on Soviet foreign aid to India oriented towards such critical questions should be awaited with great interest and anticipation. However, such research has not yet appeared. On the contrary, whitewashed accounts of Soviet aid to India, in which this aid is justified as a contribution to India's economic independence, have continued to be published.[119] What critical commentary has appeared has been directed rather to technical economic aspects such as the need for service and repair facilities.[120]

RECOGNITION OF THE PROBLEMS OF AGRARIAN OVERPOPULATION AND EMPLOYMENT

In addition to the extension of the principle of comparative advantage based on an international division of labor to their economic relations with developing countries, the Soviets also at this time

---

[118] See, B. N. Brodovich, "Koordinatsionnoe Soveshchanie po Voprosam Konkretnykh Sotsiologicheskikh Issledovanii v Razvivaiushchikhsia Stranakh," *Narody Azii i Afriki*, No. 1 (1968), 224.

[119] For a typical work of this genre, see, V. A. Kondrat'ev and L. A. Fituni, *Indiia: Ekonomicheskoe Razvitie i Sotrudnichestvo s SSSR* (Moscow, 1965).

[120] It may be parenthetically added in this regard that Soviet economists seem to have some second thoughts on the advisability of having constructed the Bhilai steel mill in a backward region of India. Addressing herself to the question of whether it was more efficacious to direct capital to the development of backward regions, which tended to retard growth tempos, or to invest in areas already possessing a skilled work force, a more or less developed infrastructure and other factors conducive towards hastened tempos of construction and exploitation, the Leningrad-based economist I. Aleshina concluded that "the problem of equalizing levels of development of separate regions cannot be solved by departing from the dynamics of economic growth tempos." See, I. Aleshina, "Planirovanie v Razvivaiushchikhsia Stranakh: Problema Vybora Tselei," *Voprosy Ekonomiki*, No. 6 (1969), 91. This statement suggests a reversal of the earlier Soviet approval of India's plan of decentralizing industrial development which had determined the Bhilai location in the first place (see above, p. 160).

began to display much greater sensitivity to the acute problem of agrarian overpopulation in the Third World. This newfound awareness affected their thinking on problems of population growth, employment and food production.

One of the immediate changes following Khrushchev's ouster was the acceptance of birth control measures and population planning as contributions to planned economic development—a position that was first advanced by Ia. Guzevatyi in 1965.[121] Yet, this alteration of orthodox Marxist "anti-Malthusianism" did not go unchallenged and, in fact, set off an academic debate which appeared in *Literaturnaia Gazeta* during the following year. Therein, academician S. Strumilin, castigating birth control programs as neo-Malthusian and downplaying the population explosion, was rebuffed by E. Arab-Ogly, defending the new approach that demographic factors must be taken into account in planning economic development and that birth control measures could be an effective supplemental means along with measures directed at basic socio-economic transformations in reducing an alarming population growth rate.[122]

While the tendency to minimize the danger of the population explosion lingered on,[123] the approval of birth control measures as a secondary means of alleviating the demographic crisis gained widescale acceptance.[124] It should be added, however, that even such advocates as Ia. Guzevatyi and A. Kvasha recognized that the effectiveness of birth control measures was largely dependent upon the ongoing cultural revolution accompanying economic modernization

---

[121] Ia. Guzevatyi, "Population and the Socio-Economic Problems of Developing Nations," *Mirovaia Ekonomika i Mezhdunarodnye Otnosheniia*, No. 8 (1965), translated in *Problems of Economics*, IX, No. 2, 50-52.

[122] See, S. Strumilin, "Polemics: Is Our Planet Threatened with Overpopulation?", *Literaturnaia Gazeta*, May 28, 1966, p. 4, and E. Arab-Ogly, "Scientific Calculation or Reliance on Spontaneity?", *Literaturnaia Gazeta*, June 11, 1966, p. 4, both translated in *CDSP*, XVIII, No. 26, 11-13.

[123] See, the comments by A. Kurshakov at the 1967 conference on industrialization contained in "Problemy Industrializatsii Razvivaiushchikhsia Stran," *Mirovaia Ekonomika i Mezhdunarodnye Otnosheniia*, No. 5 (1967), 94.

[124] See, especially, the following articles supportive of this new position: Ia. Guzevatyi, "Population Problems in Developing Countries," *International Affairs*, No. 9 (1965), 52-58; Ia. Guzevatyi, "Population and World Politics," *International Affairs*, No. 10 (1967), 59-64, and A. Kvasha, "Tvoricheskie Obsuzhdeniia Demograficheskikh Problem," *Voprosy Ekonomiki*, No. 7 (1966), 58-59.

and the disintegration of the patriarchal system. In a thorough analysis of this problem, A. Kvasha contrasted the insignificant results achieved in India with the rather successful Japanese experience in the post-war period.[125] He attributed this to the difference in socio-economic levels of development and concluded that the effectiveness of population programs was largely dependent on the depth of socio-economic transformation. Yet, while pessimistic regarding the prospects for such programs in developing countries, Kvasha nevertheless argued that birth control measures could play a positive role in economic development and should be supported.

The recognition of the severity of agrarian overpopulation also led to a basic reevaluation of the employment problem. Whereas the Soviets had earlier tended to minimize this problem or to suggest that its solution was linked to revolutionary socio-economic transformations,[126] Soviet economists now began to acknowledge that industrialization, redefined as the steady increase in labor productivity, and reducing unemployment might be incompatible.

At the important 1967 conference on problems of industrialization of developing countries, the problem of employment at last received the attention it deserved. During the discussion, V. Kollontai, who had earlier helped clarify the issue at a 1964 conference organized by the editors of *Mirovaia Ekonomika i Mezhdunarodnye Otnosheniia* (see above p. 203), now identified the contradiction in reconciling the development of highly productive industry

---

[125] A. Kvasha, "Ekonomicheskoe Razvitie Stran Azii i Afriki i Politika Ogranicheniia Rozhdaemosti," *Narody Azii i Afriki*, No. 4 (1968), 35-36.

[126] Illustrative of this genre was a 1967 article by V. A. Iashkin on the problem of employment in India. Iashkin explained that the Indian government's efforts to increase employment through the expansion of small scale production, crafts enterprises and large scale construction projects had been pursued at the expense of raising the organic growth of labor productivity, which explained why the growth of labor productivity in India had not corresponded to the levels of capital investment. Addressing himself to the problem of reducing unemployment, Iashkin felt that there were significant reserves for increasing both production and employment to be found in maximizing existent industrial capacities and broadening land irrigation programs. While citing these partial measures, Iashkin concluded by relating the solution of this problem to the deepening of the anti-Imperialist, anti-feudal struggle and the transition to the non-capitalist path of development. V. A. Iashkin, "Problema Zaniatosti i Planirovanie v Indii," *Narody Azii i Afriki*, No. 1 (1967), 48-52.

with the task of reducing overt and covert unemployment, by noting that the orientation of industrial development to labor intensive methods of production, now being conducted by many developing states, was correlated with the increase in production costs, the growth of unprofitable enterprises and the retardation of development tempos. While inviting general discussion of the problem, Kollontai recommended the adoption of a combined strategy, which would encourage the growth of labor intensive enterprises along with the simultaneous development of modern, technologically-advanced, capital intensive enterprises.[127]

One participant at the conference, A. Kurshakov, tended to minimize the significance of the problem by asserting that the "danger of the demographic explosion" had been greatly overestimated. Kurshakov reverted to the older view that only the fast growth of industry could solve this problem and concluded with the rhetorical question, "if not industrialization, then what other more radical means can fundamentally resolve the problem of employment in these countries?"[128]

Kurshakov's viewpoint constituted the last echo of the earlier, essentially optimistic attitude. Most participants at the conference, however, recognized that no "radical" solution to this critical problem was forthcoming. In fact, several discussants recommended the utilization of small scale production and crafts enterprises as a supplemental means of both increasing accumulations of capital and expanding the levels of employment,[129]—a suggestion which was endorsed by V. Tiagunenko in his concluding remarks, but only on the condition that they play a subordinate role to programs of large scale industrialization.[130]

[127] Kollontai's comments are contained in "Problemy Industrializatsii Razvivaiushchikhsia Stran," *Mirovaia Ekonomika i Mezhdunarodnye Otnosheniia*, No. 4 (1967), 112.

[128] "Problemy Industrializatsii Razvivaiushchikhsia Stran," *Mirovaia Ekonomika i Mezhdunarodnye Otnosheniia*, No. 5 (1967), 94.

[129] See, the comments of N. Savel'ev, V. Logina and S. Makarova in *Ibid.*, 101-04.

[130] *Ibid.*, 106-07. In a subsequent article, R. Andreasian and A. El'ianov discounted the utility of promoting small scale production on the grounds that it would only lead to the non-rational utilization of development funds, thereby detracting resources from highly productive large scale industry. Instead, they recommended the development of small enterprises producing semi-finished and finished components for modern industry on the basis of long term contractual agreements. See, Andreasian and El'ianov, *op. cit.*, 35.

Towards the end of the decade, Soviet scholars grew increasingly pessimistic and, in fact, somewhat alarmist regarding the dimensions of agrarian overpopulation. For example, addressing himself to such lingering ideological optimists as Kurshakov, G. Skorov, in an important 1969 article on this subject, stated,

> "It is also impossible to agree with the underevaluation of the significance of the demographic growth which was widespread at one time among some Soviet economists and demographers who tried to explain the severity of relative overpopulation in developing countries exclusively by action of the laws of capital accumulation and to view the difficulties of the solution of this problem only as a result of unfavorable socio-economic conditions. The problem of employment would never have achieved such sharpness and would not have taken such scales as in developing countries if there hadn't occurred parallel to their slow economic development a stormy growth of their population."[131]

Dramatizing the crisis even further, Skorov estimated that fully one-third of the labor resources of developing countries were superfluous to the production process.[132] The fact that employment seriously

---

[131] G. Skorov, "Zaniatost' i Razvitie," *Mirovaia Ekonomika i Mezhdunarodnye Otnosheniia*, No. 8 (1969), 39.

[132] As Skorov acknowledged, the problem of unemployment was not solely confined to the agrarian sector. Skorov noted that in India there were several thousand unemployed engineers and technicians—a phenomenon which indicated that despite India's long range needs for technical specialists, the development of education in this field (which the Soviets had assisted through the financing of the Indian Institute of Technology at Bombay and the training of technicians in both India and the USSR) had outstripped present economic demands. This was the result of miscalculations by both Indian planners and Soviet sponsors. As Skorov revealed: "It was silently assumed that the needs of developing countries for technical cadres was so great that "overproduction" of them in the near future was impossible." In light of this problem, Skorov called attention to the need for better coordination of education policy with future economic needs. *Ibid.*, 44-45. Another analyst, commenting on this problem, furnished an additional suggestion that unemployed Indian technical specialists be assigned on a temporary basis to duty in neighboring countries experiencing a shortage of trained specialists. See, G. Starchenkov, " "Utechka Umov" iz Razvivaiushchikhsia Stran," *Mirovaia Ekonomika i Mezhdunarodnye Otnosheniia*, No. 7 (1969), 53-54.

lagged behind industrial growth had shaken confidence in the view that industrialization represented the key to the solution of this problem and led economic planners in these countries to redirect their attention to agricultural development in order to alleviate this crisis. While admitting that agrarian reforms, the development of peasant cooperatives and cottage industries could mitigate chronic unemployment to some extent, Skorov nevertheless believed that at best these were only temporary palliatives. With the eventual modernization of agriculture, manpower needs would decline, which would provide a new stimulant to the expulsion of labor from this sector of the economy. Recognizing the fundamental contradiction between the social imperative of increasing employment and the economic imperative of raising labor productivity, Skorov prescribed a mixed strategy of economic development essentially identical to the one advanced by V. Kollontai at the 1967 conference on industrialization.[133]

In a subsequent article on this subject, Skorov recommended the application of intermediate technology, i.e. simple and cheap means of mechanizing hand labor, such as centrifuges for shelling nuts and mechanical adapters for cleaning rice.[134] Yet, he added

[133] Skorov, "Zaniatost' i Razvitie," 42-48. This was also the strategy recommended for India by V. Vasil'ev, in an article on Indian planning, in which he observed that for the foreseeable future, India would have to combine both intensive and extensive forms of economic development. See, V. Vasil'ev, "Ekonomika Indii : Planirovanie, Plany, Deistvitel'nost'," *Mirovaia Ekonomika i Mezhdunarodnye Otnosheniia*, No. 10 (1968), 63.

[134] G. Skorov, "Poiski Resheniia Slozhnoi Problemy," *Mirovaia Ekonomika i Mezhdunarodnye Otnosheniia*, No. 11 (1969), 54-55. This idea was later supported by S. I. Tiul'panov in an article which for the first time in the Soviet scholarly literature explored the attitudinal dimensions of the development process. Emphasizing the psychological features of the traditional social structure which resisted material stimuli and obstructed the development of modern labor discipline, Tiul'panov suggested that in these conditions it might be more efficacious to phase the transition to higher forms of production by commencing with the application of technology outmoded by modern-day standards. In Tiul'panov's viewpoint, simple technology of a crafts type would be economically more effective than the introduction of the latest equipment. See, S. Tiul'panov, "K Voprosu o Sotsial'noi Strategii Razvivaiushchikhsia Stran," *Mirovaia Ekonomika i Mezhdunarodnye Otnosheniia*, No. 7 (1970), 44-45. This, of course, represents something of a retreat from earlier expectations that modern technology might shorten the takeoff periods for economic development. For an expression of this view, see, I. M. Shatalov, "The Third World and the Scientific Technical Revolution," *International Affairs*, No. 5 (1967), 75.

that intermediate technology offered no panacea, since it could neither secure fast tempos of economic growth nor high norms of accumulation. Eventually, the need would arise to raise labor productivity to world standards. While arguing that only socialism could facilitate the solution of this problem by providing thorough, step-by-step planning, he did not suppose, as scholars had in the past, that the non-capitalist path offered any shortcut. On the contrary, he affirmed that there existed no "magical method" which could eliminate this crisis within one generation. Only partial solutions were possible. While urging his colleagues not to be fatalistic, he nevertheless concluded on the pessimistic note that there were no historical precedents to the contemporary problem of unemployment in developing countries.[135]

In light of this reassessment of the employment problem, Soviet scholars were now recommending strategies which would prolong the process of economic development irrespective of socio-political factors. Whereas in the early 1960's statements advertising the non-capitalist path as the sole means enabling developing countries to catch up with the advanced industrial states within one generation abounded in both the popular and scholarly literature, such propaganda was dropped entirely once the Soviets realized that the problems confronting non-capitalist regimes were just as real as those facing the capitalist states and that for problems such as unemployment there were no quick remedies. This new, sober approach may be seen most vividly in the remarks by A. I. Levkovskii at UNCTAD-II in 1968, when he estimated that it would take 100 years for developing countries to catch up with the industrialized states and argued that "there were no easy, real recipes for galloping through the indicated precipice, although adventuristic and illusory aspirations in this direction were strong."[136]

THE FOOD PROBLEM AND AGRARIAN REFORMS

Another major area which received considerable attention in the post-Khrushchev years was the food problem. Agricultural

---

[135] Skorov, "Poiski Resheniia Slozhnoi Problemy," 55-57.

[136] A. I. Levkovskii, "Obshchee v Ekonomicheskoi Platforme Tret'ego Mira i Vystupleniia Predstavitelei Dvadtsati Dvukh Razvivaiushchikhsia Stran Na IuNKTAD-II," *Narody Azii i Afriki*, No. 1 (1969), 223.

production was stressed during this period not only because of the pressure of population growth but also because the slow tempos of agricultural trade production had retarded economic growth in general. More specifically, not only was the domestic market for industrial goods limited by a stagnant agrarian sector, but also, to shore up food deficits, funds had been diverted from productive purposes to be spent on food imports. It was acknowledged that the one-sided emphasis on industrialization in programs of economic development (which the Soviets had earlier encouraged) was now resulting in serious branch disproportions, which had been accompanied by the growth of inflationary pressures on food prices, thereby aggravating social tensions as well.[137]

Thus, it is not surprising that the Institute of the Peoples of Asia decided to organize a conference on the food problem in June 1966. Delivering the main report, V. G. Rastiannikov noted that the food crisis in India had been compounded by speculation on the grain trade which, by holding grain off the market, had sometimes created man-made famine conditions.[138] Rastiannikov also drew attention to the U. S. Public Law 480 grain export program, through which India could pay for American grain in rupees. Although the terms of payment seemed to be advantageous for the recipient countries, Rastiannikov stressed the negative social and economic consequences of the program. In the first place, grain imports allowed the ruling classes of India and other countries to stabilize the domestic food situation and check the rising tide of

---

[137] These points were raised at the 1967 conference on industrialization by V. Kollontai and E. Bragina. See, their comments in "Problemy Industrializatsii Razvivaiushchikhsia Stran," *Mirovaia Ekonomika i Mezhdunarodnye Otnoshenii*, No. 4 (1967), 113, 116.

[138] V. G. Rastiannikov, "The Food Problem in the Developing Countries of Asia and North Africa," *Narody Azii i Afriki*, No. 1 (1967), translated in *Soviet Sociology*, VI, No. 3, 18-19. In a report at the conference on the Indian government's food policy, E. I. Mironova noted that government efforts to organize the grain trade had been ineffective due to the fact that government purchase prices had been set too low to really challenge private traders' control of the grain market. So too, the central government's programs to limit the activity of trade capital had been thwarted by the state governments under the strong influence of these trade capital interests. See her revised report, E. I. Mironova, "Gosudarstvennaia Prodovol'stvennaia Politika v Indii," in *Prodovol'stvennaia Problema v Stranakh Azii i Severnoi Afriki* (Moscow, 1968), pp. 97-105.

urban unrest; at the same time, it enabled them to postpone land reforms, thereby affording large landowners more time to convert to capitalist production methods.[139] Secondly, grain imports increased the dependence of these countries on the United States, and since Public Law 480 funds were often used to support American companies operating in the recipient countries, it oriented these countries even more to the world capitalist economy. Furthermore, insofar as the prices for imported grain were set at world market prices, which were lower than the domestic cost of production in developing countries, grain imports actually checked the expansion of domestic agricultural production in these countries.[140]

For these reasons, Rastiannikov strongly recommended that attention be turned to increasing domestic agricultural production through the transformation of the archaic agrarian social structures of these countries. Yet, his response had little in common with the stereotypical references to the need for radical socio-economic reforms of past years. While urging the gradual transition to large cooperatives marked by high labor productivity and by a high percentage of marketable product, Rastiannikov warned that precipitous measures restricting capitalist farming might have adverse effects on agricultural production.[141] In the discussion of his report which followed, Rastiannikov made the additional observation that any easing of the situation of the peasantry through agrarian reform would only increase immediate peasant consumption and even curtail to a certain extent the availability of marketed grain.[142]

The Soviets thus began to recognize that the need for agrarian

---

[139] Rastiannikov, "The Food Problem in the Developing Countries of Asia and North Africa," 20.

[140] Given the Soviet acceptance of the principle of comparative advantage, it would be reasonable to assume that they might also have become reconciled to the replacement of domestic trade grain production by grain imports. This was certainly not Rastiannikov's position, however. For an expression of a contrasting view of the food problem, which reflected the Soviet endorsement of specialization through an international division of labor, see, A. Iu. Shpirt, "Problema Obespecheniia Prodovol'stviem Razvivaiushchikhsia Stran," *Voprosy Ekonomiki*, No. 10 (1967), 101, discussed below, p. 268.

[141] Rastiannikov, "The Food Problem in the Developing Countries of Asia and North Africa," 24-25.

[142] "Prodovol'stvennaia Problema v Razvivaiushchikhsia Stranakh," *Narody Azii i Afriki*, No. 1 (1967), 223.

reform was not necessarily compatible with the task of raising agricultural productivity.[143] They began, for example, to sympathize with the reluctance of revolutionary democratic regimes to engage in radical agrarian reforms for fear of reducing agricultural production and thereby generating a political crisis.[144] Indeed, towards the end of the decade, the Soviets had grown so wary of this problem that one commentator asserted that under present conditions, real possibilities for fully reconciling the social interests of the peasant masses with the necessity of maximum rationalization of agricultural production and raising its effectiveness did not exist.[145]

However, the Soviets had by no means abandoned the struggle for agrarian reforms. Rather, they urged that agrarian reforms be preceded by thorough preparation, with consideration given to all possible economic consequences, so that optimally-sized economic units, which would raise trade output, be organized.[146] While the Soviets maintained their faith in cooperative agriculture, they abandoned the idea that the Soviet experience could serve as an exemplary model. Rastiannikov, for example, pointed approvingly to the Chinese communes, just prior to the 'great leap forward,' where significant production gains had been achieved.[147] In fact, N. Shmelev later admitted that a number of mistakes had been committed by socialist countries in the process of collectivization of agriculture and pointed instead to the more successful experiences of East Germany, Hungary and Rumania, where collectivization had taken place without a diminution of agricultural production.[148]

In contrast to the preceding period when a ritualistic reference to the need for radical agrarian reform would have sufficed, Soviet

---

[143] This conflict was authoritatively acknowledged in the editorial, "Aktual'nye Zadachi Izucheniia Problem Mirovogo Razvitiia," *Mirovaia Ekonomika i Mezhdunarodnye Otnosheniia*, No. 11 (1966), 15.

[144] See, G. Kim and A. Kaufman, "Non-Capitalist Development: Achievements and Difficulties," *International Affairs*, No. 12 (1967), 76.

[145] N. Shmelev, "Sotsial'nye Sdvigi v Sel'skom Khoziaistve Razvivaiushchikhsia Stran Azii i Afriki," *Narody Azii i Afriki*, No. 5 (1969), 20.

[146] Andreasian and El'ianov, *op. cit.*, 32.

[147] V. G. Rastiannikov, *Razvivaiushchiesia Strany: Prodovol'stvie i Politika* (Moscow, 1968), p. 96.

[148] Shmelev, "Sotsial'nye Sdvigi v Sel'skom Khoziaistve Razvivaiushchikhsia Stran Azii i Afriki," 28.

scholars now felt constrained to prescribe partial solutions of a technical economic nature in addition to thoroughly prepared and carefully executed reforms. Thus, for example, Rastiannikov advised developing countries to adopt a protectionist policy with high purchasing prices to stimulate agricultural trade production. In this regard, he commended the Japanese success in modernizing the technological base of their agriculture and in reducing production costs through the maintenance of a system of price supports on rice production in the post-war period.[149] Moreover, Rastiannikov thought that with more intensive taxation of propertied classes, India could also undertake a program of agricultural protectionism. Besides developing a system of price supports which would squeeze trade-usurer capital off the grain market, Rastiannikov also encouraged states such as India to subsidize the purchase of agricultural equipment by the peasants. While acknowledging that part of the price supports would go to consumption among the small producers, he nevertheless maintained that the sale of agricultural equipment at below-market prices would secure genuine reduction in production costs, which would stimulate production.[150] In short, Rastiannikov believed that the solution to the food problem lay in the systematic implementation of a comprehensive policy, including carefully planned agrarian reforms which would transform a backward socio-economic agrarian structure, along with the pursuance of specific technical economic measures.

While most Soviet economists were in accord with Rastiannikov on the need to increase agricultural production in these countries, they were somewhat less negative in their assessment of grain imports. Thus, for example, L. Zevin affirmed in a 1967 article that a definite part of the food aid program must be considered productive.[151] Nevertheless, he considered food imports to be only a temporary measure and stressed the need to increase domestic

---

[149] V. G. Rastiannikov, "Mirovoi Kapitalisticheskii Rynok i Vosproizvodstvo v Zernovom Khoziaistve Razvivaiushchikhsia Stran," in *Prodovol'stvennaia Problema v Stranakh Azii i Severnoi Afriki* (Moscow, 1968), pp. 222-23. He also pointed to similar successes which Turkey had achieved in the 1940's and early 1950's until that government dropped its price supports program.

[150] Rastiannikov, *Razvivaiushchiesia Strany: Prodovol'stvie i Politika*, pp. 101-06.

[151] L. Zevin, "Nekotory Tendentsii v Razdelenii Truda Mezhdu Sotsialisticheskimi i Razvivaiushchimisia Stranami," *Voprosy Ekonomiki*, No. 8 (1967), 89.

production, largely through irrigation and land drainage programs, the construction of factories producing fertilizers and agricultural machines, and the delivery of equipment to large state farms—i.e., those projects to which the USSR had directed part of its aid.

Moreover, it must be noted that there was no common viewpoint on the type of agricultural production to be developed. A. Iu. Shpirt, in a 1967 article on the food problem, advised developing countries to specialize in the production of separate food cultures—a strategy which conformed to the current Soviet emphasis on utilizing the international division of labor.[152] According to his recommendation, a country's food requirements would be met through the importation of foodstuffs from developing and socialist countries and, on acceptable conditions, from the developed capitalist states as well. This solution, with its implicit acceptance of the continued reliance of developing countries on imports of foodstuffs mainly from the West, runs counter to Rastiannikov's encouragement of government protectionism and the subsidization of general agricultural development.

Another method of increasing agricultural productivity was through the application of technological advances and discoveries. In a report delivered at the 1966 conference on the food problem, Shpirt specifically lauded the introduction of synthetic foods such as fish flour and the development of improved seed sorts.[153] Certainly, a major technological advance in this area was the development of high yield strains of wheat and rice at experimental agricultural stations in Mexico and the Philippines under the auspices of the Rockefeller and Ford Foundations.[154] The positive results achieved by the introduction of these new strains in India, Pakistan and other countries generated widespread enthusiasm over the "green revolution" sweeping Asia in the latter half of the 1960's.

---

[152] A. Iu. Shpirt, "Problema Obespecheniia Prodovol'stviem Razvivaiushchikhsia Stran," 101.

[153] Consult his revised report, A. Iu. Shpirt, "Prodovol'stvennaia Problema v Razvivaiushchikhsia Stranakh," in *Prodovol'stvennaia Problema v Stranakh Azii i Severnoi Afriki* (Moscow, 1968), pp. 19-20.

[154] The Soviets have yet to acknowledge publicly the sources of financing although they have referred to the locations at which the high yield grains were developed. See, in this regard, R. P. Gurvich, "Zelenaia Revoliutsiia v Indii: Sotsial'no-Ekonomicheskie Rezul'taty," *Narody Azii i Afriki*, No. 1 (1971), 19.

While the subject of much publicity in the West, the "green revolution" was ignored in the Soviet press for several years. The first reference to it came indirectly when S. B. Gorelik, in a 1969 article on American assessments of India's economic problems, cited Lester R. Brown's July 1968 *Foreign Affairs* article on the "green revolution" and noted without comment the American author's observations that this technological revolution had met many obstacles in its path and had generated social contradictions between landowners and landless peasants.[155]

It should be added, however, that even after the publication of Gorelik's article, the Soviets for a time continued to ignore the "green revolution." In an article which appeared in *International Affairs* several months later, A. Kodachenko explained that the expansion of food production in India in the preceding two years was due to favorable weather conditions and suggested that the gains made might only be temporary. No mention at all was made of the introduction of the new strains of wheat and rice.[156] The reluctance of the Soviets to discuss publicly the "green revolution" was not solely due to the fact that it had been the product of American and not Soviet aid. It would seem that the Soviets were more concerned over the prospects, which appeared promising at the time, that the "green revolution" might offer India and other Asian countries a way out of their food crises without undertaking agrarian reform. This hypothesis gains support from the subsequent consideration of the "green revolution" in the scholarly literature.

Thus, in the first straightforward commentary on the "green revolution," L. Bagramov, writing in *Mirovaia Ekonomika i Mezhdunarodnye Otnosheniia*, No. 4 (1970), coupled the admission that a 5 per cent annual increase in India's food production in 1967 and 1968 had been achieved as a result of the utilization of the new seeds with doctrinaire insistence on the necessity of carrying out radical agrarian reforms, though no rational argument was presented

---

[155] S. B. Gorelik, "Problemy Ekonomiki Indii v Osveshchenii Amerikanskikh Zhurnalov (1965-1968gg.)," *Narody Azii i Afriki*, No. 2 (1969), 173. Gorelik's reference was to Lester R. Brown, "The Agricultural Revolution in Asia," *Foreign Affairs*, XLVI, No. 4 (July 1968), 688-98.

[156] A. Kodachenko, "Developing Countries' Economic Prospects," *International Affairs*, No. 11 (1969), 22-23.

in support of this demand.[157] More thorough and rational evaluations of the "green revolution" came forth only in the following year with the almost simultaneous publication of two articles by the leading Soviet authorities, V. G. Rastiannikov and R. P. Gurvich.

Writing in *Mirovaia Ekonomika i Mezhdunarodnye Otnosheniia*, Rastiannikov characterized the "green revolution" as a transition to intensive capitalist agriculture, which affected only the capitalist layer of the agrarian social structure but not the traditional structure itself and, moreover, adjudged its possibilities for modernizing the traditional agrarian structure as being extremely limited.[158] While recognizing that "certain successes" in increasing agricultural production had been achieved, Rastiannikov focused his attention on the socio-economic consequences of the "green revolution," which had sharpened class contradictions in the village and strengthened regional inequalities in India, inasmuch as the new strains could be applied only in well-irrigated areas. In his estimation, the conservative classes in such countries as India had hoped to find in the "green revolution" a way out of the severe food crisis and had viewed it as the quickest method of adapting the old agrarian structure to the needs of contemporary society. Yet, Rastiannikov felt that such hopes were ill-founded. In his view, the "green revolution" did not remove but rather strengthened objective economic demands for the basic transformation of the archaic agrarian structure. Even palliatives such as the appropriation of special credits to small producers for the purchase of the new seeds and fertilizers, he warned, could not avert the mass ruination of the small producers.[159]

Further elaborating these points, R. P. Gurvich, in a *Narody Azii i Afriki* article specifically on this subject, explained that the new seed sorts, which she described as "one of the most remarkable achievements in genetics," were being utilized only by the well-off cultivators and landowners, who were now raising rents and

[157] L. Bagramov, "Prodovol'stvennaia Problema Segodnia i Zavtra," *Mirovaia Ekonomika i Mezhdunarodnye Otnosheniia*, No. 4 (1970), 117-18.

[158] V. G. Rastiannikov, "Problemy Sel'skokhoziastvennogo Rosta v Razvivaiushchikhsia Stranakh Azii," *Mirovaia Ekonomika i Mezhdunarodnye Otnosheniia*, No. 1 (1971), 57-59.

[159] *Ibid.*, 64-69.

dispossessing tenants as intensive forms of agriculture were becoming more attractive than traditional pre-capitalist forms of land tenancy.[160] Although, to be sure, the augmented supplies of marketed grain had substantially reduced the flow of grain imports, she nevertheless stressed that these grains had been purchased at the severe social costs of worsening the position of the lower peasant strata. Moreover, Gurvich concluded that given the existing tempos of population growth, the "green revolution," operating in conditions of an archaic socio-economic structure, could not meet India's long-range food requirements.

The strong focus of Soviet agrarian experts on the deleterious socio-economic consequences of the "green revolution" was not merely an instance of trying to cover up an embarrassing situation. Although this was rarely discussed in the scholarly literature, the Soviets were most likely quite concerned over the effect it might have in fomenting peasant unrest in India at a time when the domestic political situation had begun to turn in their favor. Indicative of this concern, R. A. Ul'ianovskii, in a major article in *Mirovaia Ekonomika i Mezhdunarodnye Otnosheniia*, quoted Prime Minister Gandhi to the effect that if the "green revolution" were not accompanied by a revolution based on social justice, then it would not remain green. While not mentioning the Naxalite rebellion in West Bengal by name, Ul'ianovskii raised an apparition of future peasant-armed struggle by noting that secret detachments of poor peasants had recently seized land "illegally" held by landlords.[161] It seems plausible to assume, therefore, that the Soviets feel that without the concomitant implementation of agrarian reforms, the "green revolution" might bring about the final differentiation of the peasant masses and lead to class war in the village on the Naxalite pattern—a movement already associated in Soviet minds as Maoist-inspired.[162] The Soviets may be fearful that if the Indian government does not act now to carry out a

[160] Gurvich, " "Zelenaia Revoliutsiia" v Indii: Sotsial'no-Ekonomicheskie Rezul'taty," 20-21.

[161] R. A. Ul'ianovskii, "Sovremennyi Etap Natsional'no-Osvoboditel'nogo Dvizheniia i Krest'ianstvo," *Mirovaia Ekonomika i Mezhdunarodnye Otnosheniia*, No. 6 (1971), 80.

[162] See, M. Kapitsa, "The National Liberation Movement and the Mao Group's Splitting Activity," *International Affairs*, No. 7 (1968), 12.

comprehensive program of agrarian reform, it might be too late to act in the future with a full scale peasant uprising in progress. And as the Soviets are surely aware, only the Chinese and their allies in India would benefit from this eventuality. Thus, it is precisely at a time when the "green revolution" has given a needed boost to India's economic development that the Soviets have reemphasized the importance of reforming the antiquated agrarian structure.

Although it appears that socio-political factors now motivate Soviet insistence on agrarian reforms, it should be noted that the post-Khrushchev period as a whole has been marked by the ascendance of economic over political criteria. This reorientation underlies their more cautious approach to socio-economic reform as well as the decision to utilize the principle of comparative advantage as the basis for their own trade and aid policies with the Third World. This growing emphasis on economic considerations was not an unconscious process. At the 1967 conference on industrialization, for example, I. Aleshina argued that the study of problems of industrialization should not be limited exclusively to research on socio-economic factors, since economic planning demanded reliance on technical economic criteria, such as cost effectiveness and financial capacities.[163]

REASSESSING THE POSSIBILITIES OF ECONOMIC DEVELOPMENT PLANNING

A subject which was clearly affected by the ascendance of economic realism was the Soviet view of the role of state intervention in the process of economic development. It had previously been assumed that planning and the state sector were hallmarks of a country's progress towards socialism. Given a favorable political configuration of power, planning could be directed to the attainment of general national goals. The problem of its effectiveness then was largely a political question.

As in the case of the gradual transition towards economic realism in the early 1960's (see above, pp. 201-205), the reevaluation of planning in the Third World was preceded by a perceptible

---

[163] See, her comments in "Problemy Industrializatsii Razvivaiushchikhsia Stran," *Mirovaia Ekonomika i Mezhdunarodnye Otnosheniia*, No. 4 (1967), 117.

undercurrent of resistance to new analytic positions. Paralleling Tiagunenko's 1960 condemnation of "bourgeois" theories of comparative advantage and staged economic growth (see above, p. 200), I. Aleshina, in a 1966 article on planning, disputed the view of Western economists that the character of planning and the state sector in the mixed economies of the developing countries was determined by the dominance of the private sector, and therefore, that these institutions were essentially supportive and subordinate to the latter, by reviving the hackneyed formularly that their methodology was "neo-colonialist."[164] From her perspective, with the presence of certain, mainly political, preconditions, national planning could be realized in conditions of the prevalence in the economy of the private sector without being determined by the latter.

Yet, as Soviet economists became more sensitive to the problem of rational economic planning, they began to look more critically at the relation between planning and the market. Discussing the problem of cost criteria and price formation in developing countries, N. Shmelev revealed that in recent years the view had been expressed among Soviet economists (although not publicly, however) that the free market economy was the only mechanism which could secure the most effective use of the limited resources of developing countries.[165] Not surprisingly, however, in view of his earlier positions, Shmelev was not among the advocates of this view. In fact, he argued that the "free market" was not a sound indicator of value, since administrative intervention in price formation had existed from colonial days. So too, price formation was distorted by the influence of native and foreign monopolies as well as by the working class struggle. Shmelev also questioned the utility of the criterion of profitability in determining economic policy, since for many infrastructural branches as well as for health care and science and education, the profit criterion could not be applied to investment policy. In addition, he noted that profit was inapplicable to projects designed to reduce unemployment.[166]

[164] I. Aleshina, "Planirovanie v Razvivaiushchikhsia Stranakh i Neokolonialistskie Teorii," *Voprosy Ekonomiki*, No. 5 (1966), 114-15.
[165] N. Shmelev, "Stoimostnye Kriterii i ikh Rol' v Ekonomike Razvivaiushchikhsia Stran," *Mirovaia Ekonomika i Mezhdunarodnye Otnosheniia*, No. 6 (1968), 41.
[166] *Ibid.*, 42ff.

It should be noted, however, that Shmelev was not advocating that considerations of cost effectiveness and profitability be ignored. In a follow-up article, Shmelev asserted that planning should reflect profit considerations and prices formed in market conditions of a mixed economy.[167] He, moreover, urged that planners employ a mutually supportive combination of direct and indirect methods, which would afford economic enterprises a high degree of independence.[168] Thus, while questioning the extent to which the market mechanism could be used to determine value, Shmelev, nevertheless, advocated that cost and profit criteria be applied where possible.

It was only in 1969 that the publication in *Mirovaia Ekonomika i Mezhdunarodnye Otnosheniia* of a major article by V. Kollontai brought forth widescale public discussion of the issue of planning in developing countries.[169] In contrast to earlier positive endorsements, Kollontai struck a rather pessimistic note, by observing that the real influence of plans on economic progress had been rather limited; most often plans were not implemented or were replaced by new ones following political *coup d'états*. Moreover, their effectiveness was restricted by various factors, such as climatic conditions and world market fluctuations, that were not subject to state control. Kollontai also stated that the possibilities of regulating private enterprise on the basis of "isolated administrative and economic measures" were not promising and that real subordination of private enterprise to the interests of national development depended upon structural changes in the economy.[170] On the other hand, he cautioned that there was no basis for speaking of the "uselessness" of planning despite the modest results achieved so far. Planning, he argued, not only helped to mobilize resources and expand production, but also exerted a certain influence on the social structure and, thus, could be used to evaluate the policies of the ruling circles.[171] Although planning retained some positive

---

[167] N. Shmelev, "Razvivaiushchiesia Strany: Formirovanie Khoziaistvennogo Mekhanizma," *Mirovaia Ekonomika i Mezhdunarodnye Otnosheniia*, No. 8 (1968), 55ff.
[168] *Ibid.*, 59-61.
[169] V. Kollontai, "Voprosy Planirovaniia v "Tret'em Mire"," *Mirovaia Ekonomika i Mezhdunarodnye Otnosheniia*, No. 7 (1969), 91-100.
[170] *Ibid.*, 97-99.
[171] *Ibid.*, 100.

features, Kollontai had nevertheless cast doubt on the capabilities of planning to influence the development of the mixed economies of underdeveloped countries.

The discussion which followed revealed a fairly broad consensus of support for Kollontai's position on the limitations of economic planning. Thus, for example, G. Smirnov of the Institute of Africa asserted that the role of plans should not be overevaluated lest disbelief in the very possibility of planning results.[172] According to Smirnov, the influence of planning was limited to the state sector, credit policy and in some instances foreign trade. Yet, he also drew attention to the interdependence of the state and private sectors as a factor determining the effectiveness of planning. Further elaborating this viewpoint, S. Bessonov stated that if a state sector were small and the country strongly influenced by the world capitalist market, it would be fairly easy for private capitalist elements to become dominant.[173] In addition, Bessonov warned of the danger of a development plan becoming a national symbol and a focal point of immoderate aspirations, instead of being geared to the country's real possibilities which depended on the role of the state sector in the economy. Finally, V. Kondrat'ev felt that Kollontai had been overly optimistic in assuming the victory of the idea of planning in developing countries had already been achieved. Under present conditions, he asserted, planning generated no more than certain impulses for development, setting forth its most general directions.[174]

Although Soviet economists have begun to adopt an analytic perspective on the problems of planning in developing countries that had been previously labeled "bourgeois neo-colonialist," they have by no means abandoned the idea of planning. Rather, they have emphasized that it must be placed on a sounder economic basis. In this regard, the possibility of utilizing econometric models in development planning has gained widespread interest. While

---

[172] G. Smirnov, "Vozmozhnosti i Predely," *Mirovaia Ekonomika i Mezhdunarodnye Otnosheniia*, No. 8 (1969), 75-76.

[173] S. Bessonov, "Real'nye Predposylki i Vozmozhnosti Planirovaniia," *Mirovaia Ekonomika i Mezhdunarodnye Otnosheniia*, No. 12 (1969), 90-91.

[174] V. Kondrat'ev, "Sfera Nereshennykh Voprosov," *Mirovaia Ekonomika i Mezhdunarodnye Otnosheniia*, No. 12 (1969), 93.

econometric models had been discussed as early as 1965,[175] initial assessments were rather circumspect. For example, L. Artsishevskii and B. Iaroshevskii, evaluating the work of Western economists in this field, concluded that although models could help elucidate complex economic mechanisms, for the immediate future they would remain "abstract, inanimate constructions."[176] This same skepticism was also shared by Kollontai, who, in his 1969 article, asserted that mathematical models had only "theoretical interest" and added that their practical significance for macro-economic analysis and planning would be very limited for a long time to come.[177]

However, the discussants of Kollontai's article, on the whole, took a much more positive view of the practical utility of mathematical models although no consensus of opinion was achieved. In an apparent reversal of his earlier position, L. Artsishevskii asserted that models could have immediate practical application in the selection of optimal correlations between consumption and accumulation and in the determination of the strategy and timing of capital investment. While cognizant that the construction of an optimal plan for the entire economy was impossible, largely because of these countries' economic dependence on foreign resources, Artsishevskii nevertheless maintained that models could provide several variants of a plan and allow the selection of the most optimal of these.[178] Besides Artsishevskii, the utilization of models in planning won the enthusiastic endorsement

[175] Consult, the comments of I. Aleshina at an October 1965 conference held at Leningrad University contained in "Itogi i Perspektivy Sotsial'no-Ekonomicheskogo Razvitiia Molodykh Suverennykh Gosudarstv," *Narody Azii i Afriki*, No. 5 (1966), 229.

[176] L. Artsishevskii and B. Iaroshevskii, "Ekonometrika i "Tret'ii Mir"," *Mirovaia Ekonomika i Mezhdunarodnye Otnosheniia*, No. 5 (1969), 26.

[177] Kollontai, "Voprosy Planirovaniia v "Tret'em Mire"," 96. At a 1968 conference at Leningrad University, Kollontai had also emphasized the obstacles in the path of applying mathematical models to development planning, although most of the participants felt that these difficulties were not insurmountable. See, V. V. Smirnov, "Theoretical Problems Pertaining to the Management of the Economy of Developing Countries," *Vestnik Leningradskogo Universiteta*, Seriia Ekonomiki, Filosofii i Prava, vyp. 4, No. 23 (1968), translated in *Problems of Economics*, XII, No. 3 (July 1969), 86-87.

[178] L. Artsishevskii, "Nuzhno-li Otkazyvat'sia ot Ekonomiko-Matematicheskikh Metodov?," *Mirovaia Ekonomika i Mezhdunarodnye Otnosheniia*, No. 8 (1969), 79.

of I. Aleshina and S. Kuzmin.[179]

Presenting something of a minority viewpoint, N. Shmelev accused both Kollontai and the other discussants of having pushed socio-political factors into the background.[180] He stressed that such crucial factors as the character of the political regime, the cultural level of a country and its traditions, which could not be expressed in quantitative terms, also affected the process of economic development. Even the majority of Western economists who had developed these models, he added, recognized that the effectiveness of these models was circumscribed by the influence of intangible, qualitative social and political factors. Taking this argument one step further, Shmelev stated that an "automatic and non-class mechanism" in planning did not exist. The very criteria determining optimality of development plans varied according to one's class perspective. Echoing the earlier view of planning, Shmelev stated: "Only a political decision, which has taken account of the prospective interests of the working classes and which has been accepted on the basis of a genuinely democratic discussion can guarantee the progressive...general national character of the aims posed in the plan."[181]

Yet, Shmelev's comments were not well-received by the discussants. Issuing a rejoinder to Shmelev's emphasis on non-economic factors, N. Petrakova asserted that taking account of social and political factors did not free planners from the necessity of measuring expenditures against achieved results.[182] Hence, while unanimity did not reign, most Soviet economists displayed considerable

[179] Consult, I. Aleshina, "Modeli Ekonomicheskogo Razvitiia," *Mirovaia Ekonomika i Mezhdunarodnye Otnosheniia*, No. 8 (1969), 80-83, and S. Kuzmin, "Tseli Razvitiia i Metody Planirovaniia," *Mirovaia Ekonomika i Mezhdunarodnye Otnosheniia*, No. 11 (1969), 65-66.

[180] N. Shmelev, "Politicheskie Resheniia i Ekonomicheskie Protsessy," *Mirovaia Ekonomika i Mezhdunarodnye Otnosheniia*, No. 9 (1969), 80.

[181] *Ibid.*, 84-85.

[182] N. Petrakova, "Ekonomicheskie i Politicheskie Kriterii v Programmakh Razvitiia," *Mirovaia Ekonomika i Mezhdunarodnye Otnosheniia*, No. 11 (1969), 68. She also took issue with Shmelev's earlier position, stated in his article in *Mirovaia Ekonomika i Mezhdunarodnye Otnosheniia*, No. 6 (1968), 48, (see above p. 273), that profit could not serve as the sole determinant of investment policy, by arguing that this formulation could sanction the tendency to ignore economic factors entirely in selecting variants of capital investment.

interest in econometric models as instruments assisting rational economic planning.[183]

In retrospect, the ascendancy of economic considerations in Soviet thinking on the development process could not but educe a more positive evaluation of Indian economic development. With all its difficulties, the extensive Indian planning experience attracted much Soviet attention. In the first place, it was acknowledged that India was one of the few developing countries which possessed a sufficient number of technical cadres to undertake economic planning.[184] Secondly, India was lauded as the only country which employed material balances in planning.[185] Moreover, as the Soviets became more sensitive to the complexities of the process of economic development, they also became aware that the problems and failures of Indian planning and economic development were not solely attributable to political factors. For example, once having recognized that the employment problem forced developing countries to utilize labor-intensive projects to absorb surplus labor, the Soviets can no longer claim that India's slow growth of labor productivity was due exclusively to the selection of the capitalist path of development. While the Soviets may be desirous of certain concrete social and economic reforms (especially in the agrarian sector), their reorientation towards economic considerations has undoubtedly elicited a more sympathetic

---

[183] The interest in models was not limited to economists. V. Iordanskii, at a 1968 conference, raised the possibility of utilizing mathematical models for research on urban migration in developing countries. Specifically, he mentioned that their use might facilitate the prediction of political instability induced by urban migration. See, his comments in "Sotsial'nye Sily i Perspektivy "Tret'ego Mira"," *Mirovaia Ekonomika i Mezhdunarodnye Otnosheniia*, No. 5 (1968), 94-97. It should be noted that the Soviets seem particularly sensitive to the problem of political instability generated by widescale unemployment in overpopulated cities. For a perceptive analysis of the reasons for urban unrest, consult, T. Pokataeva, "Urbanizatsiia v Razvivaiushchikhsia Stranakh," *Mirovaia Ekonomika i Mezhdunarodnye Otnosheniia*, No. 9 (1969), 51-62. Pokataeva also describes, without comment, the efforts of several governments to check urbanization by creating new employment opportunities in rural areas, which, thus far, have not produced significant results. This reportage suggests some indirect Soviet support for such programs aimed at controlling urbanization.

[184] Kuzmin, *op. cit.*, 69.

[185] Artsishevskii, "Nuzhno-li Otkazyvat'sia ot Ekonomiko-Matematicheskikh Metodov?," 79.

understanding of the problems of development in India.

CHANGING PERSPECTIVES OF SOCIO-POLITICAL PROCESSES IN THE THIRD WORLD

Another area of inquiry which underwent profound change in the post-Khrushchev era was the Soviet perspective of the social and political structures in the Third World. Up till now, the Soviets had employed the standard Marxist categories of class analysis based on the European experience. As we shall see below, in recent years the very utility of these Marxist class categories came into question as Soviet scholars began to recognize the uniqueness of the socio-economic structure and patterns of development of developing countries.

In his usual pace-setting role, G. Mirskii, in a series of articles co-authored with T. Pokataeva on the class structure of developing countries, advanced the view that the overwhelming majority of the population in these countries could not be considered either petty bourgeois or proletarian, since they were only partially drawn into capitalist relations; the term semi-proletarian working poor was advanced instead. Moreover, in many cases the semi-proletarian masses were not differentiated as a class from the peasantry or artisans and, therefore, could be considered semi-peasants, as well.[186] Occupying intermediate positions between the proletariat and bourgeoisie were employees and the intelligentsia, the latter of which represented an independent political factor. The authors warned that the political orientations of the intelligentsia should not be judged by their social origin, since, though they came from wealthier strata, they formed the leadership of the most diverse political parties from Communist to right wing. Mirskii and Pokataeva added, however, that with industrialization and the crystallization of the class structure, the independent role of the intelligentsia would diminish.[187] The authors also employed for the first time the term elite to refer to the merger of higher government officials with the big business community of many of these

---

[186] G. Mirskii and T. Pokataeva, "Klassy i Klassovaia Bor'ba v Razvivaiushchikhsia Stranakh," *Mirovaia Ekonomika i Mezhdunarodnye Otnosheniia*, No. 2 (1966), 45-46.

[187] *Ibid.*, 48-49.

countries and contrasted this elite to the minor officials and school teachers, who often played a radical role in politics, taking positions close to the proletariat.[188] A final innovative idea which Mirskii and Pokataeva introduced was the view that the new political superstructure in many developing countries had not grown organically from the socio-economic base and, in fact, displayed a large degree of independence from it. This autonomy of political power from socio-economic factors generated feelings of general national and supra-class consciousness among those in power.[189]

Although there was to be sure an undercurrent of resistance to these novel perceptions of the social and political structures,[190] Mirskii and Pokataeva's research set a trend towards the expression of even bolder views on this subject. Thus, delivering the main report at a conference on the problems of the formation of the proletariat, held at the Institute of the Peoples of Asia in February-March 1968, Iu. N. Rosaliev asserted that the proletariat could be considered a class only when it became aware of its historic role and socio-economic tasks and left little doubt of his conviction that a proletariat had yet to be formed in most developing countries.[191] Consonant with Mirskii and Pokataeva's formulation, Rosaliev stated that most hired workers should be considered semi-proletarians, since the incompleteness of the formation of new classes of capitalist society and the absence of distinct borders between social groups had impeded the delineation of the proletariat from the general mass of hired labor. Moreover, he admonished that attempts to

[188] *Ibid.*, 42.

[189] Mirskii and Pokataeva, "Klassy i Klassovaia Bor'ba v Razvivaiushchikhsia Stranakh," *Mirovaia Ekonomika i Mezhdunarodnye Otnosheniia*, No. 3 (1966), 60.

[190] At an April 1967 conference on agricultural workers, for example, G. G. Kotovskii disagreed with Mirskii and Pokataeva'a description of the small peasantry and tenant farmers as non-proletarian working poor and argued that the denial of the petty bourgeois nature of the peasantry would only lead to a distorted understanding of the social processes at work in the village. See, his comments in "Nauchnaia Konferentsiia "Sel'skokhoziaistvennye Rabochie Razvivaiushchikhsia Stran Azii i Afriki"," *Narody Azii i Afriki*, No. 6 (1967), 168. This position is also reflected in Iu. G. Aleksandrov and N. A. Simoniia, "Po Povodu Monografii "Klassy i Klassovaia Bor'ba v Razvivaiushchikhsia Stranakh"," *Narody Azii i Afriki*, No. 1 (1969), 46-50.

[191] "Nauchnaia Konferentsiia "Problemy Formirovaniia Proletariata v Stranakh Azii i Afriki Na Sovremennom Etape"," *Narody Azii i Afriki*, No. 5 (1968), 213.

identify the structure of the proletariat of the developed states with the structure of the working class of developing countries were unavoidably accompanied either by the "artificial isolation" of part of the Afro-Asian workers from the broader masses or by the inclusion in the proletarian category of people who by their general socio-economic position were semi-proletarian.[192]

The very applicability of the Marxist concept of class in the Third World context was questioned at a 1968 conference organized by the editorial board of *Mirovaia Ekonomika i Mezhdunarodnye Otnosheniia*. There, Iu. Ostrovitianov observed that the social structure was essentially amorphous and not typical of either feudal or capitalist societies.[193] In his opinion, the pre-capitalist peasantry and small producers did not constitute classes at all in the sense that classes were large groups of people tied to a single whole by the very conditions of production. Rather, the undifferentiated social groups of these societies represented, in his words, a "mosaic of...disconnectedness." From a similar perspective, M. Cheshkov argued that in most developing countries non-class or pre-class communities prevailed over class formations. Advancing an original formulation, Cheshkov stated that the basis of the social structure rested not on class antagonism but on a unique type of dualism of higher groups and lower social layers. Accordingly, the very process of social differentiation departed from the capitalist pattern of the formation of exploiter and exploited classes and was characterized, instead, by the formation of narrow leadership groups counterposed to the basic mass of toilers.[194]

The recognition that classes had not yet crystallized in the

[192] *Ibid.*, 214-15.

[193] See, his comments in "Sotsial'nye Sily i Perspektivy "Tret'ego Mira"," *Mirovaia Ekonomika i Mezhdunarodnye Otnosheniia*, No. 5 (1968), 92.

[194] *Ibid.*, 103-04. In a subsequent article, Cheshkov employed the term elite to describe these leadership groups, arguing that the class nature of these upper strata was not clearly defined. In his view, however, elites were a transitory phenomena, typical of the lesser developed states of Africa, which would disappear with the formation of classes. Dependent upon the path of development, the ruling elite would become either the nucleus of the bourgeoisie, and take on the features of bureaucratism, or leading groups representing the interests of the working class and peasantry. See, M. Cheshkov, " "Elita" i Klass v Razvivaiushchikhsia Stranakh," *Mirovaia Ekonomika i Mezhdunarodnye Otnosheniia*, No. 1 (1970), 85-91.

lesser developed states of Asia and Africa necessitated a revision of the traditional Marxist view that the state constituted the executive arm of the dominant exploiting class. Indeed, it will be remembered that Mirskii and Pokataeva, in initiating the reassessment of the social structure noted that the political superstructure did not reflect the existant socio-economic base of these countries and, therefore, constituted an independent factor. Undoubtedly, an additional impetus for the reevaluation of the role of the state was the rehabilitation, soon after Khrushchev's fall, of the concept of the Asiatic mode of production as a socio-economic formation which distinguished Oriental from Western historical development.[195] Thus, Iu. Ostrovitianov interpreted the independent role of the state as derivative from the pre-colonial Asiatic mode of production: "This traditional peculiarity of oriental states is preserved and sometimes even develops to a certain extent in contemporary countries where economically and politically prevail intermediate layers."[196] In contrast to the traditional view that political power reflected the economic base, Ostrovitianov asserted that just the reverse was true of the developing states: "Economic weakness generates strong political power."[197] Ostrovitianov also recognized the possible reversion of these states into despotic regimes. He warned that in conditions in which an "anemic" social structure co-existed with a hypertrophied state apparatus, executive power could be converted into an isolated, self-contained organism, which begot an inflated, bureaucratic caste. While sharing Ostrovitianov's

[195] The Asiatic mode of production is identified with the Oriental despotic state, which arose on the base of an irrigated type of agriculture, which required large scale public works and restricted ownership of land, to become the principal exploiter of the masses. After discussion of this concept was extinguished in the early 1930's, only five historical socio-economic formations were officially recognized. These were: primitive communism, slave holding, feudalism, capitalism and communism. Interest in the Asiatic mode of production was revived by the publication of E. S. Varga's *Essays on Problems of the Political Economy of Capitalism* (Moscow, 1964), which elicited widespread discussion of the concept during subsequent months at the Institutes of Philosophy, History and the Peoples of Asia. These discussions are summarized in L. V. Danilova, "Discussion of an Important Problem," *Voprosy Filosofii*, No. 12 (1965), 148-56, in *CDSP*, XVIII, No. 12, Part II, 1-2

[196] "Sotsial'nye Sily i Perspektivy "Tret'ego Mira"," *Mirovaia Ekonomika i Mezhdunarodnye Otnosheniia*, No. 5 (1968), 93.

[197] *Ibid.*

perception of the origin and character of developing states, R. G. Landa later viewed the potency of their political power in a more positive light. Landa suggested that a strong state would be able to maintain strict discipline and apply coercive methods when necessary in order to mobilize the masses for the urgent tasks of economic development.[198]

Although Soviet scholars spoke in general terms when discussing the social and political structures of developing countries, it may be reasonably assumed that some of these innovative concepts, such as the independent role of intermediate strata, the state and ruling elites, were not applicable to the Indian context. India was, in fact, regarded as something of an exception not only in the fact that she was governed by a viable democratic political system, which departed from the authoritarian pattern, but also because of the leadership role exercised by the bourgeoisie. The Indian state then conformed more to the traditional Marxist paradigm of the political extension of the ruling class, in this case the bourgeoisie.[199]

THE VIEW OF CASTE

It was also acknowledged, however, that the Indian social structure was hardly analogous to the Western pattern. While Soviet scholars had earlier referred to the role of caste as an impediment to the organization and formation of class consciousness of the Indian working class, in the post-Khrushchev period Soviet Indologists began to explore more fully the dimensions and impact of caste on contemporary Indian society.

An important step in this direction was the publication in 1965 of the anthology, *Castes in India*. Writing the introductory article, G. G. Kotovskii acknowledged that the caste system was not, as

[198] R. G. Landa, "O Spetsifike Sovremennykh Uslovii Klassovoi i Politicheskoi Bor'by Na Vostoke," *Narody Azii i Afriki*, No. 1 (1971), 46-47.

[199] That India represented a significant exception was acknowledged by Mirskii and Pokataeva, who observed that the dominance of the bourgeoisie suppressed the influence of intermediate social layers. Mirskii and Pokataeva, "Klassy i Klassovaia Bor'ba v Razvivaiushchikhsia Stranakh," *Mirovaia Ekonomika i Mezhdunarodnye Otnosheniia*, No. 3 (1966), 61. It may further be noted that the concept of elites as employed by M. Cheshkov would also be irrelevant to India, since the class nature of the political superstructure had already been defined there.

previously assumed, disappearing but rather adapting to modern conditions. Borrowing extensively from the work of Western and Indian scholars, Kotovskii recognized the salience of caste in electoral politics and even adopted M. N. Srinivas' concept of 'sanskritization' in describing the dynamics of upward social mobility in India.[200] Indeed, his introduction is quite remarkable in that, being a compendium of recent Western and Indian research on the subject, there is little to distinguish it from "bourgeois" scholarship.

The anthology also contained an excellent piece of original research by S. F. Levin on the evolution of Moslem trading castes.[201] Levin described how nascent entrepreneurs used their caste associations as a source of credit to finance business ventures and as a means of securing a sales market. Because of the role of caste in the formation of the modern bourgeoisie, Levin observed that capitalist competition often took the form of competition between different castes. So too, contradictions between bourgeois strata of different nationalities usually became manifest as inter-caste conflicts. Levin also noted that if contentious bourgeois elements were of different religions, religious communal tensions often ensued. Thus, caste permeated class relations on the subcontinent. As Kotovskii stated in this regard, "deep research of the social structure of Indian society is possible only through the study of its caste organizations."[202]

The influence of caste was present in the evolution of other modern social classes as well. As O. Oskolkova and Iu. Gusev, in an article on this subject, noted, the professional character of caste divisions was usually transferred to modern industry, with skilled workers emanating from the ranks of high castes and low castes filling the unskilled positions.[203] Moreover, they suggested that

---

[200] G. G. Kotovskii, "Vvedenie: Nekotorye Aspekty Problemy Kast," in *Kasty v Indii* (Moscow, 1965), pp. 37-39. For a lucid explanation of the term 'sanskritization', consult, M. N. Srinivas, *Social Change in Modern India* (Berkeley and Los Angeles: University of California Press, 1966).

[201] S. F. Levin, "Ob Evoliutsii Musul'manskikh Torgovykh Kast v Sviazi s Razvitiem Kapitalizma," in *Kasty v Indii*, pp. 233-61.

[202] Kotovskii, "Vvedenie: Nekotorye Aspekty Problemy Kast," p. 37.

[203] O. Oskolkova and Iu. Gusev, "Indiiskie Kasty Segodnia," *Mirovaia Ekonomika Mezhdunarodnye Otnosheniia*, No. 6 (1966), 131. It should be noted that Oskolkova and Gusev also made the interesting admission that the instances where class struggle prevailed over caste conflict were exceptionally rare. *Ibid.*, 130.

while caste differences dissolved with education, urbanization and industrialization, this process was neither as simple nor as automatic as previously assumed. The significance of caste had not entirely disappeared even among the urban intelligentsia, as evidenced by the fact that the incidence of inter-caste marriage did not exceed 2%. In addition, the authors drew attention to the fact that legislation intended to abolish caste was often used to strengthen caste divisions and cited, in this regard, the competitive struggles of dominant castes, such as the Kammas and Reddis in Andhra Pradesh and the Lingayats and Okkalingas in Mysore, to obtain for themselves the label "backward castes," so as to have privileged access to schools, the civil service and other advantages that had originally been intended for untouchables and other truly backward castes.[204] Thus, Oskolkova and Gusev not only showed that modern social classes in India were saturated by caste divisions but also shed doubt on the capacity of government to hasten the eradication of caste inequities by decree.

Whereas Soviet scholars had heretofore underestimated the longevity and vitality of the Indian caste structure, there was now newfound appreciation for its dynamism. As L. A. Gordon, in a revised version of a report delivered to the Seventh International Congress of Anthropological and Ethnographical Sciences held at Moscow in 1964, observed,

> "...capitalism liquidates the influence of caste remnants only in the final account. In the intermediate stages of social development caste discord, used in the political and economic struggle, not only doesn't disappear but on the contrary can be sharpened. Caste still continues to play an important role in the social life of the country."[205]

Yet, despite the publication of the volume *Kasty v Indii*, statements urging closer attention to the role of caste in modern India have

---

[204] *Ibid.*, 132.
[205] L. A. Gordon, "Religiozno-Kastovyi Sostav Naseleniia Indii," in *Kasty v Indii*, pp. 211-12.

continued to be expressed.²⁰⁶ Indeed, research on the caste system has run parallel to but independent of research on contemporary Indian society and politics without any effective symbiosis having occurred. As we have noted at the outset of this chapter, Soviet observers of the contemporary Indian political scene still use the standard class categories as if caste were irrelevant or, worse still, non-existent.

In a general perspective, then, Soviet scholars have become increasingly aware of the essential peculiarities of the dynamics of social and economic development in the Third World. In earlier days, when the process of revolutionary progress was viewed in simplistic and unilinear terms, differences in the historical conditions of each country were acknowledged, but it was assumed that these peculiarities would become insignificant as these countries advanced along the path of social and economic progress. This sense of optimism, however, began to disappear once Soviet scholars became cognizant of the severity of the crisis of agrarian overpopulation and admitted that the tasks of social and economic progress might not necessarily be compatible. Soviet scholars began to sense that traditional social consciousness in these countries strongly influenced the process of socio-economic development itself. Thus, for example, Mirskii and Pokataeva, in their 1966 study of the social structure of developing countries, affirmed that even when governments encouraged the development of private industry, the bourgeoisie still preferred to acquire land or engage in speculative activities—a phenomenon which, the authors maintained, could be explained not by economic factors but by social traditions.²⁰⁷ Expressing a similar observation with respect to the socio-economic change in rural India, G. G. Kotovskii noted that even though money was beginning to supplant natural forms of payment, this monetary compensation for the work of artisans, service workers and peasants was not determined by market values and represented, in fact, nothing more than a converted form of natural payment set according to the traditions of the jajmani system of role and

---

²⁰⁶ See, for example, A. A. Kutsenkov's remarks to this effect at the December 1970 conference of Soviet Indologists contained in "Konferentsiia Sovetskikh Indologov," *Narody Azii i Afriki*, No. 3 (1971), 221.

²⁰⁷ Mirskii and Pokataeva, "Klassy i Klassovaia Bor'ba v Razvivaiushchikhsia Stranakh," *Mirovaia Ekonomika i Mezhdunarodnye Otnosheniia*, No. 2 (1966), 40.

occupational differentiation within the village.[208]

In recent years, the view has also emerged that these traditional social structures are more or less impervious to the external influence of the state. Where modern economic development has occurred, it has run parallel to the traditional socio-economic structure without affecting the latter. This rather pessimistic view was articulated by A. Sterbalova at a 1968 conference.[209] She further argued that it was extremely difficult for capitalist relations to grow spontaneously on the base of the traditional socio-economic structure—a contributory factor to which was the enormous pressure of agrarian overpopulation, which made the continued reliance on archaic forms of hired labor more advantageous than the application of modern technology. It was largely for this reason, then, that the tempos of development of Oriental societies were extremely slow. Offering little hope of brighter future prospects, Sterbalova predicted that the "path to the socialist ideal" would consist of a "long period of zigzags, vacillations, political coups and mass disturbances."[210] Sterbalova's pessimistic conclusions, then, are suggestive of a pervasive mood of despondency over the stagnation of traditional societies. Not only was the question of which path of development a country might select less central to Soviet thinking, but Soviet experts on developing countries were now beginning to despair of the possibility of any movement towards modernization—capitalist or non-capitalist.

* * *

In retrospect, the post-Khrushchev years have been especially

---

[208] Kotovskii, "Vvedenie: Nekotorye Aspekty Problemy Kast," p. 22.

[209] Her comments are recorded in "Sotsial'nye Sily i Perspektivy "Tret'ego Mira"," *Mirovaia Ekonomika i Mezhdunarodnye Otnosheniia*, No. 8 (1968), 91-92. In a more recent elaboration of this viewpoint, A. P. Kolontaev and V. I. Pavlov have argued that the polarization of the traditional agricultural and modern industrial sectors was leading to the extreme dissociation of the two spheres of social and economic life and, hence, reduced the influence which the new structure could exert upon the old one. See, A. P. Kolontaev and V. I. Pavlov, "V. I. Lenin o Preobrazovanii Mnogoukladnykh Struktur i Chastnogo Sektora (Na Primere Razvivaiushchikhsia Stran)," *Narody Azii i Afriki*, No. 2 (1970), 14-25.

[210] "Sotsial'nye Sily i Perspektivy "Tret'ego Mira"," *Mirovaia Ekonomika i Mezhdunarodnye Otnosheniia*, No. 8 (1968), 92-93.

dynamic and fruitful ones for Soviet scholarship on developing countries. Outmoded dogmas which hampered research were discarded and the search for new ideas and concrete recommendations was encouraged. Whereas any influence which Soviet scholars might have exerted on official attitudes and decision-making in the past occurred despite expectations that they play the essentially passive role of apologists for the latest party pronouncements, the role of Soviet social scientists in the policy-making process has now been officially acknowledged and sanctioned. The most tangible results in this regard may be seen in the influence of Soviet economists in the search for new forms of economic collaboration with developing countries. Thus, for example, the December 1970 Soviet-Indian trade agreement embodies proposals for production collaboration that had been advanced by L. Zevin five years before.[211] Furthermore, the recent Soviet commitments to develop India's deep sea fishing resources and to build a fertilizer plant (see above, p. 91) reflect the growing concern over India's chronic food crisis evident in the scholarly literature. To be sure, not all scholarly recommendations have been adopted. Despite academic criticism of import substitution programs as being economically inefficient, the Soviets have deferred to Indian requests to maximize the use of Indian products in foreign-assisted projects with the result that the Bokaro steel plant will use less foreign components than any previous state sector plant. However, as suggested by the production delays and other problems engendered by the Soviet placement of orders for refractory bricks and structural materials for the Bokaro project with private Indian suppliers (see above, p. 60), the results thus far have tended to confirm the scholar's admonitions.

Although we have observed that dramatic changes have also

---

[211] It should be noted, however, that the Soviets had earlier implemented plans of production collaboration with other developing countries. The first joint production project was the 1963 Soviet-Afghan agreement for the construction of a natural gas pipeline which would be repaid by deliveries of natural gas to the Soviet Union. In addition, in late 1965 Guinea began to ship canned foods to repay part of a Soviet loan for the construction of a food processing plant. For an illuminating survey of recent Soviet aid projects in the Third World, consult, Elizabeth Kridl Valkenier, "New Trends in Soviet Economic Relations with the Third World," *World Politics*, XXII, No. 3 (April 1970), 415-32.

taken place in the scholarly perspective of the social and political structures of developing countries, by their very nature, these changes can have only an indirect and long range impact on the course of Soviet policy. However, while it is perhaps too early to discern the full extent of scholarly influence on policy resultant from the "intellectual ferment" which Soviet research on developing countries has undergone in recent years, it may nevertheless be concluded that the more realistic and, on the whole, pessimistic assessments that have been generated are likely to impose additional constraints on the conduct of Soviet policy towards the Third World in the foreseeable future.

CONCLUSION

An examination of the Soviet academic literature on India and the problems of developing countries has revealed that scholarly influence is limited mainly to areas where the requirements of expertise are high. This is quite evident in the new role which has apparently been assigned to Soviet economists in the elaboration of new forms of economic collaboration with India and other developing countries. The growing influence of economists is not surprising. It stands to reason that with the present economic leadership's concern for improving the economic efficiency and performance of their aid projects in the Third World the leaders would turn to economists for advice. As a consequence of their new tasks, Soviet scholars have now virtually set aside ideological constraints and concentrated on the generation of concrete, practical recommendations, some of which have already materialized in Soviet aid and trade programs. This reorientation not only reflects the pragmatic style of the Brezhnev leadership but also is derivative of Soviet acceptance of the responsibilities which they have assumed in the Third World.

In the historical perspective, the heightened role of Soviet scholars in Soviet policy-making represents a recent phenomenon. Thus, during the post-war Stalin years, at a time of strong ideological constraints, Soviet Indologists were reduced to playing the role of propagandists for the revolutionary line then being espoused. Indeed, much of their attention was focused on elaborating the tactical line of which elements of the Indian bourgeoisie could be included in the national democratic front. The involvement of Soviet experts in the task of promoting revolutions in Asia impeded dispassionate scholarly inquiry, as is evidenced by the distorted and overly optimistic views of the revolutionary possibilities of the working class and peasantry which appeared in the academic journals at this time. The research conducted on nationality problems in the subcontinent no more than elaborated the official policy aimed at weakening the Indian state. Even the latent pro-India bias on the Kashmir issue present in the academic literature of this period was reflective of Soviet efforts to counter Western support of Pakistan's position and did not represent an independent judgment by a Soviet Indologist. Given Stalin's inspiration, omniscience and wisdom, it is not surprising that scholarly expertise was so undervalued. What is more surprising is the fact that Soviet orientalists did not adjust to the important policy changes which began to prominently appear in the months before Stalin's death. In fact, Eugene Varga's indication that the Indian government was capable of playing an independent role in world politics—a view which was reflected in the initial Soviet overtures towards India in 1951 and 1952—represented a muted counterpoint to the solid chorus of Soviet orientalists who echoed the official line. Indeed, the anomalous situation emerged in which Varga, whose post-war conciliatory views were officially censured, seems to have gained Stalin's ear after a brief, unsuccessful interlude in the late 1940's of fomenting revolutionary activities in Asia,[1] whereas the more docile group of Soviet orientologists continued to air positions which soon became outmoded.

If during the Stalin period Soviet orientalists played a supportive role in promoting revolutionary praxis, under Khrushchev they were now expected to elaborate rationalizations for the newly-established Soviet-Indian friendship. This transition from propagandists to apologists does not connote any significant change in the expectations of the Party regarding the role of Soviet specialists. In both periods, Soviet scholars were expected to substantiate policies already made at higher levels. The difference, however, is that Stalin was more successful than Khrushchev in disciplining the Soviet academic community—a fact which is explicable in view of the relaxed intellectual atmosphere of the mid-1950's. Not only were Soviet scholars resistant to the new Khrushchev line, but, once having accepted it, they began to express reservations regarding the progressive role of the Indian national bourgeoisie and its domestic economic and social policies, and also to raise the specter of monopolist penetration of the Indian state sector years before critical commentaries appeared in the popular press. Indeed, in the academic discussions of the late 1950's a certain tension may be discerned between the official position, expounded by Ul'ianovskii and others, which defended Indian state capitalism mainly on foreign policy considerations, and the more critical, inductive analyses of the domestic situation in India presented by the younger specialists.[2] To be sure, the very fact that the popular press, which throughout the mid-1950's had virtually abandoned class analysis of the Indian government and its policies, began, starting in the early 1960's, to echo the more critical analyses of the scholarly literature strongly

---

[1] That Varga was closely connected with Stalin for a long period of time has been suggested by Robert Conquest. See, his *Power and Policy in the U.S.S.R.* (New York: St. Martin's Press, 1961), p. 88. Varga's divergent attitudes on this and other problems of post-war foreign policy are perceptively analyzed by William Zimmerman in his "The Sources of Soviet Conduct: A Reconsideration" (paper presented at the 1972 annual meeting of the American Political Science Association, Washington, D. C., Sept. 5-9, 1972), pp. 16-18.

[2] Although Ul'ianovskii enjoys the highest official standing of any Soviet specialist on developing countries, his role during the academic discussions suggests that he served more as an official spokesman in the academic community than as a representative of that community in higher Party conclaves.

suggests the presence of a scholarly influence on official thinking. However, it must be kept in mind that popular criticism of the Indian government began to appear only after the Soviets had become enamored of the more progressive Afro-Asian states, and India's standing in the Third World and her importance in global politics had begun to decline in Soviet eyes. Thus, it would seem that these intervening factors had induced the Soviet leadership to endorse the scholarly perceptions. In any event, these critical views of India, irrespective of their source, had no impact on the momentous Soviet decisions to claim "neutrality" in the Sino-Indian border dispute and then to augment economic aid and begin to supply military arms to India. As we have suggested in the text, these calculations were based on the broader Soviet foreign policy objectives of East-West detente being pursued at the time.[3]

The present reevaluation of the role of Soviet scholars was preceded by the curious period of the early 1960's when inflated expectations regarding the revolutionary possibilities of 'revolutionary democratic' regimes coexisted with a growing trend towards economic realism in the scholarly literature. While it would seem that the candidly critical assessments of the performance of the Indian state sector should have had a direct and immediate impact on the Soviet aid programs there, this was not the case. Indeed, rather than attending the problems which had already arisen in Soviet-aided state sector projects, the Soviets stepped in to assume the added responsibility of building on a turn-key basis the Bokaro

[3] It should be noted that the major decisions affecting Soviet policy towards India during the entire post-war period are devoid of any scholarly input. Thus, Stalin's sudden adoption of a hostile posture towards India in 1947 was a consequence of Cold War tensions and not even precipitated by any actions on the part of the Indian government. So too, the academic literature provides no clue to the adoption of a balanced policy in the sub-continent in the 1960's. To be sure, it would be presumptuous perhaps to expect any influence by Soviet scholars over the basic contours of Soviet policy towards India. Nevertheless, it must be added that these broad dimensions of Soviet policy have not been even critically discussed in the academic literature. The entire study of foreign relations with developing countries is a highly sensitive area. The analyses that have appeared have been either in the nature of historical research (e.g. Nikhamin's *Ocherki Vneshnei Politiki Indii*) or an elucidation of official policy (e.g. Nasenko's 1968 article). No analytic research on Indo-Pakistani relations or on recent Sino-Indian relations has yet appeared. Moreover, other topics, such as Soviet aid to India, have been treated most gingerly.

steel mill, with the result being that the Bokaro project has suffered from many of the same problems, such as production delays and administrative incompetence, earlier recorded by Soviet analysts in the years preceding the agreement. Having, thereby, shunned expert advice, it is not surprising that an ephemeral propaganda coup has become an albatross for Soviet leaders and a sore point in Indo-Soviet relations. It was only after Khrushchev's departure that the Soviets began to take steps to improve the performance of their aid projects and to adopt a more careful approach to the dispensation of aid. In marked contrast to Khrushchev's penchant for gratifying the immediate desires of Third World leaders regardless of long-range consequences, the present leadership has openly risked Indian disfavor by dispatching management teams to improve the operations of inefficient Soviet-built enterprises.

As we have already discussed in chapter 5, the recent recognition and encouragement of expert influence in the policy-making process is a consequence of the presence of a pragmatic leadership confronted, in the latter half of the 1960's, with a series of disappointments and setbacks in the Third World. The concomitant sense of disillusionment and the new found awareness of the unpredictability of the Third World have undoubtedly induced Soviet leaders to seek expert advice. This has led to the proliferation of policy-oriented recommendations, the elimination of outmoded dogmas regarding the negative character of private capital and birth control programs and the rejection of pristine views of the positive value of the state sector and planning. Not only has the quality of academic discourse and inquiry been improved by the jettisoning of ideological baggage, but, inasmuch as more accurate information and analyzes are likely to result, Soviet policy-makers must be included among the beneficiaries. However, in a political system in which ideology constitutes the essential source of legitimacy of the regime, one wonders to what extent the Party will permit the erosion of ideology in this area of academic inquiry to continue. To be sure, an alternative interpretation that the sweeping changes in Soviet perceptions of the Third World in recent years do not constitute an abandonment of ideology but only a necessary elimination of simplistic distortions of earlier years is possible. While it cannot be denied that Soviet analyzes have become much more sophisticated, the salient point is that the changes go well beyond a mere refinement of ideology. Soviet scholars have not only adopted wholesale such previously discredited Western "bourgeois" concepts as the necessity of commercial profitability of state enterprises, branch specializations based on comparative advantage and the strategy of staged economic growth, but have even abandoned traditional Marxist class categories in analyzing the social structure of developing countries. Subjecting to doubt the utility of the quintessential Marxist categories of class can only by a far stretch of the imagination be considered an exercise in "creative Marxism," and rather tends to substantiate Chinese claims of Soviet revisionism. In any event, what the increasing irrelevancy of ideology in research on developing countries portends for the long-range security of the regime cannot be clearly discerned at this time.

It is much easier to perceive, however, the implications of recent research trends for current Soviet strategy in the Third World. The present mood of caution regarding political prospects in the developing countries has not been accompanied by a withdrawal on the economic front. Although the Soviets have been more judicious and selective in the allocation of their aid, they have also pursued programs of closer economic cooperation. It may well turn out that this is a better mechanism of stabilizing relations with developing states than Khrushchev's emphasis on cultivating political ties with Third World leaders. Thus, for example, if Soviet plans for economic integration with developing countries take shape, the overthrow of a pro-Soviet regime would not necessarily result in the abrupt cessation of relations as well.

One should not, however, conclude that Soviet economic penetration would eventuate in political subversion of Afro-Asian states. In the first place, the Soviets have to a large degree abandoned their earlier aspirations of eliminating Western influence in developing countries—a consideration which dominated their thinking on aid and even determined their very concept of economic development. As the Soviets became more attuned to the monumental economic problems of developing countries and lost faith in painless revolutionary solutions for them, they also began to acknowledge the potential contributions of both foreign and native private capital in the tasks of economic development. Thus, while promoting forms of closer economic collaboration, the Soviets are no longer interested in eliminating Western economic presence. In seeking to establish a durable influence in these countries, the Soviets are apparently reconciled to sharing it with the West. This is especially true of India, whose relatively strong business community and well-established economic ties with Western countries preclude the possibility of a dominant Soviet economic influence. While alarms have been sounded in the West in the aftermath of the Bangladesh crisis regarding India's drawing closer to the Soviet orbit, it would seem that the Soviets have a more realistic appraisal of their own prospects and are content to establish stabler relations with India. The recent Soviet initiatives in solidifying economic and political ties, embodied by the 1970 economic agreements and the 1971 friendship treaty, must be interpreted against the background of anxieties over India's rightward drift, which began to be articulated in the late 1950's but which intensified during the following decade. Riding the crest of present Indian goodwill, the Soviets are taking advantage of the opportunities provided by the fortuitous events since 1969 to set their relations with India on a firmer and more permanent basis.

EPILOGUE : SOVIET POLICY TOWARDS INDIA SINCE BANGLADESH

As the elaborate welcome for General Secretary Brezhnev during his visit to India in 1973 confirms, Soviet prestige in India has remained at a quite high level since the Bangladesh crisis.[1] The strong show of Soviet support for India during that emergency has removed to a considerable degree the suspicions regarding Soviet policy in South Asia so clearly manifest in previous decades. The value of Soviet friendship having thereby been tested, the Soviet leader's visit was widely acclaimed in the Indian press. Judging from the amount of attention focused upon the visit and from the numerous instances of Brezhnev's public praise of Mrs. Gandhi and of India's role in world affairs, this perception of Soviet-

---

[1] Brezhnev was accorded full honors of a visiting head of state.

Indian friendship is a reciprocal one.[2]

Yet, despite apprehension in the Western press over the anticipated form of Indian repayment for Soviet support, Moscow has thus far not translated its prestige into concrete political advantage. Mrs. Gandhi's statement that India did not feel obligated to reciprocate Soviet support "in any tangible sense" made shortly after the December 1971 war continues to be relevant to the present state of Indo-Soviet relations.[3] To be sure, India has made minor diplomatic gestures, such as the elevation of her representation to North Vietnam to the ambassadorial level in January 1972 and the extension of diplomatic recognition to the German Democratic Republic in October 1972 and to both Korean states in December 1973, all of which have strengthened Moscow's international positions. However, considering the circumstances which surrounded these moves, their significance from Moscow's perspective should not be overestimated.[4] On balance, a review of the broad spectrum of Indo-Soviet relations since the Bangladesh crisis suggests that far from receiving concrete benefits from its support, Moscow's main achievement may have been permission to further demonstrate its support for India both politically and materially.

INDO-SOVIET ECONOMIC COLLABORATION

Certainly, there is no better indicator of Soviet support for India than the current wide-scale Soviet commitment to Indian economic development. The major economic agreements signed during Brezhnev's trip to India constitute an assurance of continued strong economic ties with India irrespective of the emerging prospects for trade with the West resultant from the process of detente. As two Soviet commentators reviewing the benefits of the Brezhnev visit affirmed, "India will be guaranteed against all kinds of

---

[2] With an entourage of 145 newsmen and journalists, coverage of the Brezhnev visit was transmitted live in color to the USSR.

[3] *New York Times*, February 17, 1972, p. 14.

[4] The naming of an ambassador to Hanoi, a step intended by New Delhi well in advance, was meant as a rebuff to Washington, which by blocking aid to India in December 1971 had forfeited its leverage to stay India's hand. The diplomatic recognition of the GDR and both Korean states was coordinated and approved by all the states concerned.

contingencies in the development of its industry."[5] It is most probable that the mutual confidence and trust invested in Indo-Soviet friendship during the Bangladesh emergency itself was a necessary pre-condition for the intensification of Indo-Soviet economic collaboration. For example, Soviet initiatives for joint production projects which had remained in the discussion stage prior to the crisis have now taken concrete form. In accordance with recent Soviet strategy of setting up projects designed to take advantage of low labor costs in the Third World, several production collaboration agreements have been signed by which the Soviets will export cotton to be converted into sewing thread and textiles, wool to be turned into knitwear, and steel to be manufactured into cutlery and nuts and bolts—with the finished products to be re-exported for the Soviet market. The production of automobile ancillaries for the Soviet market and setting up of joint projects in Third World countries are also probable in the near future.[6] While of obvious benefit to the USSR, these projects would also provide Indians with jobs and give much needed work to India's underutilized industrial plants.[7]

The Soviets have also sought through long-term projects as well as short-term agreements to alleviate India's energy problems which have become acute as a result of the oil crisis.[8] Besides providing aid

[5] G. Kudin and P. Naumov, "Days Infused with the Warmth of Friendship," *New Times*, No. 49 (December, 1973), 5.

[6] The arrangement of joint projects in Third World countries is specifically mentioned in the fifteen year agreement on economic and trade cooperation. The financing of such multilateral projects may come from Comecon's international investment bank utilizing transferable ruble accounts. This has been proposed by L. Z. Zevin in his article, "Sotsialisticheskaia Ekonomicheskaia Integratsiia i Sotrudnichestvo so Stranami "Tret'ego Mira," *Narody Azii i Afriki*, No. 2 (1972), 9.

[7] This plan also seems a way in which the Soviets hope to resuscitate some of their less successful aid projects in India. For example, the Soviet-aided surgical instruments plant near Madras, which was a poorly planned project that had been exporting most of its production to the Soviet Union, is now expected to be adapted to the production of steel cutlery for the Soviet market. *Times of India*, May 20, 1972, p. 1.

[8] A threefold increase in the price of oil since 1973 has forced India to cut back her oil imports by at least 3 million tons, which will deeply affect fertilizer, food, and overall industrial production (which is expected to decline by 20% during 1974). *New York Times*, February 4, 1974, p. 9. A recently negotiated credit for the delivery of oil from Iran, one of India's largest sources of oil imports, should help alleviate this crisis. See, *New York Times*, February 23, 1974, p. 15.

for the construction of a six million ton oil refinery at Mathura, the Soviets have also sought to meet India's immediate oil requirements for the public sector through the delivery of three million tons of crude oil in addition to the one and one-half million tons of kerosene already promised.[9] In addition, the Soviets signed a protocol providing for intensive oil drilling operations, rapid development of known oil fields and the maximum utilization of currently productive wells.[10] The Soviets have also sought to revive India's lagging nationalized coal industry with the signing of a protocol on December 27, 1973, which provides assistance for the development of three open caste mines.[11]

A notable change in the character of Soviet economic assistance to India is that with a few exceptions, such as the expansion of Bhilai and Bokaro steel plants to 7 and 10 tons annual capacity, respectively, the construction of the Calcutta underground railroad project and the Mathura oil refinery, the Soviets have announced substantial credits for India's fifth five-year plan without earmarking these funds for specific projects as in the past.[12] This flexibility suggests that Moscow may be concentrating its efforts on ensuring that projects built with Soviet aid are operating at maximum efficiency. In this respect, the recent agreement to build a 100,000 tons annual capacity refractory brick plant at Bhilai which will help India overcome a chronic shortage of refractory bricks for public sector steel plants may serve as a prototype for future Soviet assistance.[13]

Moscow is also concerned with upgrading the performance of their economic collaboration with India. The fifteen year pact on trade and economic cooperation calls for improvement in the terms of credit and methods of account, which may mean longer grace and repayment periods on credits. A separate agreement signed

---

[9] *Times of India*, January 1, 1974, p. 4.

[10] *India News*, January 25, 1974, p. 1. It has also been reported that the Soviets offered to share with India part of the production from new oil fields being built in Eastern Siberia with Japanese aid. See, *Times of India*, December 6, 1973, p. 5.

[11] *Times of India*, December 28, 1973, p. 1.

[12] Soviet credits for India's forthcoming five-year plan are estimated at around $80 million. *Times of India*, December 8, 1973, p. 6.

[13] *Times of India*, December 6, 1973, p. 5.

during the Brezhnev visit established a study group, consisting of members of the Soviet Gosplan and Indian Planning Commission, which will seek to eliminate supply bottlenecks and coordinate economic collaboration more effectively. The joint study group is also mandated to facilitate the transfer of knowledge in economic forecasting and planning methodology.

A final area of emphasis in the recent economic agreements is the effort to provide India with an independent research and design capacity within the state sector—long considered by Soviet observers to be a weakness in India's economic development. While they have thus far concentrated their attention on the engineering and design facility of the heavy industrial complex at Ranchi, the Soviets apparently have some hope of significantly limiting India's overall technological dependence on the industrialized capitalist states in the future.[14]

If these ambitious programs proceed as scheduled, the announced target of a 50 to 100 percent increase in Indo-Soviet trade by 1980, set during the Brezhnev visit, may well be within sight. Despite the fact that the December 1971 war probably gave a needed boost to Indo-Soviet trade,[15] Indian economists have felt that without a significant diversification of exports and imports there were only limited possibilities for the continued growth of trade.[16] While the growth of Indo-Soviet trade seems assured with the realization of the aforementioned joint production collaboration ventures, a more serious problem is the growing imbalance of Indian exports over

---

[14] This possibility is mentioned by G. Skorov in his article, "Problemy Ispol'zovaniia Nauki i Tekhniki v Razvivaiushchikhsia Stranakh," *Mirovaia Ekonomika i Mezhdunarodnye Otnosheniia*, No. 9 (1973), 36.

[15] Largely as a result of Soviet efforts to fill the gap left by the abrupt U.S. cessation of deliveries of non-ferrous metals, newsprint, rolled steel and fertilizer following the December 1971 war, Indo-Soviet trade expanded by more than 20% in 1972 to 451 million rubles. Ministerstvo Vneshnei Torgovli SSSR, *Vneshniaia Torgovlia SSSR za 1972g*. (Moscow, 1973). Preliminary Soviet estimates for Indo-Soviet trade in 1973 indicate a 15% increase. See, *Ekonomicheskoe Polozhenie i Obzor Kapitalisticheskikh i Razvivaiushchikhsia Stran za 1972g. i Nachalo 1973g*, 135. For a comparison with previous years, consult Table I, p. 96. If the present trade trend continues, the Soviet Union may well supplant the United States as India's biggest trade partner.

[16] See, for example, Professor Sumitra Chishti's remarks on the Brezhnev visit in *The States* (December 22, 1973), 18.

imports.¹⁷ Moreover, although their record is better than the East European countries in this respect, the Soviets have not imported proportionately as many Indian manufactured products as was intended.¹⁸ Another difficulty concerns the fact that the USSR experiences shortages of many of the very same items, such as non-ferrous metals, steel alloys, newsprint and fertilizers, which India needs most. This may have been partially responsible for recent shortfalls in Soviet exports of copper, zinc, nickel and petroleum products despite efforts to step up deliveries of these and other goods.¹⁹ To be sure, there seems to be a strong Soviet resolve to meet India's needs for these vital products as exemplified by a recent $80 million deal for 325,000 tons of Soviet fertilizer—the largest single fertilizer contract ever signed by the Indian government.²⁰ It has also been reported that the Soviets have proposed to build a pulp factory in Siberia to meet India's acute needs for newsprint.²¹

In the broader perspective, the recent expansion of Indo-Soviet economic cooperation represents not merely an effort to further perfect their economic relations but may also have the purpose of drawing India into the "international socialist division of labor" between socialist and developing countries recently advocated by Soviet economists.²² The Soviet leadership has indeed promised to adjust their own long range plans to provide for Indo-Soviet economic collaboration.²³ Yet, whether such coordination is

[17] Continuing a trend of recent years, India exported 312.5 million rubles worth of goods to the USSR in 1972 and received only 138.5 million rubles worth of Soviet imports. See, MVT SSSR, *Vneshniaia Torgovlia SSSR za 1972g.* (Moscow, 1973).

[18] The proportion of manufactured products in India's total exports to the USSR during the 1965-1970 period did not exceed 12%, whereas 40% was the planned target. See, Sumitra Chishti, "Export Boost Result of Soviet Cooperation," *The States* (November 24, 1973), 24.

[19] *Times of India*, November 5, 1973, p. 4.

[20] *India News*, February 8, 1974, p. 1.

[21] *Times of India*, December 6, 1973, p. 5.

[22] For an exposition of this strategy, see, L. Z. Zevin, "Sotsialisticheskaia Ekonomicheskaia Integratsiia i Sotrudnichestvo so Stranami "Tret'ego Mira"," *Narody Azii i Afriki*, No. 2 (1972), 3-14.

[23] See, specifically, Brezhnev's remarks on this subject during a dinner speech at the Soviet embassy honoring Mrs. Gandhi. *Socialist India* (December 8, 1973), 29-30.

eventually achieved remains highly problematic. Even though Soviet aid is earmarked exclusively for the development of the Indian state sector, dovetailing of plans may prove difficult to achieve given the generally disappointing performance of planning in India. It should be noted that economic planning, which was suspended in the late 1960's, seems destined for further troubles in the wake of the major impact which the oil crisis has had on India.[24]

Moreover, the Soviets may still encounter resistance to their initiatives from the Indian side. When, for example, the Soviets sought to sell India thermal power equipment which they could deliver within two years, officials of the Indian ministry of heavy industry, adhering to the government goal of Indian economic self-sufficiency, were interested in placing the orders with the state sector heavy machine building plant even though delivery would have taken at least 36 months.[25] Although in this instance, the Indian Planning Commission intervened to work out an arrangement for the importation of two complete Soviet turbosets and other components, one cannot be confident of such successful negotiated outcomes in the future. One is reminded in this regard that negotiations over prices have already scuttled the railway wagon deal and have delayed the textile production conversion arrangement.[26]

Even should these plans of intensified economic collaboration proceed without serious difficulties, it is highly doubtful that India would eventually become economically subordinate to the Soviet bloc. With the dependence of her industry on advanced technology and deliveries of highly sophisticated complex equipment and

[24] A probable indication of this is the resignation of the respected economist, Dr. B. S. Minhas, from the Planning Commission over what he and other economists believe to be a highly unrealistic and overoptimistic annual growth rate target of 5.5% during the forthcoming five-year plan. See, *The New York Times*, December 10, 1973, p. 10.

[25] The Soviet officials also argued that any future Indian surplus production of thermal power equipment could be exported at a later date. See, *Times of India*, December 13, 1973, p. 5. A similar report of Indian reluctance to accept Soviet equipment for the Calcutta underground railroad project has been documented by R. V. R. Chandrasekhara Rao, "Indo-Soviet Economic Relations," *Asian Survey* (August 1973), 798.

[26] *Times of India*, November 28, 1973, p. 6.

her perennial needs for grain imports,[27] India will be oriented to Western markets for a long time to come. While closer economic links should enhance the long term stability of Indo-Soviet relations in general, it cannot be assumed that Soviet political leverage in India will increase immeasurably thereby. Indeed, as the history of Indian relations with the United States (which has given India over six times the amount of Soviet aid) indicates, a country as large and as jealous of her independence as India is not likely to be significantly pressured by attempts at "ruble diplomacy."

INDO-SOVIET POLITICAL RELATIONS

An examination of current Soviet policy towards India suggests, on the contrary, that Moscow with all its economic assistance has refrained from exerting any notable political pressure on India. Soviet support for the Indian side during the protracted negotiations over unresolved issues arising from the Bangladesh crisis serves as a good case in point. While a Tashkent-type direct mediation of these issues was precluded by Moscow's partisan role during the crisis, with its prestige ascendant in both New Delhi and Dacca, Moscow might have acted to expedite a settlement through behind-the-scenes pressure.

This is most probably what Mr. Bhutto had in mind when he went to Moscow just months after the conclusion of hostilities. Although the Soviets had immediately after the conflict called for direct negotiations between the parties involved without any outside interference (i.e., China), a remark by Kosygin during an earlier visit of the Afghan Prime Minister to the effect that the Soviets were prepared to contribute to a political settlement of disputed issues in South Asia may have encouraged Bhutto to enlist Soviet support for the repatriation of Pakistani POW's and the protection

---

[27] Given the USSR's own general food deficits, it is questionable how often the Soviets may be relied upon to provide grain on as favorable terms as the two million ton interest-free wheat loan arranged in the fall of 1973.

of the Bihari minority in Bangladesh.[28] If Bhutto harbored any illusions about enlisting Soviet support for the Pakistani position, these were dispelled by the visit itself. Receiving a cool reception, Bhutto found his hosts totally unresponsive. Thus, when Bhutto pointedly referred to the POW issue and the plight of the Bihari minority in Bangladesh during a luncheon in his honor, Prime Minister Kosygin responded by passing over in silence the specific issues and reiterating Soviet concern for direct negotiations between the parties involved. Moreover, Kosygin went so far as to publicly embarrass his guest by characterizing the Bangladesh crisis as a clash of forces between a national liberation movement and an "anti-popular military dictatorship" and added: "If history were to repeat itself, we would again take the same position, because we are convinced it was correct."[29] Besides restoring Soviet-Pakistan trade and aid programs that had been broken off during the hostilities, the talks accomplished very little from the Pakistani viewpoint. That the talks were a bitter disappointment to Bhutto is clearly reflected in his remarks on his return in which he derided the Tashkent agreement (and by inference any Soviet mediatory role) and admitted that prospects for a peace settlement were as distant as ever.[30]

If any doubts remained concerning Soviet fidelity to their stated positions, these were soon laid to rest by Indian Foreign Minister Swaran Singh's trip to Moscow a few weeks after the Bhutto visit. During the discussions it was reported that a complete identity of views on the situation in the subcontinent and on the need for a lasting settlement of outstanding issues was achieved. Upon his return, the Indian Foreign Minister rejected the proposition that the Soviets ever wanted to assume a mediatory role and also denied

---

[28] See, for example, *Times of India*, March 15, 1972, p. 1. This Indian press interpretation seems to be more indicative of the state of Indian anxieties than an accurate reading of Kosygin's statement, which was coupled with a reaffirmation of the Soviet (and Indian) view that a settlement should be accomplished without outside interference. The Indian government denied that Kosygin's speech signified any change in the stated Soviet position in favor of direct negotiations.

[29] *Pravda*, March 18, 1972, pp. 1, 4, in *Current Digest of the Soviet Press*, XXIV, No. 11, 2.

[30] *The New York Times*, March 20, 1972, p. 8.

any Soviet pressure on the POW issue.[31]

Nor have the Soviets apparently sought to exert such pressure during the long course of negotiations since then. For the most part the Soviets have placed great priority on Pakistani recognition of Bangladesh as the key to normalization on the subcontinent. Thus, for example, in reviewing the July 1972 Simla agreement on delimiting a ceasefire line and normalizing Indo-Pakistani relations, Soviet commentators endorsed the Indo-Bangladesh position that tripartite negotiations on the repatriation of POW's and related issues must be preceded by Pakistani recognition of Bangladesh.[32] Even after the Indian and Bangladesh governments had made some important concessions to the Pakistani side in the April 1973 proposals for population exchanges and POW repatriation—a move which the Soviets lauded as a "positive step"[33]—the Soviets continued to stress the importance of Pakistani recognition of Bangladesh as a precondition for the solution of the unresolved issues on the subcontinent.

The fact that the return of Pakistani POW's has preceded the recent dramatic recognition of Bangladesh by Bhutto at the Lahore conference of Moslem nations attests to Bhutto's considerable political skills and is not suggestive of any major Soviet pressure.[34] The Soviets may, however, have helped the progress of these negotiations along by omitting, in recent months, any public mention of Bangladesh's demand for war crimes trials of 195 Pakistani POW's—an issue which had stood as the last remaining road-block to Pakistan's

---

[31] *Times of India*, April 7, 1972, p. 1.

[32] See, I. Borisov, "Outlook for Lasting Peace on the Indian Subcontinent," *New Times*, No. 27 (1972), 16, and G. Kudin, "The Simla Summit," *New Times*, No. 28 (1972), 8.

[33] See, the communique issued after Podgorny's visit to Afghanistan in May, 1973. *Pravda*, May 26, 1973, p. 1, in *Current Digest of the Soviet Press*, XXV, No. 21, 15.

[34] Selecting the Lahore meeting as the setting for the announcement of recognition was a particularly astute move on Bhutto's part, since it enabled him to claim that Pakistan had not submitted to big power pressure but had acted in deference to the wishes of fraternal Moslem states, thereby mollifying domestic Pakistani sentiment.

recognition of Bangladesh.[35] With diplomacy on the subcontinent at last moving towards normalization of relations among the three South Asian states, Moscow must be pleased that progress towards this desired goal has been achieved without its direct involvement.

The Soviets have been much less successful, however, in promoting their plan for Asian collective security. Originally presented as a system of security pacts designed to fill the void left by British withdrawal east of Suez and American post-Vietnam disengagement from the area with the intent of thwarting Chinese expansionism, in the face of a cool Asian reception, the Brezhnev plan has subsequently been emasculated of its security aspects. In its present form, emphasis is placed on economic and political cooperation of all Asian states including China.[36] While the Soviets, by inviting Chinese participation, have sought to disarm Asian criticism that the scheme is anti-Chinese, insofar as it projects a stabilization of Asia on the basis of the present status quo, the plan nonetheless conflicts with the interests of all "revisionist" states in the area, the most important of which is China.

If the Soviets are eventually going to make any headway with the Brezhnev plan for Asian collective security, they must of course win the support of India. Indeed, the Soviet public build-up of India's international prestige since 1972 can largely be explained in terms of their efforts to win India's sponsorship of the plan. The great attention in the Soviet media focused on Asian collective security just prior to the Brezhnev visit led many observers to believe that the Indian endorsement was

---

[35] Presumably, a tacit understanding was reached prior to recognition that the issue of war crimes trials would be dropped. While remaining silent on that issue, the Soviets have, however, pushed for the repatriation of Biharis stranded in Bangladesh by endorsing the Indo-Bengali formulation demanding mutual repatriation of Pakistanis stranded in Bangladesh and Bengalis stranded in Pakistan. The Pakistani government has so far been reluctant to take in large numbers of Biharis since this would create additional economic problems and perhaps aggravate Pakistan's tense nationality problems. See, *The New York Times*, Oct. 27, 1973, p. 7.

[36] For a review of the transformation of the Soviet concept of Asian collective security, see, Alexander O. Gebhardt, "The Soviet System of Collective Security in Asia," *Asian Survey* (December 1973), 1075-91, and Ian Clark, "The Indian Subcontinent and Collective Security—Soviet Style," *Australian Outlook* (December 1972), 315-25.

precisely one of the main aims of the visit.

Yet, despite Soviet wooing, the joint declaration concluding the Brezhnev trip conspicuously omitted any reference to Asian collective security. This does not necessarily connote any significant divergence in Indian and Soviet attitudes toward the security of Asia. In its substantive aspects, recent Soviet clarifications of the Brezhnev plan have brought it into line with the Indian view that the long range stabilization of the region could be achieved through the gradual development of trade and economic cooperation. Moreover, a comparison of comments contained in the joint declaration on the subject of stability in Asia with earlier Soviet expositions reveals a striking degree of conformity with emphasis in both placed on a reaffirmation of the famed five principles of peaceful coexistence.[37] The Soviet *Pravda* commentator, V. Shurygin, then, was quite accurate, when, in reviewing the results of the Brezhnev trip, he stated that the basic principles of the Soviet proposal for collective security were reflected in documents signed at New Delhi.[38]

The main reason for India's refusal to endorse the Soviet plan, therefore, is that no Asian country seeks to unnecessarily offend China. An Indian endorsement would have reinforced Chinese suspicions of Indian collusion in sinister Soviet designs against China—an impression which the Indians are anxious to debunk. In order to keep the door open in dealing with China, the Indian government has ostensibly sought to publicly distance itself from the Soviet Union. The Brezhnev visit itself affords graphic confirmation of this. Not only did India refuse to formally endorse collective security, but New Delhi also reportedly turned down Moscow's request that the Brezhnev visit coincide with the second anniversary of the Soviet-Indian friendship treaty and, moreover, declined to label the fifteen year economic agreement signed during

---

[37] Compare the text of the joint declaration (*Times of India*, December 1, 1973, p. 7) with Brezhnev's speech at Alma-Ata on August 15, 1973 and a follow-up *Pravda* editorial of August 24, 1973. The only noteworthy difference between the joint declaration and these earlier Soviet remarks is the inclusion in the *Pravda* editorial of a statement affirming the "impermissibility of territorial seizures through aggression"—a position certainly not detrimental to India given the current disposition of the Kashmir dispute.

[38] *Pravda*, December 14, 1973, p. 4.

the visit a treaty which the Soviets desired.[39] There is little doubt that Mrs. Gandhi's remark in a speech made at New Delhi's Red Fort that there was "no reason why friendship with the Soviet Union should be directed against any third country" was made for the benefit of the Chinese.[40] As long as she seeks to normalize relations with China, it is likely that India will continue to publicly demonstrate her independence of the Soviet Union in the foreseeable future.

THE ROLE OF GREAT POWER RIVALRIES

A review of the Soviet and Indian postures towards Asian collective security points to the salience of China as the underlying explanatory factor. Whereas New Delhi, in its desire to normalize relations with Peking, has avoided any antagonistic gesture, Moscow has promoted collective security in large part to contain Peking's expansionism in the region. It is curious that while the Soviets deny any such intention when they specifically discuss the collective security plan, they have become much more explicit in articulating their anxieties regarding Chinese "hegemonistic" ambitions in Asia—a perspective which would, after all, evoke a counter strategy of containment. The important role of India in this strategy is indicated by the Soviet view that India and the Soviet Union stand as the two primary obstacles to the realization of Chinese designs. According to this perspective, China is accused, on the one hand, of seeking to isolate India by stirring up discord between India and her neighbors and, on the other, of trying to weaken India internally by supporting guerrilla movements among the Naga hill tribes.[41] In order to bind closer to themselves Pakistan, a country which the Soviets regard as the cornerstone of

---

[39] *The States* (December 22, 1973), 12. Another index of India's desire to maximize her independence vis-a-vis the Soviet Union is her attitude toward the 1971 treaty. While the Soviets continue to attach much importance to it, the Indians denigrate the treaty's significance and consider it rather a matter of expediency dictated by the exigency of the Bangladesh crisis. (For an analysis of the contextual implications of the treaty, see above, pp. 77-79).

[40] *Socialist India* (December 8, 1973), 14.

[41] See, for example, *Moscow Radio*, December 21, 1971, summarized in *USSR and the Third World*, II, No. 1, p. 5.

Chinese policy in South Asia,[42] the Chinese are accused of seeking to prevent the normalization of the post-Bangladesh situation on the subcontinent. They have interpreted the visit of Chinese Vice Foreign Minister Chiao Kuan-hua to Islamabad in the midst of the 1972 Simla talks and the Chinese veto of Bangladesh's application for UN admission as signs of Chinese intent to obstruct a negotiated settlement of disputed issues among the South Asian states directly involved.[43]

These heightened anxieties over Chinese policy in the subcontinent have elicited stronger Soviet support for India in the post-Bangladesh period. This can be seen most clearly in the Soviet response to the communiques marking President Nixon's February 1972 visit to China. Not only was the section in both American and Chinese communiques calling for a troop withdrawal of Indian and Pakistani forces to pre-1971 positions interpreted by New Delhi and Moscow as outside interference in the affairs of the subcontinent, but the portion of the Chinese version raising the issue of Jammu and Kashmir in a provocative way was seen as an outright attempt to rekindle chauvinistic aspirations in Pakistan.[44] Perhaps as a counter to alleged Chinese interference, the Soviets openly reaffirmed their support of the Indian claim to Kashmir for the first time since the fall of Khrushchev. At a press conference soon after the Nixon Peking visit, the noted Soviet Indianist, G. G. Kotovskii, stated that the Kashmiri people had already expressed their right to self-determination through the general

[42] Besides the anti-Indian element, the Soviets also recognize the long term strategic significance of Pakistan for China. Not only does the Sinkiang-Gilgit highway provide China with the quickest outlet (via the port of Karachi) to the markets in the Near East and Africa, but a strong pro-Chinese Pakistan is geographically situated to deny the Soviet Union overland access to India through Iran and Afghanistan—a project in which the Soviets have long been interested.

[43] The Soviets, perhaps for propagandistic purposes, may have distorted the Chinese position somewhat. With respect to the Bangladesh vote, the Soviet Union reportedly pushed for a showdown whereas China sought to delay consideration to prevent an embarrassing use of the veto in Pakistan's defense. After that vote, moreover, the Chinese made an overture by stating that they had no prejudices against the people of Bangladesh—a definite indication of Chinese preparedness to recognize Bangladesh following Pakistan. See, *Times of India*, May 26, 1972, p. 10.

[44] See, *Izvestia*, March 4, 1972, p. 3.

elections recently held in that state.⁴⁵ Leaving no doubt that this was not a casual remark, G. V. Matveev, in a major article published a few weeks later in the new Soviet academic journal *Problemy Dal'nego Vostoka*, endorsed the Indian view that Pakistan invaded Kashmir in 1947 and thereby divided the principality artificially despite the popular sentiment for unification with India.⁴⁶

Even more significant than the reaffirmation of Soviet support for India on Kashmir are their recent pronouncements on the Sino-Indian border. While the Soviets may not deem Indian reluctance to endorse the Asian collective security proposal as too high a price for India's desire to normalize relations with China, they most assuredly would become alarmed if India with this aim in mind were to make territorial concessions to China—a circumstance which would undermine Moscow's own bargaining position on the Sino-Soviet border dispute. It must have surely occurred to them that the resolution of the Sino-Indian border dispute, probably on the basis of recognition of the de facto Chinese control of Aksai Chin and the Indian position in NEFA, would be easier to achieve than a settlement of Sino-Soviet territorial differences. To forestall such an eventuality, the Soviets have sought to stiffen India's resolve to resist Chinese pressure by taking a public stand for the first time in favor of the Indian position on the border dispute. In the aforementioned article on Chinese policy in the subcontinent, G. V. Matveev, while stopping short of actually endorsing Indian territorial claims, nevertheless revealed Chinese treachery in dealing with India on the border issue after the signing of the 1954 agreement on Tibet, which had lulled the Indian side into thinking that

---

⁴⁵ *Times of India*, March 31, 1972, p. 11.

⁴⁶ G. V. Matveev, "Politicheskie Makhinatsii Pekina na Indostanskom Poluostrove," *Problemy Dal'nego Vostoka*, No. 4 (1972), 39. This statement should not be interpreted as a sign of Soviet encouragement for an Indian drive on the Pakistan-held sector of Kashmir, for this would assuredly bring active Chinese and American intervention. Moreover, such an interpretation is inconsistent with the Soviet position on border questions which rules out the use of force to resolve existing territorial disputes. It seems more likely that the Matveev statement was intended to strengthen India's bargaining position to convert the present cease-fire line in the area into a permanent international border.

the border issue had been settled.⁴⁷ In recounting this episode, the Soviets were clearly forewarning India to be wary of such negotiations in the future.

It should be recalled at this point that the Soviet position on this issue is complicated by the fact that Soviet maps have traditionally acknowledged Chinese claims along the Sino-Indian border—a position for which the Soviets have been accused of "cartological aggression" by the right wing opposition in India.⁴⁸ Although the Indian government had made several formal inquiries concerning this matter to the Soviet government, Moscow has never formally altered its juridical position, perhaps out of consideration that such a unilateral action might serve as a negative precedent to be emulated by countries which have territorial claims against the USSR. The Soviets have instead sought to defuse the issue, on the one hand, by deleting the disputed areas from their maps,⁴⁹ and, on the other, by assuring the Indian government that their juridical position would not compromise their support for India in any future flare-up along the Sino-Indian border.⁵⁰ More recently, however, the Soviets have shown some signs of altering their stand in India's favor. On May 19, 1973, *Moscow Radio* broadcast that "one of the methods of Peking's anti-India policy is to put forward a baseless territorial claim."⁵¹ Whether or not the Soviets will follow this up with a formal revision of their *dejure* position on the border dispute remains to be seen. In any event, their heightened support for India on this matter

---

⁴⁷ Matveev, *op cit.*, 40. In a subsequent article in that journal, the charges against the Chinese were taken one step further by an allegation that the Chinese had been the first to attack Indian border patrols in 1959 (at the time of the border clashes, blame had not been affixed to either of the combatants). See, E. D. Kostikov, "Velikoderzhavnye Ambitsii i Pogranichnaia Politika Pekinskogo Rukovodstva," *Problemy Dal'nego Vostoka*, No. 1 (1973), 59.

⁴⁸ See above, p. 79, footnote 227.

⁴⁹ Not one of the six maps displayed in the section on India in the 1973 edition of *Bol'shaia Sovetskaia Entsiklopediia* shows the areas of the Sino-Indian border in question.

⁵⁰ When questioned about this matter in Parliament shortly after his return from Moscow in 1972, Foreign Minister Swaran Singh stated that the security clause in the Indo-Soviet treaty would become operative when India's actual line of control was threatened. See, *Times of India*, May 26, 1972, p. 10.

⁵¹ Reported in *USSR and the Third World*, III, No. 5, 306.

suggests a certain uneasiness by Moscow over the future direction of New Delhi's efforts to normalize relations with Peking. While they do not expect the Chinese to soften their attitude towards India in the near future,[52] they have nevertheless admonished India that such normalization should not be pursued to the detriment of Soviet-Indian friendship.[53]

While the perceived Chinese threat has garnered a great deal of attention in the Soviet press, Moscow also remains somewhat apprehensive regarding American policy in the region. Although it has become commonplace among Western observers to concentrate exclusively on the Chinese factor in analyzing Soviet-Indian relations to the exclusion of serious consideration of American policy on the grounds that both superpowers share fundamentally common interests in seeking political and economic stabilization in South Asia, the Soviets are not nearly as complacent. Specifically, Soviet observers are fearful of potential Sino-American collusion in the subcontinent. They point to the coordination of Chinese and American efforts on behalf of Pakistan during and after the December 1971 war as evidence of this.[54] In a recent article in the new publication of Soviet Americanists, *SShA*, the view was advanced that the Nixon administration's anti-India course was closely connected with considerations of the desire to achieve future cooperation with the Chinese in this region.[55] The Soviets apparently share India's apprehension that the United States might seek to apply

[52] This opinion has been explicitly stated by S. G. Iurkov in his work, *Pekin: Novaia Politika?* (Moscow, 1972), p. 236.

[53] See, for example, P. Kutsobin and V. Shurygin, "South Asia: Tendencies Towards Stability," *International Affairs*, No. 4 (1973), 48. It may be added that the present Indian government has responded with assurances that this would not happen. See, Swaran Singh's remarks to this effect shortly before the Brezhnev visit. *Times of India*, November 24, 1973, p. 9.

[54] It was even suggested that China's position was one of the factors which influenced the dispatch of ships of the 7th Fleet to the Bay of Bengal. *Pravda*, December 22, 1971, p. 5, in *Current Digest of the Soviet Press*, XXIII, No. 51, 6. This view is remarkably similar to that of C. L. Sulzberger, who interpreted the dispatch of the aircraft carrier Enterprise into the Bay of Bengal as a demonstration of American resolve in time of an emergency for the benefit of the Chinese. See, *New York Times*, April 21, 1972, p. 39.

[55] V. P. Lukin, "American-Chinese Relations: Concept and Reality," *SShA*, No. 2 (1973), 12-23, in *Current Digest of the Soviet Press*, XXV, No. 11, 5.

the "pattern of European diplomacy in Metternich's time" to Asia.[56] More specifically, both countries are concerned about the major military buildup in Iran and fear that already some of these arms have found their way to Pakistan. The Soviets have also been critical of proposals emanating from Pakistan for a limited collective security system including Pakistan, Iran and Turkey and patronized by the United States and China.[57] From the Soviet perspective, this is but a poorly veiled attempt to revitalize CENTO as a counterpoise to an alleged India-Soviet-Iraq axis.

Whether or not these perceptions of potential threats lead to a renewed arms race in the subcontinent cannot be discerned as of this writing. Thus far, Pakistan has been given replacements for its losses of tanks and jets in the December war from China and a very limited amount of "non-lethal" aircraft spare parts and armored personnel carriers from the United States.[58] More recently, the Chinese have reportedly supplied Pakistan with a number of outmoded TU-16 bombers which are not effective against a modern air defense.[59] While these deliveries, in themselves, would seem insufficient to cause India much alarm, the estimation of Pakistani military strength has become more complicated by Pakistan's reported acquisition of special arrangements with such Moslem states as Abu Dhabi, according to which Pakistani air force members will fly and maintain Abu Dhabi's recently purchased Mirage jets in return for their disposition by Pakistan in the event of an emergency.[60] Despite this arrangement, however, no buildup of Indian land and air forces has taken place since the December war although the Indians are now producing an improved version

[56] *Izvestia*, April 8, 1972, p. 4.
[57] *Pravda*, June 30, 1973, p. 5.
[58] Pakistan lost 220 tanks, 83 aircraft, 2 submarines, and 20 other naval vessels during the December 1971 war. For a complete estimate, consult Stockholm International Peace Research Institute. *World Armaments and Disarmament Yearbook* (Stockholm, New York and London, 1973), p. 303.
[59] *Times of India*, May 17, 1973, p. 7.
[60] *The New York Times*, December 10, 1973, p. 32.

of the MIG-21 under Soviet license.⁶¹ Judging from the denial of Bhutto's request for military aid during his September 1973 visit to Washington and from the Soviet's slow pace in processing Indian requests for additional arms,⁶² it would seem that both superpowers, for the present, are anxious to avoid an arms race on the subcontinent.

This military balance could be upset by emergent prospects for a Soviet-American confrontation in the Indian Ocean. The recent increase in the size of the Soviet Indian Ocean squadron has been countered by more regular patrols of American carrier forces into the area.⁶³ In addition, the Defense Department has recently announced plans for a $29 million expansion of the Anglo-American naval communications station at Diego Garcia into a naval air base—a move anticipated by the Soviets long in advance.⁶⁴ These recent American moves have been justified on the grounds of anticipated Soviet expansion into the area following the opening of the Suez Canal. In response, the Soviets accuse the Pentagon of deliberately fabricating a Soviet naval menace as a smokescreen for its own designs of establishing a permanent naval presence in an area of recognized strategic significance astride the Persian Gulf oil lifeline and within the range of missile-bearing submarines for targets in the USSR's southern borderlands.⁶⁵

The Soviet charge is worthy of more than cursory consideration.

---

⁶¹ It should be noted that while India is now self-sufficient in many small arms and is producing many of her own tanks and aircraft, she is still dependent upon the delivery of more complex weapon parts and military technology from supplier nations. It has been reported that the Soviets still exercise much control over the production of their aircraft in India through their exclusive possession of detailed designs and deliveries of more sophisticated components. For further elucidation, consult Stockholm Peace Research Institute. *The Arms Trade with the Third World* (New York and Stockholm, 1971), pp. 749-53.

⁶² The Indians are specifically interested in MIG-23's and SAM 6 and 7's, which proved so effective during the October 1973 Mideast war.

⁶³ Estimates of the current number of Soviet ships there vary from 20 to a high of 32, with perhaps only half of these being combat vessels. See, *New York Times*, December 2, 1973, p. 1, and December 6, 1973, p. 13. Previous estimates set the number of Soviet military vessels at 8 to 10. See, *New York Times*, June 18, 1973, p. 3.

⁶⁴ *The New York Times*, January 21, 1974, p. 3.

⁶⁵ See, for example, V. F. Davydov and V. A. Kremeniuk, "Strategiia SShA v Zone Indiiskogo Okeana," *SShA*, No. 5 (1973), 6-17.

It should be noted that one of the frequent allegations emanating from Washington is that the Soviets already have or are seeking bases along the Indian subcontinent's littoral.[66] This allegation has never been substantiated and has frequently been denied by responsible Indian and Soviet officials. The Soviets have, in fact, sought to disarm such speculation about its activity. When it was rumored, for example, that the Soviet salvage operations in the Bangladesh ports of Chalna and Chittagong were a cover for the establishment of permanent military installations, the chief of the Soviet salvage team allowed an open inspection of the operations, which led one British journalist to conclude that the Soviets were more interested in winning friends than in securing a military toehold on the subcontinent.[67] Although we cannot be sure that this open display of good faith is an accurate reflection of peaceful Soviet intentions on the whole, it nevertheless seems obvious that the recent American initiatives are bound to eventually evoke a Soviet response in kind. One must, therefore, agree with Senator Clairborne Pell of Rhode Island, who recently characterized the Pentagon's proposal to expand the Diego Garcia facility as "a Pavlovian United States response that would stimulate the very threat we fear and precipitate an escalation in the costly arms race which we can ill afford."[68]

Within the context of Soviet-Indian relations, Soviet circumspection regarding U.S. policy in the area has forced them to temper their support for India's proposal to convert the Indian Ocean into a zone of peace. In order to keep their options open to counter

---

[66] The expectation that the Soviets would demand a permanent naval base at Vizagapatnam in return for their political and military support for India during the December war was raised specifically by Admiral Zumwalt during the December 4, 1971 meeting of the National Security Council reported in the Anderson papers. See, *New York Times*, January 6, 1972, p. 16.

[67] See, William Drummond's report in *The Guardian*, January 9, 1973, summarized in *USSR and the Third World*, III, No. 1, 3. Bangladesh Prime Minister Mujibur Rahman might have also been apprehensive regarding Soviet intentions in this regard since he had tried unsuccessfully to have the UN undertake the salvage operations before he received the Soviet offer in March 1972. Respect for Bangladesh sensitivities on this matter might have led the Soviets to set a time limit for the completion of salvage work by the end of 1973. *New York Times*, April 6, 1972, p. 3.

[68] *New York Times*, February 27, 1974, p. 4.

any American initiative, the Soviet Union (along with the United States) abstained on an Indian-sponsored UN resolution setting up a 15-member committee to explore further the proposal for a demilitarized Indian Ocean.[69] It should be stressed that the Soviets do not reject the Indian plan in principle. It received the qualified endorsement of Brezhnev, when he stated during his visit that the peace zone proposal was among the initiatives inspired by a concern for the peaceful future of Asia.[70] A certain Indian sympathy for the Soviet position has also been reciprocated, as evidenced by the fact that both sides in the joint declaration concluding the Brezhnev visit expressed a desire to seek a "fair solution" to the question of making the Indian Ocean a zone of peace. Just what such a "fair solution" would mean may already have been intimated by Soviet Deputy Foreign Minister (and former ambassador to India) Pegov. He is reported to have said that the first step in the direction of turning the Indian Ocean into a zone of peace would be the dismantling of all foreign bases, including British, American and French[71]—a proposal which is certainly consonant with India's desire to eliminate a major big power presence in the area (and thereby leave herself as the dominant regional power).

Indeed, one option that the Soviets might be interested in pursuing is to back India as a military buffer in the region. Such a relatively low risk policy would certainly not provoke the type of American response that would most definitely result from direct Soviet military action in the area. There are some indications, moreover, that the Soviets may already be thinking along these lines. Since the Bangladesh crisis, the Soviets have materially assisted India's efforts to increase her naval strength by supplying several "F" class submarines, "Petya" type patrol boats and "Osa" class missile boats.[72] Vocal encouragement for this naval buildup

---

[69] *Times of India*, December 7, 1972, p. 10. It should be noted that China joined Pakistan and India in voting for the measure.

[70] *New Times*, No. 49 (December, 1973), 4.

[71] As reported in an interview with V. P. Dutt, Pro Vice-Chancellor of the University of Delhi, *The States* (November 24, 1973), 48.

[72] K. Subrahmanyan, "Top-Level Indo-Soviet Rapport Required," *The States* (November 24, 1973), 32. It should be noted that while trimming its military budget in other areas, the Indian government has earmarked substantial increases for purchase of new naval vessels and is also constructing a naval base in the Andaman Islands.

has come from Admiral Gorshkov, who, on a visit to India in April 1972, was quoted as stating that India needed a strong navy.[73] Although this information does not point conclusively to any strategic trend, the development of India as an intermediary for Soviet security objectives in the Indian Ocean would not be surprising. India and the Soviet Union, after all, have no basic conflict of interests in the region. Certainly, Soviet sponsorship of a major Indian role in the Indian Ocean would give an additional dimension to the "profound community of interests" which Soviet commentators say underlies Indo-Soviet friendship.[74]

FUTURE CONTINGENCIES AND PROSPECTS

To a large extent, then, it is the international environment which has shaped Soviet policy towards India. While the current configuration of external political forces has educed strong Soviet solicitation and support for India, this situation could change in the future. A normalization of Sino-Indian relations, including a settlement of their border dispute, might neutralize India as an ally in Moscow's confrontation with Peking. While it is conceivable that a Sino-Indian rapprochement might even initially induce Moscow to court New Delhi all the more assiduously, in the long run such a turn of events would prompt a withdrawal of Soviet support for India in some spheres. So, too, in order to meet the current American challenge in the Indian Ocean, the Soviets may decide against tying their security interests to India and rather opt for a more direct response—a decision which might sour Soviet-Indian relations in much the same manner as present U.S.-Indian relations have been strained by the growing American naval presence in the area.

Irrespective of alterations in future patterns of international relations, the reliability of Indo-Soviet relations in the long range perspective depends largely upon the economic viability and political stability of India. Despite Moscow's willingness to come to

[73] *Times of India*, April 6, 1972, p. 7.
[74] See, for example, A. Maslennikov, "A Time-Tested Friendship," *New Times*, No. 32 (1972), 8; and V. P. Iakunin, "Po Puti Ukrepleniia Natsional'nogo Suvereniteta i Progressa," *Narody Azii i Afriki*, No. 4 (1972), 12.

India's aid materially, it is doubtful that any foreign power can significantly ameliorate India's current economic and social plight. Beset by food riots, strikes, official corruption and a possible sharp downward turn in annual industrial production as a result of the oil crisis, India is experiencing her worst economic conditions since independence. This, of course, has weakened Mrs. Gandhi's political power as candidates of her party have suffered defeats in several by-elections.

The Soviets have not been oblivious to this growing trend towards economic and political disequilibrium. Doubts have begun to be expressed regarding the willingness of the ruling Congress party to carry out its 1971 electoral mandate for socio-economic reforms. Soviet commentators have observed the return of many former right wing defectors to the Congress and accused them of obstructing the implementation of progressive measures.[75] The Soviets also assert that land reforms, which are viewed as absolutely essential if the disintegrative social impact of the "green revolution" on village life is to be checked, have been blocked at the local level by many Congress leaders and government officials who are themselves landlords.[76]

Despite these criticisms, Moscow is still committed to collaborating with the ruling Congress party. Indeed, the complimentary remarks accorded Mrs. Gandhi and the Congress party by Secretary Brezhnev during his visit boosted the lagging prestige of the government within the country.[77] The Soviets apparently still believe

---

[75] E. Gryaznov, "India: Main Tendencies of Socio-Economic Development," *International Affairs*, No. 12 (1971), 56.

[76] *Pravda*, August 13, 1972, p. 2.

[77] Brezhnev's approbation of the Congress's domestic reform program could not have pleased the CPI, which has been highly critical of government mismanagement of late. However, this does not necessarily mean that the CPI and Soviet leadership are working at cross purposes. It should be emphasized that given the government's sagging popularity, it was necessary that the CPI adopt a more critical posture in order to maintain its public credibility. This policy, moreover, seems to have achieved definite benefits. The recent erosion of Congress strength in Uttar Pradesh and other states will undoubtedly force Congress state governments to rely more heavily on CPI support to stay in power. Operating through the intermediary of the CPI, Soviet leverage within India may thereby be enhanced.

that the progressive tendencies within the Congress may be brought to the forefront through closer collaboration with the unified forces of the democratic left.[78] More specifically, by their frequent references to the Communist-led united front government in Kerala as a model for the successful conduct of land reform, the Soviets are promoting the participation of Communists in state ministries where jurisdiction for land legislation resides.

In a broader perspective, by focusing their attention on the pressing needs for rapid economic development combined with social justice, the Soviets have displayed an awareness that political stability in India cannot be maintained by standing still. As they have often reminded the Congress leadership, the progressive measures outlined in the Congress's electoral platforms must be implemented if the party is to maintain its current power. If the Indian leadership does not respond dynamically to meet India's economic and social plight, then regardless of how much aid they stand ready to furnish, the Soviets may be building the foundations of their partnership with India on the shifting sands of political instability and economic chaos.

[78] See, for example, P. Kutsobin and V. Shurygin, "South Asia: Tendencies Towards Stability," *International Affairs*, No. 4 (1973), 45.

SELECTED BIBLIOGRAPHY OF SOVIET SCHOLARLY SOURCES ON CONTEMPORARY INDIA*

Books

Batalov, A. L. and Gurvich, R. P. *Mozhet li Indiia Prokormit' Sebia?* Moscow: Izdatel'stvo Vostochnoi Literatury, 1961.

Ekonomika Sovremennoi Indii. Moscow: Izdatel'stvo Vostochnoi Literatury, 1960.

Frei, L. I. *Denezhno-Kreditnaia Sistema i Mezhdunarodnye Raschety Respubliki Indii.* Moscow: Vneshtorgizdat, 1956.

Gurvich, R. P. *Indiia. Prodovol'stvie-Vozmozhnosti i Perspektivy.* Moscow: Izdatel'stvo "Nauka," 1970.

Gurvich, R. P. *Sel'skoe Khoziaistvo Indii i Polozhenie Krest'ianstva.* Moscow: Izdatel'stvo Vostochnoi Literatury, 1960.

Indiia i Afganistan, Ocherki Istorii i Ekonimiki. Moscow: Izdatel'stvo Vostochnoi Literatury, 1958.

Indiia: Stat'i po Istorii. Moscow: Izdatel'stvo Vostochnoi Literatury, 1959.

Kocharian, M. A. *Druzhba i Sotrudnichestvo SSSR i Indii.* Moscow: Izdatel'stvo Vostochnoi Literatury, 1959.

Kondrat'ev, V. and Fituni, L. *Indiia: Ekonomicheskoe Razvitie i Sotrudnichestvo s SSSR.* Moscow: Izdatel'stvo "Nauka," 1965.

Kotovskii, G. G., ed. *Kasty v Indii.* Moscow: Izdatel'stvo "Nauka," 1965.

Mamrykin, G. I. *Stroitel'stvo Natsional'noi Ekonomiki Indii (Problemy, Itogi, Perspektivy).* Moscow: Izdatel'stvo Sotsial'no-Ekonomicheskoi Literatury, 1964.

Medovoi, A. I. *Rostovshchicheskii Kapital v Sel'skom Khoziaistve Indii.* Moscow: Izdatel'stvo Instituta Mezhdunarodnykh Otnoshenii, 1961.

Mironova, E. I. *Prodovol'stvennaia Problema v Indii.* Moscow: Izdatel'stvo "Nauka," 1967.

Mironova, E. I. *Rynok Prodovol'stvennogo Zerna v Sovremennoi Indii.* Moscow: Izdatel'stvo "Nauka," 1972.

Nezavisimaia Indiia: 10 let Nezavisimosti, 1947-1957, Sbornik Statei. Moscow: Izdatel'stvo Vostochnoi Literatury, 1958.

*Articles by the same author are arranged chronologically by date of publication.

Nikhamin, V. P. *Ocherki Vneshnei Politiki Indii, 1947-1957gg.* Moscow: Izdatel'stvo Politicheskoi Literatury, 1959.

Osipov, A. M., ed. *Indiia i Afganistan, Ocherki Istorii i Ekonomiki.* Moscow: Izdatel'stvo Vostochnoi Literatury, 1958.

Pavlov, V. I. *Formirovanie Indiiskoi Burzhuazii.* Moscow: Izdatel'stvo Vostochnoi Literatury, 1958.

Pokataeva, T. S. *Polozhenie Rabochego Klassa Indii.* Moscow: Izdatel'stvo Akademii Nauk SSSR, 1960.

Problemy Ekonomicheskogo i Sotsial'nogo Razvitiia Nezavisimoi Indii. Moscow: Izdatel'stvo "Nauka," 1958.

Rastiannikov, V. G. *Agrarnaia Evoliutsiia v Mnogoukladnom Obshchestve; opyt Nezavisimoi Indii.* Moscow: Izdatel'stvo "Nauka," 1973.

Reisner, L. I. *Inostrannyi i Natsional'nyi Kapital v Promyshlennosti Indii (Shtat Uttar-Pradesh, 1947-1957).* Moscow: Izdatel'stvo Vostochnoi Literatury, 1959.

Reisner, L. I. and Shirokov, G. K. *Planirovanie v Indii.* Moscow: Izdatel'stvo "Nauka," 1969.

Shevtsova, T. I. *Natsional'nyi i Inostrannyi Kapital vo Vneshnei Torgovle Nezavisimoi Indii.* Moscow: Izdatel'stvo "Nauka," 1968.

Shirokov, G. K. *Ekonomicheskoe Razvitie Chainykh Plantatsii v Indii.* Moscow: Izdatel'stvo Vostochnoi Literatury, 1959.

Shirokov, G. K. *Industrializatsiia Indii.* Moscow: Izdatel'stvo "Nauka," 1971.

Sovremennye Problemy Ekonomiki Stran Iuzhnoi Azii. Moscow: Izdatel'stvo "Nauka," 1968.

Articles

Akhmedzianov, A. L. "Deiatel'nost' Musul'manskikh Obshchinnykh Organizatsii v Sovremennoi Indii." *Kratkie Soobshcheniia Instituta Narodov Azii*, Kn. 75 (1964), 100-117.

Andreev, N. "India's State Structure and Political Parties." *International Affairs*, No. 1 (1967), 112-13.

Avarin, V. Ia. "Indiia na Puti k Ekonomicheskoi Nezavisimosti." *Voprosy Ekonomiki*, No. 1 (1957), 73-86.

Azarkh, A. "Aktivizatsiia Ul'trapravykh v Indii." *Mirovaia Ekonomika i Mezhdunarodnye Otnosheniia*, No. 10 (1970), 70-73.

Azarkh, A. and Oskolkova, O. "Narodnosti Indii." *Mirovaia Ekonomika i Mezhdunarodnye Otnosheniia*, No. 7 (1973), 138-43.

Bagramov, L. "Zelenaia Revoliutsiia: Svet i Teni." *Mirovaia Ekonomika i Mezhdunarodnye Otnosheniia.* No. 8 (1972), 47-62.

Baikov, I. P. "O Politike Gosudarstvennogo Kapitalizma v Indii." *Narody Azii i Afriki*, No. 6 (1963), 164-70.

Balabushevich, V. V. "Indiia Posle Razdela." *Mirovoe Khoziaistvo i Mirovaia Politika*, No. 12 (1947), 41-62.

Balabushevich, V. V. "Natsional'no-Osvoboditel'naia Bor'ba Narodov Indii." *Uglublenie Krizisa Kolonial'noi Sistemy Imperializma.* Edited by V. A. Maslennikov. Moscow: Gosudarstvennoe Izdatel'stvo Politicheskoi Literatury (1953),

pp. 265-342.
Baranov, I. L. "Kastovyi Bunt v Ramnade." *Kasty v Indii.* Edited by G. G. Kotovskii. Moscow: Izdatel'stvo "Nauka," 1965, pp. 262-73.
Baskin, A. D. "O Torgovlykh Otnosheniiakh Indii s FRG." *Vestnik Leningradskogo Universiteta,* Seriia Ekonomiki, Filosofii i Prava, No. 5 (1964), 152-57.
Batalov, A. L. "Razvitie Transporta v Respublike Indii." *Ekonomiki Sovremennoi Indii.* Moscow: Izdatel'stvo Vostochnoi Literatury (1960), pp. 396-415.
Batalov, A. L. "Osobennosti Promyshlennogo Razvitiia Indii i Pakistana za Gody Nezavisimosti." *Sovremennye Problemy Ekonomiki Stran Iuzhnoi Azii.* Moscow: Izdatel'stvo "Nauka," 1968, pp. 149-76.
Bel'skii, A. G. "Kontseptsiia 'Istinnogo Natsionalizma' i ee Reaktsionnaia Sushchnost' (o Nekotorykh Osobennostiakh Politicheskoi Ideologii Indiiskogo Kommunalizma)." *Narody Azii i Afriki,* No. 4 (1966), 16-26.
Bel'skii, A. G. "Partiia 'Dzhan Sangkh,' ee Sotsial'naia Baza i Indiiskie Monopolii." *Krupnyi Kapital i Monopolii Stran Azii.* Moscow: Izdatel'stvo "Nauka," 1970, pp. 184-97.
Bessonov, S. A. "O Roli Gosudarstvennogo Kapitalizma v Ekonomicheskom Razvitii Sovremennoi Indii." *Vestnik Moskovskogo Universiteta,* Seriia VIII: Ekonomiki i Filosofii, No. 6 (December, 1962), 55-67.
Bragina, E. A. "Tretii Piatiletnii Plan i Ekonomika Indii." *Narody Azii i Afriki,* No. 2 (1963), 37-48.
Brodovich, B. N. "Rol' Kredita v Razvitii Gosudarstvennogo Sektora Ekonomiki Indii." *Kratkie Soobshcheniia Instituta Narodov Azii,* Kn. 79 (1964), 3-23.
Brodovich, B. N. and Gordon, L. A. "K Voprosu o Raspredelenii Natsional'nogo Dokhoda Respubliki Indii." *Narody Azii i Afriki,* No. 4 (1964), 157-63.
Bylov, V. G. "Indiiskie Kontseptsii Resheniia Problemy Zaniatosti." *Teorii Ekonomicheskogo Rosta Razvivaiushchikhsia Stran Azii.* Moscow: Izdatel'stvo "Nauka," 1973, pp. 211-32.
Bylov, V. G. and Pankin, M. "India's Economy." *International Affairs,* No. 9 (1967), 109-11.
Chicherov, A. I. and Kuz'michev, G. K. "Indiia na Puti Nazavisimosti." *Narody Azii i Afriki,* No. 4 (1962), 22-38.
Chufrin, G. I. "Vneshneekonomicheskie Sviazi i Nauchno-Tekhnicheskii Progress v Indii." *Narody Azii i Afriki,* No. 2 (1973), 109-16.
Chuvikov, A. "Zametki o Sel'skom Khoziaistve Indii." *Ekonomika Sel'skogo Khoziaistva,* No. 3 (April-May, 1958), 102-10.
Deviatkina, T. F. "Bor'ba Indiiskogo Natsional'nogo Kongressa za Vliianie na Molodezh'." *Kratkie Soobshcheniia Instituta Narodov Azii,* Kn. 75.
Deviatkina, T. F. and D'iakov, A. M. "Sozdanie Shtatov po Lingvisticheskomu Printsipu i Likvidatsiia Kniazhestv." *Nezavisimaia Indiia: 10 let Nezavisimosti, 1947-1957.* Moscow: Izdatel'stvo Vostochnoi Literatury, 1958, pp. 80-101.
D'iakov, A. M. "K Voprosu o Natsional'nom Sostave Naseleniia Indii." *Uchenye Zapiski Tikhookeanskogo Instituta,* Tom I (1947), 223-330.
D'iakov, A. M. "Poslevoennye Angliiskie Plany Gosudarstvennogo Ustroistva Indii." *Uchenye Zapiski Tikhookeanskogo Instituta,* Tom II (1949), 54-66.
D'iakov, A. M. "Krizis Angliiskogo Gospodstva v Indii i Novyi Etap Osvoboditel'noi Bor'by ee Narodov." *Krizis Kolonial'noi Sistemy.* Edited by

E. M. Zhukov. Moscow: Izdatel'stvo Akademii Nauk SSSR, 1949.

D'iakov, A. M. "Natsional'noe Dvizhenie na Iuge Indii Posle Vtoroi Mirovoi Voiny." *Uchenye Zapiski Instituta Vostokovedeniia*, Tom I (1959), 3-50.

D'iakov, A. M. "Indiia v Bor'be za Mir." *Sovetskoe Vostokovedenie*, No. 1 (1955), 36-43.

D'iakov, A. M. "K Voprosu o Razvitii Natsional'nykh Iazykov Narodov Indii." *Sovetskoe Vostokovedenie*, No. 3 (1958), 38-45.

D'iakov, A. M. "Po Shtatam Iuzhnoi Indii." *Indiia i Afganistan, Ocherki Istorii i Ekonomiki*. Edited by A. M. Osipov. Moscow: Izdatel'stvo Vostochnoi Literatury, 1958, pp. 239-68.

D'iakov, A. M. and Reisner, L. I. "Rol 'Gandi v Natsional'no-Osvoboditel'noi Bor'be Narodov Indii." *Sovetskoe Vostokovedenie*, No. 5 (1956), 21-34.

Dolnykova, R. N. "Fabrichno-Zavodskaia Promyshlennost' Sovremennoi Indii" *Ekonomika Sovremennoi Indii*. Moscow: Izdatel'stvo Vostochnoi Literatury, 1960, pp. 215-17.

Egorov, I. I. "Finansirovanie Piatiletnykh Planov Indii (1951-1962)." *Kratkie Soobshcheniia Instituta Narodov Azii*, Kn. 75 (1964), 3-18.

Egorov, I. I. "Natsional'nyi Dokhod Indii (ego Obrazovanie i Raspredelenie)." *Kratkie Soobshcheniia Instituta Narodov Azii*, Kn. 81 (1964), 3-13.

Egorov, I. I. "Nakoplenie Kapitala v Indii (1951/52—1960/61)." *Kratkie Soobshcheniia Instituta Narodov Azii*, Kn. 81 (1964), 24-36.

Egorov, I. I. "Gosudarstvennye Predpriatii i ikh Rol' v Finansirovanii Piatiletnikh Planov Indii." *Aktual'nye Problemy Ekonomiki Stran Azii*. Moscow: Izdatel'stvo "Nauka," 1965, pp. 77-97.

Egorov, I. I. and Rastiannikov, V. G. "Nakopleniia v Indii i Problemy ikh Realizatsii." *Narody Azii i Afriki*, No. 2 (1966), 15-26.

Egorov, I. I. Oblozhenie Sel'skokhoziaistvennykh Dokhodov v Sovremennoi Indii." *Sovremennye Problemy Ekonomiki Stran Iuzhnoi Azii*. Moscow: Izdatel'stvo "Nauka," 1968, pp. 111-26.

Egorov, I. I. "Ekonomicheskaia Effektivnost' Gosudarstvennogo Sektora v Indii: ee Faktory i Puti Povysheniia." *Ekonomicheskaia Politika i Gosudarstvennyi Kapitalizm v Stranakh Vostoka*. Moscow: Izdatel'stvo "Nauka," 1972, pp. 179-207.

Egorova, M. N. "O Nekotorykh Chertakh Rabochego Dvizheniia v Indii." *Problemy Vostokovedeniia*, No. 5 (1959), 93-103.

Egorova, M. N. "Sotsial'noe Strakhovanie v Respublike Indii." *Indiia: Stat'i po Istorii*. Moscow: Izdatel'stvo Vostochnoi Literatury, 1959, pp. 205-47.

Egorova, M. N. "Chislennost' i Struktura Fabrichnogo Proletariata." *Ekonomika Sovremennoi Indii*. Moscow: Izdatel'stvo Vostochnoi Literatury, 1960, pp. 258-83.

Egorova, M. N. "Izmeneniia Chislennosti i Struktury Profsoiuzov v Nezavisimoi Indii." *Kratkie Soobshcheniia Instituta Narodov Azii*, Kn. 75 (1964), 76-91.

Ershov, T. M. "Indiiskaia Respublika—Vazhnyi Faktor Mira." *Nezavisimaia Indiia: 10 let Nezavisimosti, 1947-1957*. Moscow: Izdatel'stvo Vostochnoi Literatury, 1958, pp. 139-54.

Gamaiunov, L. S. and Gol'dberg, N. M. "Sovetsko-Indiiskie Kul'turnye Sviazi." *Nezavisimaia Indiia: 10 let Nezavisimosti, 1947-1957*. Moscow: Izdatel'-

SELECTED BIBLIOGRAPHY

stvo Vostochnoi Literatury, 1958, pp. 116-33.
Gankovskii, Iu. "Ob Avtonomistskikh Dvizheniiakh v Stranakh Iuzhnoi Azii." *Mirovaia Ekonomika i Mezhdunarodnye Otnosheniia.* No. 8 (1970), 148-50.
Gorchakov, R. S. "Nekotorye Voprosy Razvitiia Gosudarstvennogo Kapitalizma v Indii v Sviazi s Tret'im Piatiletnim Planom." *Vestnik Leningradskogo Universiteta,* Vypusk 4, No. 23 (1961), 35-45.
Gordon, L. A. "Nekotorye Voprosy Polozheniia Promyshlennogo Proletariata." *Ekonomika Sovremennoi Indii.* Moscow: Izdatel'stvo Vostochnoi Literatury, 1960, pp. 284-317.
Gordon, L. A. "Polozhenie Promyshlennogo Proletariata Indii i Nekotorye Osobennosti Bor'by Rabochego Klassa." *Polozhenie Rabochego Klassa i Rabochee Dvizhenie v Stranakh Azii i Afriki.* Edited by A. A. Iskenderov. Moscow: Izdatel'stvo Vostochnoi Literatury, 1962, pp. 57-79.
Gordon, L. A. "Religiozno-Kastyi Sostav Naseleniia Indii." *Kasty v Indii.* Edited by G. G. Kotovskii. Moscow: Izdatel'stvo "Nauka," 1965, pp. 201-13.
Grashe, V. Ia. "Osobennosti Formirovaniia Nekotorykh Natsional'nykh Grupp Indiiskoi Promyshlennoi Burzhuazii." *Kratkie Soobshcheniia Instituta Vostokovedeniia,* Kn. 1 (1951), 51-58.
Gurvich, R. P. "Nekotorye Novye Iavleniia v Indiiskoi Derevne." *Narody Azii i Afriki,* No. 3 (1964), 16-26.
Gurvich, R. P. "Zelenaia Revoliutsiia v Indii: Sotsial'no-Ekonomicheskie Rezul'taty." *Narody Azii i Afriki,* No. 1 (1971), 17-28.
Iashkin, V. A. "Problema Zaniatosti i Planirovanie v Indii." *Narody Azii i Afriki,* No. 1 (1967), 43-52.
Iashkin, V. A. "Planirovanie v Indii: Makroekonomicheskie Modeli i Strategiia Razvitiia." *Teorii Ekonomicheskogo Rosta Razvivaiushchikhsia Stran Azii.* Moscow: Izdatel'stvo "Nauka," 1973, pp. 175-210.
Iverov, A. "Slozhnaia Obstanovka v Indii." *Mirovaia Ekonomika i Mezhdunarodnye Otnosheniia,* No. 10 (1969), 84-97.
Iverov, A. "Vnushitel'naia Pobeda nad Pravymi Silami v Indii." *Mirovaia Ekonomika i Mezhdunarodnye Otnosheniia,* No. 6. (1971), 105-11.
Kaliagin, B. A. "Sotsial'no-Ekonomicheskie Posledstviia Provedeniia Programmy Obshchinnogo Razvitiia v Indii." *Narody Azii i Afriki,* No. 6 (1965), 38-47.
Kolontaev, A. P. "Vosproizvodstvo Orudii Truda v Krest'ianskom Khoziaistve Indii v XX Veke." *Narody Azii i Afriki,* No. 4 (1966), 78-84.
Komarov, E. N. "Material'noe Polozhenie Promyshlennogo Proletariata Bengalii i Nekotorye Voprosy ego Formirovaniia." *Uchenye Zapiski Instituta Vostokovedeniia,* Tom V (1953), 3-74.
Komarov, E. N. "Kritika Burzhuaznogo Obshchestva i Egalitaristskie Kontseptsii v Indii." *Narody Azii i Afriki,* No. 6 (1967), 40-51.
Kondrat'ev, V. "Podgotovka Tekhnicheskikh Spetsialistov v Indii." *Mirovaia Ekonomika i Mezhdunarodnye Otnosheniia,* No. 8 (1958), 107-12.
Kondrat'ev, V. "Znachenie Ekonomicheskogo Sotrudnichestva Indii so Stranami Sotsialisticheskogo Lageria dlia Razvitiia ee Natsional'noi Ekonomiki." *Voprosy Ekonomiki,* No. 11 (1958), 70-78.
Kondrat'ev, V. "The Role of India's Economic Collaboration with Countries of the Socialist Camp in the Development of India's Economy." *Voprosy*

Ekonomiki, No. 11 (1958). Translated in *Problems of Economics*, I, No. 3 (March, 1959), 40-44.

Kondrat'ev, V. "Natsional'naia Burzhuaziia i Promyshlennoe Razvitie Sovremennoi Indii." *Mirovaia Ekonomika i Mezhdunarodnye Otnosheniia*. No. 8 (1959), 61-72.

Kondrat'ev, V. "Ekonomicheskie Otnosheniia Indii s Sotsialisticheskimi Stranami." *Mirovaia Ekonomika i Mezhdunarodnye Otnosheniia*, No. 11 (1960), 98-105.

Kondrat'ev, V. "Novye Tendentsii v Strukture Ekonomiki Sovremennoi Indii." *Mirovaia Ekonomika i Mezhdunarodnye Otnosheniia*, No. 7 (1961), 45-60.

Kondrat'ev, V. "Gosudarstvennyi Kapitalizm i Promyshlennoe Razvitie Sovremennoi Indii." *Kratkie Soobshcheniia Instituta Narodov Azii*, Kn. 51 (1962), 18-36.

Kondrat'ev, V. "Industrializatsiia Indii i Ekonomicheskaia Rol' Gosudarstva." *Mirovaia Ekonomika i Mezhdunarodnye Otnosheniia*, No. 4 (1964), 23-36.

"Konferentsiia Sovetskikh Indologov." *Narody Azii i Afriki*, No. 3 (1971), 219-24.

Kotovskii, G. G. "K Voprosu o Roli Rostovshchicheskogo Kapitala v Obezzemlenii Krest'ianstva v Indii." *Kratkie Soobshcheniia Instituta Vostokovedeniia*, Kn. 10 (1953), 20-34.

Kotovskii, G. G. "Sotsial'no-Ekonomicheskoe Soderzhanie Problemy Neprikasaemykh." *Uchenye Zapiska Instituta Vostokovedeniia*, Tom V (1953), 75-152.

Kotovskii, G. G. "Sistema Ekspluatatsii Plantatsionnykh Rabochikh Iuzhnoi Indii." *Uchenye Zapiski Instituta Vostokovedeniia*, Tom X (1954), 57-96.

Kotovskii, G. G. "Agrarnye Otnosheniia v Indii." *Sovetskoe Vostokovedenie*, No. 4 (1955), 66-83.

Kotovskii, G. G. "Ruchnoe Promyshlennoe Proizvodstvo i Rassloenie Krest'ianstva na Iuge Indii." *Kratkie Soobshcheniia Instituta Vostokovedeniia*, Kn. 15 (1955), 21-33.

Kotovskii, G. G. "Indiia." *Agrarnye Otnosheniia v Stranakh Vostoka*. Moscow: Izdatel'stvo Akademii Nauk SSSR, 1958, pp. 7-133.

Kotovskii, G. G. "Vvedenie: Nekotorye Aspekty Problemy Kast." *Kasty v Indii*. Edited by G. G. Kotovskii, Moscow: Izdatel'stvo "Nauka" (1965), pp. 3-40.

Kotovskii, G. G. and Pavlov, V. I. "Sel'skokhoziaistvennoe i Promyshlennoe Proizvodstvo v Respublike Indii." *Sovetskoe Vostokovedenie*, No. 1 (1956), 129-44.

Kriuchkova, T. F. "O Politike Pravitel'stva Nezavisimoi Indii po Otnosheniiu k Neprikasaemym." *Kasty v Indii*. Edited by G. G. Kotovskii. Moscow: Izdatel'stvo "Nauka," 1965, pp. 322-39.

Kudriavtsev, M. K. "Musul'manskie Kasty." *Kasty v Indii*. Edited by G. G. Kotovskii. Moscow: Izdatel'stvo "Nauka," 1965, pp. 214-32.

Kutsenkov, A. A. "Sovetsko-Indiiskie Ekonomicheskie Otnosheniia." *Nezavisimaia Indiia: 10 let Nezavisimosti, 1947-1957*. Moscow: Izdatel'stvo Vostochnoi Literatury, 1958, pp. 102-11.

Kutsenkov, A. A. "Kastovaia Obshchina Sosedstva v Indiiskom Gorode." *Narody Azii i Afriki*, No. 1 (1972), 37-47.

Kutsobin, P. "Voprosy Volnuiushchie Indiiu." *Mirovaia Ekonomika i Mezhdunarodnye Otnosheniia*, No. 3 (1968), 113-19.

Kutsobin, P. "Pravye Sily v Indii: Tseli i Metody Bor'by." *Narody Azii i Afriki*, No. 2 (1971), 16-29.

Lemin, I. M. "Fruits of Imperialist Domination in India and Pakistan." *Voprosy Ekonomiki*, No. 1 (1952), 73-89. Translated in *Current Digest of the Soviet Press*, IV, No. 11, 26-28.

Leonidov, A. "The Economy and Foreign Trade of India." *Vneshniaia Torgovlia*, No. 12 (1951), 8-14, in *Current Digest of the Soviet Press*, IV, No. 10, 29-30.

Levin, S. F. "Ob Evoliutsii Musul'manskikh Torgovykh Kast v Sviazi s Razvitiem Kapitalizma." *Kasty v Indii*. Edited by G. G. Kotovskii. Moscow: Izdatel'stvo "Nauka," 1965, pp. 233-61.

Levkovskii, A. I. "Angliiskie Upravliaiushchie Agentsva—Orudie Poraboshcheniia i Ekspluatatsii Narodov Indii." *Kratkie Soobshcheniia Instituta Vostokovedeniia*, Kn. 10 (1953), 69-80.

Levkovskii, A. I. "Sistema Upravliaiushchikh Agenstv—Orudie Poraboshcheniia i Ekspluatatsii Narodov Indii Angliiskim Imperializmom." *Uchenye Zapiski Instituta Vostokovedeniia*, Vol. 10 (1954), 161-219.

Levkovskii, A. I. "Osobennosti Razvitiia Krupnogo Kapitalisticheskogo Predprinimatel'stva v Indii." *Sovetskoe Vostokovedenie*, No. 2 (1955), 107-24.

Levkovskii, A. I. "O Nizshikh Formakh Kapitalisticheskogo Predprinimatel'stva v Promyshlennosti Indii (Na Primere Ruchnogo Tkhachestva)." *Kratkie Soobshcheniia Instituta Vostokovedeniia*, Kn. 15 (1955), 34-51.

Levkovskii, A. I. "Gosudarstvennyi Kapitalizm i Chastokapitalisticheskoe Predprinimatel'stvo v Indii." *Ekonomika Sovremennoi Indii*. Moscow: Izdatel'stvo Vostochnoi Literatury, 1960, pp. 173-214.

Lialin, V. A. "Kapitaloemkost' Proizvodstva v Promyshlennosti Indii." *Vestnik Leningradskogo Universiteta*, Seriia Ekonomiki, Filosofii i Prava, Vypusk 2, No. 11 (1970), 39-43.

Loshakov, Iu. I. "Nekotorye Osobennosti Indiiskogo Monopolisticheskogo Kapitala." *Vestnik Moskovskogo Universiteta*, Seriia Ekonomika, VII, No. 3 (1967), 62-72.

Maev, O. "Indiiskii Monopolisticheskii Kapital." *Narody Azii i Afriki*, No. 1 (1964), 21-36.

Maev, O. "Ekonomicheskaia Programma Indiiskikh Monopolistov." *Narody Azii i Afriki*, No. 5 (1964), 153-64.

Maev, O. "Indiiskii Monopolisticheskii Kapital (Zapadno-indiiskie Gruppy)," *Mirovaia Ekonomika i Mezhdunarodnye Otnosheniia*, No. 8 (1966), 120-27.

Maev, O. "Monopolies' Role in Politics." *International Affairs*, No. 1 (1967), 97-98.

Maev, O. "Indiiskii Monopolisticheskii Kapital (Vostochno-indiiskie Gruppy)." *Mirovaia Ekonomika i Mezhdunarodnye Otnosheniia*, No. 3 (1967), 118-23.

Maev, O. "Rekomendatsii Komissii po Monopoliiam i ikh Znachenie." *Narody Azii i Afriki*, No. 3 (1967), 136-45.

Maev, O. "Blow at the Monopolies." *International Affairs*, No. 10 (1969), 97-98.

Maev, O. "Monopolii, Banki i Politika." *Mirovaia Ekonomika i Mezhdunarodnye Otnosheniia*, No. 11 (1969), 58-61.

Maksimov, M. A. and Maslennikov, V. A. "Puti Resheniia Agrarnogo Voprosa v Indii." *Mirovaia Ekonomika i Mezhdunarodnye Otnosheniia*, No. 12 (1961), 52-65.

Maliarov, O. V. "Ekonomicheskaia Sushchnost' i Ekonomicheskaia Osnova Upravliaiushchikh Agentstv v Indii." *Sovremennye Problemy Ekonomiki Stran Iuzhnoi Azii.* Moscow: Izdatel'stvo "Nauka," 1968, pp. 3-40.

Maliarov, O. V. "Vliianie Inostrannogo Kapitala na Protsessy Kontsentratsii i Obrazovanie Monopolii v Indii." *Krupnyi Kapital i Monopolii Stran Azii.* Moscow: Izdatel'stvo "Nauka," 1970, pp. 148-83.

Maliarov, O. V. "Problema Monopolii v Kontseptsiiakh Sotsial'no-Ekonomicheskogo Razvitiia Indii." *Teorii Ekonomicheskogo Rosta Razvivaiushchikhsia Stran Azii.* Moscow: Izdatel'stvo "Nauka," 1973, pp. 99-157.

Mamrykin, G. I. "Finanso-Valiutnye Problemy Indii." *Mirovaia Ekonomika i Mezhdunarodnye Otnosheniia,* No. 10 (1959), 100-107.

Maslennikov, A. A. "V Kerale Likvidiruetsia Pomeshchich'e Zemlevladenie." *Mirovaia Ekonomika i Mezhdunarodnye Otnosheniia,* No. 9 (1958), 99-101.

Maslennikov, A. A. "India." *Agrarnye Reformy v Stranakh Vostoka.* Moscow: Izdatel'stva Vostochnoi Literatury, 1961, pp. 77-98.

Maslennikov, A. A. "Indiia: Bor'ba Vokrug Ekonomicheskoi Politiki." *Mirovaia Ekonomika i Mezhdunarodnye Otnosheniia,* No. 11 (1966), 104-106.

Maslennikov, A. A. "Peremeny v Indostane." *Mirovaia Ekonomika i Mezhdunarodnye Otnosheniia.* No. 3 (1973), 99-103.

Medevoi, A. "Osobennosti Kontsentratsii Proizvodstva i Kapitala v Indii." *Mirovaia Ekonomika i Mezhdunarodnye Otnosheniia,* No. 6 (1965), 38-49.

Medevoi, A. and Iashkin, V. A. "Problemy Vosproizvodstva i Planirovaniia v Indii." *Ekonomicheskaia Politika i Gosudarstvennyi Kapitalizm v Stranakh Vostoka.* Moscow: Izdatel'stvo "Nauka," 1972, pp. 152-78.

Mel'man, S. M. "Inostrannyi Monopolisticheskii Kapital v Ekonomike Indii." *Ekonomika Sovremennoi Indii.* Moscow: Izdatel'stvo Vostochnoi Literatury, 1960, pp. 131-72.

Mel'nikov, A. M. "Bor'ba Indiiskogo Krest'ianstva za Radikal'nye Agrarnye Reformy (1957-1962)." *Narody Azii i Afriki,* No. 5 (1964), 83-90.

Mel'nikov, A. M. "Agrarnoe Dvizhenie v Indii Posle Dostizheniia Nezavisimosti (1947-1951)." *Krest'ianskoe Dvizhenie v Stranakh Vostoka.* Moscow: Izdatel'stvo "Nauka," 1967, pp. 90-130.

Mironova, E. I. "Nekotorye Formy Sotrudnichestva Indiiskikh i Inostrannykh Monopolii." *Kratkie Soobshcheniia Instituta Narodov Azii,* Kn. 81 (1964), 29-34.

Mironova, E. I. "Gosudarstvennaia Prodovol'stvennaia Politika v Indii." *Prodovol'stvennaia Problema v Stranakh Azii i Severnoi Afriki.* Moscow: Izdatel'stvo "Nauka," 1968, pp. 94-105.

Mironova, E. I. "Nekotorye Voprosy Realizatsii Promyshlennoi Produktsii v Sovremennoi Indii (na primere sakharnoi promyshlennosti)." *Sovremennye Problemy Ekonomiki Stran Iuzhnoi Azii.* Moscow: Izdatel'stvo "Nauka," 1968, pp. 85-110.

Morozova, V. E. "Smeshannye Natsional'no-Inostrannye Predpriiatiia v Indii kak Forma Privlecheniia i Proniknoveniia Inostrannogo Kapitala." *Vestnik Leningradskogo Universiteta, Ekonomika, Filosofiia i Pravo,* Vyp. 1, No. 5 (1972), 24-29.

Nasenko, Iu. P. "O Deiatel'nosti Indiiskikh Pravosotsialisticheskikh Liderov." *Kratkie Soobshcheniia Instituta Vostokovedeniia,* Kn. 15 (1955), 65-76.

SELECTED BIBLIOGRAPHY

Nasenko, Iu. P. "Indiia: Evoliutsiia Politiki Neprisoedineniia." *Narody Azii i Afriki*, No. 6 (1968), 15-24.

Orleanskaia, L. K. "K Voprosu o Razvitii Proizvodstvennykh Zemledel'cheskikh Kooperativov v Indii." *Kratkie Soobshcheniia Instituta Narodov Azii*, Kn. 51 (1962), 49-59.

Orleanskaia, L. K. "Sel'skokhoziaistvennye Sbytovye Kooperativy Indii." *Kratkie Soobshcheniia Instituta Narodov Azii*, Kn. 75 (1964), 50-59.

Oskolkova, O. and Gusev, Iu. "Indiiskie Kasty Segodnia." *Mirovaia Ekonomika i Mezhdunarodnye Otnosheniia*, No. 6 (1966), 126-33.

Pavlovskii, V. V. "Krupnyi Kapital v Indii." *Krupnyi Kapital i Monopolii Stran Azii*. Moscow: Izdatel'stvo "Nauka," 1970, pp. 112-47.

Pavlovskii, V. V. "Gosudarstvennyi Kapitalizm i Perspektivy Sotsial'no-Ekonomicheskogo Razvitiia Indii." *Ekonomicheskaia Politika i Gosudarstvennyi Kapitalizm v Stranakh Vostoka*. Moscow: Izdatel'stvo "Nauka," 1972, pp. 120-51.

Petrunicheva, Z. "Natsional'no-Osvoboditel'noe Dvizhenie v Kniazhestve Kashmir." *Uchenye Zapiski Instituta Vostokovedeniia*, Tom I (1959), 157-224.

"Po Povodu Knigi M. K. Kudriavtseva "Obshchina i Kasta v Khindustane."" *Narody Azii i Afriki*, No. 4 (1972), 79-93.

Rastiannikov, V. G. "Naemnyi Trud v Sel'sko-Khoziaistve Pendzhaba." *Uchenye Zapiski Instituta Vostokovedeniia*, Tom XVIII (1957), 213-96.

Reginin, A. "Nekotorye Natsional'nye Voprosy v Nezavisimoi Indii." *Mirovaia Ekonomika i Mezhdunarodnye Otnosheniia*, No. 10 (1972), 109-12.

Reisner, L. I. and Shirokov, G. K. "Inostrannyi Chastnyi Kapital v Indii." *Problemy Vostokovedeniia*, No. 1 (1960), 44-55.

Reisner, L. I. and Shirokov, G. K. "Razvitie Ekonomicheskikh Sviazei Mezhdu Sovetskim Soiuzom i Indiei." *Ekonomika Sovremennoi Indii*. Moscow: Izdatel'stvo Vostochnoi Literatury, 1960, pp. 416-29.

Reisner, L. I. and Shirokov, G. K. "Gosudarstvennyi Kapitalizm i Chastnyi Kapital v Indiiskoi Promyshlennosti." *Aktual'nye Problemy Ekonomiki Stran Azii*. Moscow: Izdatel'stvo "Nauka," 1965, pp. 56-76.

Reisner, L. I. and Shirokov, G. K. "Promyshlennyi Perevorot v Sovremennoi Indii." *Narody Azii i Afriki*, No. 1 (1967), 5-18.

Riabchikov, A. M. "Izmeniia v Administrativnom Delenii Indii Posle Razdela." *Izvestiia Vsesoiuznogo Geograficheskogo Obschestva*, Tom 81, Vypusk 5 (1949), 513-23.

Riabinina, E. D. "Gosudarstvennye Finansy Indii v Period Nezavisimosti." *Aktual'nye Problemy Ekonomiki Stran Azii*. Moscow: Izdatel'stvo "Nauka," 1965, pp. 98-133.

Riabinina, E. D. "Novye Gosudarstvennye Instituty v Kreditnoi Sisteme Indii." *Sovremennye Problemy Ekonomiki Stran Iuzhnoi Azii*. Moscow: Izdatel'stvo "Nauka," 1968, pp. 127-49.

Rubinshtein, M. "Ob Ekonomicheskom Razvitii Sovremennoi Indii." *Voprosy Ekonomiki*, No. 10 (1955), 108-25.

Rubinshtein, M. "Vtoroi Piatiletnyi Plan Respubliki Indii." *Sovestkoe Vostokovedenie*, No. 4 (1956), 28-44.

Savel'ev, N. "Monopoly Drive in India." *International Affairs*, No. 4 (1967), 35-40.

Sedov, I. A. "Osnovye Tendentsii v Torgovle Indii s Razvivaiushchimsia Stranami Azii i Afriki." *Sovremennye Problemy Ekonomiki Stran Iuzhnoi Azii.* Moscow: Izdatel'stvo "Nauka," 1968, pp. 41-63.

Sedov, I. A. "Pomoshch' Indii Razvivaiushchimsia Stranam i Eksport Kapitala." *Sovremennye Problemy Ekonomiki Stran Iuzhnoi Azii.* Moscow: Izdatel'stvo "Nauka," 1968, pp. 64-84.

Seleznev, L. I. "O Nekotorykh Osobennostiakh Monopolisticheskogo Kapitala Indii." *Vestnik Leningradskogo Universiteta,* Seriia Ekonomiki, Filosofii i Prava, Vypusk 4, No. 23 (1964), 27-35.

Semenov, E. K. "Ekonomicheskoe Sotrudnichestvo Sovetskogo Soiuza i Drugikh Sotsialisticheskikh Stran s Indiei." *Narody Azii i Afriki,* No. 1 (1964), 53-60.

Semenov, E. K. "Razvitie Mashinostroeniia v Indii." *Kratkie Soobshcheniia Instituta Narodov Azii,* Kn. 75 (1964), 40-49.

Semenov, E. K. "O Razvitii Tiazheloi Promyshlennosti Indii za Gody Nezavisimosti." *Kratkie Soobshcheniia Instituta Narodov Azii,* Kn. 81 (1964), 14-20.

Semenova, N. I. "Bor'ba Sel'skokhoziaistvennykh Rabochikh Indii." *Krest'ianskoe Dvizhenie v Stranakh Vostoka.* Moscow: Izdatel'stvo "Nauka," 1967, pp. 131-47.

Shakov, O. S. "O Politike Indiiskogo Pravitel'stva v Rabochem Voprose." *Narody Azii i Afriki,* No. 5 (1970), 41-49.

Shevtsova, T. I. "Vneshniaia Torgovlia Indiiskoi Respubliki." *Ekonomika Sovremennoi Indii.* Moscow: Izdatel'stvo Vostochnoi Literatury, 1960, pp. 374-95.

Shevtsova, T. I. "Pozitsii Angliiskogo Kapitala vo Vneshnei Torgovle Respubliki Indii." *Kratkie Soobshcheniia Instituta Narodov Azii,* Kn. 51 (1962), 60-70.

Shirokov, G. K. "Nalogovaia Sistema Sovremennoi Indii." *Ekonomika Sovremennoi Indii.* Moscow: Izdatel'stvo Vostochnoi Literatury, 1960, pp. 345-73.

Shirokov, G. K. "K Voprosu o Deiatel'nosti Otraslevykh Ob'edinenii v Indiiskoi Promyshlennosti." *Kratkie Soobshcheniia Instituta Narodov Azii,* Kn. 51 (1962), 3-18.

Shirokov, G. K. "Nekotorye Osobennosti Lomki Kolonial'noi Struktury Indiiskoi Promyshlennosti." *Narody Azii i Afriki,* No. 4 (1964), 12-21.

Shirokov, G. K. "Indiiskaia Promyshlennost': Nekotorye Osobennosti Rosta." *Narody Azii i Afriki,* No. 6 (1969), 23-35.

Shirokov, G. K. "Indiiskaia Burzhuaziia: Izmeneniia za Gody Nezavisimosti." *Narody Azii i Afriki,* No. 2 (1972), 28-43.

Shmidt, G. "K Voprosu o Narodonaselenii Indii." *Uchenye Zapiski Instituta Vostokovedeniia,* Tom I (1950), 51-156.

Sokolov, I. "O Sel'skom Khoziaistve Indii." *Ekonomika Sel'skogo Khoziaistva,* No. 8 (1961), 117-22.

Solodovnikov, V. "Inostrannyi Kapital v Ekonomiki Indii." *Mirovaia Ekonomika i Mezhdunarodnye Otnosheniia,* No. 11 (1958), 69-81.

Sosina, N. N. "Panchaiaty i ikh Rol' v Sovremennoi Indii." *Narody Azii i Afriki,* No. 4 (1966), 216-21.

Sukhanova, V. "K Sobytiiam v Shtate Kerala." *Mirovaia Ekonomika i Mezhdunarodnye Otnosheniia,* No. 11 (1959), 108-18.

Tiul'panov, S. I. and Chufrin, G. I. "Nekotorye Voprosy Razvitiia Gosudarstvennogo Sektora Promyshlennosti Indii v Period Tret'ego Piatiletnogo Plana."

SELECTED BIBLIOGRAPHY

Vestnik Leningradskogo Universiteta, Seriia Ekonomiki, Filosofii i Prava, Vypusk 3, No. 17 (1962), 5-23.

Tiul'panov, S. I. and Veitz, G. M. "Gosudarstvennye Predpriiatiia Indii." *Narody Azii i Afriki*, No. 3 (1970), 28-37.

Ul'ianova, L. P. "Gosudarstvenno-Pravovye Formy Resheniia Natsional'nogo Voprosa v Indii." *Sovetskoe Gosudarstvo i Pravo*, No. 10 (1967), 119-24.

Ul'ianovskii, R. A. "Indiia v Bor'be za Ekonomicheskuiu Nezavisimost' (O Gosudarstvennom Sektore v Ekonomike Indii)." *Sovetskoe Vostokovedenie*, No. 4 (1957), 9-26.

Ul'ianovskii, R. A. "SShA i Industrializatsiia Indii." *Sovetskoe Vostokovedenie*, No. 4 (1958), 35-50.

Ul'ianovskii R. A. "Indiia v Bor'be za Ekonomicheskuiu Nezavisimost' (Voprosy Goskapitalizma)." *Nezavisimaia Indiia: 10 let Nezavisimosti, 1947-1957.* pp. 5-79.

Ul'ianovskii, R. A. "Ob Osobennostiakh Razvitiia i Kharaktere Gosudarstvennogo Kapitalizma v Nezavisimoi Indii." *Problemy Vostokovedeniia*, No. 3 (1960), 23-41.

Ul'ianovskii, R. A. "Reforma Agrarnogo Stroia." *Ekonomika Sovremennoi Indii.* Moscow: Izdatel'stvo Vostochnoi Literatury, 1960, pp. 52-130.

Ul'ianovskii, R. A. "Agrarnye Reformy v Stranakh Blizhnego i Srednego Vostoka, Indii i Iugo-Vostochnoi Azii." *Problemy Vostokovedeniia*, No. 1 (1961), 13-34.

Ul'ianovskii, R. A. "Agrarnye Reformy v Stranakh Blizhnego i Srednego Vostoka, Indii i Iugo-Vostochnoi Azii." *Narody Azii i Afriki*, No. 2 (1961), 14-30.

Ul'ianovskii, R. A. "Amerikanskaia Strategiia v Indii." *Mirovaia Ekonomika i Mezhdunarodnye Otnosheniia*, No. 5 (1963), 27-37.

Ul'ianovskii, R. A. "Amerikanskaia Politika 'Pomoshchi' i Neitralizm Indii (Zametki Indologii)." *Narody Azii i Afriki*, No. 3 (1963), 16-24.

Vasil'ev, I. "Indiia i 'Obshchii Rynok'." *Mirovaia Ekonomika i Mezhdunarodnye Otnosheniia*, No. 4 (1961), 107-108.

Vasil'ev, V. "Ekonomika Indii: Planirovanie, Plany, Deistvitel'nost'." *Mirovaia Ekonomika i Mezhdunarodnye Otnosheniia*, No. 10 (1968), 52-63.

Vasil'ev, V. "Mirovoi Rynok i Razvitie Natsional'noi Ekonomiki Indii." *Mirovaia Ekonomika i Mezhdunarodnye Otnosheniia*, No. 11 (1972), 78-93.

Vladimirov, V. "Indiia i Problema Ispolzovaniia Atomnoi Energii." *Mirovaia Ekonomika i Mezhdunarodnye Otnosheniia*, No. 3 (1959), 118-19.

Vladimirskii, L. A. "Nekotorye Voprosy Razvitiia Gosudarstvennogo Sektora vo Vneshnei Torgovli Indii." *Kratkie Soobshcheniia Instituta Narodov Azii*, No. 75 (1964), 60-70.

Vladimirskii, L. A. "Deval'vatsiia Rupii v 1966 godu i ee Posledstviia dlia Ekonomiki Indii." *Narody Azii i Afriki*, No. 1 (1970), 139-45.

Zhukov, E. M. "K Polozheniiu v Indii." *Mirovoe Khoziaistvo i Mirovaia Politika*, No. 7 (1947), 3-14.

INDEX

Abdullah, Sheikh M., 125
Administrative reorganization in India: Soviet view of, 117-118, 123. *See also* States Reorganization Act
Agriculture, development of, 264, 267; Soviet view of, in India, 139, 213, 218-219, 265, 265 n.140, 267-269. *See also* Agrarian Relations; "Green Revolution"
Agricultural cooperatives. *See* Cooperatives, agricultural
Agrarian overpopulation: Soviet view of, in India, 129, 153, 153 n.81, 155, 257-259, 261, 286-287; and urbanization in India, 187. *See also* urbanization
Agrarian reforms: and employment, problem of, 262, 266; and "green revolution," 269, 271-272, 319; Soviet view of, 33; Soviet view of, in India, 133, 137, 137 n.38, 139, 141, 152-155, 213, 216-221, 266-267. *See also* employment, problem of; "green revolution"
Agrarian relations in India: and cooperatives, agricultural, 214; and "green revolution," 214-215; Soviet view of, 129, 134-135, 137-139, 141, 152-155, 217-219, 286-287
Ahmed, Fakhruddin Ali, 230
Akhramovich, R. T., 131
Aleksandrov, M. A., 173
Aleshina, I., 257 n.120, 272-273, 276
Amer, Abdal Hakim, 46-47
Andreasian, R. A., 201
Andreev, N., 229
"Anti-Party Group," attitude towards foreign aid of, 25
Arab-Ogly, E., 245, 258

Arab Socialist Union of Egypt: and relations with CPSU, 46
Arkhipov, V. Ia., 182
Army, in developing countries: Soviet view of, 193, 196
Artsishevskii, L., 276
Arutiunian, A., 12
Arzumanian, A., 194
Asaf Ali, Aruna, 50 n.137
Asian Collective Security, Soviet plan of, 68, 307-308; Asian response to, 68, 307; and India, 307-308
Asiatic mode of production, 282, 282 n.195. *See also* State structure in developing countries
Atomic energy development in India. *See* Indian Foreign Policy
Avakov, R., 180 n.32, 213
Ayub Khan, Md., 51, 55
Azizian, A., 136
Bagramov, L., 269
Balabushevich, V. V., 104, 108 n.19, 112-115, 118, 120, 128, 141-143
Bandung Conference, 15
Bangladesh, 306-307; Soviet salvage operation in, 316; Soviet support for, 81, 306
Bangladesh crisis, 75-82; American reaction to, 76, 76 n.220; Chinese reaction to, 76; political issues resultant from, 304-305; Soviet position on issues resultant from, 304-306; Soviet reaction to, 75-79, 81. *See also* Soviet-Indian relations
Batalov, A. L., 175, 213
Bessonov, S. A., 176, 275
Bhutto, Z. A., 44, 306; 1972 trip to Soviet Union of, 81, 304-305; 1973 trip to United States of, 315

INDEX

Birth control: in India, 259; Soviet attitude towards, 91-92, 92 n.257, 129, 213 n.139, 257-259
Bochagov, A. K., 235
Bombay industrial exhibit (1952): Soviet participation in, 10
Bourgeoisie in India. *See* Indian bourgeoisie
Bragina, E. A., 209, 264 n.137
Braginskii, I. S., 170
Brezhnev, L. I., 74 n.215; and Asian collective security plan, 68 n.198, 307-308; position on Indian Ocean peace zone initiative of, 317; remarks on India at 23rd Party Congress of, 65; remarks on India at 24th Party Congress of 75, 75 n.217, 241; remarks at 1970 Lenin Centennial of, 240; 1973 speech at Alma-Ata of, 308; 1973 visit to India of, 297, 302 n.23, 319
Brodovich, B. N., 209, 257
Brutents, K., 233, 239
Bulganin, N. A.; and offer of cooperation in atomic energy development in India of, 160 n.104; remarks during 1955 USSR visit of Nehru, 17 n.36; visit with N. S. Khrushchev to India, 18-22. *See also* Khrushchev, N. S.
Caste system in India: and social stratification, 284-285; Soviet view of, 129, 283-286; and untouchability, 129
Chavan, Y. B., 230
Cheprakov, V., 178, 193
Cheshkov, M., 281
Chiang Kai-shek, 116
Chiao Kuan-hua, 310
China: attitude toward Bangladesh of, 310-311, 310 n.43; attitude towards India of, 64; attitude towards Soviet-Indian relations of, 22, 25-26; Communist Party of, 190; encouragement of guerrilla movements by, 64; as factor in Indian nuclear policy, 70; as factor in Soviet policy towards India, 49, 309; as factor in Soviet-Indian relations, 66-68, 309-310, 312-313; military aid to Pakistan by, 57, 57 n.161, 314; Pakistani relations with, 44; response to Soviet support on 1959 Sino-Indian border clash of, 29; revolution in and application to India, 119-120; Soviet warnings against, in South Asia, 66-67, 310
Chou En-lai: 1960 visit to India of, 28
Chufrin, G. I., 210
Communalism in India: Soviet view of, 123
Communist Party of India: differences between, and CPSU on Indian government, 16, 143; effects of 1971 election on, 74 n.216; insurrectionary activities of, 7, 113, 122; position of, during 1962 Sino-Indian border war, 36, 36 n.101; Soviet view of, 186, 197 n.86, 197-198; tactical line of, 64, 73, 113-115, 119-120, 120 n.64, 145, 319 n.77; victories in Kerala and West Bengal of, 62, 229; view of Indian government of, 176; visit of, delegation to Moscow, 74 n.215
Communist Party of India (Marxist), 64, 74, 231; effects of 1971 elections on, 74 n.216
Community Development Program in India: Soviet view of, 137
Congress, Indian National. *See* Indian National Congress
Cooperatives, agricultural: and agrarian overpopulation, 214, 264; and agrarian relations, 214-216; and employment, problem of, 261; Soviet view of, 156 n.90, 265; Soviet view of Indian, 214-216. *See also* Agrarian relations
Cuban revolution: effects of, on Soviet policy towards the developing countries, 25, 33, 48; Soviet view of, 33 n.88
Dantsig, B. M., 147

INDEX

Dastur and Co.: and Bokaro Steel Plant controversy, 44, 59, 206

Democratic Party of Guinea: and relations with CPSU, 46

Demographic policy, Soviet. *See* Birth control

Desai, Morarji, 23, 34 n.92, 42, 71, 177

Developing countries: Soviet view of, 30, 286, 295

Deviatkina, T. F., 163

Dharia, Mohan, 230

D'iakov, A. M., 102, 104-105, 108 n.19, 112-113, 117-118, 122-123, 126, 130, 147, 163

Diego Garcia, U. S. development of, 315-316

Dinesh Singh: visit to Soviet Union of, 68

Dudinskii, I., 251

Dutt, R. Palme, 122

Dzhunusov, M. S., 192

Economic aid: Soviet view of, 158-159, 254-257. *See also* Soviet economic aid

Economic aid in Africa: Soviet view of, 90

Economic development, strategies of: American, 85; Soviet attitude towards American, 85, 183, 199-200; Soviet, 85, 91, 158-159, 198-204, 243-247, 260, 262 n.134, 263-264; Soviet view of, in India, 246-247, 247 n.85. *See also* Industrialization

Egorov, I. I., 256

El'ianov, A., 201

Employment, problem of: and industrialization, 203-204, 248, 258-259, 261; Soviet view of, in India, 145 n.58, 203-204, 259 n.126, 260, 261 n.132, 263. *See also* Industrialization

Etinger, Ia., 173

Fedorenko. V. M., 147

Firiubin, N., 61 n. 177

Fituni, L. A., 200

Food problem: Soviet response to, in India, 91; Soviet view of, 33, 263-264, 267-268; Soviet view of, in India, 138, 156 n.90, 212-213, 264, 264 n.138

Foreign aid, Soviet. *See* Soviet economic aid

Foreign relations, as distinguished from policy, 1

Frei, L. I., 138 n.40

Fridman, L. A., 187-188, 190

Gafurov, B. G., 170 n.140

Gandhi, Indira, 55, 57 n.163, 58 n.165, 70-75, 82, 229-232, 319; comments after Bangladesh crisis by, 82, 298; remarks during 1973 Brezhnev visit by, 309; Soviet support for, 42, 72-73

Gandhi, M. K., 15; Soviet reappraisal of, 15, 134

Ganges River, Soviet offer to mediate Indo-Pakistani dispute over, 55

Gataullina, L. M., 237

Ghanaian coup of 1966: effect on Soviet policy towards developing countries of, 223-224, 234, 237

Giri, V. V., 67 n.195, 71, 231

Goa: Soviet support for Indian position on, 2, 10 n.11, 14, 19, 22-23, 23 n.59

Gol'dberg, D. M., 102

Gorchakov, R. S., 206

Gordon, L. A., 141, 187-190, 285

Gorelik, S. B., 269

Goriunov, V. P., 252 n.99

Gorshkov, S., 318

Gosplan (USSR), joint committee on Indo-Soviet collaboration of, 301. *See also* Indian Planning Commission

Great Britain: support for Pakistan by, on Kashmir issue, 125

"Green revolution," 268; Soviet view of, 269-272

Gromyko, A. A., 54 n.150, 68 n.199, 78, 80

Guber, A. A., 135-136, 140, 142

Gurvich, R. P., 213, 215, 270-271

Gusev, Iu., 284-285

Guzevatyi, Ia., 258
Iaroshevskii, B., 276
Iashkin, V. A., 259 n.126
Ignatenko, G. V., 195, 204
India: air exercises in, 41 n.112; Chinese view of, 26; as compared to other developing countries, 33-34, 46, 48, 190-191, 191 n.64, 240; effects of Sino-Indian border conflict on Soviet view of, 40-41; economic conditions in, 318-319; Soviet view of, 6-7, 25, 30, 33, 39, 41, 61-65, 72-74, 82, 118, 122 n.69, 127, 130, 132, 135-136, 156, 163-165, 175-177, 197, 221, 224-225, 230-232, 241, 282, 292-293; Western aid to, 161
Indian communalism. *See* Commualism in India
Indian bourgeoisie: and agrarian reforms, 220; and private foreign capital, 150-152, 165-166, 177, 180-181; Soviet evaluation of, 110-120, 131, 140-141, 155, 179-180, 292; and working class, 189
Indian economy: role of private foreign capital in, 131-132, 138 n.40, 138, 144-145, 150; Soviet view of, 132-133, 135-138, 142-143, 146, 149-152, 155, 160, 183-185, 196, 198, 256, 278
Indian foreign policy, 12-13; and atomic energy development, 138 n.42, 160, 206 n.113; towards China, 9; towards East Germany, 70 n.207, 298; towards developing countries, 11; towards Korea, 298; and nonproliferation treaty, 69; towards North Vietnam, 298; and nuclear weapons policy, 70; towards Soviet intervention in Czechoslovakia, 70-71; Soviet view of, 6-7, 12-13, 41, 49, 51 n.141, 112, 130, 165-168, 173, 221, 225-226; towards United States, 76, 173-174, 176
Indian independence: Soviet view of, 6, 70, 131, 134

Indian language policy, 228; Soviet view of, 15
Indian monopolies. *See* Monopoly capital in India
Indian National Congress: 1969 split of, 71, 224; 1971 electoral victory of, 74-75; Soviet response to 1969 split of, 72-73; Soviet view of, 110-114, 134, 141-143, 175-176, 177, 229, 318-320; Soviet view of 1969 split of, 73-74, 229-231; Soviet view of 1971 electoral victory of, 75; and working class, 189
Indian Ocean: American presence in, 315; Indian objectives in, 67-68, 317; and peace zone plan, 316-317; prospects for Soviet-American confrontation in, 316-317; Soviet attitudes towards Indian objectives in, 316-318; Soviet naval presence in, 67, 315 n.63, 315-316; Soviet view of American presence in, 315
Indian peasantry. *See* Peasantry, Indian
Indian Planning Commission, 303, joint committee on Indo-Soviet collaboration of, 300-301
Indo-Nepalese relations, 168
Indo-Pakistani relations: and Soviet posture towards, 52, 55-56, 293 n.3; and Tashkent declaration, 54-55. *See also* Pakistan
Indo-Pakistani War (1948): Soviet view of, 124, 167, 311
Indo-Pakistani War (1965), 53; American reaction to, 53; Chinese reaction to, 53, 53 n.146; reasons for, 53 n.145; Soviet response to, 52-53
Indo-Pakistani War (1971), 78; American reactions during, 81; Chinese response during, 81; Soviet support for India during, 80-81. *See also* Pakistan
Indo-Soviet economic collaboration. *See* Soviet economic collaboration with India
Indo-Soviet trade. *See* Soviet-Indian trade

Indo-Soviet Treaty of Peace, Friendship and Cooperation (1971), 77-80, 296, 308; Chinese response to, 78; implications for China of, 79; Indian view of, 309 n.39; provisions of, 77-79; significance of, 79-80; Soviet view of, 80, 309 n.39

Industrialization, process of: and employment, 203, 259-262; Soviet view of, 157-158, 183-184, 198-200, 202-203, 243-244; Soviet view of, in India, 183, 248, 249 n.90. *See also* Economic development, strategies of

Institute of Economics (USSR), 109 n.24, 114, 250

Institute of International Relations of USSR Ministry of Foreign Affairs, 109 n.24

Institute of Orientology (Leningrad), 102; Moscow division of, 103, 107 n.17; reorganization of, 103-104, 106-107

Institute of Orientology (Moscow), 119, 131, 170; 1956 conference on national bourgeoisie at, 140-143; 1958 conference on state capitalism in developing countries at, 145-149; criticism of, 133; development of, 107-109; 1958 joint conference on agrarian reforms in developing countries at, 153-156; Leningrad division of, 170; tasks of, 106

Institute of Peoples of Asia (USSR), 108; 1963 conference on private foreign investments in Asia at, 181, 183; 1964 conference on agrarian reforms at, 219-221; 1966 conference on food problem at, 264-265, 268; 1968 conference on problems of the formation of the proletariat at, 280

Institute of World Economy and International Relations (USSR), 109, 242 n.66; 1958 joint conference on agrarian reforms at, 153-156; 1962 conference on problems of the national liberation movement and socio-economic development of liberated countries at, 180 n.32; 1964 conference on problems of economic development, 202-204; 1967 conference on problems of industrialization at, 259-260, 264 n.137, 272

Institute of World Economy and World Politics (USSR), 103 n.6

Intelligentsia in developing countries: Soviet view of, 193, 196, 279-280. *See also* Social stratification

Iskenderov, A., 238

Ivanov, K., 234

Iverov, A., 231

Iudin, P., 30 n.79

Izdatel'stvo Vostochnoi Literatury, 107

Jana Sangh, 58 n.165, 62, 62 n.180, 175, 226-227, 229

Kabul, 1969 conference at, 56

Kakharov, A. K., 159

Kamaraj, K., 230

Kashmir issue: Chinese position on, 21; Khrushchev's speech at Srinagar on, 19-21; Soviet efforts to settle Indo-Pakistani differences on, 45; Soviet position on, 9, 13, 45, 50, 50 n.137, 50-52, 55, 124-125, 163, 221; and Soviet security interests, 8; Soviet support for India on, 2, 19-23, 41, 125-126, 291, 310-311; Stalin's policy towards, 8; at Tashkent meeting, 54-55; as treated by Soviet scholars, 221. *See also* Soviet policy towards India

Kerala, CPI government: Soviet view of, 22, 164; Soviet view of fall of, 29, 164 n. 121

Khan, Liaquat Ali, 7

Khrushchev, N. S.: criticism of Chinese by, 28, 38-39; defense of Soviet military aid to India by, 35; effects of dismissal of, on Soviet economic relations with developing countries, 242, 250-251; effects of dismissal of, on Soviet-Indian relations, 50 n.136; efforts to smooth Sino-Indian relations by, 28; remarks during 1964 trip to Egypt

by, 46, 195; and Soviet scholars, 292; views of developing countries of 232; views of Soviet foreign aid of, 89, 244-245; views of western foreign aid of, 84 n.236
Kim, G. F., 237
Kodachenko, A., 248-249, 269
Kollontai, V. M., 203-204, 212 n.136, 259-260, 262, 264 n.137, 274-276
Kolontaev, A. P., 287 n.209
Kolykhalova, 181, 183
Komarov, E. N., 108 n.19, 128, 142
Kondrat'ev, V., 150-151, 198, 275
Kosygin, A. N., 52-53, 55, 67 n.194; mention of arms aid to India by, 4; remarks on issues resultant from Bangladesh crisis by, 304; remarks at President Husain's funeral by, 67; remarks on Soviet-Indian relations by, 65
Kotovskii, G. G., 108 n.19, 129, 138, 141, 147, 148 n.70, 152-153, 211 n.133, 219-220, 280 n.190, 283-284, 286, 310
Krasin, Iu. A., 195
Kratkie Soobshcheniia Instituta Vostokovedeniia, 106
Krishna Menon, V.K., 40 n.110, 62,172
Krishnamachari, T. T., 23, 42
Kudriavtsev, V., 236, 238
Kulikova, F. I., 237
Kurshakov, A., 260
Kutsobin, P. V., 230
Kuzmin, S., 277
Kvasha, A. Ia., 258-259
Landa, R. G., 283
Language policy in India. *See* Indian language policy
Lazarev, N. I., 154
Lemin, I. M., 132, 159
Leningrad University: 1963 conference on problems of economic development at, 177
Levin, S. F., 284
Levkovskii, A. I., 140, 142, 146-147, 175, 210 n.128, 263
Li, V. F., 195

Lukianova, M. I., 155
MacMahon line, 36-37; Soviet position on, 39. *See also* Sino-Indian border
Maev, O. V., 172, 231
Maksimov, M. A., 139, 148, 218-219
Malaviya, K. D., 172
Malenkov, G. M., 13
Malinovskii, R. Ia., 43 n.116, 54 n.150
Mamrykin, G. I., 182, 206
Maslennikov, A. A., 218, 220, 224
Maslennikov, V. A., 131, 137 n. 38
Matveev, G. V., 311
Medevoi, A., 225
Mel'man, S. M., 112
Mel'nikov, A. M., 219
Menshikov, M. A., 11, 13 n.22
Middle East crisis of 1958: Soviet sponsorship of major Indian role after, 22
Mikoyan, A. I., 34 n.92, 45; criticism of Soviet orientalists at 20th Party Congress by, 133; remarks on trade at 20th Party Congress by, 244; toast to Nehru during 1955 visit by, 17 n.34
Military aid, Soviet. *See* Soviet military aid
Mironova, E. I., 184, 264 n.138
Mirovaia Ekonomika i Mezhdunarodyne Otnosheniia, 109; 1964 discussion of developing countries organized by, 173
Mirskii, G. I., 157-158, 180 n.32, 196, 202, 213, 233, 279-280, 282, 286
Moiseev, P. P., 219
Monopoly capital in India, 140, 142, 144-145, 149-151, 166, 174-179, 181, 224, 229, 231, 292; and 1962 Sino-Indian border war, 172; and Tibetan issue, 167-168. *See also* Indian economy, western private capital investment
Moscow Economic Conference (1952): Indian participation at, 10
Moscow meeting of 81 communist parties (1960), 32, 191

Mujibur Rahman, Sheikh, 316 n.67
Muslim League, 123; Soviet view of, 124
Naga autonomy movement: Soviet view of, 22, 162, 162 n.113, 227, 228 n.18, 309
Nasenko, Iu. P., 120, 225-226
National bourgeoisie: and agrarian reforms, 154 n.85, 154; in India, 196-197; Soviet view of, 30-31, 63, 135, 139-143, 146
National democratic state, 237; and India, 191-192; Soviet definition of, 31-32, 191-192, 195
National integration: and Indian language policy, 228; Soviet attitude towards, in India, 16, 117-118, 122-123, 162-164, 227-229
National liberation front of Algeria, 46
National liberation movement: Soviet view of, 233-234, 236, 240-241. *See also* Non-capitalist path of development
Nationalization: of banks in India, 231-232; Soviet view of, 204, 238; Soviet view of, in India, 204-205
Naxalite movement, 64-65, 271
Nehru, J.: American reaction to 1955 visit to Soviet Union by, 18 n.37; attitude towards CPI of, 16; comment on Soviet response to 1959 Sino-Indian border conflict by, 28 n.72; criticism of 1961 Soviet nuclear tests by, 29; effects of Sino-Indian border conflict on, 40 n.56; response to Soviet intervention in Hungary by, 22; response to Soviet position on 1962 Sino-Indian border war by, 37; significance of 1955 visit to Soviet Union by, 18; Soviet praise for, 14, 41; Soviet response to U.S. trip by, 7; Soviet treatment of, during 1955 visit to Soviet Union by, 16-17; Soviet view of, 110; view of Soviet state sector of, 84 n.234; 1955 visit to Soviet Union by, 16-18. *See also* Sino-Indian border dispute

Nehru, R. K., 43 n.116
Nesterov, S., 172
Nikhamin, V. P., 165-168
Nikiforov, V. N., 119
Nikitin, A. I., 177
Nikitin, Afanasy, 8 n.6
Nixon, R. M., 1972 visit to Peking: implications for India of, 310-311
Non-capitalist path of development: and African, 236; and Indian, 179, 196-197; Soviet interpretation of, 32, 193-195, 232-237, 239-240, 263; as used by Lenin, 32 n.85
Orientology, Soviet. *See* Soviet orientology
Orleanskaia, L. K., 215-216
Oskolkova, O., 284-285
Ostrovitianov, Iu., 197, 281-282
Pacific Institute (USSR), 103, 113-114, 116; merger with Institute of Orientology, 106
Pakistan: changes in foreign policy of, 44; impact of 1970 elections on, 75; military aid to, 314; relations with China, 44; relations with Soviet Union, 44; relations with United States, 13; Soviet view of, 124, 167 n. 131, 221; Soviet view of foreign policy of, 221 n.170
Pant, G. V., 23
Patel, S. V., 110
Patil, S. K., 42
Pavlov, V. I., 138, 147, 249 n.90, 287 n.209
Pearson Commission Report: Soviet response to recommendations of, 89
Peasantry, Indian: and agrarian reforms, 217-221, 265-266; effects of "green revolution" on, 270-271; situation of, 138, 153-154, 218-219, 271; Soviet view of, 128-129. *See also* Agrarian relations
Pegov, N., 317
Petrunicheva, Z., 124-126
Pigulevskaia, N. V., 170
Planning: and econometric models, 275-278; in India, 278; Soviet

evaluation of, in developing countries, 272-275, 277-278, 302-303
Podgorny, N. V., 74 n.215; letter to Yahya Khan on situation in East Pakistan by, 75
Pokataeva, T., 187 n.52, 279-280, 282, 286
Poliak, A. A., 148, 155
Political parties in developing countries: Soviet view of, 237-238
Ponomarev, B. N., 30, 33, 49
Popov, V. A., 219
Population control. *See* Birth control
Program of CPSU (1961): statements on developing countries in, 31 n.82
Prokhorov, G. M., 159, 212
Pushtunistan issue: Soviet support for Afghanistan on, 20 n.48
Radhakrishnan, S., 43
Radio Peace and Progress: broadcasts to India of, 62 n.180
Ram, Jagjivan, 230
Rashtriya Swayamsevak Sangh, 226
Rastiannikov, V. G., 108 n.19, 139, 218, 256, 264-267, 270
Regional economic development, 157-159, 249, 249 n.90; Soviet aid for, 158; Soviet sponsorship of South Asian, 55-56, 158, 249
Regional nationalism in India. *See* National integration
Reddy, S., 44 n.120
Reisner, I. M., 102, 105
Reisner, L. I., 151, 170
Revolutionary democrats, 193-194, 196-197; and agrarian reforms, 266; and India, 196, 197 n.86; role of, defined, 46; as sanctioned by Khrushchev, 46 n.124. *See also* Noncapitalist path of development
Revoliutsionnyi Vostok, 105 n.11
Rosaliev, Iu. N., 131, 280
Roy, M. N., 63 n.185
Rubinstein, M., 25, 132-133, 136-138
Rudenko, G. F., 256
Rusinova, S. I., 164
Rymalov, V., 202-203

Savel'ev, N. A., 179-180
Scientific technical revolution: Soviet evaluation of effect of, on developing countries, 245, 245 n.76
Sevastianov, A., 233
Shamrai, Iu. F., 252-255
Shaposhnikova, L. V., 163
Shastri, L. B., 41, 45; death of 55; visit to Soviet Union by, 51
Shchetinin, V. D., 200
Shirokov, G. K., 181, 184
Shmelev, N., 201, 208, 266, 273-274, 277
Shpirt, A. Iu., 268
Simoniia, N. A., 234
Sino-Indian border: Soviet position on, 79 n.227, 311-312
Sino-Indian border dispute: 26, 168, 171, 311-312; Chinese response to 1959 Tass statement on, 27; effect of, on Indian military budget 28; 1959 Tass statement on, 27; Soviet position on, 26-29; Soviet support for India on, 311-312; Soviet view of effects on India of, 172-173
Sino-Indian border war (1962) 35-36; Indian reaction to Soviet reaction to, 37, 41 n.113; reasons for, 36; Soviet response to, 35-40, 172
Sino-Indian relations, 67 n.195, 309; and Soviet Union, 308, 312-313
Sino-Pakistani relations: Soviet view of, 45 n.122, 309-310
Sino-Soviet dispute: effect on Soviet policy towards developing countries of, 46; and India, 28-29; and Sino-Indian border conflict, 37-40, 312 n.47; Soviet charges in, 28, 293; as treated by Soviet scholars, 221. *See also* Sino-Indian border war; Sino-Pakistani relations
Skachkov, S. A., 64 n.186; visit to India by, 61, 87
Skliar, M. A., 208
Skorov, G., 261-262
Smirnov, G., 275
Social science: Soviet view of, 242-243

Social stratification: and economic development, 287, 287 n.209; in India, 283, 284 n.200; Soviet view of, in developing countries, 279-282; and working class, 114, 128. *See also* Urbanization; working class
Sokolovskii, V. D., 54 n.150
Sovetskoe Vostokovedenie (1940-1949), 102
Sovetskoe Vostokovedenie (1955-1958), 106, 135, 170
Soviet economic aid to India, 9, 12-15, 19, 23, 28, 33-34, 37, 43-44, 66, 66 n.191, 83-84, 86, 90-91, 99, 205-206, 288, 299-300; approach of post-Khrushchev leadership to, 294; changes in 91-92; Chinese view of 48-49; Indian resistance towards, 23, 166 n.127; levels of, 83 n.232; objectives of, 88; problems of, 59-61, 86-88, 90, 294; rationale for, 14, 24; Soviet efforts to correct problems of, 60-61; Soviet evaluation of, 159-160, 206-207, 248 n.86, 257, 257 n.120; Soviet view of, 206; terms of, 15 n.28, 83 n.233. *See also* Soviet economic collaboration with India
Soviet economic aid to Pakistan, 57 n.160, 305
Soviet economic collaboration with India, 298-301; as component of Soviet policy towards India, 82; prospects for, 303-304. *See also* Soviet economic aid to India
Soviet foreign aid, 89, 159, 288 n.211; approach to, by post-Khrushchev leadership, 89-90, 239; beginnings of, 12, 85-86, changes in, 157; justification of, 12, 48-49; and regional economic development, 158-159; Soviet evaluation of, 156-157, 160, 212, 253 n.102; as target of anti-Party group 25. *See also* anti-Party group; Khrushchev, N. S.; Regional economic development; Soviet economic aid to India

Soviet-Indian relations, 5-6, 11, 29, 42-43, 45-46, 59, 61, 65-66, 70-71, 298, 305-306, 318; bases of, 49; historical antecedents of, 7-8; periodization of, 5-6; prospects for, 318-320; and Soviet-Indian trade, 304; and 20 year Treaty of Peace, Friendship and Cooperation, 79-80. *See also* Soviet policy towards India
Soviet-Indian trade, 24, 83, 87-88, 92-99, 301; changes in, 97-98; effects of closing Suez Canal on, 96; levels of, 24, 24 n.62, 92 n.260, 92, 95; Table 1 (96); 1953 agreement on, 11, 24 n.63; 1958 agreement on, 24; 1970 agreement on, 288, 296; problems of, 93-95, 97-99, 211 n.130, 301-303; and rupee devaluation; 62 n.179, 95; Soviet evaluation of; 254; Soviet objectives in, 93-94, 302; under Stalin, 10, 10 n.12; terms of, 92-93
Soviet Indology: character of, 138, 150; development of, 101-103, 108-109; official criticism of, 134-135. *See also* Soviet orientology; Soviet scholars
Soviet military aid to India, 34-35, 43, 43 n.116, 315, 317-318; during Bangladesh crisis, 80; early Soviet offer of, 13 n.22; effects on Soviet-Pakistani relations of, 57; Kosygin's mention of 4; offer of, 67 n.194; rationale for, 35, 43, 48; Soviet commentary on, 172, 172 n.3; Soviet defense of, 39; suspension of, during Sino-Indian border war 37
Soviet military aid to Pakistan, 57; impact on India of, 57, 58 n.166; reasons for, 58; Soviet assurances to India on, 58
Soviet orientology: character of, 104, 135, 169-170, 223, 287, 289, 291-292, 294-295; criticism of, 145, 242-243; history of, 101-102; organizational development of, 102, 106, 110. *See also* Soviet scholars

Soviet-Pakistani relations, 13, 45, 51; effects of Bangladesh crisis on, 81, 305; effects on Soviet-Indian relations of, 45, 71; and Kashmir issue, 45; and Khrushchev's 1955 speech at Srinagar, 20-21

Soviet policy towards developing countries, 47-48, 295; effects of Ghanaian coup on, 99; effects of Sino-Soviet dispute on, 46; and inter-party relations, 46; under post-Khrushchev leadership, 99; Stalin's reevaluation of, 11. *See also* Sino-Soviet dispute

Soviet Policy towards India, 21-22, 25, 99-100, 291, 296; basis of, 45-46; defining the content of, 1-2; development of, 120; effect of Cuban missile crisis on, 4; goals of 8, 24, 185; influence of Sino-Indian relations on, 318; influence of Soviet-Pakistani relations on, 4; influence of Sino-Soviet dispute on, 4; objectives of, 42, 49; official as distinguished from unofficial, 2-3; Soviet press reportage, 3; and Soviet scholars, 3, 5; and Soviet security interests, 8; Stalin's reevaluation of, 9. *See also* Soviet-Indian relations; Soviet scholars

Soviet policy towards South Asia, 50, 126, 304; changes in, 44-45; and China, 50-51; effect of Bangladesh crisis on, 81; and 1968 Soviet military aid to Pakistan, 58; as treated by Soviet scholars, 221

Soviet political system, attributes of, 2

Soviet scholars: controversy over role of Indian bourgeoisie among, 114-118; official criticism of 131-132; practices of, 149; role of, 291-295; and Soviet foreign policy. 104, 120-121, 126, 169, 288-293. *See also* Soviet orientology

Soviet trade with developing countries, 10; problems of, 252-254; Soviet view of, 250-252

Stalin, J. V., 123; invitation to Liaquat Ali Khan of, 7; and Soviet scholars, 121, 127, 291-292

Starushenko, G., 237 n.49, 238

Stasov, M., 232, 254

State capitalism, 148-149; in India, 136, 145; Soviet view of, 143-148, 174-175, 177-178, 225, 292. *See also* State sector

States Reorganization Act of 1956: Soviet view of, 163, 227

State sector: American attitude towards Indian, 85; Soviet view of, 31, 142; Soviet view of Indian, 31, 84 n.234, 84-85, 146, 149, 151, 161, 179, 212, 272-273, 275, 293; Soviet view of problems of, 207-212. *See also* State capitalism

State structure in developing countries: and Asiatic mode of production, 282-283; Soviet view of, 280-283. *See also* Asiatic mode of production

State Trading Corporation of India: Soviet view of, 210. *See also* State capitalism

Stepanov, L. V., 157-158, 162, 169

Sterbalova, A., 287

Strumilin, S., 258

Subramaniam, C., 230

Sudanese Union Party of Mali: and relations with CPSU, 233 n.33

Suslov, M. A., 45 n.122, 46 n.125, 47, 74 n.215

Swaran Singh, 305, 312 n.50

Swatantra party, 58 n.165, 62 n.180, 175, 229

"Syndicate," the (faction within Indian National Congress), 71-73, 230-231

Tashkent declaration, 54-55; Soviet view of, 55-56

Tashkent meeting, 76 n.219; characterization of, by Z. A. Bhutto, 305; origins of, 53; significance of, 54, 54 n.150, 55; Soviet reportage of, 54 n.150

Telengana, 1948 insurrection in, 8; Soviet encouragement of, 7 n.5, 113, 122

Technical assistance, Soviet. *See* Soviet economic aid

Tiagunenko, V., 194 n.75, 200, 236-238, 240, 248 n.86, 260

Tibet: 1954 Sino-Indian agreement on, 14, 167, 311; 1959 rebellion, 26, 168

Tiul'panov, S. I., 156 n.90, 175, 210, 262 n.134

Tolstov, S. P., 104-105

Twentieth Party Congress: criticism of Soviet orientalists at, 133; pronouncements on India at, 22. *See also* Soviet orientology

Uchenye Zapiski Instituta Vostokovedeniia, 106

Ul'ianova, L. P., 164-165, 227-228

Ul'ianovskii, R. A., 63, 64 n.186 73-74, 143-150, 154-155, 161, 173-175, 178-180, 183, 202-203, 213, 217-220, 271, 292; background of, 143 n.56; professional responsibilities of, 3 n.1

Unemployment, problem of. *See* Employment, problem of

United Nations Conference on Trade and Development, 2nd meeting of, 255 n.108, 263

United States: foreign policy towards South Asia of, 173; military aid to Pakistan by, 57, 315; role in Kashmir issue of, 125; Soviet view of, foreign policy towards India, 173, 313; Soviet view of, foreign policy in South Asia, 313-314

United States' Public Law 480: Soviet view of 264-265, 267. *See also* Agricultural development

Urbanization: and agrarian overpopulation, 187, 278 n.183; application of mathematical models to study of, 278 n.183; Soviet view of, 187

Vaintsvaig, N. K., 237

Varga, E., 111, 118-119, 121, 282 n.195, 291

Vasil'ev, V., 255, 262 n.133

Vladimirov, V., 160

Vladimirskii, L. A., 210

Western economic aid: to India, 161, 180; Soviet view of, 12, 144, 158-162, 200, 246. *See also* Soviet economic aid

Western private capital investment: Soviet view of, in developing countries, 181-182, 245-246, 295; Soviet view of, in India, 185, 205, 224, 239

Working class in India: situation of, 137, 145; Soviet view of, 128, 186-190. *See also* Social stratification

Yahya Khan, M., 75

Zevin, L., 244, 250, 251 n.97, 267, 288

Zhdanov, A. A., 5

Zhukov, E. M., 104, 112, 114-115, 119-120, 236

Augsburg College
George Sverdrup Library
Minneapolis, Minnesota 55454